SERENDIPITY IN RHETORIC,
WRITING, AND LITERACY RESEARCH

SERENDIPITY IN RHETORIC, WRITING, AND LITERACY RESEARCH

edited by
MAUREEN DALY GOGGIN
AND PETER N. GOGGIN

UTAH STATE UNIVERSITY PRESS
Logan

© 2018 by University Press of Colorado

Published by Utah State University Press
An imprint of University Press of Colorado
245 Century Circle, Suite 202
Louisville, Colorado 80027

All rights reserved

 The University Press of Colorado is a proud member of the Association of University Presses.

The University Press of Colorado is a cooperative publishing enterprise supported, in part, by Adams State University, Colorado State University, Fort Lewis College, Metropolitan State University of Denver, Regis University, University of Colorado, University of Northern Colorado, Utah State University, and Western State Colorado University.

ISBN: 978-1-60732-738-7 (paperback)
ISBN: 978-1-60732-739-4 (ebook)
https://doi.org/10.7330/9781607327394

Library of Congress Cataloging-in-Publication Data

Names: Goggin, Maureen Daly, editor. | Goggin, Peter N., editor.
Title: Serendipity in rhetoric, writing, and literacy research / edited by Maureen Daly Goggin and Peter N. Goggin.
Description: Logan : Utah State University Press, [2018] | Includes bibliographical references and index.
Identifiers: LCCN 2017025387| ISBN 9781607327387 (pbk.) | ISBN 9781607327394 (ebook)
Subjects: LCSH: English language—Rhetoric—Research. | Archives—Research. | Literacy—Research. | Serendipity.
Classification: LCC PE1404 .S426 2018 | DDC 808/.042072—dc23
LC record available at https://lccn.loc.gov/2017025387

Cover illustration © Ice lemon/Shutterstock.

CONTENTS

List of Figures   ix

Stumbling into Wisdom in Rhetoric, Writing, and Literacy Research: An Introduction
   Maureen Daly Goggin and Peter N. Goggin   3

I. INTERSECTIONS OF PERSONAL AND POLITICAL

1. "Oh, My God! He Was a Slave!" Secrets of a Virginia Courthouse Archive
   Shirley E. Faulkner-Springfield   17

2. Making Sense of Disaster: Composing a Methodology for Place-Based Visual Research
   Doreen Piano   28

3. Death, Dying, and Serendipity in the Scholarly Imagination
   Gale Coskan-Johnson   44

II. INTERSECTIONS OF PERSONAL AND PROFESSIONAL

4. Fortuitous Happenstance: Serendipity in Archival Research
   Lynèe Lewis Gaillet   59

5. Pre-Sentence: Researching, Reporting, and Writing
   Caren Wakerman Converse   70

6. Echoes in the Archives
   Liz Rohan   80

7. Serendipity and Memory: The Value of Participant Observation
   Kim Donehower   92

III. STUMBLING INTO THE UNKNOWN

8. The Serendipity of (Mis)Timing in Research
   Maureen Daly Goggin   103

9. Setting Out for Serendip: Of Research Quests and Chance Discoveries
   Ryan Skinnell   117

10. The Art of the "Accident": Serendipity in Field Research
    Peter N. Goggin   129

11. Reading between the Power Lines: How "Nikola Tesla Corner" Enhanced the Wireless Signals in a Rhetorical Analysis of Electricity and Landscape
    Daniel Wuebben   138

IV. METHODOLOGY AND SERENDIPITY

12. Prepare to Be Surprised: How Flexible, Methodical, and Organized Research Practices Lead to Serendipity in the Archives
    Lori Ostergaard   153

13. Playing the Name Game: Exploring Name Variations in Archival Research
    Patty Wilde   164

14. Serendipity and Methodological Willingness in Team Science
    Ellen Barton   175

15. The Sunshine of Serendipity: Illuminating Scholarship of Genre (a New Canon) and Generosity (Yes You Can)
    Lynn Z. Bloom   190

16. Serendology, Methodipity: Research, Invention, and the Choric Rhetorician
    Jennifer Clary-Lemon   205

V. TRUSTING THE PROCESS

17. The Ethics of Serendipity: Rare Events and a Need to Act
    Bill Endres   221

18. Creating Kismet: What Artists Can Teach Academics about Serendipity
    Brad Gyori   237

19. Coordinating Chaos and Befriending a Fuzzy Focus: Reflections of a Serendipitist
    Judy Holiday   247

20. The Strange Practices of Serendipitous Failure: Considering *Metanoia* as an Alternative to *Kairos*
    Zachary Beare   257

    Afterword: Serendipity and Ethics in Rhetoric, Writing, and Literacy Research
    Gesa E. Kirsch   267

    About the Authors   275
    Subject Index   279
    Name Index   287

FIGURES

1.1	Excerpt from Jacob Faulkner's Last Will and Testament	18
2.1	Post-It note memorial on the facade of the then closed Camellia Grill	37
2.2	The ruins of the Florida Projects	39
6.1	Sign at Vittum Park recently rubbed clean of graffiti	88
6.2	The drawing of Vittum on a wall in the park's recreation center	89
8.1	Elizabeth Parker circa 1830 sampler	105
8.2	Map showing Ashburnham, Catsfield, Battle, Hastings, and Fairlight	108
14.1	Youth coding	180
14.2	"Statistics Kitty"	185

SERENDIPITY IN RHETORIC,
WRITING, AND LITERACY RESEARCH

STUMBLING INTO WISDOM IN RHETORIC, WRITING, AND LITERACY RESEARCH
An Introduction

Maureen Daly Goggin and Peter N. Goggin

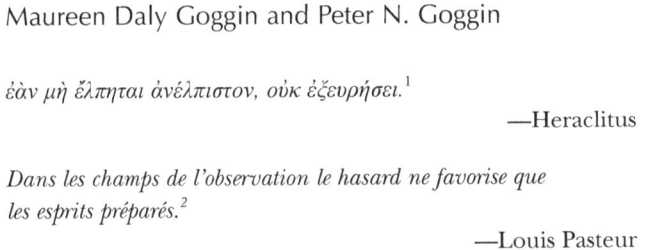
—Heraclitus

Dans les champs de l'observation le hasard ne favorise que les esprits préparés.[2]
—Louis Pasteur

When students read published scholarship and research, the path toward discovery seems clean and direct. The dead-ends, the backtrackings, the starting overs, the stumbles have all been cleared away, and it seems as though by some kind of magic the scholars were able to start at point A and arrive safely and neatly at point B. Of course, those of us who do scholarship know the path is never clear and never straight. Research and writing is messy. It is fraught with moments of anxiety and feelings of being lost. David Gold captures this feeling well when he says of researching, "I felt clueless, a feeling I have since come to learn is at the heart of the scholarly process. In academia, one is in a perpetual liminal space. As soon as you answer a research question, you ask another, your growing body of expertise simply marking the expanding edge of your ignorance" (18).

The liminal space of research stymies some students, making them want to quit the process. Yet as Heraclitus notes, "He [*sic*] who does not expect will not find out the unexpected, for it is trackless and unexplored" (Fragment 18, 106). In other words, scholars through practice, through living on the edge of ignorance, expect to find the unexpected. They learn, that is, to stay open to possibilities while they wait actively doing what it is they can do. Louis Pasteur points the way. On December 7, 1854, at a lecture at the University of Lille, Pasteur stated that "in the fields of observation, chance favors only the prepared mind." Active waiting offers the opportunity for preparing the mind. *Serendipity in Rhetoric, Writing, and Literacy Research* takes up two terms from Pasteur: "chance" as serendipity, wonder, amazement and "prepared mind" as the different kinds of work scholars, particularly those in rhetoric, writing, and literacy, need to have done to recognize a serendipitous discovery or a missed opportunity.[3]

Economist Albert O. Hirschman writes about "stumbling" into truths: "Language itself conspires toward this sort of asymmetry: we fall into error, but do not usually speak of falling into truth" (13). He argues: "We are . . . correspondingly unwilling to concede—in fact we find it intolerable to imagine—that our more lofty achievements, such as economic, social or political progress [we might add scholarly research], could have come about by stumbling rather than through careful planning, rational behavior, and the successful response to a clearly perceived challenge" (13). In research, this "falling into truth" as he calls it is far more common than many scholars admit. Hirschman terms serendipity "the Hiding Hand." He argues that researchers

> take on and plunge into new tasks because of erroneously presumed *absence* of a challenge—because the task looks easier and more manageable that [sic] it will turn out to be. As a result, the Hiding Hand can help accelerate the rate at which men [sic] engage successfully in problem-solving; they take up problems *they think* they can solve, find them more difficult than expected, but then, being stuck with them attack willy-nilly the unsuspecting difficulties—and sometimes even succeed. People who have stumbled through the experience just described will of course tend to retell it as though they had known the difficulties all along and have bravely gone to meet them—*fare bella figura* is a strong human propensity. (13, original emphasis)

Those who do admit the stumbling usually refer to it as serendipity. For instance, in describing her research project on Dr. Mary Bennett Ritter (1860–1949), Gesa Kirsch notes that it "helps to have serendipity on one's side, but that, of course, is not something one can arrange purposefully, although I am convinced one can be open to the possibility" (20).

Serendipity may be understood as an unexpected rupture, an opportunity, fortunate circumstances, and discoveries. Many of the life-saving and convenience items we use today—nylon, Velcro, Teflon, microwave oven, penicillin, X-rays, Viagra, sugar substitutes, safety glass, various plastics, and other technological advancements—were the results of such happenstance mistakes and unplanned-for discoveries (Gaughan; Hannan; Meyers; Rosen; Roberts). Thus, scientists value and write often about serendipity. As Till Düppe writes, "The rhetoric of chance is part of the self-image of scientists" (9). Medical researcher and Nobel Prize awardee Pek Van Andel dubbed serendipity "the art of making an unsought finding" (631). In *The Serendipity Machine*, David Green explores post-internet computers as serendipity machines. William Michener and colleagues recommend biological field stations as important sites of serendipity. More recently, in discussing the benefits of transdisciplinary research, Frédéric Darbellay, Zoe Moody, Ayuko Sedooka, and Gabriela Steffen argue that "serendipity is . . . capable of playing a central role in interdisciplinarity, boosting the exchange of ideas and speeding up their circulation among researchers committed to exploiting the heuristic dimension of the unexpected" (1). So commonplace are the happy accidents that scientist Vincent J. Schaefer's autobiography has at its center his fortuitous adventures in science, many of which were chance findings.

Social scientists also call attention to happenstance and fortune. In fact, the first volume of *Serendipities: Journal for Sociology and History of Social Sciences*, a publication focusing on chance discoveries, appeared in 2016. Isabelle Rivoal and Noel B. Salazar make the point that "in anthropology, serendipity, together with reflexivity and openness, is widely accepted as a key characteristic (and strength) of the ethnographic method" (178). Indeed, in the 1940s, Robert Merton was the first to call attention to the "serendipity component" in qualitative research, one that "involves the unanticipated, anomalous, and strategic datum which exerts pressure upon the investigator for a new direction of inquiry which extends theory" (506). He later authored a book with Elinor G. Barber on the origins and history of serendipity titled *The Travels and Adventures of Serendipity*, a monograph Pek Van Andel assessed as "the best study on serendipity I ever read" (633). Keith Townsend and John Burgess anthologize researchers' stories of qualitative studies in a variety of social science fields. Haim Hazan and Esther Hertzog write about serendipity in anthropological research, describing such work as "a lifelong nomadic journey of discovery in which the world yields an infinite number of unexplored issues and innumerable ways of studying them" (2). James E. McClellan III encourages historians to more fully understand and report serendipities. Emma Wild-Wood also urges historians to conduct field research from a vantage point that opens paths for serendipity, what she terms "se débrouiller," a Congolese term that means "to manage (on your own), sort things out (by yourself), cope, get by" (367). In many ways, the term itself could stand in for precisely the ways research feels as one is doing it. Serendipity, Wild-Wood suggests, comes out of moments of roadblocks, situations from which scholars have to disentangle themselves, particularly in fieldwork.

Rivoal and Salazar rightfully note that serendipity in research is more than just a happy find or accident; serendipity "requires sufficient background knowledge, an inquisitive mind, creative thinking and good time" (178). Paul André and colleagues concur; they propose that "the term serendipity itself may be ironic . . . more often than not a confluence of specific events, knowledge and attitude is needed to draw insight from chance encounters; in other words, no discovery is truly *by accident* . . . The circumstances may be termed luck, but as Gladwell states, they are generally the particular advantage of experts" (original emphasis). Given the need for both happenstance and sagacity, Craig Calhoun, in his recent book review of Merton and Barber's *The Travels and Adventures of Serendipity*, calls serendipity "accidental wisdom."

Serendipity in Rhetoric, Writing, and Literacy Research offers vignettes of scholars who have had moments of "accidental wisdom" in their research and writing processes. Thus young scholars need to come to understand that happenstance is not merely chance or accidental *phronesis*. It takes a lot of hard work to avoid or at least recognize what Van Andel termed "negative serendipity," missed opportunities. Inquisitive open minds, wisdom, knowing how to know, and dedicated hours can, however, yield wondrous surprises. The stories in this volume substantiate precisely these qualities that mark good scholarship.

What exactly is it that serendipity needs? Serendipity demands not only a prepared mind but an open mind (*sine anticipatio mentis*). Learning how to do scholarship with an open mind, however, is typically not taught directly. Young scholars thus are often flummoxed by the stubborn steep path toward nuggets of discovery and by the serendipity encountered along the difficult way. Of course, one cannot purposefully rely on serendipity, as Kirsch notes. Rather, what one can rely on is an open mind, one that is ready for the messiness and one that learns to stay comfortable within the mire of unknowing as well as a process of preparing that mind.

Students thus need to be taught the hows and whys of doing *thorough* research—of where and how to start with the understanding that there will be dead-ends, roadblocks, U-turns along the way. They need to learn how to review the scholarly literature so they understand that scholars participate in an ongoing "unending conversation," to use Kenneth Burke's metaphor. Students also need to learn and understand grounded, sound, and tested research strategies to gather data, to ponder them, to rearrange and rethink them, to generate more questions about their project, and so on. One of the goals of this collection is to help students understand the reasons for staying open and "suspending belief" during a scholarly project, as Alton Becker has argued.

While researchers in the sciences and social sciences have written a fair amount about serendipity as a normal praxis in research, no scholar in rhetoric, writing, and literacy studies has devoted a book to the topic. This proposed collection thus breaks new ground. We imagine *Serendipity in Rhetoric, Writing, and Literacy Research* as a powerful companion to the robust collection *Beyond the Archives: Research as a Lived Process*, edited by Gesa E. Kirsch and Liz Rohan, as well as that by Alexis E. Ramsey and colleagues, *Working in the Archives: Practical Research Methods for Rhetoric and Composition*. While the latter two present tantalizing scenarios of how various researchers came to define a research project, *Serendipity* will present scenarios of serendipitous moments that can occur anytime during a scholarly project. This collection also makes a good companion to other kinds of research methods texts.

The twenty scholars who penned these pages share with students the deep reality of doing research, a reality that doesn't have a prescriptive map (these don't work) or a how-to manual (these aren't often helpful either). They show what it takes to doggedly pursue a line of inquiry with an open mind that is prepared for the difficult terrain that is research in rhetoric, writing, and literacy.

A WORD ON THE ORGANIZATION OF CHAPTERS

Narrative is radical, creating us at the very moment it is being created.
—Toni Morrison

Storytelling through narrative structures is how humans relate to each other, pass along wisdom and experience, and give meaning to our lives. All too often it seems, though, that academic scholarly writing attempts to remove the fallible human element from the narrative to support the ideal of objectivity. But the concept of serendipity inherently challenges notions of objectivity, impartiality, and pure data in research. The very unpredictability and uncertainty of happenstance and "accidental" sagacity requires that we tell of such moments and occurrences as reflective stories of discovery. For academics, when or if we tell each other and our students these stories, more often they are relegated to social settings and non-scholarly publications, not to the privileged spaces of our classrooms and professional journals. *Serendipity in Rhetoric, Writing, and Literacy Research* offers a corrective to this tendency and restores the human element of storytelling about adventures in the making, unmaking, and dissemination of knowledge. In the Call for this collection, we invited proposals for essays from scholars and researchers that narrated a serendipitous transformative occasion they experienced during a research project. The result is a collection of essays that are rigorously scholarly in terms of their theoretical and methodological approaches to serendipity in research, but, in addition and perhaps even more important, they are the stories each scholar tells of his or her own experiences with exploration, discovery, and happenstance that have influenced their professional and personal lives as researchers.

Serendipity in Rhetoric, Writing, and Literacy Research is organized into five sections that represent the range of experiences with serendipity into which the authors of this collection have delved. The twenty chapters in these five sections offer insights into research conducted in multiple theoretical frames and methodologies that have benefited from serendipitous moments, including, but not limited to, archival oral histories, ethnographies, case studies, feminist practices, fieldwork, theoretical work, qualitative and quantitative research, and rhetorical and discourse analysis. These sections are, of course, not exclusive; nor do they represent the entirety of possible approaches to, and perspectives on, serendipity in research; but taken together they offer scholars of rhetoric, writing, and literacy multiple analyses and usable knowledge on the significance of serendipity in research. We have organized this rich group of stories on these significant moments of happenstance and sagacity into narrative realms through which the authors tell their stories. The first two, Intersections of Personal and Political and Intersections of Personal and Professional, underscore that research always takes place somewhere and sometime and that these contexts—in conjunction with our personal lives, local and global events, relationships, funding, authority, institution, and a host of often unforeseeable connections between place and human connections, values, and emotions—can have profound impacts on the multiple twists and turns that impact research, and vice versa.

Intersections of Personal and Political is perhaps the most deeply introspective and empowering of the five sections, as the authors explore their experiences with serendipity in their research that mark significant shifts in perspectives and identities as individuals and scholars. In the first chapter, Shirley E. Faulkner-Springfield's "'Oh, My God! He Was a Slave!' Secrets of a Virginia Courthouse Archive," the author recalls the almost overpowering emotional and embodied trauma of her unexpected discovery of a long-"lost" ancestor while conducting historical and archival research and her resulting reimaging and retelling of the rhetorics of American culture and narratives of slavery and of herself as a scholar of this area of inquiry. In "Where You See Ruins, I See

Rhetoric: Composing a Methodology for 'Making Sense' of Disaster," Doreen Piano explores how cataclysmic change opens up new possibilities for research projects and tools that may otherwise be hidden. She focuses specifically on Hurricane Katrina and its aftermath to pursue several questions: What tools do we have from our past or other aspects of our lives that we may be overlooking in our research? How can these tools help us re-conceive our research agenda, our methods, and the kinds of data we draw from? What is the significance of building one's own data collection of images from which to draw rather than seeking out more official kinds of archives? In chapter 3, "Death, Dying, and Serendipity in the Scholarly Imagination," Gale Coskan-Johnson narrates the serendipitous coalescence of events, both global and personal, associated with death and dying centered around 9/11 and President Barack Obama's subsequent announcement of the killing of Osama Bin Laden. In her chapter she explores the transformative links among the personal, the political, and the scholarly.

In the next group, Intersections of Personal and Professional, the authors recount their serendipitous experiences in academic disciplinary and institutional contexts. In "Fortuitous Happenstance: Serendipity in Archival Research," Lynèe Lewis Gaillet details the challenges of archiving the sheer volumes of records, materials, and resources and, further, knowing how and where to access the archives that do exist. She narrates her own experiences of fortuitous discoveries of archival data, often through the help of others, and the importance for scholars to recognize and take advantage of serendipitous opportunities in archival research. In chapter 5, "Pre-Sentence: Researching, Reporting, and Writing," Caren Wakerman Converse relates how a chance call to a former colleague in her previous career as a probation office sparked a new direction and perspective in her research as a rhetorician on pre-sentence investigation reports in the criminal justice system. For Liz Rohan in the next chapter, "Echoes in the Archives," high hotel prices and a long commute led her to a collection of Settlement House archives at Northwestern University. Like Converse, she highlights the importance of the "happenstance" of inquiry processes in professional contexts that can lead to unexpected caches of archived texts. In chapter 7, the final essay in this section, Kim Donehower explores what she describes as "the role of memory in serendipitous moments of analytical epiphany" in "Serendipity and Memory: The Value of Participant Observation." In her examination of connections between methodology and memory, she details her personal and professional deliberations and negotiations between her field's traditions and values and both contradictory and complementary values of another field's methodologies. Drawing from two site cases, Donehower argues for qualitative research practices that prioritize vivid memory of field data as a necessity for the "prepared mind."

Stumbling into the Unknown takes us in into the realm of exploration. In the stories and analyses in this section, the authors focus on the journeys—in some cases, literally—they have taken in their scholarly pursuits and how "the prepared mind" resulted in serendipitous discoveries, impacting not only the journeys themselves but their research trajectories in rhetoric, writing, and literacy scholarship. In the first chapter of this section, Maureen Daly Goggin's "The Serendipity of (Mis)Timing in Research," the author recounts the significance of archival research in preparing her mind to capitalize on a sequence of serendipitous moments during her field research in churchyards, post offices, pubs, and museums in the English countryside. In chapter 9, "Setting Out for Serendip: Of Research Quests and Chance Discoveries," Ryan Skinnell relates his doctoral dissertation quest and subsequent purposeful travels for archival data to Michele Tramezzino's 1557 fairy tale/allegory, "The Three Princes of Serendip." Next, in "The Art of the 'Accident': Serendipity in Field Research," Peter N. Goggin argues the need for professional education in purposeful methods of discovery and describes his own accumulation of serendipitous events in field research with his work in island studies. Wrapping up this section in chapter 11, "Reading between the Power Lines: How 'Nikola Tesla Corner' Enhanced the Wireless Signals in a Rhetorical Analysis of Electricity and Landscape," Daniel Wuebben draws on a serendipitous moment of discovery in his quest for a street sign and offers a meta-critical narrative and rhetorical analysis about shifting between places of text and context.

The five authors in the fourth group of this collection, Methodology and Serendipity, delve into the roles of scholarly organizational principles and approaches to research in rhetoric, writing, and literacy studies that draw from expectations of serendipity. They offer us their accounts and cases built on methodological preparation in anticipation of such instances and provide usable models for future studies and discovery. For Lori Ostergaard, preparing for archival research and serendipitous opportunity is the key to discovery. Ostergaard illustrates her archival discoveries in chapter 12, "Prepare to Be Surprised: How Flexible, Methodical, and Organized Research Methods Lead to Serendipity in the Archives." Next, Patty Wilde, in "Playing the Name Game: Exploring Name Variations in Archival Research," relates her experiences while investigating "rhetorical strategies utilized by women composing sensational memoirs" during the American Civil War. In her chapter, Wilde describes how her methods of preparing for searching name variations in records detailing exploits of Confederate spy Loreta Janeta Velazquez led to serendipitous discoveries. In "Serendipity and Methodological Willingness in Team Science," Ellen Barton recounts her experiences as the designated linguist on a National Institutes of Health (NIH)–funded transdisciplinary health research team and how those experiences led her to a mixed-methods approach to research. In "The Sunshine of Serendipity: Illuminating Scholarship of Genre (a New Canon) and Generosity (Yes You Can)," Lynne Z. Bloom details how she serendipitously discovered a robust literary canon of essays. This then led her to unexpectedly create a 325-volume archive of canonical textbooks. Her research project combined canon theory and quantitative research, leading to qualitative discoveries in literary analysis, pedagogy, and ethics. She then turns to how serendipity plays out in pedagogy. In "Serendology, Methodipity: Research, Invention, and the Choric Rhetorician," Jennifer Clary-Lemon draws on concepts of *chōra* as a methodology to examine the interconnectedness of serendipity across a variety of dynamic rhetorical activities. She argues that *chōra* is not something preconceived but something always ongoing, always generated, always a beginning in the making of scholarly life.

The final section in this collection, Trusting the Process, offers narratives on serendipity that underscore Rohan and Kirsch's contention of research as a *lived* process. Thus, serendipity in research is inevitable and rewarding for rhetoric, writing, and literacy scholars who are prepared and willing to step out of the comfort zone of the known and not only to recognize and capitalize on unexpected moments of discovery and opportunity in their research but to generate the situations and conditions for those moments to happen. In chapter 17, Bill Endres tackles the uncomfortable reality that sometimes the catalyst for serendipity can be a calamity or trauma. In "The Ethics of Serendipity: Rare Events and a Need to Act," Endres comes to terms with the death of a colleague whose demise provides the author with access to grant funding for a project in digitizing the early medieval St. Chad Gospels in Lichfield, England—a project he was well prepared for and able to step into under the circumstances. Next, in "Creating Kismet: What Artists Can Teach Scholars about Serendipity," Brad Gyori details how formal strategies of montage, collage, and collaboration in media production are employed to intentionally cultivate the conditions for serendipity and discusses how these techniques and strategies can be appropriated for similar purposes for rhetorical and critical analysis. Judy Holiday's approach to cultivating the conditions for serendipity in her research involves reading widely and broadly and indiscriminately all texts that come to her. Combined with talking in person widely with others and with attunement to serendipity always in mind, her approach opens any manner of potential opportunities for happenstance in her work, and she expounds on this strategy in her chapter, "Coordinating Chaos and Befriending a Fuzzy Focus: Reflections of a Serendipitist." In the final chapter in this collection, "The Strange Practices of Serendipitous Failure: Considering *Metanoia* as an Alternative to *Kairos*," Zachary Beare asks us to consider the alternative to serendipity as fortuitous alignment—everything falling into place—and imagine moments instead when serendipity involves everything going wrong. In his chapter he explores how *metanoia* (missed opportunity) as opposed to *kairos* (opportunity) should also be theorized for its serendipitous possibilities.

In her afterword to this collection, Gesa Kirsch addresses the need for humanist scholar researchers to consider the ethical dilemmas of the discoveries we make that are dependent on the past, present, and future lives and circumstances of the individuals, societies, and cultures we study and remarks on "the current age of discontent" on university campuses and across the country as a whole. As this collection was going to press, the 2016 presidential election that revealed deep ideological, cultural, and economic divisions in the United States had just concluded and the country was facing new leadership and an uncertain future. The Brexit referendum in Great Britain has threatened to destabilize the European Union (EU), and researchers and universities in the United Kingdom are facing a potential threat of massive cuts in funding depending on how the post-Brexit government will align with future EU ideals. The waves of populism and nationalism that have swept across the United States and Europe appear to have emboldened volatile discourses of intolerance and hatred and sponsored fear for many of the most vulnerable members of society. How this will play out in terms of serendipity and future developments and discovery in our research and that of our students and colleagues is uncertain, but we also recognize that resistance in multiple forms is an appropriate response to intolerance, and we hope that this collection will inspire those who read it to continue the good work. In short, we hope this collection will encourage, inspire, and prepare the minds of current and future scholars for exploration and discovery, like Princes of Serendip, as they set forth on their own adventures in these especially challenging times.

Notes

Authors' Note: We appreciate the support of Michael Spooner, editor at the University Press of Colorado. We are also grateful to two anonymous reviewers who offered productive criticism that improved an earlier version of this collection. We also thank Cheryl Carnahan for her keen eye in editing the manuscript. Of course, any errors remain our own.

1. "He [*sic*] who does not expect will not find out the unexpected, for it is trackless and unexplored."
2. "In the fields of observation, chance favors only the prepared mind."
3. Also see Mark de Rond, and Iain Morely's edited collection, *Serendipity: Fortune and the Prepared Mind*.

Works Cited

André, Paul, M. C. Schraefel, Jaime Teevan, and Susan T. Dumais. "Discovery Is Never by Chance: Designing for (Un)Serendipity." *Creativity and Cognition* 9 (2009). Web. 14 April 2015.

Becker, Alton. "A Pikean Way of Thinking." Arizona State University, Tempe. 25 Sept. 1997. Presentation.

Burke, Kenneth. *The Philosophy of Literary Form: Studies in Symbolic Action*. 3rd ed. 1941. Los Angeles: U California P, 1973. Print.

Calhoun, Craig. "Accidental Wisdom: Robert Merton's Serendipitous Findings." *Book Forum* Summer 2004. Web. 7 April 2015.

Darbellay, Frédéric, Zoe Moody, Ayuko Sedooka, and Gabriela Steffen. "Interdisciplinary Research Boosted by Serendipity." *Creativity Research Journal* 26.1 (2014): 1–10. Print.

Düppe, Till. "Serendipity in Writing the Lives of Scientists." *Serendipities: Journal for the Sociology and History of the Social Sciences* 1.1 (2016): 7–10. Web. 23 June 2016.

Gaughan, Richard. *Accidental Genius: The World's Greatest by Chance Discoveries*. London: Metro, 2010. Print.

Gold, David. "The Accidental Archivist: Embracing Chance and Confusion in Historical Scholarship." *Beyond the Archives: Research as a Lived Process*. Ed. Gesa E. Kirsch and Liz Rohan. Carbondale: Southern Illinois UP, 2008. 13–19. Print.

Green, David G. *The Serendipity Machine: A Voyage of Discovery through the Unexpected World of Computers*. Crows Nest, Australia: Allen and Unwin, 2004. Print.

Hannan, Patrick J. *Serendipity, Luck, and Wisdom in Research*. Bloomington, IN: Universe, 2006. Print.

Hazan, Haim, and Esther Hertzog. *Serendipity in Anthropological Research: The Nomadic Turn*. Farnham, UK: Ashgate, 2011. Print.

Heraclitus. "Fragment 18." *The Art and Thought of Heraclitus*. Ed. and trans. Charles H. Kahn. Cambridge, UK: Cambridge UP, 1999. Print.

Hirschman, Albert O. "The Principle of the Hiding Hand." *National Affairs* 6 (1967): 10–23. Print.

Kirsch, Gesa E. "Being on Location: Serendipity, Place, and Archival Research." *Beyond the Archives: Research as a Lived Process*. Ed. Gesa E. Kirsch and Liz Rohan. Carbondale: Southern Illinois UP, 2008. 20–27. Print.

McClellan, James E., III. "Accident, Luck, and Serendipity in Historical Research." *Proceedings of the American Philosophical Society* 149.1 (2005): 1–20. Print.

Merton, Robert K. *Social Theory and Social Structure*. 1948. New York: Free Press, 1968. Print.

Merton, Robert K., and Elinor G. Barber. *The Travels and Adventures of Serendipity: A Study in Historical Semantics and the Sociology of Science*. 1958. Princeton, NJ: Princeton UP, 2004. Print.

Meyers, Morton A. *Happy Accidents: Serendipity in Major Medical Breakthroughs in the Twentieth Century.* New York: Arcade, 2011. Print.

Michener, William K., et al., "Biologic Field Stations: Research Legacies and Sites for Serendipity." *BioScience* 59.4 (2009): 300–310. Print.

Morrison, Toni. Nobel Lecture (1993). *Nobelprize.org.* Web. 25 Jan. 2009

Pasteur, Louis. "Inaugural Lecturer, University of Lille, Douai, France, December 7, 1854." *A Treasury of the World's Great Speeches.* Ed. Houston Peterson. New York: Simon and Schuster, 1954. 473. Print.

Ramsey, Alexis E., et al., eds. *Working in the Archives: Practical Research Methods for Rhetoric and Composition.* Carbondale: Southern Illinois UP, 2010. Print.

Rivoal, Isabelle, and Noel B. Salazar. "Contemporary Ethnographic Practice and the Value of Serendipity." *Social Anthropology* 21.2 (2013): 178–85. Web. 23 June 2016.

Roberts, Royston M. *Serendipity: Accidental Discoveries in Science.* Hoboken, NJ: Wiley, 1989. Print.

Rond, Mark de, and Iain Morely, eds. *Serendipity: Fortune and the Prepared Mind.* Cambridge: Cambridge UP, 2010. Print.

Rosen, Martin F. "Serendipity and Scientific Discovery." *Creativity and Leadership in the Twenty-First Century* 13 (2001): 187–93. Print.

Schaefer, Vincent J. *Serendipity in Science: Twenty Years at Langmuir University.* Schenectady, NY: Square Circle Press, 2013. Print.

Townsend, Keith, and John Burgess, eds. *Method in the Madness: Research Stories You Won't Read in Textbooks.* Oxford: Chandos, 2009. Print.

Van Andel, Pek. "Anatomy of the Unsought Finding: Serendipity: Origin, History, Domains, Traditions, Appearances Patterns, and Programmability." *British Journal for the Philosophy of Science* 45.3 (1994): 631–48. Print.

Wild-Wood, Emma. "'Se Débrouiller' or the Art of Serendipity in Historical Research." *History in Africa* 34 (2007): 367–81. Print.

PART I

Intersections of Personal and Political

1
"OH, MY GOD! HE WAS A SLAVE!"
Secrets of a Virginia Courthouse Archive

Shirley E. Faulkner-Springfield

COME CLOSE, LET ME TELL YOU A STORY

I sat at an old wooden table with *Will Book 12* in my hands and parted the tattered pages of the 200-year-old book. As my eyes slowly crept over the exquisite scribble, *I saw it.*

I had visited the Halifax County Courthouse in Virginia numerous times and read *Will Book 12*. My investigations into the past had not revealed official evidence of Friday Faulkner's existence. However, on January 17, 2002, I saw his name. I saw "Friday" on the last page of the four-page legal document dated February 9, 1823. Was this serendipity?

I read the line over and over: "*with sundry negroes namely Friday . . . with sundry negroes namely Friday . . . with sundry negroes namely Friday . . .*" (J. Faulkner 685).

"Oh, my God! He was a slave!" I whispered disheartingly to myself. My heart dropped to my feet; my blood boiled and heated my entire body; my throat filled with a warm, acidic substance; my tear ducts flooded. Pain penetrated every layer of my skin and tore at my organs. I was paralyzed. I was speechless. Although my intellect and curiosity had commanded ancestral knowledge, my psyche and physique did not welcome the conversion they experienced on that fateful day in the archive of the Halifax County Courthouse.

For six years I had conducted archival and historical research in Virginia, in North Carolina, and on the internet with the mission of unearthing ancestral knowledge, specifically knowledge on my great-great-grandparents, Friday and Rebecca Harris Faulkner. Although their own words went unspoken, each year my extended family and I celebrated their lives and the legacy they germinated for us. The oral history that circulated within and outside my family did not include a slave named Friday Faulkner. Hence, while analyzing the rhetoric of slavery, I

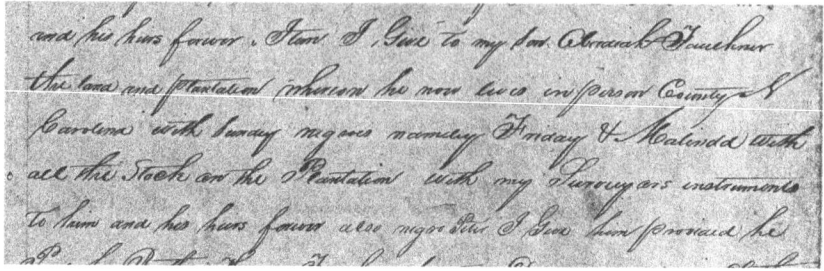

Figure 1.1. Excerpt from Jacob Faulkner's Last Will and Testament. Photo: Author.

posed one question: "Is this the lesson I was destined to learn?" Not only had I unearthed my great-great-grandfather, I had also discerned his role in the development of America and thus of American history. Friday Faulkner was a major character in one of the worst chapters in American history, which reads accordingly: *I give to my son Obadiah Faulkner the land and plantation whereon he now lives in Person County, N Carolina with sundry negroes namely Friday and Malinda with all the stock on the plantation with my surveyors [sic] instruments to him and his heirs forever* (J. Faulkner 685).

I held Friday in my hands—a life that had been placed on an eleven by seventeen piece of parchment among animals and other commodities; a life that had been directed by a white man who believed people of African descent were unworthy of autonomy, respect, and value as human beings. Reading Jacob's will overwhelmed me because I was uninformed about Friday's past, because I refused to make assumptions about Friday's life, and because I had discovered that my maternal great-great-great-grandfather and his brother were born free.

This is another story:

In October 1999, I visited the Halifax County Courthouse and searched the Register of Free Negroes for any Faulkner. Instead, I found the names "Henderson Lester" and "Elisha Lester" and learned that both of them were born free, a status that was indicative of their mother's status—a free woman: a free black woman? A free white woman? Later, I learned that Henderson Lester was my great-great-great-grandfather, my paternal great-grandmother's father. On November 27, 1848, both Henderson and Elisha A. Lester registered as freemen of color in Halifax County, Virginia (Register of Free Blacks in Halifax County, no. 404 and no. 405). Henderson was twenty-seven years old, and Elisha was twenty-six years old. Though I learned that these black males of dark complexion with curly black hair were born free, their embodied representation of "free" men was unsettling because my ancestors bore the marks of slavery: Elisha "has a scar on his left thumb," and Henderson "had a scar on his left forefinger [and] the same finger had been cut off" (Register). Was the slave-free paradox a false binary for Henderson and Elisha Lester? Given that after the year 1640 skin tone was the primary factor that distinguished a free

> human being from an enslaved human being, the writer's emphasis on physicality was imperative to my ancestors' status and survival as "free" persons of color in a slaveholding society. Furthermore, according to the 1850 United States Census, 534 "free colored Persons" resided in Halifax County, Virginia. Among a total slave population of 14,452, my maternal ancestors were among the 3.7 percent of free people of color in Halifax County.

After reading Jacob's narrative, I internalized my emotions and thought, "You cannot cry in front of these white people."

This is another story:

> I was born into a segregated southern society in 1961 during one of the African American Civil Rights movements when some people of African descent concealed their emotions from the other. In that complex society that conflicted with his ideology, my father pushed explicit and implicit racial lines back as far as he could, retaliating when called "Nigger," retaliating when refused service in public places. My parents thought they had prepared me for my racist society. They loathed the pejorative discourse that was coined for the purpose of attempting to dehumanize people of African descent, which in turn caused my mother to attempt to shape my nascent identity by helping me construct ethos and a sense of pride in myself and my African and African American legacies.
>
> "Words can't hurt you, girl," avowed my mother, who relied on her faith in God for strength and courage to avert the racially inflammatory language our foes hurled at us.
>
> However, when I struggled to chant the psychological maneuver, I surmised that I had been mis-educated. While I remembered my mother's nurturing and compassionate self each time razor-sharp racial slurs cut deeply into my soul and provoked negative emotions, sometimes I retaliated against my antagonists. On January 17, 2002, while in the courthouse, I could not retaliate and my antagonist had not called me "Nigger," but the foreign yet familiar language my eyes had forced my brain to translate hurt me. It was language that perpetuated suppression, oppression, and a sense of racial superiority. Jacob's nonverbal discourse provoked the most visceral response I had ever experienced.

Slowly and meticulously, I elevated my face to the ceiling to fight back the warm, heavy tears that engulfed my eyelid margins. My throat continued to burn. My eyes were as heavy as my heart that lay shattered at the tips of my toes. I felt the vacant cavity where my heart once resided. My body reminded me that my heart had a brain of its own, one that had experienced a psychological impediment that altered my epistemological and ontological positions on my life and my identity. My body yearned for somebody, something—a savior, a voice, answers to the inarticulate questions that were birthed in my heart, not in my head.

I fought back the tears as long as I could. Finally, I escaped and raced to the *rest*room, avoiding all eye contact. I did not want to look into anyone's eyes, nor did I want anyone to gaze into mine, for I feared the spectator would interpret my thoughts and recognize my *new* identity.

I locked the door to the small, musky space and cried hot, acidic tears. I cried with grief I had never experienced, not even when my father died. Then, I cried for me. And I cried for him again.

"Why? Why didn't someone tell me? Why didn't I know? Why didn't they fight back?" I moaned.

This is another story:

> *I was cognizant that my ancestors fought back: they resisted enslavement by using violent, physical methods such as murder and suicide; by articulating anti-slavery rhetoric; and by using other palpable, nonverbal methods. However, white racism was a white revolution that resisted black power by any means necessary, which included shooting, burning, raping, hanging, drowning, poisoning, starving, scalding, and whipping black people.*
>
> *My ancestors fought against oppression and racism as my parents and I had, and the stream of "Colored" water we drank from segregated fountains exacerbated the daily racial tensions we experienced: that stream ran "deep" and "strong" through me, carving out an immediate connection to Friday Faulkner. I also knew that if my ancestors wanted to survive, as Friday Faulkner had, they carefully chose their battles, weapons, and words, as I had throughout my research and writing processes.*

As images from visual and textual depictions of the institution of slavery populated my mind, I reconstructed Friday's life as a slave, comparing his life to my life as a young black female in a racist, sexist, and segregated society. My reflection elicited emotions that were akin to those conveyed by authors of slave narratives who did not initially recognize their destiny. Venture Smith, Frederick Douglass, Mary Prince, Harriet Jacobs, and countless others who deserve mention here told their stories of a blissful childhood naïveté that was suddenly interrupted by a painfully unanticipated reality: captivity. I, too, had been held captive by a dead man who forced me to sit at an old wooden table in a courthouse and listen to his story. In this regard, Jacob Faulkner's legacy haunted and constrained me 137 years after the abolition of slavery: by paralyzing me, by breaking my spirit, and by altering my identity. Not only did the reading of Jacob's will compel me to recall painful, suppressed, traumatic memory and repressed emotions, it forced me to recall language's ability to empower, to disempower, and to construct reality, if only temporarily.

I found "a slave." I could not deny my discovery because Friday's name was etched onto the 200-year-old legal document. I had unearthed an enslaved man, a clearer mental image of an ancestor to append my name, and equally important, I had unearthed the white family whose name I had proudly and naïvely endorsed. I channeled Malcolm X who during his six years in captivity grew so adamant about his lost African heritage that he changed his surname. My mind gradually shifted to my heritage, and I asked: Why, among "sundry Negroes," did Jacob identify Friday by name in this particular section of his will? Was Friday Jacob's trusted servant? Was Friday Jacob's son? Who was Malinda? What did Friday look like?

The succinct yet potent textual representation of Friday Faulkner exposes a harsh depiction of "colored" people, that is, as chattel. Jacob Faulkner linguistically and literally positioned Friday Faulkner among "all the stock on the plantation with [his] surveyors [*sic*] instruments" (685), thus dehumanizing him. In *Constructing the Black Masculine: Identity and Ideality in African American Men's Literature and Culture, 1775–1995*, Maurice O. Wallace asks: "Who, after all, can deny the endless and unspeakable power of so many desperate white schemes as American slavery, Jim Crow, the lynch mob, urban dispassion, and, most recently, the prison industrial complex to unman (read: dehumanize) the African American male" (2). Wallace's critique of American culture reveals a trajectory of systemic oppressive forces that enable the hegemony to maintain its dominance. Jacob Faulkner's Last Will and Testament, which commanded that his "will be done," solidified Friday Faulkner's forced social identity in the nineteenth-century milieu in which they lived and in my twenty-first-century psyche.

When I interpreted the rhetoric that manifested in Jacob's will, I acquiesced without remonstrance and accepted Friday's legal social identity as a slave, as Jacob's property. Not only did Jacob's will condemn my great-great-grandfather to perpetual slavery, a position that denied him the right and the opportunity to become a whole person or what Arlene R. Keizer calls "an autonomous liberal subject" (29), it also legitimized Jacob as a slave owner and a member of the "white-capitalist, patriarchal system of domination" (25). Therefore, a slaveholder's will—a *master* narrative—clearly defined and established Jacob's and Friday's binary positions in their nineteenth-century slaveholding society and in the master-slave relationship. Within his legal textual representation of Friday that validates how power manifests itself from the crypt, Jacob conferred his status of *owner* of Friday to his heir, Obadiah. Ultimately, all the characters in Jacob's *master* narrative, including myself, were implicated in Jacob's rhetoric, which demonstrates the power of language, how symbols form our identities, and how we take on those representations of ourselves (Bakhtin 1981). Furthermore, I was not privy to my great-great-grandfather's counter-narrative because I was too young, because I did not eavesdrop when it was told, because I was not an active listener when my family told it, or because no one told it. As a result, I did not have a narrative to juxtapose against Jacob's dominant narrative. But nothing could have prepared me for the lesson I learned on that fateful day in the archive when the discovery of my great-great-grandfather became a blessing and a curse.

Similar to the way Malea Powell encapsulates her embodied archival experience in "Dreaming Charles Eastman," I have captured my archival experience among these pages. Powell writes, "My point here is what it feels like to be in an archive not because *I* think you care how I feel, but to illustrate the ways in which meaning is sometimes held captive by the body and how we have to then walk through story to make sense of our experiences as writers, as scholars, and as humans" (117). Powell also reasons that "some events have to be walked and talked aloud, moved through, told" (117). Powell's affirmation about the link between our physical and psychological selves speaks profoundly to my embodied experience in the archive that rendered me temporarily voiceless, distressed, hapless, helpless, and fragmented.

I never thought finding Friday would hurt so *awfully*. *I had learned; I had suffered, and pain fell upon my heart, and in my own despair, against [my] will, [came] wisdom to use by the awful grace of God* (Aeschylus). After I experienced traumatic pain, powerlessness, and a sense of loss, my resurrection resulted only from confronting my immediate pain and my traumatic past, which liberated me. My transformation ceased after I dismantled Jacob Faulkner's interpellation. I had internalized white male supremacist values and attempted to articulate Jacob Faulkner's perspective of black manhood and black personhood, with a disregard for how my great-great-grandfather might have self-identified or defined black manhood and personhood in a slaveholding society.

I cleaned my face and attempted to restore myself to normalcy. That is, I gathered the fragmented pieces of myself and attempted to put them back "in all the right order" (Morrison 272–74). I found wisdom, strength, peace, and solace in the small, damp, constricted space that allowed me to provide self-therapy to my wounded soul. I had experienced bondage and freedom, and in the *rest*room I was elevated to a psychological level I had never experienced during my six-year quest for ancestral knowledge. My research necessitated new psychological and intellectual perspectives for me to continue my research and, though painful and disconcerting, tell *my* story as ethically as I could about my black and white family. However, I was also cognizant that total objectivity was impossible because of my original epistemological and ontological perspectives on enslavement and on its perpetrators.

Yet in the *rest*room I acquired the knowledge and language I needed to clearly discern, not excuse, my white family's deportment and to generate the types of responses and ask the types of questions of some white people, specifically ultra-conservatives, that merited answers that connected the puzzle of my life.

I left the small space, proudly approached the old wooden table, cradled my great-great-grandfather in my bosom, and claimed his life as a human being, as a man with a strong, prosperous progeny. Then, I carried him to the basement and requested a copy of the only written document that validated my great-great-grandfather's life, though Jacob's inscription of Friday embodied human chattel. I accepted my new identity as the descendant of an American who had been enslaved—a man who endured what Henry Louis Gates Jr. argues is "one of the most inhumane systems of social and economic oppression the world has ever seen" (vi), which I witnessed through my readings of the Faulkner family papers.

This is another story:

> I returned to the Halifax County Courthouse again and searched the archive for additional evidence of Jacob Faulkner's property, descendants, and ancestors. Not only did I learn that my great-great-grandfather is the link that connects two sets of Faulkners, one black and one white, I learned that he was a link in an international capitalist enterprise that exploited people of color in several states by ascertaining and maintaining ownership of them as real property. The Faulkner's personal papers expose their "pursuit of power, both in its economic implications for political growth and in its personal aspects in [their] own career[s]" as slave owners, planters, politicians, physicians, and educators (Koch vii). A close rhetorical analysis of the language the slave owners used in their wills exposes the formation and perpetuation of a planter aristocracy that began in Halifax County, Virginia, and extended to Person County, North Carolina, as well as to Kentucky and Georgia. It also points to members of a southern-dominant cultural group that determined the group's hegemony and how their Last Will and Testaments were used to gain access to cultural values, individuals, communities, and institutions of power that shaped the way meaning and identities were formed in Halifax County, Virginia, and Person County, North Carolina, in ante- and post-bellum America. In addition, while I could only trace my paternal ancestry to my great-great-grandfather, the five generations of slaveholders I traced were the progeny of a white servant, Thomas Faulkner, the first Faulkner who arrived in the American [Colonies] on the Mary Providence in 1622 (Hotten 251). Thomas was a twenty-eight-year-old immigrant from Great Britain and one of the two servants of M' Robart Salford, a fifty-six-year-old who arrived in New England aboard the John and Francis in 1611, according to a muster taken on January 23, 1624 (Hotten 250). M'Robart and his servants lived in Elizabeth Cittie [sic], Virginia. Thomas was among 227 people—55 men, 41 women, 129 children, and 2 servants—who "promise[d] Lord Ambassador of the Most Serene King of Great, obedience, as soon as conveniently may be, and this under the conditions to be carried out in the articles we have communicated to the said Ambassador, and not otherwise, on the faith of which we have unanimously signed this present with our sign manual" (Hotten 252). The persons signing, called the Virginia Company,

went to Virginia after taking the Oath of Allegiance or Supremacy, which was an "allegiance to the King and to conform to the rules of government established in the Church of England" (Hotten 252). The king promised land "in convenient numbers in the principal cities, boroughs, and corporations in Virginia" (Hotten 252). The Company at Elizabeth Cittie owned 3,000 planted acres and 1,500 acres of common land (Hotten 274). Thomas was a minister for the Church of England, and by June 5, 1639, he owned 350 acres of land (Hotten 274).

This is another story:

The unearthing of my great-great-grandfather had initiated a succession of methodical queries about black and white Faulkners. My newfound knowledge necessitated information on the man who became the beneficiary of land that was granted to him by King James I of England and a man whose descendants had enslaved my great-great-grandfather. In an attempt to connect the two families, on April 8, 2002, I sent an email message to one of Thomas's descendants, David Faulkner. David lives with his family in Christian County, Kentucky. David and his wife, Jan, asked, "From which Faulkner line are you descended?" After one week of careful deliberations that were mired in conflicting internal dialogue about my approach to David and Jan's inquiry, I informed them that I am the descendant of Friday Faulkner, an African American male who was enslaved by Jacob Faulkner. Since we communicated through cyberspace, I had no indication of Jan's and David's reaction to my e-response. Although I responded as amicably and sensitively as any descendent of enslaved human beings possibly could, I thought I would never hear from the couple again. However, two days after my response, Jan and David delivered this email message to the descendants of the man their ancestors enslaved:

> *There is no way to excuse Faulkners or anyone else for enslaving others. It stops me cold every time I see an old document that refers to people as property and slaves. Nothing else—not histories, biographies, essays, etc.—makes that time as starkly real to me as does a court document in the handwriting of the people of those days. To say we are sorry is inadequate, but my husband and I will do whatever I can to help you, and I greatly admire your attitude about your research. I am very much looking forward to learning more about your family.*

Jan, David, and I planned to meet one day in Halifax County, Virginia, where David's and my roots were transplanted and germinated. I emailed the couple again in 2009, but they did not respond to my inquiry. However, I received a call from Jan ten years from the time of my first email, on Monday, July 22, 2013. Jan, who is eager to read my book, inquired about its availability. I informed Jan that I lost my history book when my computer crashed and that I have not succeeded at retrieving the book from the only other electronic archive I created. Then, on Friday, August 2, 2013, Jan sent me an email message that contained the names of Faulkners of African descent whom she had contacted approximately twenty years ago when she researched the Faulkner genealogy. Jan also sent me the name of a white male who owns Jacob Faulkner's three-story mansion that was built before the Revolutionary War and suggested that I visit him and inquire about the white Faulkners. The Library of Virginia had given me an image of Jacob's mansion in exchange for a copy of my history book, which I could not deliver. On February 15, 2016, Jan invited me to view David's DNA results on Ancestry.com and encouraged me to submit my DNA results to Ancestry. What might my twenty-three pairs of chromosomes reveal? Will I discover that Shirley Elizabeth Faulkner-Springfield and David Faulkner share more than a family name?

In *Slaves in the Family,* Edward Ball writes:

No one among the [families of former slave owners] talked about how slavery had helped us, but whether we acknowledged it or not, the powers of our ancestors were still in hand. Although our social franchise had shrunk, it had nevertheless survived. If we did not inherit money, or land, we received a great fund of cultural capital, including prestige, a chance at education, self-esteem, a sense of place, mobility, even (in some cases) a flair for giving orders. By skewing things so violently in the past, we had made sure that our cultural riches would benefit all white Americans . . . The plantation heritage was not "ours," like a piece of family property, and not "theirs," belonging to black families, but a shared history. *The progeny of slaves and the progeny of slave owners are forever linked* (emphasis mine). We have been in each other's lives. They have been in each other's dreams. We have been in each other's beds. (14)

Ball describes slavery as a legacy that divides us and as a legacy that keeps us bound together, as my research demonstrates.

In this text, I, an African American archival researcher, exerted rhetorical power and wrote Friday Faulkner back into humanity. In 2002, when I considered making my story accessible to a wider audience, I agonized over publicizing my personal thoughts and experiences. Initially, I struggled to evoke a wider, diverse audience with whom I could engage in candid discourse about controversial topics that arouse various visceral and negative emotions. Furthermore, I believed I could not expose my innermost thoughts about race, enslavement, oppression, racism, and sexism to a general audience who is deeply implicated in a culture of amnesia.

I also believed that I could not expose my inner thoughts about enslavement because similar to what bell hooks experienced while writing *Talking Back,* I experienced an array of interruptions, and the most invariable interruptions were pain and fear. My rhetorical performance was painful because composing a version of my narrative for *you* forced me to relive the experiences that speak to my exigency, and I feared what both the affects and the effects of my private thoughts would have on *me,* as the personal is political. My reluctance, like my family's silence, spawned from my sense of the importance of my family history and how dangerous that history might be in the hands of people who historically have exploited people of color, psychologized people of color, and romanticized whiteness and the institution of slavery.

Eventually, I deduced that my unspeakable family secret must be reinscribed, positioning my great-great-grandfather as a resilient survivor of inhumane treatment and positioning me as a griot who articulates a contemporary narrative of slavery. My great-great-grandfather did not live in perpetual slavery, as his *master* had decreed from the crypt. Friday Faulkner died a free man at the age of seventy-seven, according to his death certificate. The oral histories I collected place Friday in the Civil War at the Battle of Nashville in 1864. However, I did not discover the role Friday played in the American Civil War; nor did I discover when or how he became a free man. Family oral history also situates Friday as an entrepreneur—a sawmill owner in Virgilina, Virginia, where he and Rebecca lived.

My textual resurrection of Friday Faulkner is the rhetorical antithesis to Jacob Faulkner's Last Will and Testament. Subsequently, Friday Faulkner's life can be read against the grain of the dominant narrative and as part of a collective cultural memory that reverberates from the crypt of a Virginia courthouse archive.

Works Cited

Aeschylus. *The Agamemnon of Aeschylus*. Trans. Gilbert Murray. London: George Allen and Unwin Ltd., 1920. Web. 3 March 2011.

Bakhtin, Mikhail M. "Discourse in the Novel." *The Dialogic Imagination*. Ed. Michael Holquist. Austin: U of Texas P, 1981. 259–422. Print.

Ball, Edward. *Slaves in the Family*. New York: Ballantine Books, 2001. Print.

Faulkner, Jacob. "Jacob Faulkner's Last Will and Testament." 9 Feb. 1823. Halifax County Circuit Court. Halifax County, VA. *Will Book 12*, 682–85. Print.

Faulkner, Jan, and David Faulkner. Email communication. 8 April 2002; 22 July 2013; 3 Aug. 2013, and 15 Feb. 2016.

Faulkner, Obadiah. Records Books, Abstracts 1792–1820, North Carolina State Archives, Raleigh; Slave Records and Bill of Slaves, Misc. Records, North Carolina State Archives, Raleigh; Book O, page 394, North Carolina State Archives, Raleigh; 1850 N.C. Schedule 2—Slave Inhabitants in Person County, page 33, Aug. 17, 1850; 1860 N.C. Schedule 2—Slave Inhabitants in Person County, page 46, Sept. 5, 1860. Print.

Gates, Henry Louis, Jr. Preface. *The Slave's Narrative*. Ed. Charles T. Davis and Henry Louis Gates Jr. New York: Oxford UP, 1985. v–vii. Print.

hooks, bell. *Talking Back: Thinking Feminist, Thinking Black*. Boston: South End, 1989. Print.

Hotten, John C., ed. *The Original Lists of Persons of Quality: Emigrants, Religious Exiles, Political Rebels, Serving Men Sold for a Term of Years, Apprentices, Children Stolen, Maidens Pressed, and Others, Who Went from Great Britain to the American Plantations, 1600–1700*. London, 1874. Clearfield, PA: Genealogical P, 1997. Print.

Keizer, Arlene R. *Black Subjects: Identity Formation in the Contemporary Narrative of Slavery*. Ithaca, NY: Cornell UP, 2004. Print.

Koch, Adrienne. Preface. *Power, Morals, and the Founding Fathers: Essays in the Interpretation of the American Enlightenment*. New York: Great Seal Books, 1961. vii–ix. Print.

Morrison, Tony. *Beloved*. New York: Knopf Doubleday Publishing Group, 1987. Print.

Powell, Malea. "Dreaming Charles Eastman: Cultural Memory, Autobiography, and Geography in Indigenous Rhetorical Histories." *Beyond the Archives: Research as a Lived Process*. Ed. Gesa E. Kirsch and Liz Rohan. Carbondale: Southern Illinois UP, 2008. 115–27. Print.
Register of Free Blacks in Halifax County, no. 404. 27 Nov. 1848. Halifax County Circuit Court. Halifax County, VA. Print.
Register of Free Blacks in Halifax County, no. 405. 27 Nov. 1848. Halifax County Circuit Court. Halifax County, VA. Print.
Wallace, Maurice O. *Constructing the Black Masculine: Identity and Ideality in African American Men's Literature and Culture, 1775–1995*. Durham, NC: Duke UP, 2002. Print.

2
MAKING SENSE OF DISASTER
Composing a Methodology for Place-Based Visual Research

Doreen Piano

> *To learn therefore means at root—at route—"to follow a track."*
> —Robert McFarlane,
> *The Old Ways: A Journey on Foot*

Driving to campus during the spring semester 2005 after the levees breached in New Orleans, flooding, then displacing residents, I passed by an abandoned rusted-out car with "Bush Lies" painted on it until one day it was gone, its disappearance a small yet significant sign that the city was recovering. On that same route to campus, located between two of the major levee breaches, I saw the remains of houses that had taken in water above their rooftops, many of them sagged and tilted at odd angles, weighed down by water. Sludge from the lake covered everything: it was a world of beige, spiked occasionally by the brashness of sunflowers that had sporadically been sown by the lake water. The university's campus, while on relatively high ground, had been an evacuation drop-off for survivors who had been stranded there for days. When rescued, they were told to leave their pets behind. The library had been vandalized and many of our offices, used as living spaces and washroom facilities, were undergoing mold remediation when campus reopened in late fall of 2005. We could enter our offices briefly to retrieve materials we needed while teaching online or at a nearby satellite campus. For many academics like me who lived on or near the Gulf Coast in August 2005, Hurricane Katrina impacted not only our personal lives but also our professional ones. Given the scale of the disaster, it was hard to ignore. In the aftermath of "the storm," as locals called it, the division between where we lived and where we worked eroded as universities and colleges in the area became part of an emerging, fragmented narrative about what had happened during and after the flood.

DOI: 10.7330/9781607327394.c002

In discussing the storm's impact on academic research along the Gulf Coast, Amy Koritz observes, "the work they pursued post-Katrina was really a mode of coping with tragedy. We fell back on what we knew how to do as the vehicle for our response to a community in crisis" (21). For some of us in English studies, this meant designing disaster-related content and assignments in our classes starting online during a truncated semester (what we called the Katrina semester) and continuing during the first few years of recovery. A book I taught in my graduate writing pedagogy seminar that spring by Derek Owens, *Sustainability and Composition: Teaching for a Threatened Generation,* became a touchstone for many of the Katrina-related place-based writing assignments I developed.

Owens's call for composition studies "to localize," by concentrating on environmental, political, and social issues that connected students to where they live, spoke to me and a graduate student whose master's thesis I was directing that focused on Katrina-related pedagogies.[1] Using Owens's work as a guide, I assigned micro-ethnographies, visual essays documenting students' neighborhoods and interviews/profiles of people they knew who had a Katrina story to tell. What I did not expect, however, was how my research would radically change over the next few years, reflecting my experiences of living in post-Katrina New Orleans. Despite the psychic and material challenges of confronting devastation on a daily basis, living in New Orleans during its protracted recovery bestowed a gift of sorts, a unique moment to engage in meaningful projects that connected my professional life to local conditions.

This chapter explores serendipity in the research process not as an "aha moment" of discovery but as a starting point for rethinking one's relationship to scholarly work in the context of disaster. In addition to exploring unexpected, fortuitous moments that unfolded during the research process, I also focus on the circumstances surrounding the storm's impact that shifted my research to what writing colleagues described as "whole body" scholarship, "disturbing the normal" and "ontological."[2] Even while serendipity is, as the editors of this collection define it, a combination of "chance" and a "prepared mind," additional elements such as "place" and "disaster"—in this case, proximity to disaster—can also perhaps paradoxically provide the conditions for rethinking one's relation to research and writing. While definitions of serendipity typically focus on timing, I make the case for place as significant to the *where* and not just the *when* of serendipity. Gesa Kirsch understands this when describing how being in Berkeley while researching her subject, Dr. Mary Ritter, "made it easier . . . to read the handwritten correspondence and diary entries that prominently featured local places and events" (22). The material world acts as a guide to the textual, allowing Kirsch to become part of the world Ritter describes. Yet what if we take the consequences of place on research further and examine serendipity within a context of disaster? How can openness to shifting material and psychic conditions in one's professional life—in my case, living and teaching through catastrophe—provide a serendipitous moment for challenging traditional scholarly methods and frameworks?

Sociologists, public health specialists, disaster researchers, historians, geographers, American studies, media, critical race, and gender studies scholars have all contributed to a growing body of Hurricane Katrina scholarship, what my late colleague in history Michael Mizell-Nelson described as "the documentary impulse" (59). Some of these projects are ones Mizell-Nelson criticizes as unsustainable, undertaken by parachute academics, many of whom dismissed local researchers, exploited residents for their own gains, or later abandoned their often funded projects. Yet, one outcome of this surge in research was how the "Katrina genre" as a whole impacted a change in the storm's description as "natural" to an "engineering disaster" (Brodine 79). Among New Orleans institutions, the documentary turn to the local often involved cross-disciplinary and cross-institutional conversations. At the University of New Orleans, colleagues in history, documentary film, sociology, and urban studies conducted a broad range of scholarly research. For some, such as Mizell-Nelson, whose research involved histories of the streetcar and the po'boy sandwich, the development of the Hurricane Memory Databank, a digital archive of storm ephemera and stories, seemed a logical step. Another colleague in sociology, Pam Jenkins, continued her work on women and community activism but within a Katrina/disaster framework. For both of these academics, writing about the storm involved what Peter Goggin and Maureen Goggin describe as "writing trauma," what Dominick LaCapra, in his work on Holocaust survivors, defines as "a working through, and acting out, by those who are first-degree witnesses" (34). Often, this included writing about their own positionality as survivors who had sustained losses.[3] Describing her methodology, Jenkins observes: "This chapter is based on a set of conversations with women I have known for two decades. We worked with each other before Katrina on very successful projects and projects that were more challenging. So, in a way, this is my story as well. Like many here, I lost my house and belongings in the flood. I was a nomad, living here and there, for nearly two years before coming back to my rebuilt house" (169).

The rhetorical move that places the researcher and researched within a shared space of experiencing trauma (in this case, displacement) is a way of knowing that can open possibilities for different kinds of knowledge production. As scholars, we are trained primarily to analyze, decipher, observe, and understand; yet as Shannon Lee Dawdy argues, "people in post-disaster situations have a heightened reflexive awareness of their relationship with landscapes, objects, and space" (paraphrased in Brodine 82). Living in a ruined landscape was akin to living in a war zone. Familiar places for many residents were unrecognizable. This new landscape required new ways of navigating. For example, mountains of trash piled on sidewalks meant that people were returning to clean, gut, and discard unusable, damaged things. Living in a city that historically has experienced cycles of death and destruction throughout its 500-year history, living in the ruins became an ontological location: How does not just "knowing" but "being" change under these circumstances?

Despite some excellent work on trauma and disaster undertaken by scholars in rhetoric and composition, much of it is based on classroom practice,[4] helpful to me as I engaged with post-disaster New Orleans was discovering scholarship in American and gender studies that had responded to New York in the aftermath of September 11. By connecting scholarly practices of analysis and reflection to non-conventional knowledge-making practices such as personal narrative, witnessing, poetry, and photography, many of the contributions in the edited collection *Trauma at Home: After 9/11* reveal that writing in the proximity of disaster, what Ann Cvetkovich describes as "the vicinity of trauma" (62), requires us to counter "academic rootlessness" by locating ourselves in the material conditions of everyday life.[5] Key to Cvetkovich's trauma theory is the relation of place to disaster: she reads trauma sites as moving beyond "the moment of impact" to explore how disaster affects the communities "in which people live with its loss" (62). Given the regular yet unpredictable occurrences of large-scale disasters and their potential for affecting academics, especially those who live in climate-vulnerable communities, Cvetkovich and other scholars represented in *Trauma at Home* provide models for exploring what ethical obligations we have to the communities in which we live and work.

For me, living in New Orleans after the storm became a moment of questioning how I could engage intellectually with the circumstances of disaster yet not exploit them. My query began there and yet now, more than a decade later, I view this period as one in which ostensibly despairing moments also revealed possibilities for not only new ways of writing, researching, and presenting but also new ways of being. These are ideas I explore in this chapter, keeping in mind that disasters and individual/community responses to them are not monolithic and that our privileged positions as scholars, our methods, and even writing itself as a representational tool can act to displace the very population and places that we as scholars feel compelled to research (Vanderberg and Clary-Lemon).[6] In addition, questions of the right to tell a story, even one's own, become part of the challenge of researching in the aftermath of disaster.

DISASTER'S POSTMORTEM: GROUNDING MYSELF IN LOSS

> But the landscape of devastation is still a landscape. There is beauty in ruins.
>
> —Susan Sontag, *Regarding the Pain of Others*

To call what happened to my post-Katrina research "serendipitous" is to diminish the loss of life, the pain and suffering that continue to mark many people's lives more than ten years after the storm.[7] It seems deeply insensitive, even scandalous. People's lives were ruined, including those of many of my colleagues, some of whom stayed during the storm and suffered immensely. An example is poet and post-colonial studies scholar Niyi Osundari, who, along with his wife, had been stuck in an attic without a hatchet for several days before being rescued. Others lost homes and pets or returned only to sell their homes. Moreover, the negative impact on the university where I teach continues over twelve years later because of a combination of continuing low student enrollment, academic brain drain, and eight years of austerity measures disguised as higher education reform under former governor Bobby Jindal. More than a decade later, the city appears to have recovered, at least in terms of attracting tourism and urban development, yet fewer visible scars confirm a false sense of recovery. The city has become a land grab for developers and out-of-towners, especially those living in cities—New York, Los Angeles, San Francisco—where buying a house is impossible without a six-figure income. Developers intent on "reinvigorating" neighborhoods such as the one in which I live ignore residents' wishes for low-density, affordable housing and lack sensitivity to the historic features; rising rents continue to push working-class people further away from the city's central neighborhoods, and violent crime ravages isolated low-income neighborhoods and tourist areas downtown.[8]

When considering these dire circumstances, reading serendipity into an overarching narrative of catastrophe, death, displacement, and gentrification (what Naomi Klein has defined as "disaster politics") may open me up to criticism, perhaps rightly so.[9] Conveying my Katrina story of challenges and hardships in comparison with those who lost their lives, family members, homes, and communities seems insignificant based on my economic status, race privilege, and mobility—my ability to voluntarily move or leave an oncoming disaster. Discussing the storm as another anniversary loomed, a friend—a nurse who had worked tirelessly for days at a hospital surrounded by floodwaters—told me, "If you got out before the storm hit, you don't get to tell me how hard it was." Yet despite the widespread loss, devastation, and displacement, particularly in working-class white communities and communities of color, stories of positive change emerged that countered the victim narratives spun by mainstream media.

A phenomenon I witnessed on my return in November was an increased investment in community by residents committed to the city's recovery.[10] As Tulane geographer Rich Campanella observes, "High-stakes concerns about flood protection, contamination, health, education, residents' right to return, economic recovery, coastal restoration, and myriad other postdiluvial issues drove the energized public discourse" (28). In the Lower 9th Ward neighborhood of Holy Cross where I now live, every structure had been flooded, and many people died because of the proximity of the compromised levee system. From these conditions arose new and returning community leaders. Active, angry, determined, and politicized as a result of government on all levels being absent, they galvanized residents and created new organizations that focused on housing, race, youth employment, and the environment to restore their communities.[11] Writer Rebecca Solnit describes these alternate civic formations created after disasters as "akin to a shadow government—another system ready to do more were they voted into power" (313). These "paradises built in hell," she observes, are "improvisational; we make them up as we go along, and in so doing they call on all our strength and creativity and leave us free to invent" (313). Solnit's sentiment, while not quite accurate—most survivors of the flood had left involuntarily and did not have the freedom to invent— manifested itself in symbolic ways as well. I attended lectures and panel discussions, hurricane-related plays, poetry readings, and civic meetings hosted by universities, churches, museums, and community centers. A colleague invited me to monthly potlucks hosted in people's homes where an invited speaker provided a new angle or challenge related to the city's recovery, such as how to organize for a stronger levee system, reinvigorate the public school system, or understand how the city's demographics would change based on the loss of African American residents who would never return. These informal presentations brought people from diverse backgrounds and interests together around a common issue of wanting to do something to ensure the city's survival.

Everything during that first year of the recovery seemed to connect to the storm and its consequences. The drive to and from campus, while ostensibly absent of human life, revealed traces of human life: hurricane graffiti was visible everywhere. Similar kinds of visual signage sprang to life on neutral grounds—artists sculpting Katrina detritus memorials, streets signs that had been destroyed replaced with new handmade ones, even the cheap plastic advertisements for recovery services placed on neutral grounds—creating (at least in my mind) a sense of hope for the city's future. While some of my colleagues were able to compartmentalize and separate their personal anguish from their professional lives, others like me conflated the two, allowing them to inter-animate each other. My background in rhetoric and literacy studies, particularly Anne Ruggles Gere's concept of "composition's extracurriculum," enabled me to view the emerging visual culture as a public literacy, a collective and timely response to disaster through the inventive use of disaster's waste.

Discarded refrigerators, flooded cars, and damaged houses all became composing surfaces, often paralleling both New Orleans's street culture in terms of collective performances and obliquely referencing more formal art institutions that exhibited found objects and amateur photographers along with professional ones in exhibits related to the storm. Among the shout-outs to the city and uplifting, often funny messages were many spray-painted signs daring looters to enter private property. In addition, more despairing hurricane graffiti with signage that read "Don't Bulldoze" and "We'll Be Back" was found in areas Campanella describes as "that other city," whose residents, "suffering the worst of times, were largely absent from the inspiring postdiluvial tableau" (27). This "other city" he refers to consisted of neighborhoods to the east and north of the city, areas that had been hit hardest by floodwaters and revealed little to no improvements for years after the storm. Partly because of their location beyond the central areas of the city and partly as a result of economics and race that created obstacles to returning and to rebuilding, many of these areas continue to languish.

Documenting the city through photography and journal writing became part of a routine of interfacing with the physical destruction of the city, its non-functioning traffic lights and bare school playgrounds echoing dysfunction and despair. Helping a friend clean her block of trash, mostly broken glass and personal items left over from the flood; participating in second lines and other commemorative activities, and volunteering to feed abandoned animals in flooded neighborhoods fueled an intimate connection to place that might have taken years to develop. Observing and participating in what was happening around me was not based on any conscious decision to convert these experiences into research; rather, the research emerged from living, teaching, learning, and surviving in the midst of a traumatized space, a visceral and emotive response to what I was seeing around me. These activities and practices had parallels in my pedagogy where I developed assignments that connected students' lives outside the classroom to what they were composing inside. I was hoping to get my students, most of them from New Orleans and the surrounding parishes, "to learn how to dwell," a spatial pedagogy theorized by Nedra Reynolds that involves "tapping into the circulation of practices that don't show up on a map or in a photograph of a village" (143). This place-based pedagogical approach to disaster eventually became fundamental to my own place-based research, one that included photographs, local/global theories, histories of New Orleans, and walking.

CHANGING LANDSCAPE, CHANGING RESEARCH, CHANGING SELVES

> Drifting purposely is the recommended mode, tramping asphalted earth in alert reverie.
> —Iain Sinclair, *Lights Out for the Territory*

Emailed to me by a colleague during my two-month evacuation was an aerial image of a flooded New Orleans. Water levels in each neighborhood were noted by gradations of gray and green hues; the specific amount could be discovered with an interactive tool. This image did nothing to vitiate my anxieties; instead, it exacerbated them. I already had intrepid feelings about returning, reinforced by members of the US Congress and political pundits arguing against rebuilding. Once back, however, that aerial image faded along with its abstracted, objectifying gaze, what Michel de Certeau describes as "the fiction of knowledge," an epistemology whose viewpoint of "looking down like a god" assumes a false totality (92). While the anxiety was still present—about the city, my job, another hurricane—photography helped flip the script, so to speak, challenging dominant narratives about the storm typically focused on victimization and helplessness. Taking up photography after many years of neglect became a coping mechanism, what Marianne Hirsch describes as an effect of trauma: "We need to place a camera between us and the sight—to use it as a form of protection and distancing" (77). Later, it became a way of moving away from despair to being aware. In a *New York Times* article about the positive influence photography had on people suffering from PTSD, trauma, and depression, more than one person interviewed claimed that taking photographs helped them stay in the present, that it brought them into the world—photography as mindfulness (Ball). I began to carry my camera with me everywhere. In my spare time, after classes or on weekends, I drifted through the city's spaces, first by car and then, as my research deepened, through walking. In some way, this minor act connected me to the city, giving me a sense of belonging and a purpose. I had not lived in New Orleans for very long before the storm and did not mourn the city's loss as did many others I knew. Within the pre- and post-Katrina paradigm in which many New Orleanians viewed their worlds, I straddled a space somewhere in between. Photography gave me a passport to record and reflect on this world.

When used in conjunction with colonial projects of domination, photography has contributed to the oppression of non-Western cultures by reifying conceptions of the Other, yet it can also subvert and challenge the colonizing gaze in its ability to evoke "information, affect, and reflection" (Rose 238). Several instances during this time stand out as moments where I began to see photography as having the potential to challenge the storm's mainstream narratives that the city had been destroyed, its residents now "refugees" who would never return. In late 2005 I accidentally discovered a pink and yellow Post-It note memorial on the facade of the Camellia Grill, a beloved "greasy spoon" for both locals and tourists that had been closed since the storm (figure 2.1). The notes ranged from expressing grief to rage— Katrina, You Bitch! was a common misogynistic epithet—to love and well-wishes toward specific employees: Marvin, come home soon. The posts began at the entrance to the diner but over several months spread across the restaurant's facade, crowding each other out in ways similar to being inside, sitting elbow-to-elbow on vinyl stools that snaked around a Formica counter where long-time waiters kept up a continual banter with each other and customers.

Another day over a year later, while biking through my neighborhood, I came across the home of artist Helen Hill, who had lived there with her husband and young child until the hurricane flooded them out. Less than a year after their return, while living in a downtown rental until

Figure 2.1. Post-It note memorial on the facade of the then closed Camellia Grill.

their house was renovated, she was murdered, her killer never found. Friends and family had placed flowers, photographs, stuffed animals, poetry, and letters addressed to her all over the facade of the house; crime tape formed a path up the stoop stairs, and a bicycle decorated with flowers leaned against the wrought iron railing. Other homages to victims of the storm were often found where bodies had been discovered months after the storm waters receded. Plastic flowers, an obituary, mementos, and family pictures were pinned to facades of houses. These spontaneous memorials capture how trauma often manifests in a need for "the visual and the tactile" (Otte 289) that intersects at the site of the body or its material extensions, such as the locations we inhabit, a city, a house, a beloved restaurant; it is where affect rather than logic prevails.

New Orleans is a performative city like no other in the United States. Its street culture is what attracts tourists from around the world. On any given day or weekend, parades, second lines, festivals, protests, block parties are part of daily life where community participation constructs meaning and desire. To become a New Orleanian meant I had to perform, a frightening prospect for a self-defined middle-aged introvert. By participating in parades and costuming traditions urged, often demanded, by friends, I began to see walking as part of this performance tradition that had the potential to be a place-based methodology, one Nedra Reynolds argues for when she describes the *flaneur* as a figure who "illustrates the connection between place and identity and emphasizes the importance of learning to see through walking and mapping" (75). While not completely abandoning traditional methods of analysis, what I experienced while walking became more central to the research I began charting out. The situation demanded I do this—in other words, there was no other position to take. From these conditions grew not only an intentionality to adopt cultural practices of the city, such as communal performance, display, costuming, and masking, but to use those experiences as a way to speak about how public performance both collectively and individually created an emotional connection to the city.

As Sarah Pink and colleagues argue, walking is a multi-modal form of knowledge making that "is in itself a form of engagement integral to our perception of an environment" (3); it has the potential to be political. Writer and lawyer Raja Shehadeh observes that the ongoing attempts to create a sustainable peace between Israel and Palestine were awash in a "rhetoric that meant nothing" (177). This conclusion stems from what he witnessed during his walks in the Palestinian countryside over several decades. "We were not supposed to look, only to blindly believe in the hollow language of peace" (177), and yet because of his walks in areas where the continual encroachment of Israeli settlements separated Palestinians from their land, he would not have seen the physical changes occurring over twenty-five years.

In similar but obviously different ways, my walks brought me into areas of New Orleans that were not tourist-driven but often the opposite, areas of the city overrun by illegal dumping, where housing developments were corralled by highway overpasses and very few commercial services were apparent, where graffiti covered and recovered abandoned flooded sites; these were parts of the city that had been neglected pre-Katrina, only now they were worse. In these areas, street art and graffiti blossomed, sometimes a kind of tourism in itself while other times taking on a political dimension, such as artist Brandon Odoms's *Project Be*, a takeover by black artists of a city housing project that combined street art, music, and performance until they were eventually kicked out (figure 2.2). These scenes undermined the positive rhetoric from City Hall about New Orleans as having recovered, with proof being the fact that it was the most popular destination for tourists. Walking provided me with a bleak counter-narrative that tempered this optimism. It also allowed me to question how the pacing of my research was out of sync with the demands of productivity and commodity demanded by the research university.

Figure 2.2. The ruins of the Florida Projects.

CONCLUSION: MAKING THE CASE FOR SLOW SCHOLARSHIP

> To photograph, we might say, is to look in a different way—to look without understanding.
> —Marianne Hirsch, "I Took Pictures: September 11 and Beyond"

During my weekly cat feedings, I watched an abandoned house, bloated by stagnant floodwaters, inch closer toward the ground until its pitched roof rested like an Alpine chalet on a nest of wood planks. This incremental pull of gravity paralleled my own protracted understanding that photography and walking were central to whatever was compelling me to research locally. Physically and psychically experiencing loss and destruction as well as uncertainty about what I was seeing prevented me from too quickly assessing what I was seeing. It demanded another kind of observing, one Kathleen Stewart theorizes when she writes "it would mean displacing the premature urge to classify, code, contextualize, and name long enough to imagine something of the texture and density of spaces of desire that proliferate in Othered places" (26).

Serendipity—my moving three weeks before the storm, while often observed by many as a professional disaster—allowed me to rethink my connection to place and to others, often strangers, who had similar experiences. The hurricane graffiti, the second lines, my first Mardi Gras all provided moments of connection to others through place. In his research about graffiti memorials that emerged in Tel Aviv after Prime Minister Rabin's assassination, Yaacov Vertzberger observes that "traumatic events not only affect communities but sometimes also create them, so that otherwise unconnected persons who share a traumatic experience seek each other and develop a form of fellowship based on the strength of that common tie" (864).

Alternative modes of scholarly inquiry called to me during this time—returning to photography and incorporating walking worked in tandem with both personal and scholarly explorations into the material and psycho-geographic effects of disaster. Before the storm, I would describe my research and writing goals as circumscribed, the audience mainly academic. In the years after the storm I began publishing more broadly, using my writing in the service of local activists, collecting student texts written during the recovery, and using photography to document where I lived—projects I had never considered as an academic. Rethinking conventional scholarly genres as advocating for activists and writers and the city itself, I wrote or compiled essays about the post-hurricane visual culture emerging in New Orleans and my volunteer work feeding abandoned pets, an interview for a major women's studies journal with a New Orleans activist advocating for sex workers' rights, a review of a book on post-Katrina social justice movements, a multi-authored Katrina-related teaching narrative, several photo essays, and a collection of student writings about the storm. Writing these essays allowed me "to pull the pin on the binary opposition between theory and practice" (Conquergood 145) and opened an exploratory space in my research that I hadn't felt for a long time.

In their collaboratively written essay "For Slow Scholarship: A Feminist Politics of Resistance through Collective Action in the Neoliberal University," Alison Mountz and colleagues examine the significance of slow research not only as resistance to the increasingly managerial (aka neo-liberal) academic workplace but also as a change in approach, a certain consciousness that occurs "even before the writing begins, in research design, community engagement, and pursuit of personally and politically meaningful work" (1244). Meaningful work for me was to learn about the city in which I lived from others who knew it well, whether that was through face-to-face contact; reading books about the city's history, environment, flora and fauna, and culture; or walking areas of the city that had been forgotten except by those who lived there. It was about joining in the dialogue about the recovery, becoming part of community through engaging with monumental issues facing the city. But it was also about re-envisioning and working with uncertainty as a generative space or a productive position from which to begin new research.

Acknowledgments

The author wishes to thank members of her writing group, Laura Carroll, and Lisa Costello for their sensitive and constructive feedback and Kristine Blair for her helpful feedback at a critical moment of this work's genesis.

Notes

1. This graduate student eventually presented her work on a panel with Derek Owens at the 2008 4Cs.
2. I'm indebted to Kris Blair for reading an early draft of this chapter and to Laura Carroll, Lisa Costello, and Noel Radley for encouraging me to frame my work using these terms.
3. See Jenkins.
4. See Borrowman.
5. As Cvetkovich explains in "Trauma Ongoing," "I'm interested not just in what happened on one day in September but also in how that shock is absorbed into the textures of our ongoing lives" (65). Other feminist scholars writing about the World Trade Center attacks include Hirsch, Kirshenblatt-Gimblett, and Taylor.
6. Vanderberg and Clary-Lemon remind us, "The habituation to 'study'—an obligation to assume the examiner's stance—constructs a conceptual displacement, endangering reciprocity" (98).
7. Journalist Gary Rivlin, writing about New Orleans eleven years after the storm, observes, "The child poverty rate in New Orleans is now 4 percent—that's higher than it was before the storm, and more than double the national average. The income disparity between rich and poor is so great that last year Bloomberg declared New Orleans the country's most 'unequal' city."
8. See Flaherty for a thorough discussion of social justice movements in New Orleans after Katrina and the consequences of displacement for many poor, working-class African Americans. Also see David and Enarson, Penner and Ferdinand, and Weber and Peek.
9. Klein's book *The Shock Doctrine: The Rise of Disaster Capitalism* begins in a New Orleans hospital during the initial crisis. The term "disaster politics" conveys how neo-liberal policies exploit particular moments of psychic distress and confusion invoked by a cataclysmic event (such as wars, economic meltdowns, natural and manmade disasters) in already vulnerable parts of the world. Klein describes in visceral terms how this process occurs: "It is in these malleable moments, when we are psychologically unmoored and physically uprooted, that these artists of the real plunge in their hands and begin their work of remaking the world" (25). Also see Adams for a site-specific ethnography of how nonprofits and charities contribute to, rather than alleviate, economic instability during disaster.
10. See Campanella, Flaherty, Penner and Ferdinand, Tang, and Wooten.
11. See Flaherty, Piano, and Wooten.

Works Cited

Adams, Vincanne. *Markets of Sorrow, Labors of Faith: New Orleans in the Wake of Katrina.* Durham, NC: Duke UP, 2013. Print.

Ball, Aimee Lee. "Photography as a Balm for Mental Illness." *New York Times*. 24 July 2014. Web. 7 Jan. 2018.
Borrowman, Shane. *Trauma and the Teaching of Writing*. Albany: SUNY Press, 2005. Print.
Brodine, Maria T. "Struggling to Recover New Orleans: Creativity in the Gaps and Margins." *Visual Anthropology Review* 27.1 (2011): 78–93. Print.
Campanella, Rich. *Bienville's Dilemma: A Historical Geography of New Orleans*. Lafayette: Center for Louisiana Studies, 2008. Print.
Conquergood, Dwight. "Performance Studies: Interventions and Radical Research." *Drama Review* 46.2 (2002): 145–56. Print.
Cvetkovich, Ann. "Trauma Ongoing." *Trauma at Home: After 9/11*. Ed. Judith Greenberg. Lincoln: U of Nebraska P, 2003. 60–66. Print.
David, Emmanuel, and Elaine Enarson. *The Women of Katrina: How Gender, Race, and Class Matter in an American Disaster*. Nashville, TN: Vanderbilt UP, 2012. Print.
de Certeau, Michel. "Walking in the City." *The Practice of Everyday Life*. Trans. Stephen F. Rendall. Berkeley: U of California P, 1988. 91–110. Print.
Flaherty, Jordan. *Floodlines: Community and Resistance from Katrina to the Jena Six*. Boston: Haymarket Books, 2010. Print.
Gere, Anne Ruggles. *Writing Groups: History, Theory, and Implications*. Urbana, IL: Conference on College Composition, 1987. Print.
Goggin, Peter N., and Maureen Daly Goggin. "Presence in Absence: Discourses and Teaching (in, on, and about) Trauma." *Trauma and the Teaching of Writing*. Ed. Shane Borrowman. New York: SUNY Press, 2005. 29–51. Print.
Hirsch, Marianne. "I Took Pictures: September 2001 and Beyond." *Trauma at Home: After 9/11*. Ed. Judith Greenberg. Lincoln: U of Nebraska P, 2003. 69–86. Print.
Jenkins, Pam. "Gender and the Landscape of Community Work before and after Katrina." *The Women of Katrina: How Gender, Race, and Class Matter in an American Disaster*. Ed. Emmanuel David and Elaine Enarson. Nashville, TN: Vanderbilt UP, 2012. 169–78. Print.
Kirsch, Gesa E. "Being on Location: Serendipity, Place, and Archival Research." *Beyond the Archives: Research as Lived Process*. Ed. Gesa E. Kirsch and Liz Rohan. Carbondale: Southern Illinois UP, 2008. 20–27. Print.
Kirshenblatt-Gimblett, B. "Kodak Moments, Flashbulb Memories: Reflections on 9/11." *Theatre and Drama Review* 47.1 (Spring 2003): 11–48. Print.
Klein, Naomi. *Shock Doctrine: The Rise of Disaster Capitalism*. New York: Picador, 2007. Print.
Koritz, Amy. (2009). "Coping with Disaster." *Civic Engagement in the Wake of Katrina*. Ed. Amy Koritz and George J. Sanchez. Ann Arbor: U of Michigan P, 2009. 20–22. Print.
LaCapra, Dominick. *Writing History, Writing Trauma*. Baltimore: Johns Hopkins UP, 2001. Print.
Mizell-Nelson, Michael. "Not Since the Great Depression: The Documentary Impulse Post-Katrina." *Civic Engagement in the Wake of Katrina*. Ed. Amy Koritz and George J. Sanchez. Ann Arbor: U of Michigan P, 2009. 59–77. Print.
Mountz, Alison, Anne Bonds, Becky Mansfield, Jenna Loyd, Jennifer Hyndman, Margaret Walton-Roberts, Ranu Basu, Risa Whitson, Roberta Hawkins, Trina Hamilton, and Winifred Curran. "For Slow Scholarship: A Feminist Politics of Resistance through Collective Action in the Neoliberal University." *ACME: An International Journal for Critical Geographies* 14.4 (2015): 1236–59. Print.
Otte, Marline. "The Mourning After: Languages of Loss and Grief in Post-Katrina New Orleans." *Journal of American History* 94 (2007): 828–36. Print.
Owens, Derek. *Composition and Sustainability: Teaching for a Threatened Generation*. Urbana, IL: NCTE, 2001. Print.
Penner, Diana R., and Keith C. Ferdinand. *Overcoming Katrina: African American Voices from the Crescent City and Beyond*. New York: Palgrave Macmillan, 2009. Print.

Piano, Doreen. "Working the Streets of Post-Katrina New Orleans: An Interview with Deon Haywood, Exec. Director, Women with a Vision, Inc." *Women's Studies Quarterly* 39 (2011): 201–18. Print.

Pink, Sarah, Phil Hubbard, Maggie O'Neill, and Alan Radley. "Walking across Disciplines: From Ethnography to Arts Practice." *Visual Studies* 25.1 (2010): 1–8. Print.

Reynolds, Nedra. *Geographies of Writing: Inhabiting Places and Encountering Difference.* Carbondale: Southern Illinois UP, 2004. Print.

Rivlin, Gary. "White New Orleans Has Recovered from Hurricane Katrina; Black New Orleans Has Not." 29 August 2016. Web. 15 Oct. 2017.

Rose, Gillan. *Visual Methodologies: An Introduction to the Interpretation of Visual Methods.* 4th ed. Thousand Oaks, CA: Sage, 2006. Print.

Shehadeh, Raja. *Palestinian Walks: Forays into a Vanishing Landscape.* New York: Scribner, 2007. Print.

Solnit, Rebecca. *A Paradise Built in Hell: The Extraordinary Communities That Arise in Disaster.* New York: Viking, 2009. Print.

Stewart, Kathleen. *Space on the Side of the Road.* Princeton, NJ: Princeton UP, 1996. Print.

Tang, Eric. "A Gulf Unites Us: The Vietnamese Americans in Black New Orleans East." *American Quarterly* 63.1 (2011): 117–49. Print.

Taylor, Dana. *The Archive and the Repertoire: Performing Cultural Memory in the Americas.* Durham, NC: Duke UP, 2003. Print.

Vandenberg, Peter, and Jennifer Clary-Lemon. "Looking for Location Where It Can't Be Found: Possibilities for Graduate Pedagogy in Rhetoric and Composition." *The Locations of Composition.* Ed. Christopher J. Keller and Christian R. Weisser. Albany: SUNY Press, 2007. 91–105. Print.

Vertzberger, Yaacov Y.I. *Risk Taking and Decisionmaking: Foreign Military Intervention Decisions.* Stanford: Stanford UP, 1988. Print.

Weber, Lynn, and Lori Peek, eds. *Displaced: Life in the Katrina Diaspora.* Austin: U of Texas P, 2012. Print.

Wooten, Tom. *We Shall Not Be Moved: Rebuilding Home in the Wake of Katrina.* Boston: Beacon, 2012. Print.

3

DEATH, DYING, AND SERENDIPITY IN THE SCHOLARLY IMAGINATION

Gale Coskan-Johnson

THE PREPARED MIND

I am from the United States, but I have lived outside that nation's borders for most of my adult life. I experienced 9/11 from Ankara, the capital city of Turkey. On that day, I was attending a conference on Teaching English as a Second Language (TESOL) at Middle Eastern Technical University (METU). I was surrounded by Turkish friends and colleagues, a few North Americans, and some Brits. All of us were English teachers. The keynote speaker was from Manhattan. We were assembling in the lobby for a wine and cheese reception when a ripple passed through the crowd. What? A plane? New York City? Is this a joke? And then the terror that such a tactic intends to inspire circulated in the crowd as everyone began to work out who in their lives might be near the attack. My closest family members were in New England, but I had friends in Manhattan as well.

From Turkey, the images of 9/11 looked very much like the images of the earthquake that struck Izmit, near Istanbul, on August 17, 1999—an earthquake in which well over 17,000 people were killed in one night. In many cases, older homes were left standing while newer buildings "pancaked," evidently because to save money contractors had built them with cheap cement corrupted by sea salt. Corporate terrorism?[1] On the way back to my apartment, the taxi driver had tears in his eyes and asked me, "Amerikali'misin? Cok gecmis olsun" (Are you American? I am so sorry). For once regretting my neo-Luddite refusal to purchase a television and connect it to cable, I spent the rest of the day searching for English-language news on my friend's two-way radio. A day or two later, while finally taking the oft-given but never taken advice to "register" at the American Embassy, on the sidewalk surrounding the building I saw candles, piles of flowers, and cards that Turkish schoolchildren,

DOI: 10.7330/9781607327394.c003

individuals, and civic groups had written and signed to tell the people of the United States that Turkey was sorry for their loss. From Ankara, I experienced a world that heaved in sorrow and reached out its arms to the United States in response to the attacks of 9/11. And then the US president, mobilizing a discursive pattern in which "terrorism," a tactic, becomes "terrorist," an essential way of being, gave a speech in which he said to the world, "either you are with us, or you are with the terrorists" (Bush). That speech did damage because it cut off lines of solidarity that were just beginning to form.

THE PREPARED MIND

In this chapter I work through the perhaps paradoxical but also necessary relationship between openness and the prepared mind that allows a researcher to recognize (or produce?) *serendipity* in the scholarly process. Mine is the story of a research project, a presidential speech, and a conference Call for Papers (CFP), and it explores the research process as a negotiation among the personal, the political, and the scholarly. I begin by describing a serendipitous event, and I follow by exploring the ways my mind was prepared by scholarship, personal experience, and political conviction to receive that event as serendipitous. I conclude by discussing, and perhaps troubling, the (yet crucial) notion of openness that characterizes the scholar's ability to negotiate the path(s) of a research project.

Preparation

It is spring of 2011, and I am working on a research project on the rhetorics of immigration in the US state. My key term is "illegal" when it is used to modify the word "immigrant." I am interested in examining government documents, mainstream media reporting, and images passed around on social media sites that are publically available online and that make reference to the figure of the "illegal" immigrant. I organize my reading around an examination of Arizona Senate Bill 1070, Arizona's "papers please" law, and the federal suit US president Obama filed in opposition to that law (see Bolton). For this project, I am especially interested in what the rhetorical analysis of such documents reveals about US public perceptions of the deaths of immigrants on the border between Mexico and the United States. Deaths had increased precipitously following the militarization of the border through Operation Gatekeeper in 1993.[2] I had noticed that reports of immigrant death appear as front-page news stories when the circumstances are spectacular; however, the ongoing, repetitive, year-in-year-out deaths by exposure in the desert, evidently caused by the US policy of building walls (Jimenez 7), are rarely remarked upon—and then they are more likely framed by rhetoric of *sorrow* rather than *outrage* or *calls to action*. At the same time, I am shaken after having identified enough videos, memes, blog posts, and forum comments to understand that although immigrant death is rarely in the news, "the people," as represented in such media, are aware of the deaths.

In this project, I am led to ask this key question: What causes the people of a constitutional democracy to acquiesce in a form of border security that relies on militarized bordering practices that predict the deaths of people who attempt to cross the border without the permission of the US state? I frame my question inside a recognition of the heavy dependence of the US state's economy on non-status migrant labour.[3] I give a paper at the CCCC convention on April 6, 2011, in which I present my work-in-progress. I write an article for an online journal called *Present Tense*. My position at this point is that AZ 1070 participates in a wider, pedagogical discourse, a national imaginary that teaches a practice of citizenship that accepts the deaths of non-status individuals as an acceptable price to pay for the *perceived* safety of status citizens (Coskan-Johnson).

Disruption

On May 2, 2011, President Barack Obama announces to the "American people" that Osama Bin Laden is dead, killed in a Navy Seals operation. News footage depicts an "American people" responding by singing and celebrating that death. The president of a constitutional democracy announces publicly that the state has assassinated an enemy, and the people publicly celebrate. I am, well, flabbergasted. I experience an intense but incoherent sense that this is *wrong*. This is all wrong. The US president, as orator, and his people, as audience, work together to produce assassination as, well, normal. Socially acceptable. Okay by me. I experience fleeting moments of golden age rhetoric: this isn't the country I grew up in. What happened to *Free to Be You and Me?* At least Dwight Eisenhower's CIA had the dubious grace to hide the 1954 coup and assassination of Guatamala's democratically elected president, Jocobo Arbenz, behind a cloak of secrecy and classified information.[4] Hadn't Barack Obama been a community organizer? In Chicago . . . a man of the people. The betrayed white liberal in me whines, "He was supposed to be *good*." And finally, *a simple question:* Why doesn't President Obama need to hide state-based killing from the public? I understand very clearly that Obama's speech is a key text in the public discourse of a post-9/11 US national imaginary. This speech will tell an "us" something about the stories "we" are trying to tell "ourselves" about "ourselves." But mostly, I am angry and frustrated and probably more than a little bit self-righteous. And I don't really know what to do about it. My work these days is about the rhetorics of migration.

How do we make sense of the ways serendipity circulates in scholarship in the discipline of rhetoric and composition? The insights we make and the ideas we pursue depend on a lifetime of preparation, but we do not pretend, even at the end, to discover the "Truth" of the objects we observe. Much as Gary Fine and James Deegan characterize ethnography, "It is not that [we] accidently stumble on truth but that [we] can find accounts that others find useful in making sense of the world" (3). We think and read and think and read all sorts of texts, and then we write and invite our peers to engage in "the sweetness of critique that always finds the remainder, the forgotten, the hidden and, thereby, exposes as illusion that sense of control, that sense of a ruling self in control" (Cintron 231). Our work, while it may be more or less precise, more or less well sourced, more or less well written, defies objective measures of truth, accuracy, and correctness. Our experiments cannot be replicated because they are contingent upon and emerge from "the formation of an effective community of minds" (Perleman and Olbrechts-Tyteca 14). In other words, we are "relational" beings "whose early and primary relations are not always available to conscious knowledge" (Butler 20). We may experience "moments of unknowing" about ourselves (Butler 20) that both trouble and enrich our stories about how we came to be the ones who made a particular insight. Reflective practices like tracing paths of preparation or telling stories about how we came to be ones who recognized a serendipitous event are necessarily partial and uncertain affairs. We are liable to misread even ourselves, but such reflection is worth doing, if only because it might alert to us to some of that remainder—forgotten or hidden under our illusions of control.

Serendipity

Then, into my inbox drops a Call for Papers for an interdisciplinary conference in the Czech Republic. The conference is called Thinking About: Dying and Death. The CFP invites papers for which "areas of interest will focus on different kinds of dying and death, the experience of careers and care workers, the changing role of medicine, palliative care, the work of the hospice movement, the work of the funeral industry, and the nature of grief and mourning. Interest will also focus on philosophical, ethical, and legal issues, which surround the processes of dying and death, the role of religion, and the diverse range of historical, social, and cultural perspectives and practices" ("Dying and Death").

I nearly delete the message. Interesting, but what relevance would such a conference have for me or my work on rhetoric and immigration? But the title keeps coming back to me. Thinking About: Dying and Death. At the same time, I happen to be reading Michel Foucault, and I am trying to figure out what he was really trying to say over time about the notion of sovereign power, a key term in my work. First, he tells us that sovereign power was an "old" power characterized by the "right [to] take life or let live" (Foucault and Macey 241). In previous centuries, the king could behead or pardon his subjects. He had the right to take lives or give them back. But then Foucault says, in adjectives that suggest chronology, another kind of power appears "in the second half of the eighteenth century" (Foucault and Macey 242), and this power has the ability to "make live and let die" (241). The new power, he calls it *biopower*, works to produce a strong and healthy nation, and in the process, some people will have to die. For Foucault, state-based racism would organize this process (Foucault and Macey 254). But I also notice that in later work, Foucault allows that these "techniques of power" may exist simultaneously (Foucault and Burchell 107). The right to *take life*. The right to *let die*. Thinking about death and dying.

What if death itself has become a pedagogical figure in the US national imaginary? What if death is not just a regretful by-product but rather acts as a central trope put to work in stories told on the border and in speeches like the one announcing the death of Osama Bin Laden? "Philosophical, ethical, and legal issues which surround the processes of dying and death" says the CFP. Suddenly, this chance CFP, when faced with my "sagacity," my preparation (my openness?), made death itself my object of study, and it set me to exploring the rhetorical processes embedded in the discursive links between a hyper-visible rhetoric of death that celebrates assassination (sovereign power?) and a quiet, commonsense acknowledgment of immigrant death that is the cost of keeping America safe and its economy running (biopower?). A research project, a speech, a CFP, and a scholar. They come together and shift my research focus unexpectedly. But can I really account for the preparedness of serendipity so easily and with such transparency? How did I become one who would see things like that?

The Prepared Mind

A literature review signifies a particular kind of preparation. There is the mass of sources identified in a painstaking search and categorized carefully in terms of their relationship to a project. But there are the little serendipities that circulate in the research process, too—a book assigned in a graduate seminar that sits in the mind and percolates, a citation pursued to an obscure archive that turns out to be a treasure trove, a scholarly article consulted through a "quick-and-dirty Google search" made simply to define a single word but that instead opens up a previously unforeseen path of inquiry. Though it can include extended periods of isolation, scholarship is fundamentally collaborative because it rereads, develops, extends, rejects, or embraces arguments made by one's peers. Sources teach us about a topic; they represent positions taken in relation to a topic; they contain "facts," inspiration, and arguments that need to be negotiated before we enter a scholarly conversation. Particular lines of scholarship have captured my imagination in a fundamental sense and become barely conscious elements of the ways I confront future problems. These ways include writers I imagine writing *with*—I have been especially influenced by work that stops trying to understand or rescue others and instead asks questions about why there is this self-styled "us" that keeps pestering all these "others," and could it maybe come to construct itself differently? Here, I will work through a series of texts that mark key moments of invention in my wider research process, texts that have stuck with me and helped me to see what I had to account for and how I might go about doing so. I can look back through this series of books as a prism through which my writing has passed, and I find their traces throughout the project I am describing here—these are writers who love language and who write with conviction, reflexivity, and sometimes with irony and who have given me more than "facts," though they also give me that, and whose layered writings act as places I can still go and spend time. Or, put more simply, I like writers who get angry because, contra the history of Western philosophy and as Aristotle's *Rhetoric* still teaches us, anger is a rational response to an unjust situation.

Gloria Anzaldúa's *Borderlands: The New Mestiza* has had a transformative effect on theories of the border. She turns the space of the borderlands into a text, into poetry, into a site of agency and guarded celebration—without ever losing site of the materiality and brutality of its violences. Her border is a place of temporal, linguistic, embodied, and topographical intersections rather than a line cleanly dividing parts. It is a multidimensional site of mestiza invention, and her multilingual text works to disorient its monolingual/monocultural readers who are not her target audience anyway, and ironically. While her book traverses metaphorical boundaries of race, gender, language, and sexuality, she never allows her reader to lose sight of the material, geopolitical border dividing the United States and Mexico and underpinning the divisions that multiply in its borderlands. In a perfectly decentering move, she speaks to her target audience as if "we" are not in the room and suggests that "instead of surreptitiously ripping off the vital energy of people of color and putting it to commercial use, whites could allow themselves to share and exchange and learn from us in a respectful way" (90). Though Anzaldúa published *Borderlands* in 1987, her scholarship continues to energize border studies across disciplines. The fierceness of her voice, the fearlessness of her prose, and her lack of respect for "us" give me hope and caution me to think very hard about the arguments I make in relation to any "us" and "them" seemingly divided by a border.

Sara Ahmed's *Strange Encounters: Embodied Others in Post-Coloniality* begins with the deceptively simple assertion that strangers are not strange because they are *un*familiar but rather because they are recognized as strange: "The stranger is *some-body* whom we have *already recognized* in the very moment in which they are 'seen' or 'faced' as a stranger" (21, italics in original). Strangers are determined, she says, by the "social demarcation of spaces of belonging" (22). Thus, a sociocultural imaginary constructed in film, education, government, literature, and day-to-day conversation allows us to recognize, on the one hand, extra-terrestrial life in the form of *little green men* and, on the other hand, young black men in hoodies as strangers in gated communities. Ahmed argues that through social interaction, "we" are taught who belongs and who does not. I encountered Ahmed's text in a graduate seminar years ago, but her formulation exploring how strangers are produced inside the nation to purify the stories it tells about itself shadows my analyses and circulates in my study of death. She leads me to wonder to what extent the *figure* of an assassinated Osama Bin Laden is *useful* to public discourse as a monstrous stranger through which a "we" can valorize its own capacities for and histories of violence.

Bonnie Honig's *Democracy and the Foreigner* explains that democratic theorists have long focused their inquiry on this central question: "How should we solve the problem of foreignness" (1). She then frames her own study by inverting that question and asking instead, "What problems does foreignness solve for us? Why do nations or democracies rely on the agency of foreignness at their vulnerable moments of (re)founding, at what cost, and for what purpose" (4). She finds that Western narratives are oddly rife with stories about foreigners who (re)found the nation. Her analysis plays across borders of genre when she reads iconic texts of political philosophy, Rousseau's *Leviathan*, Freud's *Moses and Monotheism*, and *The Book of Ruth* alongside products of pop culture such as *The Wizard of Oz*, *Shane*, and *Dirty Dancing*. She allows all six to become exemplars of the stories "we" tell about foreigners in order to solve *our* problems. For my own purposes, her two most important insights are, first, that the xenophilic view of the foreigner (e.g., "we are a nation of immigrants") inevitably transforms into xenophobia (e.g., "immigrants are taking our jobs") because "we" cannot stop thinking democracy from inside the frame of the nation-state, which inevitably produces the figure of the foreigner whether it is celebrated or not. Second, she insists that the spectre of the foreigner as "taker," or one who takes from the nation what he or she does not deserve, needs to become a model for democratic citizenship rather than the story of a monster. What is the most intriguing about her argument is that she proposes a practice of citizenship that would be modeled on the nineteenth-century female gothic because "the best female gothic heroines are takers" (118). In other words, rather than view the state as her heroic protector, the citizen ought to always keep in mind that it may love her madly or it might be about to cut her throat. Honig, like Ahmed, turns the gaze of her audience back upon itself.

I still remember the first time I read Chandra Talpade Mohanty's "Under Western Eyes: Feminist Scholarship and Colonial Discourses." In this iconic text of transnational feminism, Mohanty dismantles the Western savior narrative. She does so by discovering it in the arguments of white, Western feminists who have constructed themselves as plural, liberated, and free by producing "the image of an 'average third world woman'" who is "ignorant, poor, uneducated, tradition-bound, domestic, family-oriented, victimized, etc." (22). Like Ahmed's stranger who allows the neighborhood to construct itself as pure and good through the body of the recognized stranger, Mohanty puts a mirror up to the white, Western feminist subject intent on saving her oppressed, third world "sisters." Mohanty urges feminist scholars to finally give up the comfort of essential categories and ahistorical claims of "sisterhood," which "freeze women into 'objects who-defend-themselves,' and men into 'subjects-who-perpetrate-violence'" (24). While such violence certainly begs to be interrogated, solidarity across lines of difference will only emerge in the face of situated, "concrete historical and political practice and analysis" (24).

This series of scholars, among others, not only present me with citations and useful ideas. This is scholarly work with which I have developed a sense of solidarity. But then, how did I become the person who would bring them together and read them in my own particular idiosyncratic way? Do I need to work back farther to unearth the path of my preparation?

The Prepared Mind

My perception of borders persists in underlying my work even when I think I have left it behind, and it is necessarily the product of a (life)long process, imperfectly remembered. My interest has long been drawn to cross-border movement in its many forms. Immigrants, asylum seekers, migrant workers, human trafficking. Or watching with big childhood eyes as Chief Joseph, in *I Will Fight No More Forever*, races with his people away from the US Cavalry toward Canada, his movement arrested, fatally, on *this* side of the line. Listening with teenage angst and lights turned off as Bruce Springsteen's highway patrolman slows down his car and lets his delinquent brother cross over into Canada and freedom because "nothin' feels better than blood on blood" (Springsteen). Thelma and Louise, euphoric feminist heroes, race for Mexico but end up leaping instead into the Grand Canyon to their outlaw deaths. Or Monarch butterflies cross the North American continent on their unfettered journey from Canada to Mexico. Borders are human constructions, but so many of us, myself included, seem to have internalized a persistent belief in the border as a meaningful object that really does separate unlike entities. They work to force "us and them" upon us all. And they are all that—even though they also are not. Still, many people do "risk everything" to cross over borders. Scenes imperfectly remembered.

A phrase floats up from my early childhood: "Boat People." People packed into tiny boats *swarming* the shores of the United States. The boats are from Cuba. Haiti? Fleeing communism. Poverty? Fleeing communism is good. Fleeing poverty, not so good. Good immigrants and bad immigrants. To be embraced ("we are a country of immigrants") or to be turned away ("It was *their* choice. It's not *our* problem"). Until rumors that Castro has emptied his jails and filled boats with criminals bound for the US state. So, they were *all* bad? I can still find traces of memories, anxieties, feelings that must have been produced by front-page photographs and overheard conversations. Thousands of tiny boats filled with countless black bodies leaping ashore, swarming the beaches . . . In 2014 African American comedian Chris Rock gave an interview. He pointed out that his kids "are going to be the first black children in the history of America to actually have the benefit of the doubt of just being moral, intelligent people" (Rich). Rock insists that his kids are enjoying the benefits of "white progress," not "black progress." He explains, "There have been smart, educated, beautiful, polite black children for hundreds of years," only now "[his] children are encountering the nicest white people that America has ever produced. Let's hope America keeps producing nicer white people" (Rich).

At fifteen I get a job cleaning rooms at the Catchpenny Chalet. I have to walk to the other side of Route 128. It is still Lexington, Massachusetts, but it always feels like leaving town. There is a thin black man, always dressed in colorful clothing, whom I often (sometimes? I don't really remember, perhaps it was only once or twice) pass on the way to work. He smiles at me when I walk by. For some reason, I recognize him as Haitian, and I "know" what that means . . . kindof. Though we never speak or even occupy the same side of the road, I am afraid of him. You see, Chris Rock is right. It is white people who have needed to make progress.

THE OPEN MIND

In my introduction I imply that I am uncertain about the term "open mind," though I also insist on it. How does a mind classify as open? How can we tell if we are "keeping" one? Open must mean open *to some extent.* Right? No mind can be absolutely open because a research project is also a process of cutting, limiting, focusing, discarding, closing. An expansion is followed by a contraction. But it must also be true that preparing one's mind and keeping one's mind open are processes that work both with and against each other. At the same time, both constitute processes of invention and both prepare us to, say, detect serendipity. But how do I become open to my own blindness if my preparation itself blinds me? Rhetorical theorist Kenneth Burke famously called such blinders *terministic screens.* He suggests, "Work both reflects our interests and forms them" (240). He points out that one's occupation (or one's preparation) might cause one to "adopt measures of expression so exclusively attuned to this single situation that [one] will greatly outrage persons who, though present, are living in a totally different situation" (240). In other words, what makes perfect sense to me might really piss you off. Thus, our specializations shape us as targets "for the sweetness of critique" (Cintron 232). Burke's words recognize that to be prepared is not to be capable of seeing all that is there; rather, it is about being prepared to find a particular way of seeing as useful while recognizing and remaining open to the liberating inevitability that there will be other ways, equally useful, of seeing that same object.

I have tried here to work reflectively through the narrative of a serendipitous event that occurred in my research. I was engaged in a project exploring the rhetorics of immigration, and then something happened out in the world—a president announced a death. That speech interrupted my momentum. It left me unsure of what to do next. Then an email, a CFP, that could easily have never arrived appeared and provided me with a new way of thinking about that disruption. But that *new way* had been previously shaped and prepared for by the life I had lived and the scholars I had read. All these factors came together in a mess of disruption, frustration, and new connections that, serendipitously, set me on a new research trajectory.

Notes

1. More than twelve contractors were arrested on corruption charges following the earthquake, and one, Veli Göçer, went into hiding but was eventually arrested and was referred to as "the contractor of death" (see Kinzer).
2. For a comprehensive examination of Operation Gatekeeper, its histories, and its consequences, see Nevins.
3. For a brilliant analysis of the ways migrant death is embedded as an essential component of the US economy, see Mitchell.
4. For more information, see the unclassified Central Intelligence Agency (CIA) report posted on the official CIA website (Barrett).

Works Cited

Ahmed, Sara. *Strange Encounters: Embodied Others in Post-Coloniality.* London: Routledge, 2000. Print.

Anzaldúa, Gloria. *Borderlands: The New Mestiza = La Frontera.* San Francisco: Spinsters/Aunt Lute, 1987. Print.

Aristotle. "The Internet Classics Archive / Rhetoric by Aristotle." *The Internet Classics Archive / Rhetoric by Aristotle.* Web. 28 Feb. 2015.

Barrett, David M. "Congress, the CIA, and Guatemala, 1054." United States of America, Central Intelligence Agency. 3 Aug. 2011. Web. 25 Aug. 2011.Berlin, James A. *Rhetorics, Poetics, and Cultures: Refiguring College English Studies.* Urbana, IL: National Council of Teachers of English, 1996. Print.

Bolton, Susan R., United States District Judge. "In the United States District Court for the District of Arizona: United States of America, Plaintiff vs. State of Arizona; and Janice K. Brewer, Governor of the State of Arizona, in Her Official Capacity." Scribd. 28 July 2010. Web. 15 April 2016.

Burke, Kenneth. *Permanence and Change: An Anatomy of Purpose.* 3rd ed. Berkeley: U of California P, 1992. Print.

Bush, George W. "Transcript of President Bush's Address." CNN. Cable News Network, 21 Sept. 2001. Web. 5 May 2016.

Butler, Judith. *Giving an Account of Oneself.* New York: Fordham UP, 2005. Print.

Cintron, Ralph. *Angels' Town Chero Ways, Gang Life, and Rhetorics of the Everyday.* Boston: Beacon, 1997. Print.

Coskan-Johnson, Gale. "Troubling Citizenship: Arizona Senate Bill 1070 and the Rhetorics of Immigration Law." *Present Tense: A Journal of Rhetoric and Society*. 1 Jan. 2011. Web. 28 Feb. 2015.

"Dying and Death." INTER-DISCIPLINARY.NET: *A Global Network for Dynamic Research and Publishing*. INTER-DISCIPLINARY.NET. Web. 27 Feb. 2015.

Fine, Gary A., and James G. Deegan. "Three Principles of Serendip: Insight, Chance, and Discovery in Qualitative Research." *International Journal of Qualitative Studies in Education* 9.4 (1996): 434–47. Print.

Foucault, Michel, and Graham Burchell. *Security, Territory, Population: Lectures at the Collège De France, 1977–78*. Basingstoke: Palgrave Macmillan, 2007. Print.

Foucault, Michel, and David Macey. *Society Must Be Defended: Lectures at the Collège De France, 1975–76*. New York: Picador, 2003. Print.

Honig, Bonnie. *Democracy and the Foreigner*. Princeton, NJ: Princeton UP, 2001. Print.

I Will Fight No More Forever. Wolper Productions, 1975. Film.

Jimenez, Maria. "Humanitarian Crisis: Migrant Death at the US-Mexico Border." *Aclu.org*. American Civil Liberties Union, 1 Oct. 2009. Web. 1 Mar. 2015.

Kinzer, Stephen. "Turkey's Political Earthquake." *Middle East Quarterly* (Fall 2001): 41–48. Print.

Mitchell, Don. "Work, Struggle, Death, and Geographies of Justice: The Transformation of Landscape in and beyond California's Imperial Valley." *Landscape Research* 32.5 (2007): 559–77. Print.

Mohanty, Chandra Talpade. "Under Western Eyes: Feminist Scholarship and Colonial Discourses." *Feminism without Borders: Decolonizing Theory, Practicing Solidarity*. Durham, NC: Duke UP, 2003. 17–42. Print.

Nevins, Joseph. *Operation Gatekeeper and Beyond: The War on "Illegals" and the Remaking of the US-Mexico Boundary*. 2nd ed. New York: Routledge, 2010. Print.

Perleman, Chaïm, and Lucie Olbrechts-Tyteca. *The New Rhetoric: A Treatise on Argumentation*. Trans. John Wilkinson and Purcell Weaver. Notre Dame, IN: University of Notre Dame Press, 1969. Print.

Rich, Frank. "In Conversation: Chris Rock." *Vulture*, 30 Nov. 2014. Web. 8 Dec. 2018.

Springsteen, Bruce. "Highway Patrolman." Metrolyrics. Web. 27 Jan. 2015.

Thelma and Louise. Percy Main Production(IS), Pathé(IS), Percy Main Production, Pathé[Italia], MGM/UA Home Video, 1991. Film.

PART II

Intersections of Personal and Professional

4

FORTUITOUS HAPPENSTANCE
Serendipity in Archival Research

Lynèe Lewis Gaillet

In 1754, Horace Walpole coined the term "serendipity"—a combination of "accidents and sagacity" that leads to great discoveries one never anticipated. I like tracing "serendipity" to the eighteenth century, since much of my work is grounded in that period. My investigations of revolutionary Scottish educator George Jardine, who taught moral philosophy classes at the University of Glasgow for more than fifty years (1774–1827), illustrate both Walpole's definition of "serendipity" and co-editors Goggin and Goggin's focus in this collection on interdisciplinary instances of serendipity. Lawyer and archivist Michael H. Hoeflich stresses lessons learned from interdisciplinary examples of spectacular archival finds (including James Boswell's journals, the Dead Sea Scrolls). Hoeflich explains how being lucky is in many ways a more desirable trait in an archivist than smarts (813). Of course, even the fortuitous among us must be open to the possibilities of chance, willing to divert from established research questions to pursue the fortunate find, and tenacious enough to stay on the trail. As we are reminded in most discussions of serendipity, happy accidents don't occur for those who aren't resolute and brave enough to seek out and be in fortuitous places.

Like other contributors to this volume, I wish to share my own serendipitous experiences both working in the archives and discovering a career path grounded in investigating the history of rhetoric and composition pedagogy. For many scholars of my generation, that is, those seeking degrees in the 1980s, I fell into what was becoming a cutting-edge field—the resurgence of historical research into the burgeoning field of rhetoric and composition. Indeed, many of us made the jump in graduate school to rhetoric and composition from literature studies, creative writing, and education. In my case, the shift from studying eighteenth-century literature to studying eighteenth-century rhetoric and composition was a very natural move given the period's focus on the genre of the essay and bellestristic rhetoric's concerns with style and what was then called moral philosophy. Over the years, my interests have shifted to nineteenth-century studies and the origins of composition instruction. To that end, I will conclude this chapter by briefly suggesting ways in which archival pedagogy, including an exploration of serendipity and curiosity, both negates the common assumption that archival research is dusty/boring/solely historical and addresses current concerns in composition studies, including issues such as helping students find an authentic voice, transference, avoiding plagiarism, and writing-across-the-curriculum.

MY EXPERIENCES "WORKING IN THE ARCHIVES"

In the 2010 collection *Working in the Archives: Practical Research Methods for Rhetoric and Composition,* Lori Ostergaard interviewed seven archivists to explore the role serendipity plays in archival research; these mini-interviews were interspersed throughout the chapters of the collection to illustrate the role chance plays in the research process. I was happy to be a part of that group, which included Lindal Buchanan, David Gold, Peter Mortensen, Jessica Enoch, Kathryn Fitzgerald, and Kenneth Lindblom. Ostergaard asked these questions of interviewees:

- Describe a time when you inadvertently struck gold (great or small) in the archives, or tell us about a time when you were looking for one thing and discovered something else.
- Fleming recognized the potential in his moldy Petri dish. How did you know when you inadvertently struck gold in the archives?
- Have you ever temporarily suspended work on one project to follow a serendipitous lead? If yes, when has this happened, and where did the lead take you?
- Have you ever talked about serendipity when describing your own archival work? Have you ever told readers or listeners about your chance discoveries in the archives? If yes, which projects did you discuss, and how did you describe your good fortune?

These excellent questions served as heuristics for interviewees, prompting us to overtly consider archival research methods, not just methodologies, and to codify the role serendipity might play in archival investigation for both ourselves and readers. Just like learning a new word, consciously thinking about a concept often leads one to notice ubiquitous illustrations of that idea. Building on the earlier interview and the "serendipitous experiences" I shared about my investigation of Jardine, I want to now contextualize subsequent moments of serendipity in the archives—occasions for interdisciplinary research that led me to new finds and, on one occasion, a goldmine. Specifically, in this chapter I describe the role serendipity played in my experiences researching Jardine's influence in America, highlight the increased chance of serendipity striking when researchers work across disciplines and investigate records housed outside their usual repositories, and, in the process, explore the relationship among preparedness, smart/hard work, and serendipity.

First, who is George Jardine? Today, Jardine's rhetorical and pedagogical theories resonate with scholars of both Scottish and American rhetoric. Jardine, one of Adam Smith's favorite students at the University of Glasgow in the eighteenth century and friend of Thomas Reid and John Millar, instructed many influential Scots (i.e., Francis Jeffrey, Sir William Hamilton, Christopher North, and J. G. Lockhart), some of whom later immigrated to North America and held prestigious positions in higher education and religious circles. These educators brought to American education Reid's commonsense philosophy based on an epistemology of sensation and free will (in part developed in opposition to Hume's skepticism and Locke's views of personal identity) exemplified in Jardine's insistence that students must develop habits of thinking and study that lead to communicative competence and "usefulness" in their local communities (*Outlines* 108)—educational philosophies and practices ideally suited to a democracy that values individual judgment and personal freedom. But perhaps the most notable and novel "habit" Jardine instilled in his students was the practice of writing in all disciplines to improve written communication skills and make meaning of new knowledge. Epistemic writing (including sequenced writing assignments and peer evaluation) became the cornerstone of Jardine's teaching plan, and this pedagogy was widely adopted in the major Scottish universities.[1]

In researching the work of Jardine, I visited every possible archival source I could find in Scotland. To use Walpole's terms, I "sagaciously" and at other times "accidentally" found and examined a long list of archival resources. Here is one of my best Scottish serendipitous finds—one I shared in the *Working in the Archives* interview:

> I happenstanced upon a reference to Jardine's letters. After some digging, I found a University of Glasgow library notation of 136 letters that Jardine had written. In these letters, written throughout his lifetime to a college friend, Jardine discussed personal events but also worked out some of his early teaching ideas. The librarians took forever to find the letters, and when they brought them to me (in a crushed in, flimsy cardboard box), it was with a sense of reverence. For you see, I don't think anyone had taken

a look at these letters since they were initially archived. The stack was tied with a red (faded to pink) satin ribbon, and I carefully opened the folded pages with a due sense of awe and respect. Five years later when I returned to the library, I requested the letters out of a sense of nostalgia more than a need for research. They were brought to me bound in a large notebook, each one catalogued and secured in a plastic slip cover—not exactly a repeat of my earlier experience. (Ostergaard 149–50)

Hoeflich tells us that a successful historian must "be lucky and . . . have a knack for serendipity" (827), but scholars must also be diligently prepared to recognize a find when they see it. While I applaud making archival materials available electronically for all the now-known reasons (cost, ease of researching, unfettered access to materials), researchers do lose something in this process, not only in regard to the loss of sensory experiences—there is nothing quite comparable to smelling old books, working on sacred ground where our subjects once tread, and handling primary materials owned or created by our research subjects—but also because the serendipitous nature of chance finds is not always possible in digital searches. Perusing the shelves and card catalogs (yes, I date myself) often revealed related but unexpected finds, particularly when working with boxes of manuscript materials as in the case of Jardine's letters. Perhaps most important, conversations with manuscript librarians led to untold numbers of unexpected finds; these conversations aren't usually possible in online searches.

After returning from researching materials in Scotland, I knew from previous archival investigations and published references that Jardine had definitely influenced American education; however, I couldn't document this influence—until serendipity stepped in. Back in the States, a Disciples of Christ minister, Thomas H. Olbricht, contacted me out of the blue one day, asking if I was the researcher interested in George Jardine. He had encountered my work, which dovetailed with his own scholarly interests, through the research of Carisse Berryhill, a scholar with whom he shared a research interest. The minister was researching Disciples of Christ founder Alexander Campbell and had found, through Berryhill's investigations, that both Campbell and his father, Thomas, were Jardine's students in the moral philosophy class at Glasgow before they immigrated to America—thanks to another set of serendipitous circumstances: twenty-year-old Alexander attended Glasgow University providentially to wait out a terrible storm season when his boat to America (enroute with his family to join his father in Philadelphia) was shipwrecked and forced to detour to Glasgow. Campbell could not book passage on another ship until the next season, and while his family lodged in Glasgow, Alexander Campbell attended Glasgow University, enrolling in Jardine's class (see "A Shipwreck" in Wrather for a full account of this incident). An inconvenient trip delay for the Campbell family led to a serendipitous find for me, two centuries later.

Alexander Campbell's papers are located at the national Disciples of Christ library in Nashville, Tennessee—only 225 miles from my front door. I researched the library's holdings online, called the manuscript librarians, drove up one morning, and found the mother lode of American documents I had sought for two decades. Not only were these materials housed relatively close by, but serendipitously, everything had been transcribed and typed up by a minister/researcher from Ohio on the occasion of Campbell's 200th birthday—a real coup given the difficulty in reading the ornate handwriting that characterized the time period. Furthermore, the manuscript librarians in Nashville (who usually worked with ministers and church historians) were happy to have an educator interested in the materials. They had prepared a set of all the data housed in the Alexander Campbell collection pertaining to Jardine (along with other select library holdings referencing Jardine), and photocopies of everything were waiting for me upon my arrival. This Nashville find was certainly serendipitous, yes, but my published works, which Professor Olbricht found through internet resources, also led him to contact me. This find can be largely attributed to digital finding aids and search resources, efforts of scholars interested in interdisciplinary research, and knowledgeable and extremely helpful manuscript librarians.

Since my earlier research expeditions to Scotland, I have found many resources in America to support claims that Jardine influenced American education, but none as powerful as the manuscripts housed in Nashville. Included in the Alexander Campbell papers is a set of student notes from Jardine's class, dated 1809. Finding any set of student notes from this time period is quite a discovery, but in this case each lecture is also dated, offering insight into the pacing of Jardine's course. Campbell's student notes add a third example to the two existing copies of Jardine's lecture notes (1783 and 1793) housed in the Glasgow University manuscript library. These notes provide three opportunities for studying Jardine's lectures, and this serendipitous find in additional offers an early nineteenth-century set of notes for analysis.

Teachers often lament the lack of historical student work available for studying educational practices, institutional histories, and the communities in which students studied and lived. In the eighteenth century, scholars are fortunate that universities often awarded prizes for the best sets of student notes, leaving us extant copies of lecture notes from the period.

We do have significant caches of nineteenth-century student writings, collections such as those compiled by Erika Lindemann at Chapel Hill, but I fear the continued loss of student writing for a number of reasons. We simply can't save everything, and yet the abundance of student work in some ways makes it less rare and valuable to collectors.

As a historian, I bemoan the loss of student work, yet I am also guilty of not keeping much of it. Just this year, my rather large English department relocated to a new building. Our new offices have considerably less storage capacity (a trade for windows and better vistas), and in the days prior to the move, huge stacks and piles of student work filled the department's recycling bins. When forced to choose between saving our own research files and the work of our students, it seems as though faculty members in my department made similar choices. And digitization, while one alternative to throwing away student writing, doesn't ensure that we will preserve student work for very long. Archivists are extremely overworked and underfunded; even digitized materials will be lost if we don't update our storage methods and provide information for readers to access digitally cataloged information.

Now-famous debates over the storage of newspaper and other archives, ignited in part by Nicholson Baker in *Double Fold: Libraries and the Assault on Paper* in 2001, are ongoing. In thirty-eight chapters, with titles such as "Destroying to Preserve," Baker vehemently outlines potential problems with recovering digitized records of archives that no longer exist in their original forms. The lack of preserved primary materials in the first place, combined with difficulties in locating online finding aids and not having the means to access digitized materials, certainly decreases the likelihood of serendipitous discoveries and makes discovering student writing an even more monumental task. In Jardine's case, we have a known set of student notes found in America because of the significant impact his pedagogical theories and practices made on a student who happened to become quite famous.

SERENDIPITY AND "WAYS OF MAKING IT IN RHETORIC AND COMPOSITION"

Serendipity is certainly an important element of archival work, as this volume attests, but until recently researchers didn't discuss the role of happenstance in archival research overtly as a part of methodology and method discussions. Gesa Kirsch and Liz Rohan's important 2008 collection, *Beyond the Archives: Research as a Lived Process*, breaks this pattern by pointedly calling attention to the role serendipity plays in primary research. They include a section in this work titled "When Serendipity, Creativity, and Place Come into Play," which includes chapters authored by David Gold, Kirsch, Christine Mason Sutherland, and Alisha Nitecki. These well-known archival researchers locate serendipitous moments in their research experiences, explaining ways in which chance encounters with materials and one's own curiosity can translate into substantive scholarly work. They expand conceptions of serendipity in historical research to include "a willingness to follow all possible leads, an openness to what one may encounter, and flexibility in revising research questions and the scope of a project" (5). This concept of serendipity—one that includes joy, research for its own sake, and one that is intuitive and connected to personal interests—"results in more meaningful and reflective lives," according to Kirsch and Rohan (9). Connections between joyful research and meaningful lives/careers is important and underexplored in the scholarship.

In *Women's Ways of Making It in Rhetoric and Composition* and *Living Rhetoric and Composition: Stories of the Discipline,* important scholar-teachers in rhetoric and composition discuss the role serendipity played in their careers—careers that later led to important primary investigation and published scholarship. For example, in Roen, Brown, and Enos's collection of life stories, Edward Corbett explains how he "serendipitously discovered rhetoric" while working on a master's degree sponsored by the GI Bill (3), and Richard Lloyd-Jones admits that his training "as a teacher of writing was a matter of serendipity" (120). In *Women's Ways,* Sharon Crowley tells how, as a PhD student in literature, she signed up for classes in rhetoric and "the rest, as they say, is history" (Ballif, Davis, and Mountford 219), and while Cindy Selfe was grateful for her good luck, she explained that she still took full advantage of every opportunity presented to her (305). In these academic cases and many others, fortuitous circumstances at school and at work opened pathways for novel primary research. Leading archivists, when describing their relationships to archival materials under investigation, often discuss the role serendipity played in their careers, but good fortune alone—in work and research—isn't always enough. In addition to hard work, serendipitous encounters with the right archivist, librarian, researcher, or teacher may provide the catalyst for new projects and career opportunities.

In my case, serendipity guided my research and subsequent career as well, placing me in the path of Winifred Bryan Horner, a wonderful mentor who introduced me to archival research. I had applied to two universities in the Dallas/Fort Worth area and was accepted at one, enrolling in classes and reading over the summer in preparation for the fall term. Two weeks before fall classes started, Gary Tate at Texas Christian University called, explaining that someone in the program had left to write a dissertation from afar, thereby making room for me to enter—a fortuitous happenstance indeed. I spent the next three years studying under Horner, learning from a master archivist various ways to conduct archival research in Scottish rhetoric and composition studies.

Professor Horner's generation of scholars initiated a new era of research into archival research methods and methodology—especially with regard to composition studies. While primary research has undoubtedly always been the hallmark of scholarly writings, Horner invited scholars to overtly discuss the ways they conducted archival investigations. Dr. Horner was proud that new scholars carried on her work investigating primary holdings in Scottish libraries, as she explained in a 1994 interview: "I think the mark of [the importance of nineteenth-century rhetoric] is an increasing number of young scholars in this area . . . It's a wonderful feeling, and I think it will just open up new things. There's a lot of material just waiting to be looked at in Scotland and in this country too" (Gaillet and Aley 20). She encouraged historians to not only explore existing holdings in library collections but to also become archivists themselves, to follow unexpected finds and new trails in ways that lead to novel/alternative collections, compiled for perhaps different reasons than originally intended. As a result, primary materials can be used for knowledge making rather than merely as a repository of materials that hold preconceived secrets to be gleaned by the researcher. In my case, the Scottish materials belonging to the teachers of eighteenth- and nineteenth-century moral philosophy professors cast a bright light onto contemporary American composition practices, certainly not a research trajectory anticipated by Scottish manuscript librarians and collectors. In particular, the serendipitous find of Jardine's letters in Scotland and his student notes in the United States are helping me compile a set of documents that support claims of Jardine's influence on American educational practices.

PREPARING FOR SERENDIPITY: ARCHIVAL PEDAGOGY

Scholarship such as *Working in the Archives*, the 2012 special issue of *College Composition and Communication* (CCC) focused on research methodologies (which featured four articles addressing archival research), the 2016 Landmark Essays volume (Gaillet, Eidson, and Gammill) dedicated to archival research, and this edited collection all reflect the growing interest in overtly discussing facets of archival research methods. The increase in works addressing archival pedagogy brings together many of my interests in primary research. For example, "Training in the Archives: Archival Research as Professional Development" (Beuhl, Chute, and Fields) offers a comprehensive course plan for graduate students, including curriculum and syllabi suggestions grounded in recent archival methods scholarship and work with actual archives. And the adoption of archival methods instruction throughout an undergraduate vertical writing curriculum addresses many concerns in composition classes: helping students find original topics, becoming an authority on a topic, writing across the curriculum, and plagiarism—to name but a few. The training of new scholars needs to address more esoteric components of primary research (including serendipity) and should also encourage researchers to connect to their personal experiences and community memberships (broadly defined). As Kirsch and Rohan explain, "If new researchers censor this very real and useful aspect of the research process, they might not learn to trust or recognize their own hunches" (4).

My institution has just approved a split-level (4000/6000-level) undergraduate/graduate course specifically addressing archival research methods and methodologies. In the past, we have offered separate, special topics courses in archival research at both levels, but the approval of a regularly offered course—one now officially on the books—is especially exciting. And archival/primary research is appealing to first-year students as well: Michelle Eble and I have coauthored a first-year textbook grounded in archival research methods, *Primary Research and Writing: People, Places, and Spaces*. Over the years, I have taught writing courses grounded in archival research at all levels, and in every section, serendipity has come into play. Undergrad students in particular find archival research initially daunting, but once they begin to explore materials embedded within or associated in some way with communities to which they already belong or aspire to join, they become excited about the research. Curiosity guides students' archival research, and for most, serendipity plays a role in their topic selections: students often find interesting family documents and pictures, they happen upon little-known facts or connections within their existing spheres, or they discover new cultural and familial stories while interviewing community or family members. Through this (re)discovering of the inherent pleasures in browsing and by recognizing curiosity as an important heuristic for their research projects, students' work was naturally novel and self-satisfying.

CONCLUSION

A combination of curiosity and serendipity led to now-famous scientific discoveries and innovations (Fleming/penicillin, Plunkett/Teflon, Pemberton/Coca-Cola, Spencer/the microwave). In other fields, curiosity and serendipity are not rare occurrences; "Science and Serendipity: Happenstance and Other Factors Underlying Accidental Discoveries," the Joint Speakers Event held in June 2014 at the new Chicago Innovation Exchange, highlighted the role chance plays in scientific discoveries and business. Focusing on collaboration, the participants and speakers recounted historical fortuitous discoveries and suggested opportunities for fostering contemporary serendipitous finds. As Jessica Kankel, professor of surgery and chief of pediatric surgery at Comer Children's Hospital, explained, for current researchers "being too restrictive is the enemy of new knowledge" (quoted in Borzo). Perhaps the best takeaway for rhetoric and composition researchers from this scientific conference was stated by Rick Stevens, professor of computer science and associate lab director for computing, environment, and life sciences at Argonne: "The common features of serendipity include working in collaboration with others rather than in isolation, not being at risk of immediately losing your funding, and being confident and fearless of failure" (quoted in Borzo). Collections like this one demonstrate ways in which rhetoric and composition scholars and students can prepare for serendipitous opportunities—when they arise—by faithfully following our own interests and curiosity, working together, and keeping an open mind. Perhaps most exciting to me is the overt focus on training a new generation in the methods of archival research, including the role serendipity plays in that process.

Note
1. This identifying paragraph is taken from my article "Writing in the Disciplines."

Works Cited

Baker, Nicholson. *Double Fold: Libraries and the Assault on Paper*. New York: Random House, 2001. Print.

Ballif, Michelle, D. Diane Davis, and Roxanne Mountford, eds. *Women's Ways of Making It in Rhetoric and Composition*. New York: Routledge, 2008. Print.

Berryhill, Carisse. "A Descriptive Guide to Eight Early Alexander Campbell Manuscripts." Guided research paper presented to Professor John Mark Hicks, Harding University Graduate School of Religion, Memphis, TN, as a requirement in Course 570 Guided Research in the Historical/Doctrinal Division. 2000. Web. 28 March 2016.

Beuhl, Jonathan, Tamar Chute, and Anne Fields. "Training in the Archives: Archival Research as Professional Development." *College Composition and Communication* 64.2 (2012): 274–305.

Borzo, Greg. "Scholars and Scientists Explore Factors Underlying Serendipitous Discoveries." *UChicagoNews*. 19 June 2014. University of Chicago. Web. 30 Dec. 2014.

Brown, Stuart C., Duane H. Roen, and Theresa Enos, eds. *Living Rhetoric and Composition: Stories of the Discipline*. Mawah, NJ: Lawrence Erlbaum, 1999. Print.

Campbell, Alexander. "B Manuscript 'C' Newspaper Cuttings of 'Clarinda,' Lecture Notes at Glasgow Uni." 1809. Trans. Earl Eugene Eminhizer. Disciples of Christ Historical Collection. Disciples of Christ Historical Society, Nashville, TN. Archival Material.

Gaillet, Lynèe Lewis. "Writing in the Disciplines: America's Assimilation of the Work of Scottish 'Pedagogic' George Jardine." *Writing across the Curriculum Journal* 20 (2009): 91–105. Print.

Gaillet, Lynèe Lewis, and Shelley Aley. "An Interview with Winifred Bryan Horner." Reprint with new introduction. *Composition Studies* 42.2 (Fall 2014): 11–27. Originally published in *Composition Studies* 22.2 (1994): 15–29. Print.

Gaillet, Lynèe Lewis, and Michelle F. Eble. *Primary Research and Writing: People, Places, and Spaces*. New York: Taylor and Francis, 2015. Print.

Gaillet, Lynèe Lewis, Diana Eidson, and Donald Gammill Jr., eds. *Archival Research Methods*. Landmark Series. Series eds. Krista Ratcliffe and James Murphy. Carbondale: Southern University UP, 2016. Print.

Hoeflich, Michael H. "Serendipity on the Stacks, Fortuity in the Archives." *Law Library Journal* 99.4 (2007): 813–27. Print.

Jardine, George. Lectures to the Logic Class at Glasgow University. MS Gen 166. University of Glasgow Manuscript Library, Scotland, 1783. Archival Material.

Jardine, George. Lectures to the Logic Class at Glasgow University. MS Gen 737. University of Glasgow Manuscript Library, Scotland, 1793–94. Archival Material.

Jardine, George. *Outlines of Philosophical Education, Illustrated by the Method of Teaching the Logic, or, First Class of Philosophy in the University of Glasgow*. 2nd ed. Edinburgh: Oliver and Boyd, 1825. Print.

Kirsch, Gesa E., and Liz Rohan, eds. *Beyond the Archives: Research as a Lived Process*. Carbondale: Southern Illinois UP, 2008. Print.

Lindemann, Ericka. "True and Candid Compositions: The Lives and Writings of Antebellum Students at the University of North Carolina." *Documenting the American South*. 2002. University of North Carolina at Chapel Hill. Web. 28 Aug. 2014.

Ostergaard, Lori. "Interview: Lynèe Lewis Gaillet—the Unexpected Find." *Working in the Archives: Practical Research Methods for Rhetoric and Composition*. Ed. Alexis E. Ramsey, Wendy B. Sharer, Barb L'Eplattenier, and Lisa S. Mastrangelo. Carbondale: Southern Illinois UP, 2010. 149–51. Print.

Ramsey, Alexis E., Wendy B. Sharer, Barb L'Eplattenier, and Lisa S. Mastrangelo, eds. *Working in the Archives: Practical Research Methods for Rhetoric and Composition*. Carbondale: Southern Illinois UP, 2010. Print.

Walpole, Horace. Letter to Horace Mann. 28 January 1754.

Wrather, Eva Jean. *Alexander Campbell: Adventurer in Freedom, a Literary Biography*, vol. 1. Ed. D. Duane Cummins. Fort Worth: Texas Christian UP, 2005. Print.

5
PRE-SENTENCE
Researching, Reporting, and Writing

Caren Wakerman Converse

I was ambivalent about my decision to study the genre of pre-sentence investigation reports (PSIs). While I knew the reports played a critical role in the administration of justice, I was uncomfortable in my role as researcher. As a former probation officer, I had been a practitioner of what I was now studying. I could not help but wonder if I was violating some ethical code by examining a system I had been part of and a genre I had written thousands of times. Would I be able to separate myself from something in which I had been so deeply involved? I reviewed everything about conducting qualitative research, trying to find an appropriate label for myself and what I was doing. I was not, however, a practitioner researcher, a label popular in education, since I had not worked in the criminal justice system in decades. Further, I was not an ethnographer, since my participation was in the distant past. For a short time I thought of myself as an analytical autoethnographer since, as explained by Leon Anderson, prior experience was playing a role in my endeavor but was far from my sole data source.

I decided to forget about labels and proceed with my research as though I had no prior knowledge. But it kept stalling. One problem was the paucity of academic discussion concerning PSIs; scholarly articles about the PSI as a genre were almost nonexistent. Russell Rutter, who wrote the only article I could find in a journal devoted to writing, maintained that probation officers were unable to write "clear enough to communicate the message immediately" (290). What I was able to piece together came primarily from law journals and contradicted everything I thought I knew. Probation officers and the reports they wrote were not receiving much praise. An article dating back to 1928 described probation officers as "inadequate and unsuccessful individuals" (Chute 515). John Rosecrance, a former probation officer himself, argued that the

DOI: 10.7330/9781607327394.c005

reports were of poor quality and attributed this to what he described as officers using the reports to advance their own agendas. He described the writing as "bland and prosaic" (171) and often minimal because of burned-out and passive probation officers. A paper by Stephen A. Fennell and William N. Hall described the PSI as "the most important document in the federal criminal process" (1615), but then warned of the inaccuracies that were prevalent. Qualified praise was also offered by Peter Pope, who acknowledged that the reports provided the judge with "likely the most complete written version of the offense" (378) and then asserted that a lot of information was omitted, incorrect, or slanted to the officer's bias. A survey of court personnel by Michael D. Norman and Robert C. Wadman in 2000 found less than half ever even read the report.

I eventually realized that I was stubbornly clinging to the misguided notion that personal experience could not be considered a valid source of knowledge in the research process. I found Robert K. Yin's work on case studies in which he applauds *Head Start: The Inside Story of America's Most Successful Educational Experiment* for its insightfulness, "possibly because it is based on [the author's] personal experiences with the program" (98). I located an article by Robert Bogdan and Sari Biklen in which they explicitly support personal experience as a source of knowledge in the research process. They acknowledge that "no matter how much you try you cannot divorce your research and writing from past experiences, who you are, what you believe and what you value. Being a clean slate is neither possible nor desirable" (34). Subjectivity in qualitative research is not the problem. As Alan Peshkin cautions, the problem is failing to acknowledge it.

Not only did I acknowledge it, as my research progressed, I embraced it. I came to realize that I had a unique perspective available to me, and rather than consciously avoid it so as not to make my research suspect, I needed to use it as an additional lens. It was only by utilizing every tool at my disposal that I was able to see the connections I had not expected to find. It was in that spirit that I made a phone call to a former colleague.

As I waited for him to pick up, I asked myself why I had decided to call. For months I had been scouring journals that contained anything on the subject of PSIs. I thought I had read everything on workplace writing, genres as social action, and qualitative research methods. The New York State Criminal Procedure Law had become my bedtime reading. Yet, my analysis seemed incomplete. Why, though, had I contacted someone I knew, especially someone I had not spoken to in many years? I told myself that I was just calling to make sure things had not changed much in the years that had passed. Plus, it was an opportunity to touch base with an old colleague. But what could he possibly tell me that I did not already know? By the time we had exchanged pleasantries, I was certain that the call had been a waste of time, at least in terms of my research. Then he casually mentioned that I would be miserable if I was still working there: "We don't write the reports in paragraph form anymore. Only outlines or lists."

Allow me to provide some context. Few outside the criminal justice system know what probation officers are or what they do; people often confuse them with parole officers who supervise individuals following their release from prison. Probation is a sentence that is an alternative to incarceration, and probation officers provide supervision in the community to those who receive that sentence. They also do a lot of writing. On an annual basis, probation officers in federal and county probation departments prepare tens of thousands of PSIs, which are required in every criminal case following conviction of a felony and prior to sentencing and whenever a defendant is going to receive a probation sentence. A PSI is also frequently ordered by the court in misdemeanor cases. Whenever I was asked about being a probation officer I would, to the listener's surprise, explain that the position required writing ability. Before embarking on my research, I had compared writing a PSI to writing someone's biography. I would tell whoever asked that the report contained the defendant's personal, social, family, and legal history. But it was more than the facts of someone's life. It required an evaluation of the individual's needs and a sentencing recommendation. I was proud of the reports I had written; I always felt my ability to present someone's life story made the person three-dimensional to the judge who would be imposing the sentence. I was convinced that each word, each sentence, each transition mattered; it was a way of piecing together the story of someone's life. The process of writing helped me think about that person so as to arrive at what seemed the only natural conclusion in the form of recommending the most appropriate disposition from an array of sentencing options. When I originally decided to study the genre, it was motivated in large part by my selfish wish to let people know how important those reports were; few things are that simple. Returning to the scene of the crime is what often leads to a perpetrator's arrest, and it was with a similar arrogance that I returned to the PSI (Converse, "A Qualitative Study" 15–16). I had assumed the process would be simple and straightforward, but I learned otherwise.

Given all the negative commentary I had been immersed in, it was not too surprising that hearing of the demise of paragraphs initially felt like just one more punch to the gut. My old colleague bemoaned probation officers' inability to write coherently and explained that the department's new policy of merely listing or outlining the information had gone into effect in hopes of removing the burden of "fumbling for good prosaic composition" or worrying about correct punctuation. It had been decided that "less time on how to write things correctly and more time on getting things right" was the way to go. "We're producing a tool that fits the bolt that needs to turn." A tool! It fits a bolt! Something needs to be turned! What was he talking about? Maybe I had been foolish to believe that my writing had had any impact on a defendant's future. Obviously, that one department's decision to forgo narrative writing was nothing more than the manifestation of someone's idiosyncratic decision-making process. I moved on.

For months I had been reading genre theory, specifically New Rhetoric (also known as North American Genre Theory). It was Carolyn R. Miller who, in 1984, redefined the rhetorical genre. It would no longer be defined by simply its content or form but rather by what it was doing. A rhetorical genre would henceforth be seen as "a conventional category of discourse based in large-scale typification of rhetorical action; as action it acquires meaning from situation and from the social context in which that situation arose" (Miller 163). Charles Bazerman also wrote about genre's social purpose, about "patterned, typical, and therefore intelligible textual forms" (*Shaping Written Knowledge* 323) that have grown out of a particular need to serve a particular purpose. I reviewed studies of workplace writing, such as Amy Devitt's 1991 study of texts produced in an accounting firm and Anthony Paré's work with Canadian social workers. I realized that I had to stop being so concerned with the superficial features of the PSI and go beyond the words on the page. "A new dimension, social motive, transcends what many of us have come to accept as good or bad writing" (Converse "Unpoetic Justice" 450).

That necessitated widening the lens from looking only at the text to considering the context. Was it something tangible and, if so, what was it? If, as Bonnie A. Nardi pointed out, "context is not an outer container or shell" (38), where would I find it? I turned to activity theory, which shifts the analysis of genre to how, as a tool (a term even my former colleague had applied to the PSI), the genre mediates an activity. The activity "is made up of those involved in the system, the rules and norms, the community, a division of labor, a desired object, and an outcome—all of which experience gradual or sudden change" (Converse "Unpoetic Justice" 452). The activity was sentencing; the system was the criminal justice system.

Over the next few months I went back to the beginning. I learned about the emergence of Probation in nineteenth-century Boston and how the earliest probation officers were volunteers. I read Edward Sefton Porter's memoir of his twenty-seven years as a probation officer. Hired in 1926 for his self-proclaimed writing ability, Porter regarded the writing of PSIs as helping "to make genuine justice possible" (11). I consulted procedural statutes dating back to the early twentieth century and compared them to those in the twenty-first century. I learned about the medical model of criminal justice and the more recent justice model. Guidelines from the New York State Division of Probation for writing the report were reviewed, as well as sentencing guidelines and laws of criminal procedure. I was fortunate to obtain a small corpus of PSIs that had been written over a forty-year span, from 1967 to 2007, and I examined them section by section.

What became increasingly clear was that the genre was changing. Even with a limited number of PSIs at my disposal (rife with redactions because of the confidential nature of the reports), the differences were there. When I employed a variety of analytical lenses (genre analysis, activity theory, textual analysis), patterns began to appear. The section headings had changed. More to the point, the changes corresponded to the shifts in the ideology of the criminal justice system. Gone was the section on the defendant's Social History; in the early 1980s it was replaced with Social, Family, and Personal Data. By 2007 it became Social Circumstances. Beginning in the early 2000s a new heading appeared: DNA Indexing. In 2007 Financial Responsibilities was added. The story that was emerging was of a genre being controlled by outside forces. The public had demanded harsher sentences and less judicial discretion; the politicians responded. Sentencing became more complicated but more predictable. As the criminal justice system became concerned more with letting the punishment fit the crime than with trying to understand the offender or how to facilitate rehabilitation, the content of the reports shifted from an analysis and evaluation of factors that led to unlawful behavior to a presentation of often disconnected present circumstances that might contribute to future unlawful behavior.

I had also been reading about mathematically structured sentencing guidelines that had been growing in popularity since the 1980s, guidelines that determined the sentence based on a score. The Minnesota Sentencing Guidelines, considered a role model, instruct the user that "the presumptive fixed sentence is found in the Sentencing Guidelines Grid at the intersection of the column defined by the criminal history score and the row defined by the offense severity scale" (20). Points are allotted for a variety of factors, and the total score provides the judge with the presumptive sentence. Also gaining widespread acceptance by probation departments since the 1990s were assessment instruments, scientifically based tools that utilize predetermined criteria for evaluating the defendant. Boxes are checked by the probation officer; the result is a calculation of the defendant's chances for success based on criminogenic needs, risk factors, and predicted recidivism. The finished product takes the form of bar graphs or concentric circles depending on the particular instrument. I set out to learn more about these new technological tools, reading everything from empirical research articles about their effectiveness to the manufacturers' websites. Overall, the responses were positive. The scientifically based tools were praised for taking the guesswork out of sentencing. Recommendations were no longer potential victims of a probation officer's bias; the process was objective.

I started to write. I produced a rough draft that traced the PSI from its beginnings. I analyzed the criminal justice system and the role of the PSI in the administration of justice. I made tables and figures to show how the report's focus had changed over time. But a couple of things kept nagging at me. The first was that one department's decision to remove narrative writing. The second was the proliferation of scientific assessment instruments. Was there a connection between bar graphs and lists and, if so, what was it? My mind was getting too cluttered; I knew I needed to step back and leave it alone for a while.

Fast-forward several weeks to another glorious California day. I sat out on my balcony and stared into space. I should have been relaxed and relieved that I had managed to get something down on paper, but my mind would not quiet down. I decided to read through my draft again; it was probably the twentieth time I had done so. I began to notice that references to objectivity, subjectivity, and science kept popping up. Throughout the literature, PSIs were criticized for lacking objectivity. Evidence-based assessment tools, in contrast, were lauded for their objectivity. Irving Halpern, former chief probation officer of the Court of General Sessions of the County of New York, had articulated his goal of making probation "a scientific form of correctional treatment" (24) as far back as 1939. Northpointe Institute for Public Management, Inc., the software manufacturer of an assessment instrument, has as its slogan "evolving practice through scientific innovation." All the references to objectivity and subjectivity started sounding familiar, so much so that I began to wonder if I had read it all before and had plagiarized my entire paper. *Stop and focus*, I told myself. *Don't get sidetracked.* I read on. I started second-guessing everything, repeatedly asking myself if what I had written could even be considered research. I was a fraud. I was not a social scientist. I was a former probation officer pretending to be a social scientist. And then the lightbulb went on. What I had been doing as a qualitative researcher was not that different from what I had done years before as a probation officer. PSIs did not require citing sources using APA format, but sources of information did have to be verified and the appropriate boxes checked on the cover sheet. I had gathered information from documents, interviewed people, read more documents, analyzed, and evaluated. Then I wrote my report. When I was a probation officer I was a practitioner of the social sciences.

At first it seemed a stretch, but it turned out not to be. I went back and reread what I had written about activity theory, how a genre could be part of more than one activity. My paper, however, was focused on only one activity: sentencing. What was I missing? Maybe nothing. There was no requirement for an additional activity, just the possibility. Still, I knew I was onto something. What followed was not unlike playing a game of connect-the-dots. Probation officers had to consider sociological, criminological, economic, and psychological factors in their assessments. Weren't those all social sciences? PSIs were often criticized for lacking objectivity. Weren't social scientists concerned with that as well? Hadn't Charles Bazerman pointed that out? "The terms 'human sciences,' 'behavioral sciences,' 'cognitive sciences,' and 'social sciences' express a shared aspiration to produce statements of knowledge of the kind and authority reputed to come from the natural sciences, statements that seem to rise above rhetoric" ("Codifying" 125).

I decided to free the genre from the context of the criminal justice system and reexamine it in the context of the social science debate between the relative merits of quantitative and qualitative research. Rather than view the PSI as a tool confined to the activity of sentencing, I started looking at it as a tool in the activity of conducting social science research. So much of what I had read by qualitative researchers (Alan Peshkin, Clifford Geertz, Joseph Maxwell, to name a few) had characterized what they were doing in terms of storytelling and its rich, descriptive, narrative qualities. And narrative is rhetorical; Aristotle had recognized that more than 2,000 years ago. I returned to my corpus of PSIs and applied the lenses of narrative and rhetoric. I saw that forsaking paragraphs was not just a way to compensate for inadequate writing ability; it was about the pursuit of objectivity.

Everything fell into place after that. PSIs, modeled on medical case histories in which "narrative . . . cultivates the power of observation" (Hunter 157), had evolved into grids and lists and bar graphs where the rhetoric was supposedly removed. A rhetorical analysis of the reports demonstrated ongoing attempts to ensure objectivity by standardizing their format and depersonalizing the language through "distention devices" (Eisner). This was taken one step further when one department decided to remove the rhetoric altogether by no longer using narrative. While I doubt anyone there was familiar with genre theory or Amy Devitt's assertion in "A Humanistic Rationale for Technical Writing" that writing may never be able to achieve objectivity, it nonetheless appeared that objectivity was the goal. Probation was falling in line with much of the social science community, convinced that quantification was superior. Although qualitative researchers have remained true, sadly, Probation decided to forsake its qualitative roots and go to the other side.

Personal knowledge can be a double-edged sword. Sometimes it got in my way. When I first learned the reports could be lists or outlines, I took it as a personal affront. I became bogged down with what I could see only in terms of good versus bad writing. Later, when I initially saw the similarities between what I had done as a probation officer and what I was doing as a researcher, my reaction was to dismiss it. Yet, it afforded me insights that might otherwise have been overlooked. In their discussion of serendipity in qualitative research, Gary Alan Fine and James G. Deegan describe it as more than chance, as "the interactive outcome of unique and contingent 'mixes' of insight coupled with chance" (434). Had I not had those insights, those serendipitous moments might have gone unnoticed.

I have finally come to terms with having been a probation officer who wrote PSIs who, years later, decided to embark on a qualitative research project about PSIs. I have wondered what my research would have looked like had I not contacted someone at that particular probation department, if he had never mentioned the forsaking of paragraphs, if he had been away from the office that day and I had spoken with someone else. I also realize that my prior experience was a plus. It wasn't baggage; it was an additional lens. My knowledge as a practitioner complemented my theoretical approach. As Leon Anderson asserted, it "gives the researcher an added vantage point" (388). I reminded myself of what Gary Fine had written in "Ten Lies of Ethnography: Moral Dilemmas of Field Research":

> Qualitative researchers need not be warned about the difficulty, if not the impossibility, of pretending objectivity. Objectivity is an illusion—an illusion snuggled in the comforting blanket of positivism—that the world is ultimately knowable and secure.
>
> Alas, the world is always known from a perspective. (286)

If only Probation had been familiar with those words. But that's another story.

Works Cited

Anderson, Leon. "Analytic Autoethnography." *Journal of Contemporary Autoethnography* 35.4 (2006): 373–95. Print.

Barrett, David M. "Congress, the CIA, and Guatemala, 1954." Central Intelligence Agency, Website of the United States of America Central Intelligence Agency. 3 Aug. 2011. Web. 11 Jan. 2017.

Bazerman, Charles. "Codifying the Social Scientific Style: The APA Publication Manual as a Behaviorist Rhetoric." *The Rhetoric of the Human Sciences.* Ed. John S. Nelson, Allan Megill, and Donald N. McCloskey. Madison: U of Wisconsin P, 1987. 125–44. Print.

Bazerman, Charles. *Shaping Written Knowledge: The Genre and Activity of the Experimental Article in Science.* Madison: U of Wisconsin P, 1988. Print.

Bogdan, Robert, and Sari Knopp Biklen. "Ten Common Questions about Qualitative Research." *Qualitative Research for Education: An Introduction to Theory and Methods.* 3rd ed. Ed. Robert Bogdan and Sari Knopp Biklen. Needham Heights, MA: Allyn and Bacon. 1998. 32–42. Print.

Chute, Charles L. "The Development and Needs of Probation Service." *Journal of the American Institute of Criminal Law and Criminology* 18.4 (1928): 514–21. Print.

Converse, Caren Wakerman. "A Qualitative Study of the Pre-Sentence Investigation Report." Diss. UC Santa Barbara. 2010. Ann Arbor: UMI, 2010. Print.

Converse, Caren Wakerman. "Unpoetic Justice: Ideology and the Individual in the Genre of the Presentence Report." *Journal of Business and Technical Communication* 26.4 (2012): 442–78. Print.

Devitt, Amy. "Intertextuality in Tax Accounting: Generic, Referential, and Functional." *College Composition and Communication* 44.4 (1991): 573–86. Print.

Devitt, Amy. "A Humanistic Rationale for Technical Writing." *College English* 40.6 (1979): 610–17. Print.

Eisner, Elliot W. "Objectivity in Education Research." *Curriculum Inquiry* 22.1 (1992): 9–15. Print.

Fennell, Stephen A., and William N. Hall. "Due Process at Sentencing: An Empirical and Legal Analysis of Presentence Reports in Federal Courts." *Harvard Law Review* 93.8 (1980): 1613–97. Print.

Fine, Gary Alan. "Ten Lies of Ethnography: Moral Dilemmas of Field Research." *Journal of Contemporary Ethnography* 22.3 (1993): 267–94. Print.

Fine, Gary Alan, and James G. Deegan. "Three Principles of Serendipity: Insight, Chance, and Discovery in Qualitative Research." *Qualitative Studies in Education* 9.4 (1996): 434–47. Print.

Halpern, Irving. *A Decade of Probation: A Study and Report.* Montclair, NJ: Patterson Smith, 1969. Print.

Hunter, Kathryn Montgomery. *Doctors' Stories: The Narrative Structure of Medical Knowledge.* Princeton, NJ: Princeton UP, 1991. Print.

Miller, Carolyn R. "Genre as Social Action." *Quarterly Journal of Speech* 70 (1984): 151–67. Print.

Minnesota Sentencing Guidelines Commission. 2009. Web. 3 Jan. 2010.

Nardi, Bonnie A. "Studying Context: A Comparison of Activity Theory, Situated Action Models, and Distributed Cognition." *Context and Consciousness: Activity Theory and Human-Computer Interaction.* Ed. Bonnie A. Nardi. Cambridge: MIT P, 1996. 35–52. Print.

New York Division of Criminal Justice Services. 2010. Web. 4 Jan. 2010.
Norman, Michael D., and Robert C. Wadman. "Utah Presentencing Investigation Reports: User Group Perceptions of Quality and Effectiveness." *Federal Probation* 64.1 (2000): 7–12. Print.
Paré, Anthony. "Writing as a Way into Social Work: Genre Sets, Genre Systems, and Distributed Cognition." *Transitions: Writing in Academic and Workplace Settings.* Ed. Patrick Dias and Anthony Paré. New York: Hampton, 2000. 145–66. Print.
Peshkin, Alan. *Places of Memory: Whiteman's Schools and Native American Communities.* London: Routledge, 1997. Print.
Pope, Peter. "How Unreliable Factfinding Can Undermine Sentencing Guidelines." *The Sentencing Process.* Ed. Martin Wask. Aldershot, England: Dartmouth, 1986. 361–86. Print.
Porter, Edward Sefton. *Conscience of the Court.* Upper Saddle River, NJ: Prentice-Hall, 1962. Print.
Rosecrance, John. "A Typology of Presentence Probation Investigators." *International Journal of Offender Therapy and Comparative Criminology* 31.2 (1987): 163–77. Print.
Rutter, Russell. "Teaching Writing to Probation Officers: Problems, Methods, and Resources." *College Composition and Communication* 33.3 (1982): 288–95. Print.
Yin, Robert K. *Case Study Research: Design and Methods.* Thousand Oaks, CA: Sage, 2003. Print.

6
ECHOES IN THE ARCHIVES

Liz Rohan

In the winter of 2012 I received a grant to pursue a research project about a historical Detroit-area settlement house, the Tau Beta Community House, founded in 1916 in the immigrant enclave of Hamtramck, Michigan, by the wives and daughters of Detroit's early auto moguls, who were members of the women's club Tau Beta. The club's roster at the time included Eleanor Clay Ford, wife of Edsel Ford, Henry's son. Ford was a longtime director of the Tau Beta Settlement's board and at an especially influential time during the Great Depression. Evidence also suggests that Ford's older sister, Josephine Clay Kanzler, inspired her fellow Tau Betas to develop this settlement project (Plumb 139). Considered premiere in its heyday (Alexander 1), the settlement did not survive post–World War II when the large dwellings that housed settlements were deemed white elephants, women's agency as volunteer philanthropists waned, and men took over as leaders of a growing social service bureaucracy (Stewart 15; Trolander 29). The Tau Beta Community House closed in 1957, just three years after Kanzler accidentally drowned in a swimming pool. The part of her inheritance donated to the settlement was apparently not enough to save it ("Tau Beta Gets $50,000").

    I had grown up near the Edsel and Eleanor Ford estate in the Detroit suburb of Grosse Pointe but only learned about Tau Beta's settlement work about a decade ago during an exploratory visit to the Grosse Pointe Historical Society because I was looking for a local project. On a tour of the house on the estate that day, the docent mentioned that Jane Addams had been a role model for Ford, and so I went banging on office doors at the house post-tour hoping its curators would be interested in a research project about Ford's progressive-era work that I would spearhead. The research project would be close to home, quite literally, and also close to my heart. Ford had donated part of the family's estate for

DOI: 10.7330/9781607327394.c006

a park with a pool where I spent nearly every summer day of my youth. My interest in teaching was sparked by my first job at this pool as a swimming instructor. The university where I teach in Dearborn, Michigan, is also part of a Ford estate—Henry's. Furthermore, my longtime research features the backdrop of the US progressive era, which has included studying the work and writing of Addams.

I eventually gathered a relatively significant amount of material to write about the Tau Beta Community House, which resulted in a couple of talks. But my access to primary sources about the settlement had been limited. Tau Beta still exists as a women's civic organization. The club's archives are private, and Tau Betas' well-heeled contemporary members want to keep them that way. A month or so after I sent board members of Tau Beta a proposal outlining my research and requesting a look at the archives, I got a phone call from the octogenarian-sounding historian. She crisply informed me that I hadn't the clout to be a member of the club or, as it turned out, to look at the Tau Beta archives. A local writer, who had written an article about the historical Tau Beta Community House, had warned me that the contemporary Tau Betas were tough to deal with. He surmised that the values that shaped the work of this contemporary group did not mirror those of their predecessors, which would be considered left wing in contemporary contexts. Perhaps amnesia was necessary to maintain the status quo for contemporary Tau Beta members during this cultural moment.

Fair enough, I thought, if I could not work my way into the project from the "inside out" my favorite way—gathering impressions from ordinary documents—I'd instead work my way into it from the "outside in," using other primary sources from which I'd garner a larger picture about US progressive-era settlements. The grant included some travel funds, so I planned a trip to the University of Illinois at Chicago to look at the Hull-House Settlement House archives and also a trip to the University of Minnesota in Minneapolis, which houses the extensive archives for the National Federation of Settlements.

The serendipity that took me on a different research trajectory emerged first as a hassle. My research trip to Chicago coincided with the 2012 NATO conference that May, doubling the cost of the already high-priced hotel rooms in the city. A stay at an independent hotel in nearby Evanston was affordable but would require a long El ride across town to the Hull-House archives. On a whim, I checked the Northwestern University online holdings catalog to learn that Northwestern University has an existing settlement and that its archival material fills 110 boxes. So I decided to dedicate at least a day of work to perusing this archive.

At the library, which I could walk to from the hotel, my research was "curated" by a former historian of the Northwestern University Settlement, Doris Overboe, and the four boxes that hold evidence of her extensive historical work, much about the settlement's longtime director, Harriet Vittum. Overboe completed this work during the course of a decade or so between 1990 and 2000, as she planned a book on Vittum and before Alzheimer's disease stymied her momentum. That day at the archives, Overboe's research provided a heuristic and also some heart for an otherwise intimidatingly large archive. I'd learn that the depth of this Northwestern University Settlement archive vis-à-vis my lack of access to the Tau Beta archives, if perhaps an interesting juxtaposition, was no coincidence. Overboe's passion for history and her skill at negotiating with various donors who may have otherwise held back their contributions had heavily shaped the collection process for this archive (Ellert Overboe).

While the tale of two cities—Detroit and Chicago—as well as two settlements, the Tau Beta Community House and the Northwestern University Settlement, remains a relevant and ongoing research project, the abundance of materials historicizing Northwestern University Settlement's history, including Overboe and Vittum's professional histories, meanwhile showcases some questions unto themselves about two other interdependent but perhaps under-theorized processes: the collection of material memory and the researcher accessing these archives, or not, in the second place. Also, significant, sad, and thematic, a woman who spent the last ten years of her life losing her memory had contributed substantially to a project preserving memory through a range of methods including but not limited to research, writing, and collecting. Overboe promoted the memory of *her* historical hero, Vittum, but as I perused the work that Overboe collected, *she* became my hero, especially when I saw that the folder of her research included work at the National Federation of Settlement archives in Minneapolis where I'd be going in two weeks. The old biddies in charge of the Tau Beta archives had locked me out of their archives. Overboe had thrown me a key to these.

THE RESEARCHER AS WITNESS

Overboe had died just four months before my visit to the archives, and when reading her online obituary I looked at the ceiling. *Yep*. This wasn't the first time I'd be called to witness the work of deceased writers whose work might otherwise be lost to history. My dissertation subject, Janette Miller (1879–1969), was a longtime expatriate American missionary to

Angola and was no longer in contact with her living relatives when she died. My recent research subject, John Price (1899–1972), was estranged from his children, partly because he worked nights during his long career as a newspaper editor, and these children were not much interested in the diaries I edited—diaries he originally compiled so his children could know him better. Overboe was childless. Plus, she clearly became ill before she was finished with her life's work. I had a double recovery project on my hands—promoting the memory of Harriet Vittum, per Overboe's passion, and witnessing this passion itself. Jessica Enoch ("A Woman's Place") employs Nedra Reynolds's observation that places have layers which are like a "palimpsest," embodied "with histories and stories and memories" (2) to theorize the historical and rhetorical spaces embodied and developed by historical women. The archival materials compiled by Overboe about her work on Vittum that I was perusing could be a metaphor for this layering as well as its rhetorical effects. In this case the effects were upon me—the audience and interpreter of Overboe's work—as I constructed and reconstructed Vittum's life work and vision on location in Chicago. As Enoch also argues, "We should pursue the possibility that women's words might gain new and meaningful effects outside their original rhetorical situation . . . Historians, then, would not limit their study to the immediate context of a rhetorical exchange but would continue their search and investigate who *else* was listening" ("Survival Stories" 25, emphasis added).

Overboe had been listening to Vittum. Now I was listening to Overboe listening to Vittum. As Jaqueline Royster and Gesa Kirsch interpret Enoch's point, "Enoch . . . suggests the importance of taking a longer view of tales twice (or even more) told—and remembered" (104). Broadening boundaries of a rhetorical situation to a longer view, these next tales once and twice told feature the layers of women's work embodied in the Northwestern University Settlement archives that showcase the work of Overboe and Vittum, separately and collectively.

ABOUT DORIS P. OVERBOE (1934–2012)

Overboe's longtime historical work for the Northwestern University Settlement or the Northwestern Settlement Organization (which refers to its management) began just a few years after she received her master's degree in history from Northwestern University in 1958. After serving on several of the settlements' boards beginning in 1965, she eventually became the settlement's historian and worked with writer Mark Wukas to research a book about the settlement's history in honor of its centennial, *The Worn Doorstep* (1991). Working on *The Worn Doorstep* ostensibly sparked Overboe's interest in Vittum's life and in writing about this life, which included a section about Vittum in *The Worn Doorstep* and also a lengthy entry on Vittum in the anthology *Women Building Chicago 1790 to 1990* (Olsen 1–3). Before poor health kept her from continuing her work as a historian, editor, and writer, Overboe was working on a book about Vittum's life. She enlisted her husband, Ellert, in her archival adventures, which included visits to Vittum's hometown of Canton, Illinois. Overboe's advocacy for Vittum's legacy also included a revitalization of Vittum's memory at a Chicago park that was named for Vittum in 1955, the same year another Chicago park was named for Jane Addams. Initially named Vittum Park, visitors and park employees reportedly hadn't known who Harriet Vittum was and had assumed that Vittum had been a man. Overboe arranged for the park to be named Harriet Vittum Park. In conjunction with the park's rededication as such in 1996, Overboe also arranged for a drawing of Vittum to be installed in the park's recreation center, including a sidebar of biographical information about Vittum's legacy as an activist for the people of Chicago ("Vittum Park Honors").

Overboe was furthermore instrumental in having Vittum's hometown library in Canton, Illinois, add a biography of Vittum on its website (Bunner). Overboe's research methods for the book she was researching included queries to people who could provide details about Vittum's childhood, which she accessed in cooperation with Vittum's nephew, Daniel. Overboe's systemized data collection process shows how deeply she pursued knowing every available detail of Vittum's life and influence. Although Overboe's health obviously hindered her from achieving her goal as an author, it is my assessment that her thorough approach to data collection may have also held her back from getting the project fully off the ground. As my newspaper reporter dad often put it, "Research is endless." Overboe might have also or instead studied some of the broader trends that shaped Vittum's life and rhetoric, a methodological approach that might be mine in the next tale retold.

ABOUT HARRIET E. VITTUM (1872–1954)

During the heart of her career, Vittum was considered Chicago's second woman, the first being Jane Addams. In 1937, two years after Addams died, the *Chicago [Herald] Tribune* named Vittum "the most useful woman" in the city. Vittum began her career as a nurse but became an active Chicago suffragist, social worker, and political leader after an uncle recruited her for a job during Chicago's 1893 World's Columbian Exhibition, two years after the Northwestern University Settlement was founded in 1891. Serendipity perhaps led to Vittum's eventual and long career as a settlement leader. When a free clinic she was working for closed, she took a volunteer position at the Northwestern Settlement House and worked her way up to head resident of the house in 1906, a position she retained until she retired in 1947 (Doris Overboe 913–14; Wukas 25–26). Like Hull-House and many settlement houses springing up across the country during America's progressive era, the Northwestern University Settlement was run by college-educated professionals who developed education, recreation, and job training programs, in this case for the mostly Polish working-class immigrants in a Chicago neighborhood. The Northwestern Settlement House was founded by a handful of Chicago-area leaders who consulted Addams about the need for a second settlement in the city. Among these first important stakeholders for the Northwestern University Settlement were President Henry Wade Rogers, his wife, Emma, and a University of Chicago–trained sociology professor Charles Zueblin, an espoused feminist and also an alumnus of Northwestern University whose passion for founding a settlement was fueled after staying at London's Toynbee Hall Settlement, the same settlement that had inspired the founding of Hull-House (Wukas 7–8). In decades to come, more settlement houses would proliferate in the city per the trend in the United States as a whole.

Customary at the time, settlement work required that middle-class volunteers and the paid professionals working for the settlement live at the settlement house to foster cross-class collaborative and co-generative problem solving. Vittum explained the purpose of settlement living in a 1914 speech: "Perhaps the greatest claim the settlement can make to its part in the *culture of family life* is that the settlement is part of the neighborhood, its residents live there. If the street crossings are bad[,] the residents in the community suffer the same as other people living in the street; if the streets are dirty, it is the same for the settlement residents as for the others" ("Culture" 111, original emphasis). Relatedly, Vittum described her methods as a social worker and social activist most roughly as "organized friendliness," claiming also that she "ha[d] always been interested in folks and would not care to live on a desert island or alone in a penthouse" (Cranston N1). Scholar Shannon Jackson situates "locality" among progressive-era settlers in a feminist context, arguing that "for bourgeois female settlers in particular, such a proximate epistemology [living in the settlement] drew from a discourse of domesticity, a nineteenth century formation that positioned women as sympathetic interpreters of the microperformances of every day life" (6). Vittum coined this progressive-era settlement ideal as "practical citizenship," which "presupposes a knowledge of our form of government, the technique of voting, and the relation of our daily lives to city, state, and national government" ("Politics" 423). According to Vittum, practical citizenship can result in substantive material transformation of local spaces when the politically engaged advocate for better material resources in their neighborhoods.

Vittum's leadership transcended her work at the settlement through her speeches and also through her affiliations with other Chicago activists such as Margaret Drier Robins, Jane Addams, and Mary McDowell; through her affiliation with such organizations as the Chicago branch of the Women's Trade Union League, and as president of the Woman's City Club of Chicago. While working as head resident at the settlement house, Vittum ran for office twice, first as an alderman and once for a spot on the Cook County Board of Commissioners ("Harriet Vittum Dies"). Of her time as a progressive and also perhaps ahead of her time, she fought for the civil rights of African Americans after the 1919 Chicago Race Riot by calling a conference to address and reduce racial tensions. When the Great Depression strained relations between conservative board members of settlements and the more left-leaning settlement workers, Vittum advocated for New Deal resources for her constituents (Doris Overboe 915–16). The end of Vittum's career at the Northwestern University Settlement when she retired at age seventy-five paralleled the waning heyday of female-run settlement culture when immigration laws eased nativist anxiety and made settlement projects seem less imperative.

Meanwhile, social workers took over the jobs once held by volunteers, who had most often been privileged upper-middle-class women, and some neighborhoods disappeared altogether as a result of urban renewal projects such as the building of highways. Services for the poor were centralized through sprawling nonprofits like the United Way but also outside of particular neighborhoods. As services became centralized, as mentioned, the onsite and ambitiously large houses that expanded along with the settlement movement were considered costly white elephants (Trolander 29; Haar 4). The relevance of settlements to the college-educated was disregarded, to the extent that the neighborhood surrounding Hull-House was emptied out to make way for building the University of Illinois at Chicago (Haar 81). The Northwestern University Settlement did, however, survive this cultural transformation in an unusual way. The spirit of progressive-era settlement culture was maintained through Vittum's successor, Michael Rachwalski, who grew up in the neighborhood surrounding the settlement, which remained a stable port of entry for immigrants. During his long career from 1947 through 1981, Rachwalski lived at the settlement with his wife, Helen, who was the assistant head and then associate director of the settlement during these years (Wukas 63–69).

VISITING HARRIET VITTUM PARK

The twofold recovery process I underwent during the May 2012 research trip in Chicago culminated in my visit to Harriet Vittum Park, an errand I undertook out of both curiosity and my new-felt responsibility as Overboe's witness. This errand seemed to embody the layered legacies I was uncovering. The park, southwest of downtown very close to Midway Airport, sits in a neighborhood of close-together bungalows on tiny lots with tidy lawns.

The spring afternoon was bursting with light and promise during my visit, but the park was otherwise absent of people. Impressed by the size of the park as I walked around its entirety, I was disappointed with the park signage Overboe had lobbied for. I had initially misread some of the documents in the archive that described the plans for this signage and expected that Vittum's face would be on the park signs, along with biographical information about her, as with contemporary museum didactics. Every one of the park signs I inventoried was in some stage of being tagged or cleansed of graffiti (figure 6.1). Overboe's efforts to resurrect or maintain Vittum's legacy at this park were seemingly futile or at the very least not sustainable. I recalled my long walks through London parks during my trip to that city a few years earlier when I was disturbed by the ubiquitous statues of commanding leaders of empires who were holding guns or riding horses or both, like the Nat Rocket statue in Hyde Park. Pacing around Harriet Vittum Park that afternoon, I wondered what it might take for people walking through a park named after you to get it through their heads that you had been big stuff.

I found the drawing Overboe had arranged to be hung in the park's recreation center only accidentally when looking for the bathroom at the end of my park visit (figure 6.2). The drawing was located in a rather marginalized spot, hanging at the top of tall bookcases amid a collage of sports plaques and trophies. I chatted briefly with a female employee when gazing up at this drawing, perhaps saving the woman some embarrassment and myself from more disappointment when, not waiting to

Figure 6.1. Sign at Vittum Park recently rubbed clean of graffiti. Photo: Author.

hear her answer, I asked her if she knew who Harriet Vittum was. Mid-question I blurted out, "She was the second Jane Addams." The woman nodded blankly, saying, "Um, yeah, that's right, the second Jane Addams."

I left Harriet Vittum Park with mixed emotions. Overboe's efforts as a historian were at odds with a culture indifferent to a memorial that might require extra interpretation or thought or perhaps were at odds with a culture simply not rewarded for maintaining this type of memorial—unless removing graffiti from a park sign might qualify. At the same time, while learning about Vittum's legacy and witnesssing Overboe's hard work at maintaining that legacy, I became hooked.

I hadn't considered the connection exactly during my first visit to the Northwestern University Settlement archives, but the goal of interfacing community activism with university work that in part shaped the founding of the Northwestern University Settlement long ago in 1891 historicizes some of the service learning work I was doing at my self-described "Metropolitan University," just outside Detroit. When researching the

Figure 6.2. The drawing of Vittum on a wall in the park's recreation center. Photo: Author.

settlement era, which at one time included the founding of a few other university settlement houses, I ascertained that the material goals and rhetoric of historical settlement stakeholders promote a historical case of what we might call self-reflexivity today, when the privileged are encouraged to acknowledge their positions in society and to see themselves in the Other. Scholars writing for the contemporary service learning journal the *Michigan Journal of Community Service Learning*, in fact, argue that service learning practices began with ideals and projects promoted by Addams (Daynes and Longo).

Significantly, after the much appreciated introduction to Overboe and Vittum during my first visit to the Northwestern University archives, I struck gold during a second visit the following summer when I unearthed 700 pages of writing from a 1930–31 service learning course sequence taught at the university and at the settlement when Vittum was in charge. Students in two sociology classes gathered data at the settlement and ran clubs for children. The students reflected on this work by writing term papers in which they outlined their projects and also through the lessons learned when working with a population of people who lacked their privileges as middle-class college students. These data further a richer look at the history of service learning that has origins in the work and rhetoric of women leaders like Addams and like Vittum, which I am pursuing.

CONCLUSION

My research on the Northwestern University Settlement has taken a turn that does not necessarily feature Overboe's work, but I am indebted to her efforts, her insights, and her spirit. My detour to the Northwestern University archives was serendipitous because it led me to a new research project for which the data are rich while providing one lesson about how an archive might become rich or not. That is, this detour, including a trip to Harriet Vittum Park, was instructive about the agency of archives, archivists, and researchers who embody, build, and preserve legacies, in this case the legacies of women. Moreover, the double lives of Vittum and Overboe, inscribed in the archives, which drew me in as a witness, explicitly feature an archive as a layered, rhetorical space with a history and a set of processes shaping it.

My experience researching the historical settlement work of Tau Beta clubwomen provides additional context for theorizing witnesses'/researchers' affordances and constraints, especially when these researchers embrace memory making and legacy preservation as part of their methods. Information that might help generate histories that can productively inform the present—such as Eleanor Clay Ford's admiration for Jane Addams—can be controlled or even censored by powerful others. Or individual legacies can simply be lost to history because of scant records, as in the case of Josephine Clay Kanzler, Ford's sister, who died young. Luck might lead a researcher on a fruitful journey with the exciting short-run result, for example, of witnessing the work of productive women like Overboe and Vittum. But researchers are also reliant on the goodwill, foresight, and political savvy of those holding the keys to resources in the first place and in my case the second place, as a side trip to a new archive led to a brand-new project.

Works Cited

Alexander, Frances Sibley. "The Tau Beta Association: Its Accomplishments of Twenty-Five Years and Its Future Plans." *Citizen's Weekly.* 17 Nov. 1941. 1. Print.

Bunner, Kimberly. Letter to Ronald R. Manderschied. Doris Overboe Papers. Box 2, Folder 13. Northwestern University Settlement Association, Northwestern University Archives, Evanston, IL. Archival source.

Cranston, Bernice. "Miss Vittum's Career Is One Long Crusade." *Chicago Daily Tribune.* 25 Nov. 1935. N1. Print.

Daynes, Gary, and Nicholas V. Longo. "Jane Addams and the Origins of Service-Learning Practice in the United States." *Michigan Journal of Community Service Learning* (Fall 2004): 5–13. Print.

Enoch, Jessica. "Survival Stories: Feminist Historiographic Approaches to Chicano Rhetorics of Sterilization Abuse." *Rhetoric Society Quarterly* 35.3 (2005): 5–30. Print.

Enoch, Jessica. "A Woman's Place Is in the School: Rhetorics of Gendered Space in Nineteenth-Century America." *College English* 70.1 (2008): 275–95. Print.

Haar, Sharon. *The City as Campus: Urbanism and Higher Education in Chicago.* Minneapolis: University of Minnesota Press, 2011. Print.

"Harriet E. Vittum, N. U. Settlement Chief, Selected as City's Most Useful Woman." *Chicago Herald and Examiner.* 1 June 1937. Page unavailable. Print.

"Harriet Vittum Dies; Pioneer Social Worker." *Chicago Daily Tribune* 17 Dec. 1953. C13. Print.

Jackson, Shannon. *Lines of Activity: Performance, Historiography, Hull-House Domesticity.* Ann Arbor: U of Michigan P, 2000. Print.

Olson, Janet. Finding Aide for "Doris Overboe Papers, c. 1990–2000." Northwestern University Settlement Association, Evanston, IL. Archival source.

Overboe, Doris P. "Vittum, Harriet Elizabeth." *Women Building Chicago 1790–1990.* Ed. Rima Lunin Schultz and Adele Hast. Bloomington: Indiana UP, 2001. 913–16. Print.

Overboe, Ellert. Personal Interview. 12 Oct. 2013.

Plumb, Mildred. *History of Tau Beta.* Detroit: Evans-Winter-Hebb, Inc., 1938. Print.

Reynolds, Nedra. *Geographies of Writing: Inhabiting Places and Encountering Difference.* Carbondale: Southern Illinois UP, 2004. Print.

Royster, Jacqueline, and Gesa Kirsch. *Feminist Rhetorical Practices: New Horizons for Rhetoric, Composition, and Literacy Studies.* Carbondale: Southern Illinois UP, 2012. Print.

Stewart, Evelyn S. "Hamtramck to Lose 'the House of Hope.'" *Detroit Free Press.* 23 Jan. 1953. 15. Print.

"Tau Beta Gets 50,000 in Will." *Hamtramck Citizen.* 29 April 1954. 1. Hamtramck Library Archives, Hamtramck, MI. Archival source.

Trolander, Judith Ann. *Professionalism and Social Change: From the Settlement House Movement to Neighborhood Centers 1886 to the Present.* New York: Columbia UP, 1987. Print.

Vittum, Harriet. Culture of Family Life from the Social Settlement Standpoint. Conference on Charities and Correction, Memphis, TN, 1914. Doris Overboe Papers. Box 4, Folder 13. Northwestern University Settlement Association, Evanston, IL. Archival source.

Vittum, Harriet. Politics from the Social Point of View. Conference of Social Work, 1924, Toronto, ON. Harriet Vittum E.: Speeches/Writing. Box 67, Folder 16. Northwestern Settlement Association, Evanston, IL. Archival source.

"Vittum Park Honors Harriet Vittum. Doris Overboe Papers c. 1990–2000. Box 1, Folder 2. Northwestern University Settlement Association, Evanston, IL. Archival source.

Wukas, Mark. *The Worn Doorstep: Informal History of Northwestern University Settlement Association, 1891–1991.* Chicago: Northwestern University Settlement Association, 1991. Print.

7

SERENDIPITY AND MEMORY
The Value of Participant Observation

Kim Donehower

I went to graduate school at the peak of the postmodern critique of anthropology, exemplified by James Clifford and George Marcus's *Writing Culture* (1986), Clifford's *The Predicament of Culture* (1988), and Renato Rosaldo's *Culture and Truth* (1993). These texts were assigned in a graduate seminar called Ethnography as Culture Critique that I took from Robin Brown in the fall of 1993. Our focus was on the representation of culture through ethnographic writing, and we read studies such as James Moffett's *Storm in the Mountains* and Shirley Brice Heath's *Ways with Words,* alert for the ways the author-researchers tried to both analyze and explain a culture and share space on the page with a culture without overwriting "native" voices with the author's perspective.

In *The Predicament of Culture,* Clifford documents the rise of "an efficient ethnography based on scientific participant observation . . . between 1920 and 1950" that created ethnographic texts that were a "peculiar amalgam of intense personal experience and scientific analysis" (33–34). The results are works that can be persuasive on both narrative (aesthetic) and analytical grounds and that exhibit a strong tendency to speak for, and not about, the subjects of study. "After objectivism," as Rosaldo describes it in *Culture and Truth,* ethnographers attempted to resolve this dilemma by creating accounts that are "dialogic" (Clifford) or "polyphonic" (Rosaldo "From the Door"). But these, too, have problems. Rosaldo writes of "the false ethnographic authority of polyphony," in which the ethnographer's "voice and peasant voices [appear] equally heard" but direct quotes from "peasants" are selected and presented by the ethnographer to suggest "that he and his subjects inhabit similar psychological worlds" ("From the Door" 82–84). In addition, the act of writing up an ethnographic account positions the ethnographer to "transform the research situation's ambiguities and diversities of

DOI: 10.7330/9781607327394.c007

meaning into an integrated portrait" (Clifford 40), making dialogism or polyphony on the page extremely difficult to achieve.

Ethnography as Cultural Critique was my favorite class as a graduate student, but coming out of it, ethnography and its hallmark practice, participant observation, seemed to me a methodological minefield I was not willing to cross. It is twenty-two years since I took the class as I write this, and I still refuse to use the "e-word" to describe what it is I do. I carefully say that I am a qualitative researcher who conducts interviews with people about their literacy histories, beliefs, and practices. Do not accuse me of "writing culture" or of anything associated with it. I am trying to enrich our understanding of literacy and the ways it can function in particular contexts. I am not writing to enrich our understanding of certain cultures. If the ethical concerns weren't enough, even Shirley Brice Heath—whom Brown referred to in class as "the grandmother of us all"—acknowledges in the introduction to *Ways with Words* that when we do "write culture," we're only writing the culture at the moment at which we researched it. She cautions readers that by the time they hold the book in their hands, "the ethnographic present never remains as it is described" (9).

So, no participant observation or claims to "ethnography" for me. Deborah Brandt's work, which culminated in *Literacy in American Lives*, gave me an alternative to Heath's participant observation. I would conduct interviews with individuals about literacy in their lives and work to create nuanced "thick descriptions" (Geertz) that highlighted themes that emerged across the interviews. There was no participant observation in my first study, in a small Appalachian community, and I planned none for my second site, a North Dakota town I call "Hammond." But when one of my interviewees in Hammond invited me to attend as a participant her book group's discussion of comedian Steve Harvey's *Act Like a Lady, Think Like a Man*—a manual, essentially, for catching a husband—I accepted without a second thought. The chance to observe and experience people reading and not always be at one remove from that reading seemed too good to pass up. Also, the complexities of a group of rural white women in their fifties dissecting Harvey's younger, urban, African American–centered text promised intriguing, rich data.

The content of the meeting was indeed fascinating, but what was most striking was the sensory and emotional impression the event made on me. The book group was part of a larger women's club organized around needlework, and the organizer had purchased a defunct café in a nearby dying town to use as the club's headquarters. For me, this meant a drive of eighteen miles out of Hammond, across a golden, rolling prairie landscape. I remember the sensation of dipping down into a river bottom after traveling across the high plateau—my signal that a turn on an obscure road was coming up. The town housing the café was down to a population of twenty-some people and was as silent when I arrived as though it housed zero. The café sat sparkling white along one side of a grassy town square, with a large banner proclaiming it the "House of Fun," the women's name for their group. Inside were the hallmarks of a small-town café, but the glass-front cabinets held stacks of quilting fabric instead of pies, and an antique Singer sewing machine sat where a counter or cash register may have once stood. I remember the contrast between the sun-flooded front of the café, where customers once sat, and the darker kitchen behind, where group members laid out refreshments for the meeting.

Six years have passed since that book club event, but I still recall where I and each of the other participants sat around the long table. I remember feeling myself drawn into the discussion of the book and wondering in the moment whether my ratio of participation to observation was leaning too much toward the first to get "reliable data." And I remember not caring because the interactions about the book, among the women themselves and myself and the women, were so involving.

Regardless of whether my data from the event remain reliable, experiencing literacy in Hammond compared to asking people about it set up the conditions for a moment of serendipity in my research. Four years after my site visits, I was asked by a group of Brandt's former students to submit an abstract for a *Festschrift* they were putting together to commemorate her retirement. While writing my proposal for the collection and looking at the well-thumbed copy of *Literacy in American Lives* that sits next to my computer, I hatched a strategy for acceptance: everyone, I suspected, would be writing about *LAL*. I would propose something on *Literacy as Involvement*, Brandt's first book, a difficult text that one of my graduate professors had confessed to me she could not understand.

I had read the book as a graduate student, before *Literacy in American Lives* came out, in my quest to read everything Brandt had written to that point. I had read the text the way graduate students do: latching on to keywords, connecting other texts I had read to those keywords, nodding even though no one was watching me, desperate to convince myself that I understood everything Brandt was saying. I came away with a clear understanding of what she meant by "strong text" models of literacy and the problems with those models, and I knew that a rhetorical idea of literacy could lead one to a different model, which Brandt was calling "involvement." But that was all I understood.

I didn't understand what Brandt was saying might really mean until vivid memories of the book club meeting in Hammond reasserted themselves as I was rereading the book. *Literacy as Involvement* lacks the kinds of examples with which most of Brandt's readers are familiar—Dwayne Lowery, who illustrates the idea of sponsors of literacy; Sam May and Charles Randolph from "Accumulating Literacy," and others. *Literacy as Involvement*'s examples are textual, such as Brandt's brilliant unpacking of a newspaper article reporting the results of a baseball game. But what we cannot yet see in *Literacy as Involvement* is how literacy might work in Americans' lives. My memory of the book club now offered itself as a potential example, with vivid scenes from the event popping into my head to illustrate various claims in the text.

The experience was not at first a "eureka" or lightbulb moment. It was a slow and tenuous hanging on to the word "involvement" and how it seemed to capture what I can only describe as the "atmosphere" of the book club meeting I joined. There was an intensity, a focus, a feeling—for me at least—of being very much in that specific place at that specific time. I'll return to the inherent methodological problem in that "for me at least" later. The point is that in an aesthetic way, Brandt's choice of the word "involvement" seemed to capture something about a memorable experience that I could not articulate.

Ultimately, rereading *Literacy as Involvement* with the memory of the book club fresh in my mind was a revelation. Brandt writes of the ways reading and writing work to "sustain the processes of intersubjective life" for individual readers and writers (103). I started seeing the involvements Brandt was describing as happening among groups: the group memberships implied by the book club women meeting in a rural café surrounded by antique sewing machines, bolts of fabric, and pie cases and the very different urban, largely African American readership assumed by Harvey. I had begun my Hammond project with a goal of mapping the various literacy sponsors that intersected in the town. Now my focus began to shift to the role literacy might play in sustainability, in "sustaining the intersubjective life" of a town of readers and writers. In short order I began to see the connection of "literacy as involvement" to issues of rural out-migration, rural schooling, rural rationality, social capital—all threads I had been chasing as I outlined and re-outlined the book I wanted to grow out of my Hammond research. I could see a continuity with earlier work I had done on literacy and the management of identity.

I argue that this was because of memory, and the kind of memory that can only be created by a full, present experience such as is possible in participant observation. For whatever reasons, that book club meeting had impressed itself on my emotions, senses, and intellect. This trifecta brought the memory—of some specifics but also of an overall gestalt—back to stand next to *Literacy as Involvement* as I reread it. Vivid experience provided the "prepared mind" of my serendipitous moment; the opportunity to get a publication in a collection honoring my favorite scholar provided the "chance" re-encounter with Brandt's earlier work.

The memories that were not available to me during my rereading of Brandt were those of the data I had collected in Hammond solely through observation (a youth Bible study group I had observed but not participated in) or collection (interviews). In those instances, I can remember elements of the settings in which I conducted the observations and interviews: the paneling in the living room where the Bible study was held; the comfortable antiquity of a farmhouse table where I interviewed an amateur historian. I have some recall of the mood and tenor of my interactions with some of my interviewees. These impressions are important, but interviews and observations are not fully experienced in the way participant observations are. At the youth Bible study, I was supremely conscious of being unobtrusive while rapidly taking notes. During interviews, I was focused on simply getting my interviewees to say as much as possible, all the while keeping an eye on the interview script to be sure I had covered everything but also following seeming tangents in the conversation to yield more and more data.

My richest experiences with the data I gather from observation and interviews come after the moments of collection, while transcribing, listening and re-listening, coding, and analyzing them. All of these tasks are done back in Grand Forks in my attic office, with a view only of the slanting beige wall in front of me. It is not a setting in which embodied experience creates memories that stick and assert themselves later when one does not expect it. It is, in fact, a setting designed—by me—to limit sensory and emotional input so I can concentrate on the task at hand and screen out the household and interpersonal duties that would assert themselves were I to turn away from the beige wall.

And yet . . . can I trust my impressions of that book club meeting as literacy-as-involvement? Brandt's term nailed down the nature of the experience for me, but was this how the event was experienced by the others in the room? I saw the "text" of that meeting—what participants were doing with Harvey's book, the kinds of questions they were asking, the experiences they were relating, and what seemed to be their objectives in the two-hour session—as echoing Brandt's analysis of the newspaper article reporting on the baseball game. But can I make claims—as I have in my published work—about the psychological work that kind of reading and discussion is doing? Or am I assuming, in Rosaldo's words, that I and my "subjects inhabit similar psychological worlds" (84)?

Participant observation as a method is still quite fraught. A few years after my course in ethnography, Brenda Jo Brueggemann summed up the dilemma of "the mythical participant-observer" this way: "'Self-reflexivity' has . . . been lauded as an antidote to . . . colonizing discourse. Yet . . . such self-reflexivity . . . risks turning representation into a solipsistic, rhetorical position in which the researcher . . . once again usurps the position of the subject . . . And . . . if we choose to be reflexive, to put the roles and representations of our subjects and our selves under scrutiny, we cannot possibly be chimeric, both/and, distanced yet near, objective yet subjective, participant-observer[s]" (19). In other words, the reflexivity that lent ethnographic authority to those working in the field after the critique of objectivity that Rosaldo describes in *Culture and Truth* raises a whole new set of problems. It runs the risk of making the research all about the researcher's self, and it creates a metacognitive load that mitigates against what Brueggemann argues good participant observers do: "We can be neither exclusively participant nor wholly observer . . . We must instead 'work the hyphen,' traverse the terrain of what is 'happening between' participant and observer" (20).

"Working the hyphen"—a quote from Michelle Fine—captures well what many of the debates about how to ethically do participant observation have centered on since the postmodern critiques of Clifford, Marcus, and Rosaldo. How much participation and how much observation should be in the mix? Essays such as "From Participant Observation to Observant Participation" (Moeran) and "The Active Participant Observer" (Johnson, Avenarius, and Weatherford) push toward the participation side of the equation. Both argue that certain kinds of data and understanding can only be obtained through participation. In contrast, Gary Alan Fine argues that "a peopled ethnography"—one that offers "a rich and detailed account of the world being observed" rather than "the inclusion of a few instances of data to bolster one's analytical points" (45)—is "based on extensive observation" (53). How to navigate this tension? Patrick McCurdy and Julie Uldam offer one solution—our old friend reflexivity, which Brueggemann so ably unpacks.

Sigh. There still seems no way out of the participant observation labyrinth, especially for a researcher working from humanist goals and perspectives with methods drawn from social science. What's a non-anthropologist to do?

All I know is this: serendipity of the sort I experienced does not happen in front of the beige wall. Vivid sensory input, strong emotional impressions, and intense intellectual experience were all required to store the book club event in my brain in such a way that it emerged when I was supposedly doing a one-off project on Brandt's *Literacy as Involvement.*

When we teach and conduct research, we seldom address the issue of memory sufficiently. How many of us pick up a book we read only a year or two before and stare at our own underlinings as though someone else had written them? How often do we read our own writing after the passage of some time and think, "Huh, I forgot that I thought that. That's pretty useful." My coauthors for *Rural Literacies* once laughed at me for liking a particular passage in the introduction and told me, "You should. You wrote it." I had no recollection of putting those words and ideas together in that way.

If serendipity is an encounter between chance and a prepared mind, how prepared is a mind that forgets or fails to retrieve a memory? Psychologists assert that we are more likely to remember experiences and information with an emotional charge attached (Christianson); while there is debate about the accuracy of memories related to emotional events, "slowed forgetting of emotional events comes from the extra attention and rehearsal that these events receive. Emotional materials are, by their nature, often worth thinking about" (Heuer and Reisberg 171). Furthermore, vivid sensory impressions—a particular kind of observation—melded with the emotions involved in participation may help certain memories more firmly take root.

When my doubts about participant observation creep up on me, I keep in mind its role in providing the moment of serendipity that has transformed the direction of my research. I also remind myself that ultimately, I am indeed most interested in articulating the nuances and possibilities of literacy, not in writing a definitive study of the culture of Hammond. But literacy is an abstraction, and staying at the level of abstraction in my research leaves me facing the beige wall. Participant observation brings life, memory—and the potential for serendipity—to that work.

Works Cited

Brandt, Deborah. "Accumulating Literacy: Writing and Learning to Write in the Twentieth Century." *College English* (1995): 649–68. Print.

Brandt, Deborah. *Literacy as Involvement: The Acts of Writers, Readers, and Texts.* Carbondale: Southern Illinois UP, 1990. Print.

Brandt, Deborah. *Literacy in American Lives.* Cambridge: Cambridge UP, 2001. Print.

Brueggemann, Brenda Jo. "Still-Life: Representations and Silences in the Participant-Observer Role." *Ethics and Representation in Qualitative Studies of Literacy.* Ed. Peter Mortensen and Gesa Kirsch. Urbana, IL: National Council of Teachers of English, 1996. 17–39. Print.

Christianson, Sven-Ake, ed. *The Handbook of Emotion and Memory: Research and Theory.* Hillsdale, NJ: Psychology Press, 1992. Print.

Clifford, James. *The Predicament of Culture: Twentieth-Century Ethnography, Literature, and Art.* Cambridge, MA: Harvard UP, 1988. Print.

Clifford, James, and George Marcus, eds. *Writing Culture: The Poetics and Politics of Ethnography.* Berkeley: U of California P, 1986. Print.

Fine, Gary Alan. "Towards a Peopled Ethnography: Developing Theory from Group Life." *Ethnography* 4.1 (2003): 41–60. Web. 14 Nov. 2016.

Fine, Michelle. "Working the Hyphen: Reinventing the Self and Other in Qualitative Research." *Handbook of Qualitative Research.* Ed. Norman Denzin and Yvonna S. Lincoln. Thousand Islands, CA: Sage, 1994. 70–82. Print.

Geertz, Clifford. *The Interpretation of Cultures.* New York: Basic Books, 1977. Print.

Heath, Shirley Brice. *Ways with Words: Language, Life, and Work in Communities and Classrooms.* Cambridge: Cambridge UP, 1983. Print.

Heuer, Friderike, and Daniel Reisberg. "Emotion, Arousal, and Memory for Detail." *The Handbook of Emotion and Memory: Research and Theory.* Ed. Sven-Ake Christianson. Hillsdale, NJ: Psychology Press, 1992. 151–80. Print.

Johnson, Jeffrey C., Christine Avenarius, and Jack Weatherford. "The Active Participant Observer: Applying Social Role Analysis to Participant Observation." *Field Methods* 18.2 (2006): 111–34. Web. 13 Nov. 2016.

McCurdy, Patrick, and Julie Uldam. "Connecting Participant Observation Positions: Toward a Reflexive Framework for Studying Social Movements." *Field Methods* 26.1 (2014): 40–55. Web. 14 Nov. 2016.

Moeran, Brian. "From Participant Observation to Observant Participation: Anthropology, Fieldwork, and Organizational Anthropology." *Creative Encounters* 2007. Web. 9 Dec. 2017.

Moffett, James. *Storm in the Mountains: A Case Study of Censorship, Conflict, and Consciousness.* Carbondale: Southern Illinois UP, 1988. Print.

Rosaldo, Renato. *Culture and Truth: The Remaking of Social Analysis.* Boston: Beacon, 1993. Print.

Rosaldo, Renato. "From the Door of His Tent: The Fieldworker and the Inquisitor." *Writing Culture: The Poetics and Politics of Ethnography.* Ed. George Marcus and James Clifford. Berkeley: U of California P, 1986. 77–97. Print.

PART III

Stumbling into the Unknown

8
THE SERENDIPITY OF (MIS)TIMING IN RESEARCH

Maureen Daly Goggin

Language itself conspires toward this sort of asymmetry: we fall into error, but do not usually speak of falling into truth.
—Albert O. Hirschman (13)

In the fields of observation, chance favors only the prepared mind.
—Louis Pasteur (473)

I have . . . become interested in how one teaches about research. If one accepts that there is some element of mystery, paradox, and strangeness about research, how is one going to teach it as part of a pedagogic activity which can be seen also as adjacent to research as in "research and teaching."
—Arjun Appadurai (169)

Economist Albert O. Hirschman writes about "stumbling" into truths. He argues that "we are . . . correspondingly unwilling to concede—in fact we find it intolerable to imagine—that our more lofty achievements, such as economic, social, or political progress [I might add scholarly research], could have come about by stumbling rather than through careful planning, rational behavior, and the successful response to a clearly perceived challenge" (13). In research, this "falling into truth," as he calls it in the epigraph above, is far more common than many scholars admit. Those who do talk about it call it "serendipity" of research. The question is, if there are moments of serendipity, how does one teach for these instances? How, as Arjun Appadurai asks, does one teach "some element of mystery, paradox, and strangeness about research" (169). To start teaching this aspect is to admit and explore how serendipity—how falling into truth—plays out in all sorts of research spaces and to prepare students for it in their own research. Of course, to recognize something as a finding or a truth, one needs, in Louis Pasteur's words, a "prepared mind" (473). In this chapter I discuss how I "stumbled" into truths after a substantive amount of archival research and review of scholarly literature gave me a "prepared mind."

In 2000–2001 I took a year-long sabbatical to research the literacy practices of needlework samplers. I had long thought of stitching as a literate practice, as one needs to know how to read the material—the different kinds of cloth and threads and their effects—and how to write with a needle. Although a few scholars had written on needlework, none had looked at the practice of stitching as a literacy. I set out to shift attention away from the stitched visual artifact as interpreted text—what a few other scholars had done—toward the material practices that construct, circulate, and repurpose it. More specifically, in this line of inquiry I wanted to examine needlework as a form of meaningful mark making and a method for creating knowledge—a polysemous system of writing and knowledge making. Needlework is a huge topic, so I decided to limit it to English sampler making from the seventeenth century to the nineteenth century. To do this, I needed to set my sights on the actual pieces that had been stitched, and so I began contacting museums in the United States and abroad to make appointments with curators who would let me study pieces that were not on display.

Among the stitched pieces I was examining was one from the Victorian and Albert Museum (V&A) in London that mesmerized me. This remarkable piece offered a rare window into the life of an early nineteenth-century lower-class English girl named Elizabeth Parker and her family (figure 8.1). At first glance, this piece of stitching—variously called a "piece of old handmade linen with its strange 'confessions,'" "a self-imposed penance," and a "human document" by Mrs. Lily Griffiths, the woman who sold it to the V&A in 1956—appears to be an ordinary plain-stitching sampler exercise. Plain-stitching samplers were a domestic and domesticating exercise undertaken by young women to equip them with skills that would enable them to secure employment, especially in domestic service. On closer inspection, Parker's sampler is anything but ordinary or plain. On a large piece of tightly woven linen, measuring approximately 30 inches wide by 34 inches long, Parker cross-stitched in red silk her poignant life story in forty-six lines of excruciatingly small letters. (See the appendix to this chapter for a full transcript of her text.)

Aimee Newell would describe the kind of stitching Parker did as "both biographical (conveying a life story) and epistolary (employing words on the object, whether written, stitched, or applied, to tell that story)" (140). Parker devotes the first thirteen lines to the autobiography of her then brief life of seventeen years, focusing especially on the

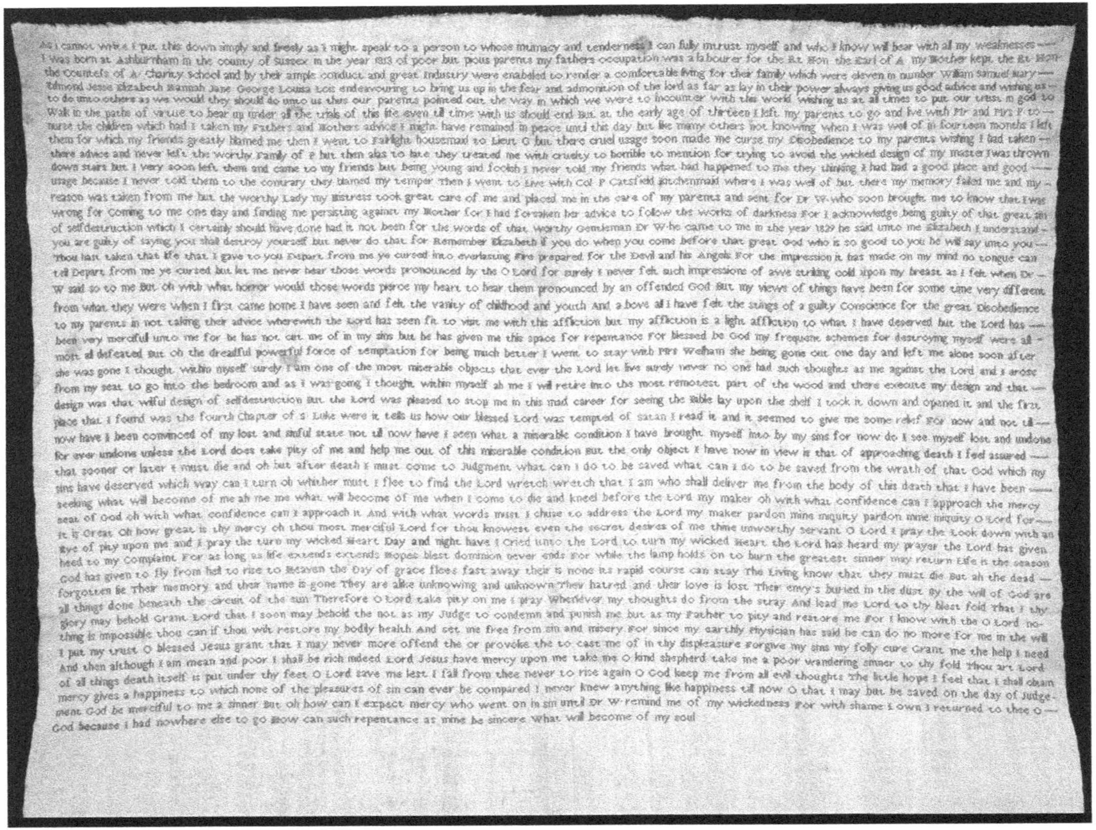

Figure 8.1. Elizabeth Parker ca. 1830 sampler. © V&A Images/Victoria and Albert Museum, London.

last four years. She tells us when she was born, who her parents and siblings are, and what her parents did for a living and how they parented her. Parker was born in Ashburnham in 1813. In 1826 her parents found her a position as a live-in nursemaid. Fourteen months later she had tired of the position and sought another position on her own. In 1828 she became a housemaid to Lt. G in Fairlight, a small village just nine miles southeast of Ashburnham. It was there that she was treated "with cruelty to[o] horrible to mention," and while "trying to avoid the wicked design of [her] master [she] was thrown down stairs" (lines 10–11). Shortly after this horrific experience, she found yet another live-in position as a kitchen maid for Col. and Lady P in Catsfield, almost three miles southeast of Ashburnham. There her "memory failed [her] and [her] reason was taken from" her (lines 11–12)—classic symptoms of what would today be diagnosed as severe depression. Col. and Lady P sent for a doctor for Elizabeth and then sent Elizabeth home to recover. She thus returned to Ashburnham.

Parker narrates what poet Diane Wakoski would call a finger story of sexual violation and physical abuse at the hands of her employer Lt. G. These horrific experiences leave unnamed physical, psychological, emotional, and spiritual scars that paralyze her. Her paralysis is compounded by persistent dark thoughts of suicide that carried heavy religious and legal consequences (MacDonald and Murphy). In the remaining lines, she stitches her struggle against, in her words, "the great sin of self destruction" (line 15) that becomes for her a "dreadful powerful force of temptation" (line 23) against which she fights almost daily. She prays for God's guidance and mercy but is not convinced she is worthy of either. After suturing 46 lines, 1,722 words, 6,699 characters (averaging 146 characters per line), she stops abruptly midway down the cloth, mid-line, with a powerful plea: "what will become of my soul" (line 46). I became obsessed with finding out what became of her.[1]

I arranged for a two-month-long stay in Lewes, England, a southeast Sussex town near the three villages Parker named in her sample and where the East Sussex Records Office stood that held some of the archives relevant for my search. I was determined to find out as much as I could about this extraordinary needleworker, as well as the people and places in her life. I spent seven weeks in the East Sussex Records Office poring over birth, baptismal, death, and census records along with personal and professional papers of Lord and Lady Ashburnham (for whom both of Elizabeth's parents worked), as well as newspapers, maps, and photographs of the period. I also spent time at the West Sussex Records Office to find information on Elizabeth's siblings; at the Public Records Office in Kew, Surrey, to scrutinize military records; and at the Family Records Centre in London to secure a death certificate for Elizabeth Parker. Parker—in accordance with nineteenth-century convention—named individuals in her sampler by initials only. It took time to identify each of the twenty people she named. I also explored the V&A Museum archives for information on the source of the donation of the Parker sampler to the museum. The archival work was slow but yielded important information. After locating records on and identifying every person named on Parker's sampler and, most important, after locating records that revealed Elizabeth found the strength to resist the dreadful force of self-destruction, living to the ripe old age of seventy-six, I was determined to visit and walk the villages she named in her sampler to do place-based research.[2] As Liz Rohan points out from her own research, "Sharing the physical context of a subject by visiting the places where a subject lived and worked allows researchers to strengthen a bond with this subject, which teaches researchers how to think better about this subject" (233). Rohan notes that this is what Christine Mason Sutherland calls "living the research" (233). For me, "living the research" means retracing the steps of those whose lives one is reconstructing and to do so as ethically and faithfully as possible.

(MIS)TIMING

I had to plan my trips to the three villages—Ashburnham, Fairlight, and Catsfield—very carefully because I had to rely on public transportation, and only one week of my time in Lewes remained (figure 8.2). Of the three places, Fairlight is the most accessible, served by one bus that runs several times a day out of the next largest town, Hastings. But the other two villages, Ashburnham and Catsfield, are served by only one bus of out Battle—the same bus that runs a circuit between the two villages one day a week, Thursdays, with a morning run and an afternoon run only. I had to be especially prudent in planning my trip to these two villages. Moreover, of the places named in the sampler, I only had nineteenth-century census data in which addresses were in the form of house names, so I had no street names or house numbers for any of the places I hoped to find. Finally, I knew precious little about any of the villages other than what I had gathered from reading about them in histories and guidebooks; all I knew was that these villages are so small that all they contain are a local village store, a pub, and one or two churches. Moreover, I didn't know whether the nineteenth-century

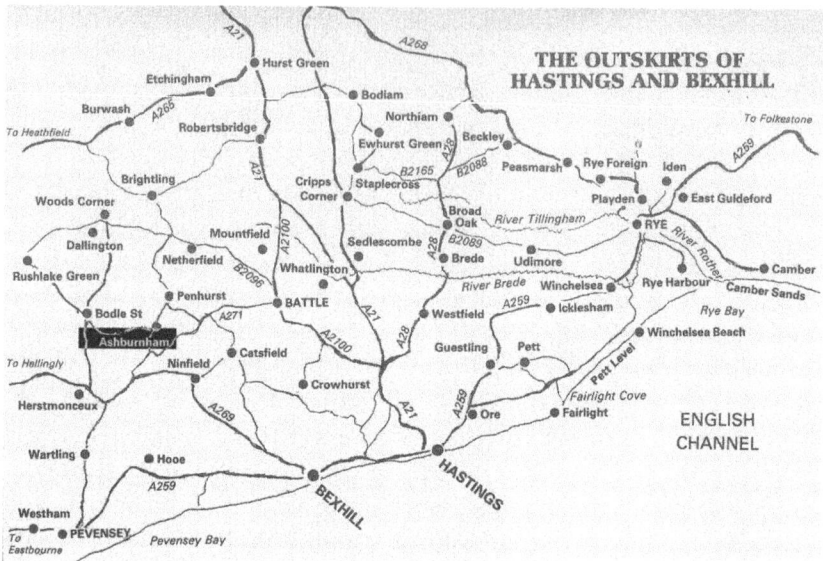

Figure 8.2. Map showing Ashburnham, Catsfield, Battle, Hastings, and Fairlight. Photo: Author.

buildings I was looking for would still be standing. The two best places to begin with in any small English village are the local village store and post office and the local pub, as these places often have people with long memories and historical interests. The post office has staff who know the local routes well, and the landlords of the pubs are familiar with many of their patrons and where they live. Historical communities are present in many small villages with people who gather together to keep abreast of the past.

Since I only had one day—Thursday—to go to both Ashburnham and Catsfield, I decided to go first to Fairlight on Monday morning. The bus dropped me off in front of the Cove, the Fairlight pub. With little information other than the nineteenth-century name "Coastguard Cottages," I asked those who worked at the Cove along with a few customers what they knew about the Coastguard Cottages and whether they still existed. With much enthusiasm, they told me the cottages were still standing. Armed with their directions, I made an easy two-mile trek across the cliffs from the pub to the cottages.

Fairlight is situated on the coast of the English Channel in East Sussex. It is a place of both extraordinary beauty and an important military stronghold. In fact, when Elizabeth moved there, it had only recently become a crucial site for the then newly formed Coastguard.

(The Coastguard service was set up in 1822 to combat smuggling and the Napoleonic threat.) Given its stunning scenery, one might fully understood why Elizabeth Parker may have wanted to live and work there. Today, the Coastguard Cottages still stand, now named the "Old Coast Guard Cottages," high on a cliff along the English Channel.

Elizabeth tells us she served as a housemaid to Lt. "G"—whom I had identified through military records as Lt. Ghallard, as he was the only lieutenant with a last name beginning with "G" who was stationed at Fairlight from 1826 to 1831. The Old Coast Guard Cottages are a connected series of five houses—four two-story buildings attached to a fifth three-story building. As the highest-ranking officer during that time, Lt. Ghallard no doubt lived in the three-story cottage at the far end facing the English Channel. The top floor would have been reserved for servants and would have been where Elizabeth stayed. What's not clear is which of the two staircases Lt. G had pushed her down. I spent time taking pictures and breathing in the scenery. Having found the site, I was ready for and pretty confident about finding places in the next two villages.

I decided to go to Catsfield first and from there catch the afternoon bus to Ashburnham and then the last of the circuit from Ashburnham back to Battle. From Battle, I could catch the train that would take me to the cottage I had rented in Lewes.

I arrived in Catsfield around 9:30 a.m. on a Thursday morning and began this time at the Catsfield Post Office and Village Store to ask about the places I wanted to find: Col. and Lady Pilkington's manor named Catsfield Manor, where Elizabeth had worked, and the St. Lawrence Church where I hoped to find Pilkington's gravesite. The postmaster was familiar with both sites. With his guidance, I walked the less than half a mile to find the manor whose pillars still bear the old name "Catsfield Manor." Right next door is St. Lawrence Church. After I spent a bit of time outside the gate of Catsfield Manor (it is now private and I had not secured permission to go on the grounds), I made the trek to the church and began walking the grounds searching for the Pilkington family plot.

While I was in the churchyard searching for Sir Andrew Pilkington's grave, an older woman with a flowered scarf tied around her hair and a bucket in her right hand asked if she could help me. I explained what I was looking for; she said she wouldn't know, but we could ask Basil: "Basil knows everything." She unlocked the church door and let me in, calling out for Basil. When Basil came out from the backroom, I again explained that I was looking for Sir Andrew Pilkington's grave, and Basil said he'd look in his records to see if he could find the site. As I waited, I saw a rack of post notes and a booklet with a short history of the church. The sign beside them read "Donation: 25p." I thought that a bit cheap, so I put a pound coin in the box. After about twenty minutes, Basil came out and apologized. He said he would need more time, as some of the records were housed elsewhere and the graveyard had been moved sometime in the nineteenth century to another site in Catsfield, but I could call him later to see what he found out. I thanked him and went back outside to continue my search of headstones.

A few minutes later, Basil came out and asked, "Well, you saw the plaque dedicated to Sir Pilkington in the church?"

"No" I said.

He reopened the church and showed me a plaque "dedicated to Sir Andrew Pilkington for his service to the church." I eagerly snapped pictures, thanked him again, and returned to the churchyard to continue my search.

About ten minutes later, Basil came back out. "Well, you saw the stained glass window dedicated to Sir Andrew Pilkington in the church, didn't you?"

"No," I exclaimed.

He reopened the church and showed me the middle panel of a large stained glass window in the south nave dedicated to the memory of Lt. General Sir Andrew Pilkington. It was commissioned by his firstborn daughter, Maria Georgia Pilkington Haybury. I snapped more pictures. Again, I thanked him profusely and returned to the churchyard to continue my search. This was my fourth venture on this pathway into the yard. As I went along the path directly from the door—the one I had already walked several times—there on my left was Pilkington's headstone along with those of his wife and children. How I had missed them I don't know. I knelt down to take the picture of Col. Pilkington's headstone, and at my knee I found a pound coin. Though it may have been a coincidence, it felt as if it were a sign from Elizabeth or Pilkington himself. I snapped pictures of the headstones and hurried off to the bus stop, but I had missed the bus. I wasn't sure what I could do since the village was so small and tucked away. But there across the street from the bus stop was the White Hart Pub of Catsfield.

I ran across the road and spoke to the landlord about my dilemma. He offered to call me a cab. He called several companies, but no one wanted the fare. Then he stopped, "Hey, my cigarette vendor is here. Perhaps he could take you when he is done." He spoke with him and arranged it. The vendor was wonderful. He told me he knew how to get to Ashburnham and asked where I wanted to go. I told him to the pub or the post office, since these were the places where I was getting my best information. We came to the outskirts of the village of Ashburnham, and he turned down the first street we came across on the right. "I'm not sure that this is the right road. I know how to get to the village but not which street the pub or post office is on."

We drove a short distance down a small, windy, tree-lined road.

"I don't think this is the right street."

Just then we passed a house with a sign "The Old School House."

"Wow," I exclaimed. "That is where Elizabeth grew up."

The vendor was becoming less sure that he had taken the right road. A bit further along, we drove past a row of cottages named the Old Alms Cottages, where Elizabeth had lived and eventually died.

"Double wow," I said.

And a bit further along, we drove past Pigknoll's farm where one of her brothers had worked.

"Triple wow!"

The vendor, now visibly frustrated that he had no doubt taken the wrong road, asked, "Where do you want to go?"

"Here at the Old School House."

He drove me back to the Old School House. I told him I could walk from there to the pub or the local village store. I thanked him profusely and snapped pictures, first of the duplex Old School House and then, just up the road, of the Old Alms Cottages. There was a road crew working just outside the cottages. As I snapped pictures, the workers watched me. Finally, curiosity got the best of one of them, and he asked me what I was doing. I explained my project and told them I was off to the pub and post office next. Could they give me directions?

"You're not walking," one of them said.

"Sure, I've been walking all these villages. It's no problem."

"Well, it's over five miles from here and all uphill."

"Ahhhhhh . . ." was all I could manage to get out. "Well, I have no choice."

Just then a cab drove up to the Old Alms Cottages to drop off a passenger. "Look," the man behind the ditch digger shouted. "Maybe he could take you where you want to go." The cab driver did just that. He took me to the seventeenth-century Ash Tree Pub in Ashburnham that probably looked in Elizabeth's day much as it does today, both inside and out. And just outside the pub was the bus stop where I was able to catch the bus back to Battle and then the train to Lewes.

I chose to write about this anecdote not because it led to some ground-breaking, dramatic intellectual discovery—it's a small piece of the much larger research puzzle—but because it vividly illustrates the paradox of chance and preparedness of serendipity, something that happens much more frequently in research than scholars seem willing to admit. Had I not missed Pilkington's grave in the churchyard at first, I would not have met Basil and I would have missed the plaque and the stained glass window dedicated to Pilkington inside the church. Serendipity. Had I taken the bus to Ashburnham—which did go to the pub, as it turns out—or driven myself, it is highly unlikely that I would have found the homes of Elizabeth and her family or the Old Alms Cottages or her brother's farm—at least not on that visit. Serendipity. On the other hand, had I not spent countless hours poring over archival records and historical accounts, I would not have recognized that these were the places I was looking for. Preparedness for serendipity. Creativity is at the heart of preparation and serendipity.

Albert Hirschman observed in his landmark essay "The Principle of the Hiding Hand"[3] that *"creativity always comes* [as] *a surprise to us; therefore we can never count on it and we dare not believe in it until it has happened. In other words, we would not consciously engage upon tasks whose success clearly requires that creativity be forthcoming. Hence, the only way in which we can bring our creative resources fully into play is by misjudging the nature of the task, by presenting it to ourselves as more routine, simple, undemanding of genuine creativity than it will turn out to be"* (13, original emphasis). Hirschman's words give us a map to share with our students. Creativity is at the center of all scholarly work. And in many ways, my scholarly process is very similar to that which I engage for my art craft projects. Sometimes my best work comes when my best-laid plans are disrupted. These are the beautiful surprises of creativity in both research and stitching.

APPENDIX
Transcription of Text Stitched on Elizabeth Parker's ca. 1830 Sampler (T6-1956)

I have tried to remain faithful to the original and have thus retained original spelling and include only punctuation marks that were stitched. Line numbers are indicated in brackets.

[1] As I cannot write I put this down simply and freely as I might speak to a person to whose intimacy and tenderness I can full intrust myself and who I know will bear with all my weaknesses [2] I was born at Ash-

burnham in the county of Sussex in the year 1813 of poor but pious parents my fathers occupation was a labourer for the Rt Hon the Earl of A my Mother kept the Rt Hon [3] the Countess of A Charity School and by their ample conduct and great industry were enabled to render a comfortable living for their family which were eleven in number William Samuel Mary [4] Edmond Jesse Elizabeth Hannah Jane George Louisa Lois endeavouring to bring us up in the fear and admonition of the Lord as far as lay in their power always giving us good advice and wishing us [5] to do unto others as we would they should do unto us thus our parents pointed out the way in which we were to incounter with this world wishing us at all times to put our trust in god to [6] walk in the paths of virtue to bear up under all the trials of this life even till time with us should end But at the early age of thirteen I left my parents to go and live with Mr and Mrs P to [7] nurse the children which had I taken my Fathers and Mothers advice I might have remained in peace until this day but like many others not knowing when I was well of in fourteen months I left [8] them for which my friends greatly blamed me then I went to Fairlight housemaid to Lieu. G but there cruel usage soon made me curse my Disobedience to my parents wishing I had taken [9] there advice and never left the worthy family of P but then alas to late they treated me with cruelty to horrible to mention for trying to avoid the wicked design of my master I was thrown [10] down stairs but I very soon left them and came to my friends but being young and foolish I never told my friends what had happened to me they thinking I had had a good place and good [11] usage because I never told them to the contrary they blamed my temper Then I went to live with Col. P Catsfield kitchenmaid where I was well off but there my memory failed me and my [12] reason was taken from me but the worthy Lady my mistress took great care of me and placed me in the care of my parents and sent for Dr. W who soon brought me to know that I was [13] wrong for coming to me one day and finding me persisting against my Mother for I had forsaken her advice to follow the works of darkness For I acknowledge being guilty of that great sin [14] of self destruction which I certainly should have done had it not been for the words of that worthy Gentleman Dr W he came to me in the year 1829 he said unto me Elizabeth I understand [15] you are guilty of saying you shall destroy yourself but never do that for Remember Elizabeth if you do when you come before that great God who is so good to you he will say unto you [16] Thou hast taken that life that I gave you Depart from me ye cursed into everlasting fire prepared for the Devil and his Angels For the impression it has made on my mind no tongue can [17] tell Depart from me ye cursed but let me never hear those words pronounced by the O Lord for surely I never felt such impressions of awe striking cold upon my breast as I felt when Dr [18] W said so to me But oh with what horror would those words pierce my heart to hear them pronounced by an offended God But my views of things have been for some time very different [19] from what they were when I first came home I have seen and felt the vanity of childhood and youth And above all I have felt the stings of a guilty Conscience for the great Disobedience [20] to my parents in not taking their advice wherewith the Lord has seen fit to visit me with this affliction but my affliction is a light affliction to what I have deserved but the Lord has [21] been very merciful unto me for he has not cut me of in my sins but he has given me this space for repentance For blessed be God my frequent schemes for destroying myself were all [22] most all defeated But Oh the dreadful powerful force of temptation for being much better I went to stay with Mrs Welham she being gone out one day and left me alone soon after [23] she was gone I thought within myself surely I am one of the most miserable objects that ever the Lord let live surely never no one had such thoughts as me against the Lord and I arose [24] from my seat to go into the bedroom and as I was going I thought within myself ah me I will retire into the remotest part of the wood and there execute my design and that [25] design was that wilful design of self destruction But the Lord was pleased to stop me in this mad career for seeing the Bible lay upon the shelf I took it down and opened it and the first [26] place that I found was the fourth Chapter of St Luke were it tells us how our blessed Lord was tempted of satan I read it and it seemed to give me some relief For now and not till [27] now have I been convinced of my lost and sinful state not till now have I seen what a miserable condition I have brought myself into by my sins for now do I see myself lost and undone [28] for ever undone unless the Lord does take pity of me and help me out of this miserable condition But the only object I have now in view is that of approaching death I feel assured [29] that sooner or later I must die and oh but after death I must come to judgment what can I do to be saved what can I do to be saved from the wrath of that God which my [30] sins have deserved which way can I turn oh whither must I flee to find the Lord wretch wretch that I am who shall deliver me from the body of this death that I have been [31] seeking what will become of me ah me me what will become of me when I come to die and kneel before the Lord my maker oh with what confidence can I approach the mercy [32] seat of God oh with what confidence can I approach it And with what words must I chuse to address the Lord my maker pardon mine iniquity pardon mine iniquity Oh lord for [33] It is Great. Oh how great is thy mercy oh thou most merciful Lord for thou knowest even the secret desires of me thine unworthy servant O Lord I pray the Look down with an [34] Eye of pity upon me and I pray the turn my wicked Heart Day and night have I Cried unto the Lord to turn my wicked Heart the Lord has heard my prayer the Lord has given [35] heed to my Complaint For as long as life extends extends Hopes blest dominion never ends For while the lamp holds on to burn the greatest sinner may return Life is the season [36] God has given to fly from hell to rise to Heaven the Day of grace flees fast away their is none its rapid course can stay the Living know that they must die But ah the dead [37] forgotten lie Their memory and their name is gone They are alike unknowing and unknown Their hatred and their love is lost Their envy's buried in the dust By the will of God are [38] all things done beneath the circuit of the sun Therefore O Lord take pity on me I pray whenever my thoughts do from the stray And lead me Lord to thy blest fold that I thy [39] glory may behold Grant Lord that I soon may behold the not as my Judge to condemn and punish me but as my Father to pity and restore me For I know with the O Lord no- [40] thing is impossible thou can if thou wilt restore my bodily health And set me free from sin and misery For since my earthly Physician has said he can do no more for me in the will [41] I put my trust O blessed Jesus grant that I may never more offend the or provoke the to cast me of in thy displeasure Forgive my sins my folly cure Grant me the help I need [42] And then although I am mean and poor I shall be rich indeed Lord Jesus have mercy upon me take me O kind shepherd take me a poor wandering sinner to thy fold Thou art Lord [43] of all things death itself is put under thy feet O Lord save me lest I fall from thee never to rise again O god keep me from all evil thoughts The little hope I feel that I shall obtain [44] mercy gives a happiness to which none of the pleasures of sin can ever be compared I never knew anything like happiness till now O that I may but be saved on the day of Judge-[45]ment God be merciful to me a sinner but Oh how can I expect mercy who went on in sin until Dr W reminded me of my wickedness For with shame I own I returned to thee O [46] God because I had nowhere else to go How can such repentance as mine be sincere what will become of my soul [. . .]

Author Note: I want to acknowledge the generous assistance of Clare Browne, curator of textiles and dress, Victoria and Albert Museum, London, who kindly answered numerous questions, shared materials with me, and gave me access to rare samplers. I also acknowledge the following people for their invaluable help: Chris Marsden and the staff at the Victoria and Albert Museum Archives, Jennifer Nash and the staff at the East Sussex Records Office in Lewes, the staff at the West Sussex Records Office in Chichester, the staff at the Family Records Centre in London, and the staff at the Public Records Office in Kew.

Notes

1. Almost nothing was known about the identity of Elizabeth Parker when I began researching her life. The only other person who had taken interest in her life was British historian Nigel Llewellyn, who in 1992 was researching the *Art of Death* exhibition at the V&A and was shown Elizabeth Parker's sampler. Llewellyn was so struck by this textile that he searched the East Sussex parish records to firmly establish that Elizabeth Parker had indeed lived when the sampler was stitched, but that was all he found out. He wrote about it in his "Elizabeth Parker's 'Sampler': Memory, Suicide, and the Presence of the Artist," a piece that appears in the anthology that came out of the conference on Material Memories held at the V&A in 1998. Like others who had seen her sampler, Llewellyn had assumed Elizabeth had committed suicide.
2. For the full story of Parker's life and those of the people she mentioned on her sampler, see Goggin.
3. "Hiding Hand" is an allusion to Adam Smith's "invisible hand" in economics.

Works Cited

Appadurai, Arjun. "The Right to Research." *Globalisation, Societies, and Education* 4.2 (2006): 167–77. Print.

Goggin, Maureen Daly. "One Nineteenth-Century English Woman's Story in Silken Ink: Filling in the Missing Strands in Elizabeth Parker's *circa* 1830 Sampler." *Samplers and Antique Needlework Quarterly* 29 (Winter 2002): 38–49. Print.

Hirschman, Albert O. "The Principle of the Hiding Hand." *National Affairs* 6 (1967): 10–23. Print.

Llewellyn, Nigel. "Elizabeth Parker's 'Sampler': Memory, Suicide, and the Presence of the Artist." *Material Memories*. Ed. Marius Kwint, Christorpher Breward, and Jeremy Aynsley. Oxford: Berg, 1999. 131–42. Print.

MacDonald, Michael, and Terence R. Murphy. *Sleepless Souls: Suicide in Early Modern England*. Oxford: Clarendon, 1990. Print.

Newell, Aimee E. *A Stitch in Time: The Needlework of Aging Women in Antebellum America*. Athens: Ohio UP, 2014. Print.

Nominal File: Mrs. Lily Griffiths. Documents related to acquisition T.6-I956. Victoria and Albert Archives. Blythe House, London. Print.

Pasteur, Louis. "Inaugural Lecturer, University of Lille, Douai, France, December 7, 1854." *A Treasury of the World's Great Speeches*. Ed. Houston Peterson. New York: Simon and Schuster, 1954. 473–78. Print.

Rohan, Liz. "The Personal as Method and Place as Archives: A Synthesis." *Working in the Archives: Practical Research Methods for Rhetoric and Composition*. Ed. Alexis E. Ramsey et al. Carbondale: Southern Illinois UP, 2010. 232–47. Print.

Wakoski, Diane. "Medieval Tapestry and Question." *In Her Own Image: Women Working in the Arts*. Ed. Elaine Hedges and Ingrid Wendt. Old Westbury, NY: Feminist Press, 1980. 38. Print.

9
SETTING OUT FOR SERENDIP
Of Research Quests and Chance Discoveries

Ryan Skinnell

[W]e would do well to remember that there are no smooth, unified stories. The stories are rough and bumpy with false starts and misleading paths.
— Lisa Mastrangelo and Barbara L'Eplattenier

As a guiding concept for contemporary researchers, "serendipity"—defined in the modern sense as "happy chance" or "fortunate discovery"—is undoubtedly a valuable one. Serendipity implies a moment of success for researchers, a sudden epiphany about how to solve what has seemed like an unsolvable problem. Considered historically, however, the concept of serendipity may be even richer for considering the research process than the modern sense suggests. The concept itself is commonly traced back to the eighteenth century when it was coined by scholar, author, and polymath Horace Walpole in a letter to his friend Horace Mann. To borrow a phrase from Walpole, in my estimation, serendipity is enlightened as much "by the derivation [of the term as] by the definition" (quoted in Remer 6). As Walpole makes clear, the word "serendipity" derives from a much older quest narrative, *The Three Princes of Serendip*.[1] In the sixteenth-century Persian fairytale, the protagonists—three princes from the kingdom of Serendip[2]—are compelled by the king (their father) to leave the kingdom. As a result, the princes embark on a long journey, one that does not have a specified duration or destination. In the course of their travels, the princes make a series of unintended but ultimately fortuitous observations that result in their advancement to high positions in the courts of other kingdoms. In due time, the princes prove their mettle and are able to return home with honor.

The specific details of *The Three Princes of Serendip* are not especially important for my purposes, but I reference the story here because the

DOI: 10.7330/9781607327394.c009

connection of unintended-but-fortuitous discovery to purposeful-but-undirected journeying is an especially generative one for twenty-first-century researchers. On one hand, it allows for the modern sense of serendipity as "chance discoveries" aided by careful preparation. On the other hand, it reintroduces the senses of aimless wandering, steady progression (if not necessarily "progress"), obstruction, deviation, and unpredictable destinations that research often comprises. Serendipity's perambulatory undertones are worth emphasizing when we consider the concept in relation to the research process because they have important explanatory power, which is not always captured in the modern uses of the word. Although moments of serendipity are often narrated in terms of the satisfying realization of a fortunate discovery, in fact, the historical concept illustrates the discovery of a new path in the middle of a journey rather than the discovery of a lost treasure at the end. In addition, such discoveries nearly always open up a new series of different paths that require researchers' further exploration. In other words, if we characterize the research process as an extended journey, serendipity distinguishes decision points along the route as much as, and maybe more than, reaching the final destination.

Put another way, the centuries-old echoes that haunt the concept of "serendipity" might be read to suggest that chance discovery is not just a function of *being* prepared—serendipity is also built into the process of *getting* prepared. Though certainly no guarantee, sometimes simply setting out on a journey clears the way for "discoveries, by accident and sagacity, of things which [the discoverer was] not in quest of" (Walpole, quoted in Remer 6). Of course, such discoveries do not end the quest—to the contrary, they often reshape and extend it. However fortuitous they may be, serendipitous discoveries do not protect against detours, deviations, or dead-ends. Inasmuch as serendipity points to new paths along the journey, it entails new risks that researchers must accept if they mean to realize the potential of discovery. In this chapter, then, I contend that serendipity helps to explain happy chances and fortuitous discoveries, but it also reminds us that those discoveries are embroiled in a quest—one that requires us to follow new paths, accept unanticipated risks, and pay careful attention as we go. As such, the concept of serendipity is both an invitation to novice researchers to set out on a quest and a reminder to experienced researchers to keep an eye out for untrod paths that might take them in new directions. In keeping with this combination of intentional journeying and unintended discovery, I offer a serendipitous travelogue of sorts—a series of unintended but fortuitous discoveries I was not in quest of when I set out on my research path but which have radically influenced my work as an archival historian of rhetoric and composition.

APRIL 1–6, 2008: NEW ORLEANS, LOUISIANA

In the spring of 2008, I was finishing my first year as a doctoral student at Arizona State University (ASU) in Tempe, Arizona, and I arranged to travel to New Orleans, Louisiana, to attend the Conference on College Composition and Communication (CCCC). I was presenting a paper that year at the main conference based on work I had done as a master's student, but I also decided to register for a half-day pre-conference workshop focused on revealing and preserving local histories in rhetoric and composition. I registered for the workshop because, although I was an aspiring historian of rhetoric and composition, I was struggling to make better sense of both the theoretical and the practical aspects of historical research in the field. Therefore, I set out to learn what I could about doing history in rhetoric and composition. To be clear, I was not actually engaged in any specific research when I traveled to New Orleans—the paper I was presenting at the conference was based on research I had already completed. Nevertheless, I was anticipating a quest as a PhD student, and my attendance at the workshop was intended as preparation for embarking on my (as yet undefined) next research path.[3]

The CCCC workshop certainly helped me in some of the practical and theoretical ways I anticipated, in particular by helping me think specifically about some of the challenges entailed in archival research and theory. But my attendance at the workshop also resulted in serendipitous discoveries of things I was not in quest of. Two in particular stand out. The first was that the workshop organizers repeatedly exhorted attendees not to let retiring professors dispose of their old materials, such as lecture notes, professional correspondence, essay drafts, and more. According to Robert Schwegler, a founding director of the National Archives of Composition and Rhetoric (NACR) and one of the workshop organizers, such materials simply do not exist anywhere but in the filing cabinets and desk drawers of the field's practitioners. But at the end of momentous careers, on the presumption that no one could possibly care about such idiosyncratic materials, many scholars empty their filing cabinets into wastepaper bins and head off into the sunset.

One goal of the workshop was to draw attendees' attention to the need to preserve such materials when possible to develop rhetoric and composition's archive, and the workshop leaders encouraged attendees to reach out to anyone who might make such a contribution. As chance would have it, I was enrolled in two classes at Arizona State University that semester taught by Sharon Crowley, an icon in the field of rhetoric and composition.[4] Dr. Crowley had notified the students in her classes that they would be her final two classes—she was retiring at the end of the year. While I was sitting in the workshop, I started planning to approach Professor Crowley to ask about her plans for preserving her professional materials.

Before I left the workshop, however, I made another serendipitous discovery. This second discovery was related to my dissertation topic—specifically, I found one. Four of the workshop organizers—Katherine E. Tirabassi, Amy Zenger, Michelle Niestepski, and O. Brian Kaufman—introduced their work with the NACR by discussing the local historical work they had done or were doing at their own institutions. All four conducted locally focused archival research to write their dissertations, and all four advocated additional local archival research as a way to extend the historical grasp of the field. Although I had not attended the workshop with the goal of discovering a dissertation topic, it occurred to me as I listened to them talk that I had potentially found one. I thought it might be an interesting and potentially worthwhile project to compose a local history of ASU's writing program, which had employed many influential rhetoric and composition scholars and had been the site of a number of important advances in the field of rhetoric and composition studies. In fact, broadly construed, this is what my dissertation turned out to be when I completed it three years later, although as I describe below I took a rather circuitous route to arrive back where I started. In the meantime, I returned to Arizona from New Orleans with two promising new paths to travel.

Travelogues, of course, are merely intended to narrate a person's travels and experiences, but as traveloguers are wont to do, I cannot resist looking for lessons in this first entry before proceeding to the next. In retrospect, the most important parts of my trip to New Orleans—these two serendipitous discoveries I made in a half-day workshop—were accidents. I was not looking for them; I did not even know they existed to be found. The things I set out to find (historical methods and theories) were not insubstantial, but finding them did not constitute discoveries of the serendipitous variety. They were, rather, discoveries of the treasure hunt variety—I knew generally what I was looking for, and I was happy but essentially unsurprised to find them. Serendipity, on the other hand, was finding that which I was not in quest of.

In addition, what I thought of as a practice of *getting prepared* to go on a research quest in fact turned out to be part of the quest. In other words, the trip to New Orleans was a leg of the trip I did not even know I was on, and while I was stumbling along, I happened to discover some obscured trails. Because I did not really know where I was headed anyway, I figured I would see where they took me. Serendipity often works in this way, opening up different paths to those who are willing to risk following them rather than simply opening up surprise ways to stay on a path a researcher has been intending to travel.

MID- TO LATE APRIL 2008: ARIZONA STATE UNIVERSITY, TEMPE CAMPUS

As chance discoveries go, the two I happened upon in a workshop in New Orleans—recognizing a unique opportunity to save important materials and finding a dissertation topic—were noteworthy. But ultimately, the discoveries were not accomplishments in and of themselves. Both indicated initial points of departure, not destinations, and both required additional efforts on my part to bring the discoveries to fruition. In truth, however, I did not have a strong sense of how to proceed along my dissertation path, since at that point I did not even have a committee chair. I had a better idea of how to proceed along the other path I had chanced upon.

Soon after I returned from New Orleans, I contacted Dr. Crowley to ask if she had plans for donating her papers when she retired. We met in her office the following week, and I explained to her (probably too exuberantly) the concern expressed by the CCCC workshop organizers about rhetoric and composition scholars' materials being unceremoniously disposed of. During our discussion, Dr. Crowley informed me that she did not have specific plans for preserving her materials, and she graciously agreed to allow me to find a home for them.

On the heels of my discussion with Dr. Crowley, I sent an email to Arizona State University's Archives and Special Collections Department:

> My name is Ryan Skinnell, and I am a PhD student in ASU's English department. As part of my preliminary dissertation research, I have begun to talk to some faculty members in my department who are retiring or moving to new schools about collecting their papers and other assorted ephemera as they clean out their offices. Eventually I hope to be able to write my dissertation about the development of ASU's writing program, which is now the largest in the country.
>
> However, I am also in the earliest phases of learning to work in and with archives, and I want to make sure that the materials I collect are cared for and maintained where they will be most valuable. So, I wonder if you [or] someone [could] tell me if ASU libraries might be interested in the

kinds of materials I'm collecting, if there is already a writing program archive, or if the possibility exists for me to propose or create an archive as I collect things. There are other options that exist for me in terms of archives, but in terms of access and local value, I hope ASU libraries finds this project useful and necessary.

I include this email in its entirety because it effectively captures my insecurity about how to proceed in light of my earlier serendipitous discoveries. I was proceeding along wherever the path(s) led me, but I was not exactly sure where I was headed. Although it is perhaps too grandiose to describe it as questing, I kept stumbling forward in the hope I would find something worthwhile.

After a series of emails with ASU's archivists, I arranged to meet with the head archivist to discuss options for housing Dr. Crowley's papers. What I learned in that meeting was that ASU's archives were not the right place for Dr. Crowley's papers because of certain institutional constraints.[5] I also learned that there were no materials in ASU's archives related specifically to the writing program as such. In my discussion with the head archivist, it became clear that there were materials related to ASU's English department and its faculty over the years, but there was nothing that he (or anybody) could point to as related to the writing program as an entity apart from the English department. I would need to do a lot more preliminary research before I could make informed choices about exploring the archives. In fact, it also became clear that I was using the term "writing program" in a way that did not make sense to many of the people I spoke with. The head archivist, for instance, was mystified by many of my questions until I clarified that I was talking about the first-year writing program. He thought, and probably for good reason, that I had been talking (bizarrely) about the creative writing program. I left that meeting feeling rather frustrated because I did not discover what I set out to discover. In fact, when my research path seemed most clear, I hit an impasse.

One kind of serendipity narrative would explain how I made my way over, under, or around the impasse; but actually I didn't. Instead I turned back, hoping to find a different trailhead. In more concrete terms, I went back to my office and considered what other options existed for Dr. Crowley's materials besides the university archives. Ultimately, I emailed the NACR to see if they would be willing to accept Dr. Crowley's donated papers, which they said they would be happy to do. But this was not a chance discovery of how to proceed along my chosen path—it was backtracking and rerouting to a different path altogether. My trip to ASU's archives was not without value, of course—it was a necessary step to exploring the initial path I was on. Here again, though, is a good reminder that serendipity does not prevent dead-ends; more likely, as with any worthwhile quest, it requires them. As my discovery about the various meanings of "writing program" aptly demonstrates, I wandered rather aimlessly into the archives, only to discover that I did not have a way to move forward.

APRIL–MAY, 2008: TEMPE, ARIZONA

Although I did not know it, Sharon Crowley was not the only professor planning to leave Arizona State University in 2008. I discovered this fact when I was making tentative steps to follow up on my second serendipitous discovery from New Orleans. I arranged to meet with Greg Glau, ASU's writing program administrator, to see if I could get guidance about how I might embark on my dissertation research. Among other useful direction(s), Dr. Glau informed me that David Schwalm, an administrator on ASU's Polytechnic campus, was winding up his career after three decades of professing, researching, and administering rhetoric and composition at ASU. Dr. Schwalm had been hired to administer ASU's writing program in the mid-1980s, so Dr. Glau suggested that I might contact him both to inquire about preserving his materials, as I was doing with Dr. Crowley's, and to discuss the local history of ASU's writing program. I did not know Dr. Schwalm except by reputation, but I dutifully contacted him. We exchanged a few emails, and Dr. Schwalm agreed to save whatever files he came across that he thought might be of value to the NACR. He also agreed to allow me to interview him later in the summer about his tenure as ASU's writing program administrator. In the meantime, there was little I could do but wait.

At this point, all my efforts, at least in my own mind, were distinct from what I thought of as my "research." Facilitating the donation of materials to NACR was at best tangential to what I intended to research, an unexpected detour; and I considered my discussions with various people about the history of the writing program to be preparatory to the real research I expected to conduct for my dissertation. Rather, I was questing in the sense that I was exploring new territories without a good sense of what I hoped, much less expected, to find. I suppose I had some general sense of what I was questing for, but I did not have a real destination or even a good sense of what to look for on the journey. I was simply trying to pay attention. With the exception of the trip to New Orleans, I did not physically travel far from home, but it was nevertheless a sort of conceptual analog to the journey to parts unknown undertaken by the three princes from Serendip. I followed some paths and undoubtedly bypassed others with the sort of deliberate lack of certainty about where I should be going that makes the initial stages of research particularly fun. And way led to way.

MAY 20–25, 2008: TEMPE AND MESA, ARIZONA

If April was characterized by questing, May was characterized by stasis. I was taking two courses and teaching two courses, I was applying for conferences and summer jobs and writing a book proposal, and I had a partner and a child who demanded my attention. Throughout April and May, I exchanged emails with various people regarding donations to NACR and about possible steps I could take to begin my dissertation research, but my exploratory adventures were largely on hold while I met my more immediate obligations. In addition, since Dr. Crowley and Dr. Schwalm were not retiring until the end of the semester, they were not yet finished with the materials they agreed to pass along to me. So things moved forward as they are bound to, but my quest was nevertheless effectively on hold. Likewise, the opportunities for serendipitous discovery were significantly reduced.

Then toward the end of May, as the semester wound to a close, I took another important step forward in my quest. I emailed Duane Roen to ask if he would be my dissertation committee chair—another risk, since although I had met Duane, I barely knew him. I asked him to chair my committee because he had published in the history of rhetoric and composition, he was a former writing program administrator at ASU, and he had a reputation as a supportive chair. I knew he would be able to help me map out the project I had in mind.

Duane agreed to serve as my chair, and we met at a coffee shop where I pitched my dissertation idea to him. He was very receptive, and we started to plan how I might proceed. It is fun, in retrospect, to think of my early discussions with Duane as plotting a research itinerary. He suggested research paths in the field of rhetoric and composition that I might follow. He helped me put together a list of people, including Drs. Glau and Schwalm, who I might venture to see to ask about their recollections of the writing program's history. He directed me to necessary research protocols (in this case, because I was interviewing people, I needed Institutional Review Board approval). Perhaps most important, Duane focused my attention on a particular territory—a specific time frame with specific issues to consider. In other words, Duane took on the important role of directing and focusing my research trajectory. In so doing, he helped me begin a different, more defined sort of quest.

Formalizing a research itinerary is, of course, a necessary part of any research process because at some point purposeful-but-undirected journeying must give way to arriving at a destination if a researcher is to make a genuine contribution to the field. All the same, as I became more resolute about which direction I was heading, I also became proportionally less open to momentously serendipitous—read unexpected—deviations. We might usefully recall *The Three Princes of Serendip* here to illustrate the point. In the narrative, the three princes set off and followed paths as they appeared. They were questing without a clear sense of destination. But as the narrative progresses and they proceed along certain paths, their goals become more concrete—they have to prove their innocence, woo a queen, and rescue a kingdom. And as their goals become more concrete, the princes become proportionally less amenable to the sorts of radical deviations that defined their early questing. In the beginning, the emphasis of their purposeful-but-undirected journeying was on *undirected*, but eventually the emphasis shifted to achieving a specific purpose (though without totally abandoning the possibility of redirection, if necessary). In the story, unintended-but-fortuitous discovery gives way to deliberate and purposeful decision-making.

So, too, with my research process. I left that first meeting with Duane with a much clearer sense of what directions I might travel and also with a much clearer sense of the consequences entailed in following unexpected detours. I was no longer wholly undirected. In the shift of emphasis from primarily *undirected* to more intentionally *purposeful*, it became clear to me that changes in course entail much higher stakes once a destination has been mapped. Which is not to say that productive deviations are precluded—only that detours may be harder to recognize, and choices to follow unexpected paths may be less easy to make, when the ultimate destination is more or less settled.

SUMMER 2008-SPRING 2011: TEMPE, ARIZONA

Beginning in the summer of 2008 and continuing for the next three years, I embarked on a series of short trips. I visited the homes, offices, and haunts of several of ASU's former writing program administrators and faculty members. I formally interviewed eight of them, beginning with Dr. Schwalm in July 2008. The interviews I conducted took me back to ASU's archives, outfitted this time with more specific knowledge about what to look for and how to look. I logged more than 150 hours exploring the archives over the course of about eight months. I made several serendipitous discoveries—discoveries, by accident and sagacity, of things I was not in quest of. Among the more interesting discoveries I made was that English faculty at Arizona State University (many decades before it was officially ASU) had first begun publishing about the teaching of writing in professional journals in 1911 (see Felton). I discovered that, as of 2008, ASU was the institutional home of three former CCCC chairs (Jerome W. Archer in 1955, Frank D'Angelo in 1980, and Akua Duku Anokye in 2007). And I discovered that the introduction of first-year composition proper into the curriculum in 1927 helped save the school (then a normal school transitioning into a teachers' college) from being decommissioned.

Each serendipitous discovery I made along the way was intimately connected to the sort of purposeful-but-undirected journeying that marked my initial trip to New Orleans (and from which the concept of serendipity derives); but because my destination was set, such discoveries were also rather more modest than those that marked the early parts of that particular quest. Often, I would set specific research goals for myself that turned out to be impractical, but by taking steps to prepare for research—even those that took me in unexpected directions—I was primed for serendipitous discoveries of things I was not in quest of. All the while, I tried to maintain a focus on my final destination. Eventually, approximately three years after I set out on my initial quest and with the indispensible help of several research/travel guides, I finally arrived at my destination (i.e., a finished dissertation). It is easy to look back and celebrate the accomplishment of arriving at a destination, but in retrospect, it seems to me that the serendipitous questing was crucial for me to discover the paths that made the final destination visible on the map. Which is to say, if I had set my destination too early, I might have found myself stranded in an inhospitable place; likewise, if I had never chosen a destination, I might have found myself endlessly unsettled.

2011–2016: VARIOUS LOCATIONS

The funny thing about destinations is that they eventually begin feel like home, and whether because of coercion (as in the case of the three princes from Serendip) or because of an insatiable wanderlust, many people begin new quests soon after they have finished old ones. In many cases, the real joy of research is setting out on a new, yet-to-be-determined path, rife with the promise of detours and dead-ends.

In the years since I completed my dissertation, because of a combination of coercion and wanderlust, I am off on new journeys. My destinations have become less clear again, and my journeying has taken me further afield, both geographically and intellectually, than I had previously traveled. I have been to archives across the country—from Denton, Texas, to Cambridge, Massachusetts, to Berkeley, California, and several points in between. I have ventured into different fields of study—sociology, history, and archival science, to name a few. These sorts of quests, away from familiar territory, have been integral to my research in the past several years, which has moved in strange and unpredictable directions. I have followed detours I could scarcely have imagined, much less planned. I recently finished a book manuscript about the institutional history of college composition—a project that would have been inconceivable to the first-year PhD student who traveled to New Orleans to learn about theories and practices of historical research. In the summer of 2014, I journeyed to Islamabad, Pakistan, where I taught a two-week course on writing for publication at the National University of Modern Languages. I learned more in those two weeks about my own place in the academy and the world than I learned in thirty years of formal education. And I co-curated a special exhibit on the constructive uses of bureaucracy, *Bureaucracy: A Love Story*, for the University of North Texas's rare books and archives department with four of my colleagues. I have truly been in unexpected territory, often without any real sense of a destination.

I have at times felt lost. I have at other times come in off the road, as it were. In less whimsical terms, for all the time I have spent traveling to different geographical and conceptual locations, I have spent as much or more time at home, attending to my daily responsibilities and deepening my engagement with my field, my students, and friends and family. I have become more aware as a result of how important purposeful-but-undirected questing is to the work I do and to the discoveries I can make. The last eight years of my career have been the consequence of serendipitous discoveries of things I was not in quest of—things I could not likely have stumbled upon if I wasn't wandering along. The path I have been on is a function of happy chances, and it has resulted in ever more serendipitous discoveries.

This, to my mind, is one of the real promises of serendipity as a concept for researchers. It reminds us—novice researchers and experienced researchers alike—that there is a thrill in the undirected quest and that setting out makes fortuitous discoveries possible. Not knowing the final destination, at least for a while, is both exciting and necessary to the research process because it frees researchers to see unanticipated diversions—new paths, choked with rabbitbrush, that we might overlook if we focus too intently on arriving. And eventually, in the process of journeying and with the help of mentors and mapmakers, researchers may begin to get a better sense of a destination.

I am beginning now to formulate my next quest—into institutional and organizational theory, sociology, and governance, to begin with. Strange and foreboding regions, to be sure. No doubt, I will end up in bizarre new places without the aid of intelligible maps but, it is hoped, with sagacity and fortune on my side. Wherever I end up, I know that embarking on the quest is as important as reaching a destination, and I am wise to pay attention as I travel.

Notes

1. *The Three Princes of Serendip* was first published in Italy in 1557 under a title more literally translated as *Peregrination of the Three Sons of the King of Serendip* (Remer). The centrality of journeying, then, was explicit in the "original" title. But even as I write "original," it is important to note that the tales collected in the *Peregrinaggio of 1557* are apparently translations of Persian tales that had circulated in other parts of the world long before they found a home in Italy. In other words, journeying is both overt in the title and inherent to the story's centuries of existence.
2. What was Serendip in the sixteenth century was known as Ceylon in Walpole's time and is now known as Sri Lanka.
3. It is interesting to reflect on that conference after a few years. My master's thesis committee chair, Irene L. Clark, organized the panel I was on that year, which included me, her, and two other very well-known rhetorical genre scholars, David Jolliffe and Richard M. Coe. A significant number of conference attendees came to our panel to see the prominent scholars who were presenting, and as a result I presented to probably my largest audience to date. But despite the auspicious circumstances of that presentation, nothing came of it for me as a researcher. The workshop was much less obviously auspicious, but it stands as one of the most significant moments in my career as a researcher.
4. As I write this chapter, the Conference on College Composition and Communication Executive Committee has announced that it will honor Dr. Crowley with its most prestigious award, the CCCC Exemplar Award, awarded annually "to a person whose years of service as an exemplar for our organization represents the highest ideals of scholarship, teaching, and service to the entire profession" and "whose record is national and international in scope."
5. ASU's university archives, like any archive, have certain guidelines used to appraise a potential donation. To make the most of limited resources, including space, archives are typically selective about what they can accept, and in this case, ASU's archives could have accepted some but not all of Dr. Crowley's materials. Since keeping her materials together was an important goal, ASU's archives were not the place for them.

Works Cited

Felton, James Lee. "Difficulties in English Composition." *Arizona Journal of Education* (1911): 139–44. Print.

Mastrangelo, Lisa, and Barbara L'Eplattenier. "Stumbling in the Archives: A Tale of Two Novices." *Beyond the Archives: Research as a Lived Process*. Ed. Gesa A. Kirsch and Liz Rohan. Carbondale: Southern Illinois UP, 2008. 161–70. Print.

Remer, Theodore G., ed. *Serendipity and the Three Princes, From the Peregrinaggio of 1557*. Norman: U of Oklahoma P, 1965. Print.

10
THE ART OF THE "ACCIDENT"
Serendipity in Field Research

Peter N. Goggin

Sometimes, no matter how prepared the mind, the exact moment of serendipity is hard to pin down. For Alexander Fleming, was it when he reportedly sneezed on a lab culture and saw that the enzymes in lysosome killed germs? When he decided to go on vacation, leaving his lab closed up during the heat of August? When his lab assistants forgot to clean the Petri dishes? When he saw the fungus in one of the dishes and identified it as *penicillium notatum*?

We recognize that it was a combination of Fleming's experience, acquired scientific knowledge, and researcher's perspective that allowed him to recognize the significance of this confluence of events. Yet the question remains, how do we as researchers know accidental discovery when we see it, and, more important, how can we learn to anticipate such moments of accidental discovery?

I've had difficulty pinpointing my own moment of serendipity that has led me to my current work in environmental rhetoric and islands studies. If my memory serves me, the best I can come up with was watching a 1992 broadcast of *Primetime Live* in which Sam Donaldson brought his trademark attack journalism to bear on the US naval air base in Bermuda, which he "disclosed" as an upscale vacation getaway for military officers, paid for with tax dollars. As a Bermudian it was an interesting story for me personally, but I was teaching writing full-time and did not see then how this event was significant beyond that personal interest. Then in 1995 the base was closed by the US Congress, in great part as a result of Donaldson's "exposé" followed by controversy over the massive cost to clean up decades of accumulated hazardous military waste. By now I was doing graduate studies in rhetoric and composition, but still I had no sense at the time of the significance these developments would hold for me other than personal interest. My academic attention was elsewhere.

DOI: 10.7330/9781607327394.c010

A few years later I was on tenure track and had just secured a contract for my monograph on literacy theory. As I was halfway through my tenure process, I was looking for that "new research trajectory" that would be crucial to getting tenure at a Research 1 university. I still was not looking at the US base closure issue. But then I got a call for proposals for an international conference on argumentation, and suddenly it clicked for me that the Bermuda/US Baselands controversy was a possibility. The situation there had just come to a head with a standoff by the UK, Bermuda, and US governments over responsibility for cleanup costs.[1] Not really knowing if there was anything to this that would pan out, I read everything I could find on environmental remediation. Two key things happened. First, I discovered there was such a thing as environmental rhetoric, an area of inquiry I had not known existed, and second, I realized that I would have to go back to Bermuda and for the first time conduct research that did not rely solely on analyzing extant digital and print texts. A whole new area of inquiry and approach had opened up for me. Luck? Perhaps. A prepared mind? I guess so. What remains for me is the question that the idea for this collection on serendipity in research has inspired. I hadn't considered the role of serendipity in my work prior to this. Why didn't I recognize the significance of these serendipitous occurrences, these accidents of discovery, while they were happening? I suspect it is because I had never actually learned to look during my formal education. Something in all those years as a student, scholar, teacher, and researcher was missing.

When it comes to academic research, I think it is safe to say that very little is intentionally left up to "serendipity" alone in the sense of pure chance or the luck of happenstance. Yes, such moments do happen, but what is significant about serendipity in academia is that it is dependent on scholarship, methodology, and planning for expectations of discoveries yet to be made. Like Fleming's famed Petri dishes and my own incremental awareness for a new research trajectory, serendipity is generally not one momentous happenstance but an accumulation of discoveries and events that emerge from purposeful exploration. In this chapter I discuss the nuances of purposeful discovery and the "happy accident" of serendipity in place-based research and make a case for ways rhetoric, literacy, and writing scholars might draw on scientific methods to learn the art of "accidental sagacity" in our own approaches to exploration.

PLACE-BASED RESEARCH

Early in my turn to place-based research in rhetoric and literacy studies, I had recently returned to my university from field inquiry on small island literacies in the Isles of Scilly (a small archipelago off the coast of Cornwall, United Kingdom). I was invited by the conservation warden of the local wildlife trust to go to a far end of St. Mary's Island to observe a small herd of cattle used for the local conservation grazing program. The program had stirred a great deal of controversy over island identity, traditions, access, and sustainability; and the cows had become the focal point of heated discourse among the human residents.[2] On the return trip, on a rough trail I stumbled and sprained an ankle.

It was a long, painful trip home. Back at my university, as I hobbled to my office, I encountered some geography colleagues I had previously worked with who inquired about my limping. This set them off on lengthy recollections about their own and other colleagues' various injuries incurred while conducting research in canyons, active volcanoes, sinkholes, swamps, ice floes, and so forth. I felt very much like Captain Brody in the scene from *Jaws* when Quint and Hooper compare their dramatic injuries and Brody embarrassingly examines his own appendix surgery scar. Up to this point, it occurred to me that the most traumatic thing that was likely to have happened in my research as a humanist scholar was a paper cut or a heavy library book falling on me. Let me make it clear that I am not advocating reckless or dangerous approaches to field research here but rather emphasizing how the physical is as relevant to discovery as the cerebral. For my scientist colleagues, it seemed that such occurrences were expected, if not specifically anticipated—an integral part of exploration and discovery literally situated in the landscapes and methods of their scholarly research. Even if such moments were not included in their published scholarship, they played a significant role in conversational knowledge sharing within their community of field researchers.

My work on environmental rhetoric and sustainability, which often brings me into proximity with sustainability scientists, engineers, and social scientists, has confirmed this for me. Importantly, what the encounter with the geographers brought home to me in a very clear moment of awareness was the inherent materiality of research even in textual analysis. While a sprained ankle is not a desirable accident, it is part and parcel of what can happen during place-based research, as much as a chance encounter with a local resident who provides a key lead to a mother lode of new information one was not expecting to find or coming across an un-archived artifact that opens up new directions of inquiry. Good research is about exploration that leads to discovery; whether in the field, the laboratory, the library, or the classroom, exploration always involves interactions in and with material and social contexts that affect discoveries—the "happy accidents" that we call serendipity. Place-based research requires that the scholar welcome the relative chaos and disorder such moments can bring to disrupt otherwise well-laid plans. Risk analyst Nassim Nicholas Taleb refers to this view of disruption or volatility as a positive attribute of knowledge invention as "antifragile."[3] This is not an easy thing for graduate students to grasp or for faculty to teach in disciplines and institutions where order, structure, and stability are often sustained by traditional reward systems.[4]

Humanist scholars in general are very proficient with reflection and resistant to volatility in their studies. The prevalent emphasis on analyzing texts in various forms as stand-alone artifacts provides a relatively stable source of inquiry that is relatively dependable even while interpretations of those texts are fluid. Even the most ephemeral digital and material texts are often archived in stable alternate forms, image files, photocopies, PDFs, and so forth, even after the original is no longer viable. Thus, the tendency is to consider findings and discoveries in interpretations of the text-as-object to be more significant than contexts and processes that played vital roles in the creation and subsequent interpretations of those texts. Serendipity in humanist research does happen, of course, but it is for the most part not seen as integral to process and is thus a mystery we rarely talk to each other about or account for. The chapters in this collection challenge that assumption and demonstrate that while we can appreciate the mystery and unpredictability of serendipity, we cannot afford not to pay attention to the extended connectivity of texts, time, place, authors, sponsors, and the unexpected twists and turns in the exploration processes. More important, awareness of the role disruption as well as resilience in place-based inquiry plays in influencing discovery provides researchers with ways to consider how planning for such "accidents" should be built into our own humanist methodologies for exploration. Being in the right place at the right time, expecting the unexpected, and welcoming disruption as a positive aspect of research is not merely happenstance or instinctive; it is a way of knowing, an art, and thus can be learned.

EXPECTING THE YET-TO-BE

The idea of predicting or forecasting serendipitous moments in academic research seems counterintuitive, a bit like a self-fulfilling prophesy that one can conveniently point to in hindsight. Truly serendipitous moments are supposed to happen "when the penny drops," when all that planning for a project comes together in a confluence of happenstance during the research process and one's prepared mind recognizes a singular opportunity, a new direction, a "happy accident" that instantly transforms one's way of seeing and approaching a hitherto unrecognized question. Robert Merton and Elinor Barber suggest that scientists and other professional researchers "seem to have a special proclivity for 'accidental sagacity,'" as Walpole described the concept of serendipity (9). My work in place-based environmental rhetoric, sustainability, and, in particular, field research in small island locales has taught me that big-bang serendipitous moments are rare, if not downright elusive. It is through purposeful exploration that one invites the accumulation of those multiple mini-serendipities, sometimes by literally falling and stumbling during data gathering that generates the new ideas, directions, and opportunities. Being an observational packrat in the field pays dividends sometimes long after the original project has been completed. But that proclivity for "accidental sagacity" in preparation for capitalizing on serendipity has its roots in purposeful exploration, even if it appears pure happenstance or luck. It is less a matter of simply (some might say "mysteriously") being in the right place at the right time and more a matter of intending where to be and when.

Research is not magic, and even what may appear pure luck is often purposeful, even if minimally. For example, while the chances of winning a state lottery are infinitesimally small, one still needs to buy a ticket for that minimal possibility to occur. Although discovery may often appear to be a matter of luck or accidental happenstance—being in the right place at the right time—such a view is likely to forget or ignore that such happenstance may also result in less desirable variations (e.g., right place/wrong time, wrong place/wrong time) or an absence of discovery. It was perhaps serendipitous that I found out about the conservation grazing controversy on the Isles of Scilly by actually visiting the place and hearing about it from local residents while in transit by helicopter from Penzance. This happenstance would lead me to an interest in animal/human relationships in small island contexts and an eventual publication on rhetoric and animal agency. However, the same happenstance put me in a situation that contributed to me spraining my ankle and thus having to cancel a planned excursion to some of the "off-islands" that are part of the Isles of Scilly archipelago and forego whatever discoveries might have happened as a result. I would like to say that the sprained ankle led to some other serendipitous moment, but all I am aware I got out of it was a lot of pain for the next few months.

For the scholar researcher, the possibility for discovery through serendipity must begin with the intent of discovery through exploration, a process not only of purposeful method but also of purposeful awareness, keeping in mind that this is not a linear process and that exploration may itself be initiated through serendipity. Of course, like serendipity, exploration itself is an often uncertain process. One only knows that there is an initial goal, plan, and preparation to explore something, somewhere; but what one will actually find is often a matter of calculated chance or prediction based on extrapolation from already existing knowledge, and the latter can range from solid data to pure speculation.

EXPLORATION VERSUS SERENDIPITY?

So, is there really a difference between exploration and serendipity? Robert Stebbins argues that despite a close relationship between the two, there is a definite difference. Referring to exploration and serendipity as "cousins," he says that they "constitute two distinct forms of discovery. Serendipity is the quintessential form of informal experimentation, accidental discovery, and spontaneous invention." By contrast, he describes exploration as "a broad-ranging, purposive, systematic, prearranged undertaking" (4–5). For Stebbins, although exploration and serendipity are related, the difference between the two forms in terms of discovery depends on to which of two groups a person is inclined to belong. Accidental serendipity, he argues, is primarily the realm of people engaged in casual leisure—"people at play . . . sociable conversationalists, and the seekers of sensory stimulation." For these folks, discovery can only occur from serendipity. For those engaged in "serious leisure and professional work," that is, those folks who routinely explore to produce new ideas (artists, scientists, entertainers), discovery is more selective and "although occasionally serendipitous, is nonetheless far more likely to flow from exploration" (4).

While I get where Stebbins is coming from in his move to establish a systematic methodological approach to social science exploratory research, I find his sharp dichotomies of exploration and serendipity and of casual leisure people and serious leisure people reductive in terms of actual research experience and in contrast with the perspectives on serendipity in this collection. Even professional research built on the strictest methodological adherence, clinical observation, and objective analysis is rife with stories of accidental discovery. The "eureka" moments of happy accident that changed the world as we knew it. Alexander Flemings's big sneeze and the discovery of penicillin is a fine example. Many others, including safety glass, X-rays, the Big Bang, Viagra, are the success narratives that exalt the significance of serendipity in scientific research. Yet Stebbins's concern here is well taken. The assumption of a pure chance accident of serendipity risks diminishing the rigor of exploratory processes that provided the opportunity for discovery as mere happenstance both in the public mind and, perhaps more troubling, in the perception of research investors.

From the ways Merton and Barber describe this phenomenon, the value of serendipitous discovery for its own sake as a desirable long-term outcome in academic research has decreased as costs for doing research have increased. Serendipity has become to some extent a calculated and expected short-term or immediate result, particularly in such disciplines as the sciences and engineering. Thus, the value of the process of accumulation of knowledge and experience through exploration conflicts with the value of the product of that accumulation. As Merton and Barber explain: "Serendipity magically collapses the time frame of this process: In the narrative of serendipitous discovery, the search (or research) and the *objet trouvée* appear immediately linked. And yet, the elements of the narrative—the far-ranging freedom of basic research, the search for applicable findings, the role of chance, and the role of the mind—all have their costs. As sponsoring institutions—private-sector laboratories, universities, government agencies—evolve, the practical strategists see serendipity either as an alchemist's stone, a shortcut to useful answers, or as fool's gold" (xvi). Academic researchers and scholars walk a fine line when it comes to exploratory research, it appears, especially when outcomes are increasingly linked financially to the expectations of investors and sponsors who anticipate specific products of discovery and results.

Most stories of accidental discovery have less headline-grabbing cachet yet are equally important, at least for disciplinary fields of inquiry if not the public arenas. For fields less tied to expectations of funded sponsorship—and most of the humanities including rhetoric, I suspect, fall into this category—exploratory research likely has a bit more latitude for creative process. But the perception of the "magical" aspect of serendipity is still problematic and undermines the long-term accumulation of sagacity that allows the "magic" to happen. It may be that the more interpretive methods of knowledge creation that are valued in humanistic research, for instance, may be perceived by those both in and outside the disciplines as though serendipity is less a matter of rigor and sagacity acquired through systematic methods of inquiry and more attributable to innate ability and luck. Merton and Barber underscore this point, observing that "the making of accidental discoveries by collectors and literary scholars has on several occasions been attributed to a personal trait that they happened to be endowed with" (203). They continue:

> Though collectors and literary scholars, like scientists, actually have to be prepared to make accidental discoveries—they must know in a general way where to look and what to look for—their stock of knowledge does not have the systematic quality of science, and the fact of their preparedness may, consequently, be less visible. Also, the nature of the happy accidents that befall them consists, frequently, of unexpectedly locating a desired item or of the unhoped for anticipation of others in the recognition of a valuable item; the human drama of such events may serve to conceal (as it does in some accidental scientific discoveries) the knowledge and effort necessary for making the discovery. (203)

It is incumbent, then, for humanists to make serendipity from their processes of preparedness, exploration, and discovery more visible and learnable—something the essays in this collection are doing. For placed-based rhetoric, this means taking attunement into account as an integral component of the research process. Place matters; so do environment, ecology, the weather, time, the landscape, and personal encounters and experiences. The differences among a hotel, a B&B, or a short-term apartment rental can make a difference in something as mundane as having a refrigerator or a kitchen, thus impacting in perhaps significant ways how one interacts in the local context. In my own fieldwork, making connections and getting tips and inside information from an innkeeper, at the local pub, and at the local market can pay dividends in accumulating new leads, stories, gossip, opinions, experiences, and places not on any maps. The divide between discovery though purposeful exploration and serendipity is not so clear-cut as Stebbins argues, and the relationship is often far more fluid and dynamic than his dichotomy suggests. Whether the process is highly structured in methodology or more open-ended and subject to creative interpretation, the key to successful research is to focus on cumulative exploration and thus invite serendipity into the process itself.

Notes

1. A full account of the controversy and rhetorical standoff titled "When Governments Collide: The Rhetoric of Competing National Arguments and Public Space" (Goggin) appears in the published proceedings of the Fifth Conference of the International Society for the Study of Argumentation at the University of Amsterdam, held in 2002.
2. For a more detailed account of the Scilly cow controversy, see "Rhetorical and Material Boundaries: Animal Agency and Presence in Small Oceanic Islands" (Goggin).

3. Taleb's notion of antifragility is that the inherently unpredictable, or the "outliers" as he refers to them in his books *Antifragile* and *The Black Swan*, are necessary for a strong, evolving social system that must necessarily be stressed and fractured to regrow, as opposed to a robust system that recovers and sustains itself without changing. His argument as it relates to serendipity is that while society cannot design unpredictability, it should not resist or attempt to eradicate such stresses (that would be a fragile system) but rather anticipate and profit from them.
4. Academic audiences and the contributors to this collection are no doubt well aware of disconnects between a desire for creative and "innovative" research and the risks associated with such desire in actual practice related to tenure and promotion, even at institutions that purport to value such approaches. An opinion article in *The Scientist* by professor of medicine Fred Southwick titled "Academia Suppresses Creativity" (2012) effectively details the dilemma. The article continues to resurface in academic social media networks.

Works Cited

Goggin, Peter. "Rhetorical and Material Boundaries: Animal Agency and Presence in Small Oceanic Islands." *Rhetoric across Borders*. Ed. Anne Teresa Demo. Anderson, SC: Parlor Press, 2015. 23–34. Print.

Goggin, Peter. "When Governments Collide: The Rhetoric of Competing National Arguments and Public Space." *Proceedings of the Fifth Conference of the International Society for the Study of Argumentation*. Ed. Frans H. van Eemeren, J. Anthony Blair, Charles A. Willard, and A. Francisca Snoeck Henkemans. Amsterdam: Sic Sat International Center for the Study of Argumentation, 2003. 393–96. Print.

Merton, Robert K., and Elinor Barber. *The Travels and Adventures of Serendipity: A Study in Sociological Semantics and the Sociology of Science*. Princeton, NJ: Princeton UP, 2006. Print.

Primetime Live. ABC News. ABC News Headquarters, New York. December 1992. Television.

Southwick, Fred. "Opinion: Academia Suppresses Creativity." *The Scientist*. N.p. 12 May 2012. Web. 15 June 2016.

Stebbins, Robert A. *Exploratory Research in the Social Sciences*. Thousand Oaks, CA: Sage, 2001. Print.

Taleb, Nassim Nicholas. *Antifragile: Things That Gain from Disorder*. New York: Random House, 2012. Print.

Taleb, Nassim Nicholas. *The Black Swan: The Impact of the Highly Improbable*. New York: Random House, 2007. Print.

11
READING BETWEEN THE POWER LINES
How "Nikola Tesla Corner" Enhanced the Wireless Signals in a Rhetorical Analysis of Electricity and Landscape

Daniel Wuebben

PART 1. MIDTOWN STATIC

One brisk morning in November 2010, while walking from the Times Square subway station to the New York Public Library (NYPL) Main Branch, I stopped at the northeast corner of Fortieth Street and Sixth Avenue, leaned back, and stared at nothing. Just beyond the empty air capturing my gaze were a few examples of New York City's perpetual metamorphoses. Above and to my left, the sixty-story building at 1095 Avenue of the Americas had recently received a $260 million facelift. Further down the block, the $1 billion Bank of America Tower, the sixth tallest building in the United States, added another looming, shimmering piece to the city's iconic skyline. To my right, Bryant Park was undergoing its seasonal makeover: Christmas decorations, an ice rink, and hundreds of temporary shopping kiosks. I could have been looking at any number of the millions of changes taking place in that environment. In addition, I could have been imagining the thousands of invisible waves and wireless beams that intersected that "empty" space as the shot from Manhattan to every corner of the planet. The vacancy, and my puzzled look into it, also contained the mysterious history of Nikola Tesla.

In 1901, around the time when plans to build the New York Public Library's Main Branch were finalized, Tesla rented a nearby office space for his new corporation, Worldwide Wireless. In the pre-digital age, Tesla may have predicted that the most ambitious high-tech company on the planet would need proximity to the nation's greatest archive. By the time the Main Branch opened in 1911, Tesla's plans for wireless transmissions had spectacularly failed, and he was on verge of bankruptcy. He lived in various hotels in the area for the rest of his life and in his later

DOI: 10.7330/9781607327394.c011

years spent hours reading inside the library and feeding pigeons near this spot in Bryant Park.

In that moment, I did not see the construction, I did not think of wireless signals, and I did not know of Tesla's history in this specific spot. I stood at Fortieth and Sixth Avenue staring into empty space because the "Nikola Tesla Corner" street sign that had previously adorned the northeast corner of the intersection was gone.

For more than a year, looking up and acknowledging the Nikola Tesla Corner sign had been the first act of my pre-research routine. Next, I touched the concrete base of the lion statue (the lion named "patience," south of the main steps), opened my satchel for the guard at bag check, and finally heard the beep of my access card and click of the lock to the thick wooden door of the Wurtheim Study. The routine was accompanied by my dissertation mantra: "Read, Write, Defend, Deposit." That morning, however, the sign was missing. The routine had been broken. I was looking at nothing. Had it been stolen? Taken down for cleaning? Permanently removed as a result of budget cuts?

At the time, the Tesla sign's absence was annoying but not critical. In hindsight, acknowledging the sign's absence that day transformed my research practice and my understanding of what it means to do rhetorical analysis. Rhetorical analysis often moves back and forth, from close readings of a text's meanings to more open evaluations of the relationships among author, communicative acts, and audience. The metaphors for describing this broad and flexible methodology often hinge on the visual. For example, Charles Bazerman explains that rhetorical analysis "can make visible the complexity of participation by many people to maintain the large projects of the disciplines" ("From Cultural Criticism" 64). Jack Selzer, building from Kenneth Burke's notion of "trained incapacity," describes rhetorical analysis as "as much a way of not seeing as it is seeing" (302). Making evident certain aspects of meaning and purpose requires "not seeing" others. As it happened, my rhetorical analysis of that space did not hinge on the visual. Neither the Tesla sign nor the Tesla speeches and essays I analyzed inside the library effectively skirted the razor-thin line between the "seen" and "unseen." The sign, the texts, and the author remained the same—the frequency with which I received them changed. The serendipity in my rhetorical analysis was not a result of a text that suddenly materialized before my eyes or of a clue I stumbled across in the stack; the serendipity was the new kind of frequency with which I approached my subject. Following this model, the first serendipitous signal, received while standing on a street corner, looking at a blank space, was a ripple of static, a momentary break in my research cycle. Eventually, the break was followed by a hissing, buzzing, inchoate white noise that inspired me to adjust the dial, so to speak, and retune my circuits.

Eventually, reaching a new frequency and finding the Tesla sign changed my view of this complex, multilingual scientist and inventor. The sign led me to the realization that Tesla's rhetorical moves deserve the kind of contextual consideration and discourse analysis offered to his contemporary, Thomas Edison, by Bazerman's ground-breaking study *The Language of Edison's Light* (1999). Like Edison, Tesla was much more than researcher and inventor—he was a writer who had to negotiate different languages, conventions, and rhetorics to bring ideas to fruition.

PART 2. TESLA IN A NETWORK OF "ELECTRICITY" AND "LANDSCAPE"

When the Tesla sign disappeared, I was dialed in and committed to finishing my dissertation, "Power-Lines: Electricity, Landscape, and the American Mind." "Power-Lines" was charged by experiences far from the city and strung upon a single, sinewy conceptual thread that, when linked to subsequent threads, eventually comprised a broad network. In fact, my ability to more fully receive Tesla's visions for a wireless planet and read *between* the power lines only occurred after I had spent years tracing, connecting, and untangling those lines.

I began my research process examining representations of telegraph, telephone, and power lines in essays, novels, poetry, and other cultural texts. To better understand this ambivalence between "ugly" overhead lines and the necessary technologies, groups, and cultural traditions they served, my research spread from representations of overhead wires to explore the overlaps between the history of electric technologies and popular rhetoric: How did the meanings and practices of "electricity" and "landscape," as materials and metaphors, evolve in philosophy, literature, and the visual arts, from the time of Benjamin Franklin's first electrical kite experiments through the gradual deployment of overhead wires to every corner of the nation?

The methods were loose, the materials legion and unwieldy. Nikola Tesla's place in all this was modest. In fact, in the summer of 2010, a few months before the sign disappeared, the audience's response to a public lecture I gave at the Midtown Manhattan branch of the NYPL made me feel it would be better to *delete* Tesla from the dissertation altogether. My talk concerned the interdisciplinary overlaps among the inventor Tesla, the psychologist and philosopher William James, and the historian Frederick Jackson Turner. For instance, Tesla and James were two of the most prominent Americans theorists to write about the relationships among electricity, sense perceptions, and automatons (James in "Are We Automata?" and Tesla in "On the Problem of Increasing Human Energy"). Meanwhile, Tesla and Turner each made epochal presentations at the 1893 Columbian Exposition in Chicago—Tesla with his patented alternating current system, and Turner with his now famous "frontier thesis" regarding the closing of the West in 1890. Turner's thesis presented America's tendency for expansion in terms of an inherent "energy." Even if the physical frontiers were closed, Turner predicted, "American energy will continually demand a wider field for its existence" ("Significance of the Frontier" 37). Tesla, who was accomplishing materially what Turner spoke of metaphorically—widening the possibilities for the production, transmission, and consumption of "American energy"—couched the "pioneering" of electrification in frontier rhetoric when he asked in 1897: "For where is there a field, in which [the electrical engineer's] God-given powers would be of a greater benefit to his fellow-men than this unexplored, almost virgin, region, where, like in a silent forest, a thousand voices respond to every call" ("On the Problem" 103). For Turner, the "virgin region" was geographic; for Tesla, it was electric. Putting James, Turner, and Tesla into conversation highlighted an interdisciplinary tendency of late nineteenth-century thinkers to use electrical metaphors to consider both the innermost landscapes of the mind and the seemingly endless landscapes of westward (and electrical) expansion.

The majority of the eighty-plus attendees seemingly ignored my thesis about American intellectual history; they heard about Tesla. Following my presentation, an open question-and-answer period was dominated by questions about Tesla, which evolved into comments and eventually the voicing of random, Tesla-related conspiracy theories. The evening was entertaining, but further research about this polarizing figure seemed like unnecessary baggage for me to take on in my rhetoric-focused dissertation.

Perhaps this was a mistake. Tesla has been neglected by histories of science and technology (and entirely overlooked in rhetoric and writing studies). In 1888, six years after immigrating to the United States, this tall Serbian with piercing eyes, who spoke six languages, invented and displayed an alternating current system that sparked the process of worldwide electrification. Between 1891 and 1900, in his late thirties and early forties, Tesla-the-inventor obtained dozens of patents, helped win the "battle of the currents," and became as famous as Thomas Edison. Meanwhile, Tesla-the-scientist was compared to other major figures in physics and electrical engineering including William Crookes,

James Clerk Maxwell, and Heinrich Hertz. After 1900, Tesla's career began to disintegrate. In 1943 he died poor, discredited, and alone in his room at the New Yorker Hotel (less than a mile from the future Nikola Tesla Corner).

Tesla's somewhat mysterious demise and the recent realization of some of his vision for wireless technologies and artificial intelligence have helped transform this tragic figure into a cult hero. That figure is what the audience at the NYPL wanted to hear about; however, at the time, Tesla was not getting serious scholarly attention. Most of my colleagues only recognized Tesla as the character played by David Bowie in the science-fiction film *The Prestige* (2006), in which "Mr. Tesla" invents a magical duplicating machine and is hounded by Edison's cronies. Others were familiar with his name because of Tesla Motors, which in 2010, as I was writing and making daily acknowledgments of the Tesla Corner sign, was about to make an initial public offering on the New York Stock Exchange. Amid this period of increased Tesla popularity, the sign, perplexingly, disappeared.

Further research regarding Tesla was not my priority, but when I saw that the sign was missing, I wanted answers. As I wrote emails to the New York City Department of Transportation, Department of Parks and Recreation, and the Bryant Park Corporation, I tried to mimic the outrage I imagined would have been felt by one of the Tesla conspiracy theorists I had met at my lecture. I wrote that I was appalled that the sign had been removed or stolen, outraged by "this disgrace to the memory of Nikola Tesla," and certain that "significant parties interested in Tesla's legacy" would not rest until this mistake was corrected. A few days later I received a response from the management company responsible for a renovation of Bryant Park:

> Daniel:
>
> The Tesla sign was inadvertently removed when we installed the new Bryant Park style illuminated street name sign. I am retrieving it from our contractor. Your sign would be very much improved and dramatic if it shared the design/style as ours. Would you be interested in purchasing one of these illuminated signs so that it matches ours? If so, I will provide you with the cost and schedule for this. Thanks and our apologies for accidentally removing the Tesla sign.

From the white noise of my mind, a signal became discernible. "Yes," I responded, "please send the cost and schedule." I tried to conceal my excitement and ended, "thank you for helping to restore this important honor to Tesla." I kept reading the email, coming back to the same line and one specific word, over and over: "*Your* sign would be very much improved . . ."

I had tried to sound authoritative in my email, but I had no real responsibility for the sign or the resources to purchase a "much improved and dramatic" replacement.[1] Fortunately, a week later, rather than the cost and schedule, I received an email saying that the management company had ordered a new sign (and they did not expect me to pay). Along with this came an inquiry from Craig LaCuruba, the person from the management company responsible for the renovation project: "I just read a book about Edison. What's the first one I should read about Tesla?"

The signals were being received—and strengthening. The new sign was ordered, Mr. LaCuruba seemed personally concerned, and the "Edison versus Tesla" rivalry had been activated. I responded enthusiastically, citing two popular Tesla biographies and concluding with what seemed like a long shot: "ps. Is there a plan for the old sign? Could it be purchased?" Mr. LaCuruba quickly responded: "I'll hold onto it for you."

For the next few months, I continued my routine and focused on the last two commands of my dissertation mantra: Defend, Deposit. In April 2011, shortly after the new Nikola Tesla Corner sign was installed and the dissertation was defended, Mr. LaCuruba and I met on the steps of the NYPL. I offered him a copy of the most accessible Tesla biography available at the time, *Tesla: Man Out of Time* by Margaret Cheney. He handed me the older Nikola Tesla Corner sign with white lettering on a reflective blue background. A few weeks later, I deposited the dissertation and then received my doctoral diploma. Today, the Nikola Tesla Corner sign with interior illumination (which is indeed much improved) stands over the corner of Bryant Park. Another, smaller Nikola Tesla Corner sign with white letters on a reflective green background has been mysteriously sited across Sixth Avenue. The former Nikola Tesla Corner sign hangs above my fireplace.

PART 3. INCREASING TESLA'S WIRELESS SIGNALS

Investigating the missing Tesla sign and then receiving this special artifact was certainly serendipitous. The experience renewed my interest in Tesla and his writing and taught me two lessons about research: first, negotiating the tensions between the archive (which included Tesla's essays, lectures, and interviews) and the environment (from which the Tesla sign disappeared) can be critical. Second, a rhetorical analysis, like the alternating currents Tesla mastered, can be enhanced by alternating from close readings and the "wired" connections between authors and their texts to ephemeral contexts and the more socio-cultural "wireless" forces that influence communication acts at certain times and places. To clarify the dialectics between archive and environment, text and context, this final section turns to Tesla's place in the network of metaphors, definitions, and various manifestations of electricity and landscape discussed in "Power-Lines" and how my attention has since been returned to see Tesla as a rhetorician promoting wireless ideas in a particular, pre-wireless context.

In addition to being an inventor and visionary, Tesla was a fairly prolific writer and frequent public speaker between 1888 and 1901. In my initial readings of Tesla's writings and speeches, I was pleased to find beautifully poetic views of electricity, nature, and sense perceptions. For example, in "On Light and Other High Frequency Phenomena," Tesla describes the incredible sensitivity of the human eye and its close relation to intellect. He ruminates, "In no way can we get such an overwhelming idea of the grandeur of Nature, as when we consider, that in accordance with the law of the conservation of energy, throughout the infinite, the forces are in a perfect balance, and hence the energy of a single thought may determine the motion of a Universe" (*The Inventions* 298). Such poetic claims may not be scientifically accurate or practical, but for my study they clearly registered as akin to popular representations of electricity and nature in American literature, especially those composed by Ralph Waldo Emerson.[2] Tesla and Emerson envisioned the potential for "a single thought" to have far-reaching consequences and used electricity as a way to present the pervasiveness, intensity, and evanescence of such thinking. For example, in "Nature," Emerson relates the act of reasoning to "an instantaneous in-streaming causing power" (47); in "The Divinity School Address," he urges us to "see how this rapid intrinsic energy worketh everywhere, righting wrongs, correcting appearances, and bringing up facts to a harmony with thoughts" (77); and in "The Poet," published in 1844, the same year Samuel F.B. Morse sent the first official electromagnetic telegraph message, Emerson states that the poet has a "dream-power" that must be transmitted: "a power transcending all limit and privacy, and by virtue of which a man is the conductor of the whole river of electricity" (467).

Emerson advised poets to act as "conductors"; Walt Whitman followed suit with his song of the "body electric." A half century later, Tesla, inspired by his readings of contemporary scientists including Heinrich Helmholtz, Edmund Spencer, Carl Stumpf, and Ernst Mach, took the idea a step further, and concluded that if he could decipher and then re-create the electric vibrations and currents he believed initiated all thoughts and sensations in the human nervous system, then he could use attuned frequencies to produce and control the circuits and "thoughts" of an external mind ("On the Problem of Increasing Human Energy" 27). Novelists and poets in the second half of the nineteenth century often acknowledged electricity in their bodies, in nature, and in the national "body electric"; Tesla wanted to design and program an *artificial* body electric. This remote-controlled automaton, he predicted, would be "a machine embodying a higher principle, which will enable it to perform its duties as though it had intelligence, experience, judgment, a mind" ("On the Problem of Increasing Human Energy" 23).

These primarily textual connections seemed to "wire" Tesla into the humanist network of American thinkers, including Emerson, James, and Turner. Additional literary and philosophical connections have since been revealed in Bernard Carlson's thorough biography, *Tesla: Inventor of the Electrical Age* (2013). Carlson shows the importance of Tesla's upbringing in the Serbian Orthodox Church and his lifelong appreciation for poetry, including the work of Goethe and Jovan Jovanovic' Zmaj (whose work Tesla translated from Serbian into English). As Tesla's closest friend, Robert Underwood Johnson, explained in a letter to faculty members of Columbia University urging them to award Tesla an honorary doctorate (which they did): "I may say that he knows the language and is widely read in the best literature of Italy, Germany and France as well as much of the Slavic countries, to say nothing of Greek and Latin. He is particularly fond of poetry and is always quoting Leopardi or Dante or Goethe or the Hungarians or Russians. I know few men of such diversity of culture or such accuracy of knowledge" (quoted in Carlson 204). Tesla's "diversity of culture" can be witnessed throughout his writing, and the sweeping success of his early speeches, patents, interviews, and essays provides critical *context* for understanding his rhetorical successes as well as his professional failures.

Neither this context nor a full analysis of Tesla's rhetoric can be developed here. The Tesla sign nevertheless sparked my interest, Carlson's biography "stepped up" the signals, and my vision of a Tesla-focused rhetorical analysis has changed. The foundation for this new project is the fact that between 1888 and 1893, years before he began his attempts to send power across the Atlantic, Tesla, his financiers, and his patent lawyers composed powerful arguments for Tesla's AC inventions. As Carlson explains, "By carefully shaping the discourse about Tesla's motor, they effectively altered the ways in which electrical engineers thought about motors in the utility industry and thus created a 'space' for Tesla's invention" (116). Crafting such a space requires diction, images, and metaphors that resonate appropriately with an audience. For a time, Tesla was a master rhetorical craftsman. In 1891, during a lecture at Columbia College (which at the time was on Forty-ninth Street and Park Avenue), Tesla explained to an awed audience that the electrostatic forces he had harnessed to illuminate lightbulbs without the use of wires provided merely a glimpse of the dynamic, ephemeral, and transcendent presence of "nature's immeasurable, all-pervading energy" (Carlson 145). Nature's electric forces, Tesla explained, "ever and ever change and move, like a soul animates an innate universe" (145–46). After speaking for almost three hours, waving glowing bulbs and touching magnetic induction coils with his bare hands, Tesla concluded by again evoking the audience's wonder: "We are whirling through endless space with an inconceivable speed, all around us everything is spinning, everything is moving, everywhere is energy" (197). The future health and welfare of mankind depended on "availing ourselves of this energy more directly" (197). Simultaneously sparking the imagination with his words and touching the coils with his bare hands, Tesla generated a feverish expectation that he might soon tap the potential of nature's pervasive energy and usher in an electrified *and* wireless society.

More immediately, Tesla's 1891 speech and demonstration turned the tide in the "battle of the currents" between his alternating current and Edison's direct current systems. During this publicity battle, both Tesla and Edison used multi-modal arguments to sway diverse audiences. Edison, Bazerman explains, was "savvy enough as a rhetorician to use . . . material arguments" such as night lighting, electrocutions, and consistent service to show electricity's wonder, power, and profitability to financial backers, patent offices, and the press (*Language of Edison's Light* 3). Tesla seemed poised to have similar success. In response to his 1891 lecture, the *New York Times* article "Wireless Electric Lamps" praised Tesla for combining "the most occult branches of theoretical electricity" with "layman's descriptions" of how electric currents were used in lighting systems. A writer from *Harper's Weekly* also focused on Tesla's presentation skills and congratulated the foreign scientist for describing complex theories in "pure, nervous English" during a three-hour "rhetorical performance" (Wetzler).

Tesla's rhetorical performances continued, even as his empirical research and financial backing faltered. In 1900 Tesla published a 22,000-word manifesto "On the Problem of Increasing Human Energy," which included theories related to human intelligence, fertilizers, fighting machines, and wireless devices that could be used to communicate anywhere on the planet. While imploring for sanitation reform, Tesla argued, "for every person who perishes from the effects of a stimulant, at least a thousand die from the consequences of impure drinking water" (11). The idea seems valid, but how did Tesla reach this figure? Without a clear answer, an op-ed in a New England newspaper complained, "Mr. Tesla [is] more of a rhetorician than a scientist." The biting critique continues, "When Mr. Tesla, who has managed to get a reputation as a scientific man, goes into the realm of rhetorical sentiment and calls it science he does a grave injustice to men who are less showy, but more dependable" (*Evening Standard*). Indeed, by the turn of the twentieth century, it seemed that Tesla's rhetorical prowess had in some sense begun to overshadow his scientific reputation and practical inventions.

The shift from text to context in my rhetorical analysis has helped to boost my appreciation for the "wireless" signals surrounding Tesla. Analyzing the entirety of those signals and the ways they intersected Tesla's rich cultural diversity, his willingness to engage popular culture, and the expectations of his audiences (tabloid and trade journal readers, scientific peers, patent lawyers, and financiers) will require additional research. Yet, in addition to gaining a better understanding of the wired and wireless forces networks that shaped Tesla's writing and its reception, it might also be helpful for scholars to consider the signals Tesla received from his environment. Indeed, as Tesla fed pigeons near the corner of Fortieth Street and Avenue of the Americas almost a hundred years ago, he may have looked up to see a web of wires. Beginning in 1888, many of Manhattan's telegraph and telephone wires were buried in the tunnels being dug for the subway, but as Tesla was promoting wireless transmission of power, power lines were just beginning to stretch across the planet. Years after his plan for wireless transmission systems failed, Tesla may have sat near the site where his sign would someday disappear, glanced at the wires hanging over Sixth Avenue, and imagined how his life may have been different if his wireless systems had made this wiry clutter obsolete. Then again, had Tesla's visions for wireless come true, subsequent overhead wires may have been absent from our planet, leaving fewer threads for researchers like me to serendipitously follow through the landscape and one less set of lines to read between in the archive.

Notes

1. I still do not know who initiated the process to commemorate Nikola Tesla Corner. As of January 2015, the New York City Department of Transportation has attached a *second* Nikola Tesla Corner sign to a street pole on the northwest corner of Fortieth Street and Avenue of the Americas (the original location is the northeast corner). This duplication implies that the initial statute for honoring Tesla with a street corner (now corners) may be unclear.
2. Emerson is discussed at varying lengths in many new studies of electricity and nineteenth-century culture, including Eric Wilson's *Emerson's Sublime Science*, Sam Halliday's *Science and Technology in the Age of Hawthorne, Melville, Twain, and James: Thinking and Writing Electricity*, and Paul Gilmore's *Aesthetic Materialism: Electricity and American Romanticism*, which examines Emerson as part of a "distinct strain of romantic thinking" that emerged from literary, popular, and scientific understandings of electricity (6).

Works Cited

Bazerman, Charles. "From Cultural Criticism to Disciplinary Participation: Living with Powerful Words." *Writing, Teaching, and Learning in the Disciplines.* Ed. Anne Harrington and Charles Moran. New York: Modern Language Association, 1992. 61–68. Print.

Bazerman, Charles. *The Language of Edison's Light.* Cambridge, MA: MIT P, 1999. Print.

Carlson, Bernard. *Tesla: Inventor of the Electrical Age.* Princeton, NJ: Princeton UP, 2013. Print.

Cheney, Margaret. *Tesla: Man Out of Time.* New York: Touchstone, 1981. Print.

Emerson, Ralph Waldo. *Essays and Poems.* Ed. by Joel Porte. New York: Library of America, 1996. Print.

Evening Standard. New Bedford, MA. July 5, 1900. Clipping found in folder for *Century Magazine.* New York Public Library Archive Division, New York, NY. Archival source.

Gilmore, Paul. *Aesthetic Materialism: Electricity and American Romanticism.* Stanford, CA: Stanford UP, 2008. Print.

Halliday, Sam. *Science and Technology in the Age of Hawthorne, Melville, Twain, and James: Thinking and Writing Electricity.* New York: Palgrave Macmillan, 2007. Print.

James, William. "Are We Automata?" *Mind* 4.13 (1879): 1–22. Print.

James, William. *The Complete Works of William James: The Principles of Psychology.* Cambridge, MA: Harvard UP, 1981. Print.

Jefferson, Thomas. *The Life and Selected Writings of Thomas Jefferson.* Ed. Adrienne Koch and William Peden. New York: Random House, 1998. Print.

Morse, Samuel F.B. "'Academies of the Arts; a Discourse.' delivered on Thursday May 3, 1827, in the Chapel of Columbia College, before the National Academy of Design on Its First Anniversary." New York: G. and C. Carvill, 1827. Reprinted in *North American Review* 26.58 (January 1828): 207–24. Print.

Selzer, Jack. "Rhetorical Analysis: Understanding How Texts Persuade Readers." *What Writing Does and How It Does It: An Introduction to Analyzing Texts and Textual Practices.* Ed. Charles Bazerman and Paul A. Prior. Mahwah, NJ: Lawrence Erlbaum Associates, 2004. 279–308. Print.

Tesla, Nikola. *The Inventions, Research, and Writings of Nikola Tesla.* 1893. New York: Barnes and Noble Books, 1992. Print.

Tesla, Nikola. "On the Problem of Increasing Human Energy: With Special Reference to Harnessing of the Sun's Energy." *Century Magazine* 1900. Reprinted as *The Problem of Increasing Human Energy.* Belgrade, Serbia: Nikola Tesla Museum, 2000. Print.

Turner, Frederick Jackson. "The Significance of the Frontier in American History." *Rereading Frederick Jackson Turner: "The Significance of the Frontier in American History," and Other Essays.* Ed. John Mack Faragher. New Haven, CT: Yale UP, 1998. 31–60. Print.

Wetzler, Joseph. "Electric Lamps Fed from Space, and Flames That Do Not Consume." *Harper's Weekly.* July 11, 1891. 524. Print.

Whitman, Walt. *Complete Poetry and Collected Prose.* Ed. Justin Kaplan. New York: Library of America, 1983. Print.

Wilson, Eric. *Emerson's Sublime Science.* New York: St. Martin's, 1999. Print.

"Wireless Electric Lamps: Mr. Tesla's Experiments with High Frequency Alternations." *New York Times.* July 9, 1891. Print.

Wuebben, Daniel. "Power-Lines: Electricity, Landscape, and the American Mind." Diss. Graduate Center of the City University of New York. 2011. Print.

PART IV

Methodology and Serendipity

12

PREPARE TO BE SURPRISED
How Flexible, Methodical, and Organized Research Practices Lead to Serendipity in the Archives

Lori Ostergaard

> *The most fortunate of all are those who are blessed with serendipity, whose research paths are filled with fortuitous byways, and who have the knack of finding the happy accident. But serendipity and its relations do not come uninvited to the scholar's table. Rather, serendipity visits those scholars and researchers who set out with open minds and the flexibility of plan that allows them both to recognize the fortuitous discovery and to pursue it to its logical end.*
>
> —Michael H. Hoeflich

From time to time, I make a serendipitous discovery in my historical research, finding new "fortuitous byways" like the ones legal historian Michael H. Hoeflich describes in the epigraph above (813). Serendipitous moments in the archives are rare, but, as Hoeflich notes, they are more likely to result when researchers set about their work with "open minds" and a willingness to change their research plans (813). Composition historian David Gold similarly contends that archival scholars need to have a "beginner's mind" so they may keep themselves "open to accidental discoveries" (43). In this chapter I discuss research practices that can lead to productive serendipitous discoveries in the archives. Archival scholars delight in those unanticipated discoveries that take them down new paths with their research and help them reframe their research questions or challenge their assumptions. But methodical yet flexible research practices are required if the researcher wishes to move beyond the accidental discovery to develop new knowledge from an archive.

DOI: 10.7330/9781607327394.c012

ACCIDENTAL CONNECTIONS: SERENDIPITY OUTSIDE THE ARCHIVES

During a recent visit to the city of Houghton in Michigan's Upper Peninsula, I discovered an artifact that promised a new line of inquiry for my research. I was browsing through items at an antique shop when I discovered an early twentieth-century copy of the local high school's literary magazine. On its own, this magazine was not especially interesting. As in many of these high school publications, students submitted poetry, satire, and short stories; and they likely compelled the local printer to publish their work for free. I might not have given this high school magazine a second glance were it not for the fact that during this same trip I noticed several fliers announcing a local conference about the 1913 copper miners' strike in the area. The literary magazine was published a decade after the strike, but holding this artifact in my hand led me to wonder how high school students in Houghton may have reacted to a strike that involved their classmates, parents, neighbors, and community members. I wondered if Houghton teenagers wrote about the strike in their school newspaper, classroom essays, and literary journals. The connection I made that day was serendipitous. I was not looking for a new archival research project at the time, but by connecting the document in my hand to the fliers I had seen around town, I discovered a new line of inquiry.

This topic seemed like a promising extension of my research agenda, which examines late nineteenth and early twentieth-century high school and normal school (teachers' colleges) writing instruction. I suspected that other scholars in my field who work at the intersections of history, rhetoric, class, and labor politics would be interested to learn how high school students responded to a strike at the local copper mine. Such a study could uncover important insights into how those students developed public, activist voices.

Archival scholars relish moments of fortunate discovery in their research, but such moments are also quite rare. Hoeflich identifies the three elements required for serendipity in archival research: "opportunity created by the preservation [of documents]; the happy accident of discoveries; and the sagacious minds necessary to recognize the importance of the discoveries" (817). For the most part, discovery work in the archives results not from accident or good fortune but from what Hoeflich describes as "*sitzfleisch*, that lovely German term for the ability to sit long hours poring over often boring documents" (827). In her book *The Allure of the Archives*, Arlette Farge warns that "one cannot overstate how slow work in the archives is," but she celebrates the creativity that may be inspired by "this slowness of hands and thought" (55). While those long, slow hours in the archives can be tedious, it is important to be methodical with this type of research. By taking good notes and making copies of anything and everything that appears even remotely germane to their topics, archival researchers safeguard against having to spend even more long hours trying to rediscover a source. By enduring long hours examining documents, they also open themselves up to accidental and fortuitous discoveries.

WHAT IS AN ARCHIVE?

Archives serve a number of different individuals and communities and thus take a variety of forms. Your personal archive might be the boxes filled with old photos, class papers, journals, and yearbooks you have saved from your childhood. Community archives, like those maintained by local historical societies, often contain the personal papers of citizens of that community, community newspapers, photos, and documents related to important local events. High school or university archives may house course catalogs, yearbooks, school newspapers, department or club minutes, faculty files, course or program proposals, and building plans. And organizational archives typically hold the founding documents of that organization and its constitution, operational materials, agendas and meeting minutes, scrapbooks, and promotional materials. While the communities these archives serve differ, all of them have one thing in common: each archive has been deliberately constructed by individuals or groups empowered to make important decisions about which artifacts of the individual's, community's, institution's, or organization's history are worthy of preservation and which artifacts should be discarded.

The choice of what to keep and what to eliminate from an archive naturally determines what historical researchers can find and the kinds of claims they can make. For example, while delving into the files of Illinois State University president David Felmley, I discovered a copy of a letter Felmley wrote in 1918 in which this university president defended his belief that women were not as intelligent as men and outlined his stance on the education of women. This letter supported a thesis I had developed while researching the meeting minutes of a women's literary society at the same university, and so "discovering" this letter in the president's university papers was serendipitous. But more than luck was involved in the "discovery" of this letter: upon Felmley's retirement in 1930, someone at the university chose to preserve rather than discard this letter. During the intervening decades, the university stored Felmley's documents in secure, dry, climate-controlled conditions.

While I might wish that more of Felmley's letters on this topic had been preserved and it would be interesting to know if he reversed his opinion about women's education later in his career, it is fortunate that this one letter was deemed important enough to warrant its preservation.

Hoeflich reminds us that our ability to make "undreamt of" discoveries in the archives is dependent on "the selection criteria" of the people who created those archives: someone in authority must believe the materials are important before they will advocate that those materials be preserved (824). Generally speaking, the documentary record of people who are considered the most significant to a community, organization, or institution—like a university president—is considered worthy of preservation. The artifacts of lesser-known individuals—like the students, staff, and custodians of a university—are often discarded. High school and university archives may include faculty files, for example, but rarely do they hold the papers students wrote in their classes, course syllabi, or assignment descriptions. Some student writing may be preserved if it originally appeared in official school publications such as student newspapers, literary magazines, and yearbooks; but this is written work that was initially selected as an example of excellence, and it may not accurately represent students' everyday kinds of writing. Such day-to-day materials documenting the work and operations of a school have historically not been valued by the people who curate institutional archives, although they are valued by people in the field of composition-rhetoric who wish to study the papers students wrote at different points during our disciplinary history.

SERENDIPITY IN THE ARCHIVES

As suggested in the epigraph to this chapter, researchers who approach the archives with "open minds and [a] flexibility of plan"—those who work inductively to determine what the archive might hold rather than deductively to find materials that support preconceived opinions—may be more inclined to experience and make use of serendipitous finds. In this section I describe three serendipitous discoveries that positively disrupted or transformed my own research plans.

Scenario One: A Flexible Research Agenda

I undertook my first archival study for my doctoral dissertation in 2004. My sum experience with archival research at the time comprised a few lazy afternoons browsing through the special collections at a small university library. I had very little understanding of how to approach archival research, little knowledge of how to identify and make use of archival materials, and no experience analyzing historical sources. At the time, I also had no idea how significantly serendipity would intervene in my historical research practices. That first day I entered the Illinois State University (ISU) archives armed with a single research question I hoped to answer—how did nineteenth-century faculty at this former normal university (teachers' college) respond to abolitionist and suffragist movements? What I initially liked about this topic was that I believed I already knew the answer. In my preliminary research into normal schools, I learned that their faculty were more liberal in their politics than the general population, especially with regard to emancipation and women's voting rights. Armed with both a research question and an answer, I believed my only tasks would be to locate documentary evidence to support my thesis and offer an analysis of the rhetorical appeals normal university faculty made in support of these causes. My methods at the outset were primarily deductive: I entered the archives knowing what I wanted to look for and what I needed to find.

Fortunately, my first foray into the archives was shaped—as these trips typically are—by the university's archivist. I had emailed ISU's archivist, Dr. Jo Ann Rayfield, the week before to arrange the visit, but I told her only that I wished to examine the papers of some early faculty at the university. That first afternoon she brought me a single box of documents from English professor June Rose Colby's university files. This box held some of Colby's work related to literature and writing instruction, but it did not contain any of the works she had written in support of suffrage. At this point I explained my project to Dr. Rayfield, and she agreed to pull another of Colby's files after she attended to a request by another researcher. While I waited, I decided to take a closer look at the first set of documents, and my attention was drawn to one folder labeled "Shall the Courses in Composition and Literature be Divided? Yes." Inside the folder was a 1916 article manuscript in which Colby argued against the practice of using literature to teach writing. Colby asserted that the purpose of a composition course was not to teach students to appreciate great works of literature but to "put boys and girls into the way of getting possession of their thought, organizing it, and then putting it into words" (12–13). This was a seemingly unusual stance for an English professor to take, as most composition histories agreed that literature instruction in the composition classroom was de rigueur by the turn of the twentieth century. For example, Sharon Crowley maintains that during this time, English teachers used literature to teach composition because they were "unable to comprehend that writing instruction might involve anything other than literary study" (102–3). But Colby argued vehemently against the seemingly universal practice of using literary works to teach writing. By the time I finished reading the first few pages of this essay, I knew that the question "how did normal school faculty approach writing instruction" would be the defining question of my dissertation. There was no guarantee that I would discover other faculty who shared Colby's progressive and seemingly forward-looking views about writing pedagogy, but I knew that working from this question and exploring the archives in a more open way could sustain my interest much more than my original plan of researching the archives merely to prove what I already suspected to be true would have done.

While archival scholars sometimes apply deductive research methods—determining the questions they wish to ask of the archive and anticipating the kinds of answers they may find—most strive to remain flexible in their research, to ask broad questions that may be supported, challenged, or refuted based on further study. It is little wonder that archival scholars like David Gold praise the detective conceit of the "grizzled veteran who always notes the importance of not jumping too quickly to a conclusion based on limited or even overwhelming evidence, lest one ignore clues that don't fit one's theory" (44). For Lindal Buchanan, remaining flexible in her archival studies means paying attention to, rather than dismissing, "information that makes [her] think 'That's odd' or 'That's interesting.'" (255). In my own research, I have found that being open to evidence that contradicts my own assumptions has helped me discover unanticipated but serendipitous leads.

While I remained flexible enough in my first foray into the archives to recognize that the topic of normal school writing instruction would be a more personally fulfilling and viable dissertation topic, I remained curious about how faculty like Colby, a self-proclaimed suffragette, advocated her political positions in her curricular and extracurricular work at the school. As I researched Colby's writing pedagogy, I also made copies of any materials that happened to be related to women's rights and emancipation on campus. Those materials eventually came to fill their own file boxes in my office, and Colby's work with the women's literary society at her university has formed the basis of several of my research presentations and articles over the past several years.

Scenario Two: A Methodical Approach

This second scenario begins with my research examining the work of June Rose Colby's most accomplished student, Essie Chamberlain, a national figure in the discipline of English studies in the 1910s and 1920s. She served as interim president and president of the National Council of Teachers of English. She also served as president of the Illinois Association of Teachers of English, and she led a number of informative classroom research studies. I ran across Chamberlain's name for the first time in Colby's university papers. Preserved among those papers was a tribute Chamberlain wrote on the occasion of Colby's retirement. After that initial discovery, I learned more about Chamberlain through the university's yearbooks and alumni magazines and, eventually, in the meeting minutes of Colby's women's literary society. Learning of Chamberlain through my research into Colby was serendipitous, as Chamberlain provided me with an example of a normal-university–educated postsecondary teacher who claimed to have been directly influenced by Colby's instruction. While Chamberlain was not a significant avenue of research during my dissertation project, I still made copies of any discoveries related to her and assigned them to their own files.

My post-dissertation research into Chamberlain did not initially involve many archival sources beyond those I had already discovered while researching Colby. Instead, I focused my study on Chamberlain's regional and national publications to demonstrate her innovative proposals for a scientific approach to classroom instruction. Truth be told, I assumed there would be little in her high school archive, since high schools rarely work to preserve their past. Instead, I collected what I believed to be all of the publications, presentations, and ephemera available on Chamberlain, using internet searches and library databases. I also made use of interlibrary loan for obscure educational journals and purchased some of Chamberlain's publications on eBay and Amazon. A few days before submitting an article examining Chamberlain's classroom research studies, I decided to do one final online search. Since historical organizations, institutions, and even Google regularly upload new digital archives, a final check for research by or about Chamberlain seemed prudent. This time, in addition to the search terms I had used in the past, I added the phrase "digital collections," hoping to find a new online collection of works by or about Chamberlain. What I found instead was the personal archive of poet Edith Nash, who had attended Chamberlain's high school in the late 1920s. Included with her personal correspondence was a letter titled "Homework Excuse," in which a teenage Nash had written to her teacher, Chamberlain, requesting an extension on an assignment. Nash's excuse for not having her homework prepared on time was that she had spent the previous evening visiting with Ernest Hemingway, an alumnus of Chamberlain's high school. Fortunately for me—and perhaps only because it documented her encounter with this famous writer—Chamberlain had returned the letter to Nash, and Nash had preserved the letter for nearly seventy-five years and donated it to the University of Wisconsin Digital Collections.

My decision to conduct a final online search for references to Chamberlain and my discovery of the magical sequencing of search terms that revealed this document was serendipitous. At that moment, I believed Chamberlain's possible connection to Hemingway might make only an interesting footnote to my article, so I emailed a friend who studies Hemingway to ask if he knew the names of any of Hemingway's high school teachers. While waiting for a reply, I searched some library databases for information about the Oak Park and River Forest High School (OPRFHS) where Chamberlain taught and Hemingway studied. That search revealed that two of the high school's librarians, two of the town's historical society archivists, and at least one Hemingway biographer had published histories of the school. The existence of these histories suggested that Chamberlain's high school may have worked to preserve its past. The database search further revealed a number of other promising articles by English teachers at the school. In other words, by following a lead to discover if Hemingway was one of Chamberlain's students (a lead that initially seemed only footnote-worthy), I "uncovered" a beautifully maintained and rich high school archive.

Scenario Three: An Organized Approach

Serendipity followed me into this high school archive as well. In preparation for my first visit to the archive, I purchased the histories of the high school to do some background research. One of these books, *Hemingway at Oak Park High*, was a compilation of Hemingway's published high school writing. This book included a number of images from the high school's archive, including a photograph of the school newspaper Hemingway and his sister, Marcelline Hemingway Sanford, wrote for. That photo included a single-column story from January 27, 1916, titled "Girl's Club Organized" (Maziarka and Vogel 19). I had completed research into the archival record of Colby's women's literary society just two years earlier, and what I learned about the work of that postsecondary women's society made me curious about the mission of a secondary school girls' club. Coincidentally, the OPRFHS Girls Club had been founded by Essie Chamberlain.

I was aware of this club and of Chamberlain's association with it before my Hemingway scholar friend and I began our research at the high school's archive, so I was on the alert for any information pertaining to the club. Over the next several months, I duplicated newspaper clippings and yearbook descriptions of the club, but I was careful to keep these documents separate from the artifacts I collected that pertained to the high school's writing faculty, students, and curriculum. Information about the Girls Club eventually took up its own file box in my basement and became the subject of another article.

Farge advises that researchers allow themselves to "soak up the archive; to remain open" to what is contained in an archive so that in addition to looking for specific information, the researcher may become attuned to items "that were not *a priori* of interest" (69). Soaking up the archive requires studying materials related to your topic but also recognizing the value of those artifacts that are only ancillary to your initial research questions. Over the course of many visits to the archives at this school where Chamberlain taught and Hemingway studied, I made a number of other serendipitous discoveries, each one resulting from my willingness "to sit long hours" and methodically examine historical artifacts (Hoeflich 827).

CONCLUSION: FORTUNE AND MISFORTUNE IN THE ARCHIVES

A broad array of resources informed my research at the OPRFHS: the school's archive of student publications, published histories of the school, and the articles written by the early English faculty. I also made use of the materials available in the town's historical society, public library, and Hemingway Society archive. While the history of the school was well preserved, the only examples of student—in process—drafts we were able to locate were the high school papers of Ernest and Marcelline Hemingway. These handwritten drafts containing margin and endnotes from the siblings' teachers had been preserved only because Marcelline chose to donate her personal files to the Hemingway Society. Most educational institutions do not make a practice of preserving student work in progress, choosing instead to safeguard the best of their past, those artifacts that demonstrate accomplishment rather than effort: for example, photos of an annual school pageant, jerseys worn by their most famous athletes, debate trophies. Rarely will those charged with preserving the past protect the artifacts representing the messy or mundane lived experiences of everyday people. Oral historians at work today recognize the importance of preserving the everyday experiences of ordinary people, but such accounts are typically missing from decades- and centuries-old archives.

While the OPRFHS archive lacked those messy and mundane artifacts of daily life at the school, it was also one of the most well-preserved archives I have had the privilege of visiting. That first serendipitous moment would not have resulted in more than a footnote were it not for the fact that Oak Park, an affluent village just outside Chicago, has always had the resources to protect its historical artifacts. Having graduated one of the greatest novelists of the twentieth century may have also motivated this high school to preserve and celebrate its past, unlike many other high schools from the same era.

Unfortunately, the experience of researching in such a beautifully maintained archive is more the exception than the norm for the type of research I do. The day after my discovery of the literary magazine at the Houghton antique shop and the serendipitous connection of that artifact to the copper miners' strike, I contacted the local high school's principal, requesting an opportunity to examine their archive. During my visit, the librarian showed me their collection of high school yearbooks, but despite the fact that the school was more than 130 years old, the yearbooks dated back only to the late 1970s. I asked the librarian if the older artifacts had been donated to the local university archives or historical society, and she told me that when they moved into the new school building in 1989, the school's administrators "took the approach of out with the old and in with the new." Even if the school had preserved the documents of its past, chances are good that most of the documents I needed would have been destroyed by a fire in 1921. At this high school where I had hoped to find unique evidence of students' rhetorical responses to a copper miners' strike, I instead encountered a sadly more familiar scene: the absence of history. As this final story demonstrates, our archival research may be directed and shaped by serendipity, but no amount of luck can make up for the misfortunes of history.

Works Cited

Buchanan, Lindal. "Making Fortunate Connections." Interview with Lori Ostergaard. *Working in the Archives: Practical Research Methods for Rhetoric and Composition.* Ed. Alexis R. Ramsey, Wendy B. Sharer, Barbara L'Eplattenier, and Lisa S. Mastrangelo. Carbondale: Southern Illinois UP, 2010. 253–55. Print.

Colby, June Rose. "Shall the Courses in Composition and Literature be Divided? Yes." 1916. June Rose Colby Papers. Box 1. Dr. Jo Ann Rayfield Archives. Normal, IL. Print.

Crowley, Sharon. *Composition in the University: Historical and Polemical Essays.* Pittsburgh: U of Pittsburgh P, 1998. Print.

Farge, Arlette. *The Allure of the Archives.* Trans. Thomas Scott-Railton. New Haven, CT: Yale UP, 2013.

Gold, David. "On Keeping a Beginner's Mind." Interview with Lori Ostergaard. *Working in the Archives: Practical Research Methods for Rhetoric and Composition.* Ed. Alexis R. Ramsey, Wendy B. Sharer, Barbara L'Eplattenier, and Lisa S. Mastrangelo. Carbondale: Southern Illinois UP, 2010. 42–44. Print.

Hoeflich, Michael H. "Serendipity in the Stacks, Fortuity in the Archives." *Law Library Journal* 99.4 (2007): 813–27. Print.

Maziarka, Cynthia, and Donald Vogel. *Hemingway at Oak Park High: The High School Writings of Ernest Hemingway, 1916–1917.* Oak Park, IL: Oak Park and River Forest High School, 1993. Print.

Nash, Edith. "Homework Excuse." *Practice the Here and Now: Selected Writings of Edith Nash.* Ellison Bay, WI: Cross Roads P, 2001. Web. 17 Feb. 2015.

13
PLAYING THE NAME GAME
Exploring Name Variations in Archival Research

Patty Wilde

In "Being on Location: Serendipity, Place, and Archival Research," Gesa Kirsch describes several fortunate finds she uncovered while researching Dr. Mary Bennett Ritter.[1] Kirsch attributes her many interesting discoveries to serendipity, noting that it "is not something one can arrange purposefully, although I am convinced one can be open to the possibility" (20). As she reveals in her discussion of her archival endeavors, though, Kirsch was persistent in her pursuit of Ritter, making multiple trips to Ritter's archives over the course of several years. Put another way, Kirsch's extensive efforts enabled her to recognize such serendipitous finds when she happened upon them.

Kirsch's diligence inspired me as I researched Loreta Janeta Velazquez, author of *The Woman in Battle* (1876). Velazquez was one of many women to publish a personal narrative about her experiences during the American Civil War;[2] her account, however, is particularly memorable, as it describes her work as a cross-dressing soldier and spy for the Confederate Army.[3] Elizabeth Leonard estimates that between 500 and 1,000 women fought in the war (165). Velazquez, though, is one of the rare few to write publicly about such experiences.[4] Interested in exploring Velazquez and her rhetorical approaches, I began to search for archival documents to fill in some of the gaps of her life and work. My initial efforts entailed exploring libraries, museums, and databases using "*The Woman in Battle*" and "Velazquez" as key search terms. This yielded some scholarly publications on Velazquez, several website sources, and a few archival documents, but overall I did not find much new information. In expanding my search terms—particularly in regard to how I spelled Velazquez's name and aliases—I encountered moments of serendipity similar to what Kirsch experienced when researching Ritter. Although I acquired documents slowly from a spectrum of sources,

DOI: 10.7330/9781607327394.c013

searching different names and spellings enabled me to locate several artifacts related to Velazquez that had not been previously discussed in scholarship. In an effort to answer Barbara L'Eplattenier's recent call to "talk about the methods we use to access our information" (68), I will retrace my own archival research journey in this chapter to show how "playing the name game" led to exciting new finds on Velazquez and her sensational rhetoric.

GETTING STARTED: *THE WOMAN IN BATTLE*

The first phase of my research centered on Velazquez's discussion of her life as recorded in *The Woman in Battle*. In her sensational account, she explained that she was born in Havana, Cuba, in 1842 to a wealthy Spanish official and his French American wife. As a young girl, however, she was sent to New Orleans to live with her aunt and attend school. In her discussion of her early life, Velazquez revealed her desire "to see some real warfare, to engage in real battles, to do some real fighting" (95). As she noted, the American Civil War gave her the opportunity to realize this ambition. She "'unsex[ed]' herself, donning men's clothing in order to fight for the 'cause of Southern independence'" (53). In her narrative, Velazquez detailed her transformation to Harry T. Buford and the battles she fought at Bull Run, Ball's Bluff, Fort Donelson, and Shiloh. Her disguise was eventually discovered, however, and she was subsequently jailed for her gender transgressions. She then pursued other work for the Confederacy, first as a blockade runner and then as an emissary who, acting as a double agent, got involved in the production of counterfeit money. After the war, Velazquez traveled extensively. In the last portion of her book, she detailed her adventures in Europe, South America, the Caribbean, and the American West.

After reading and analyzing *The Woman in Battle*, I turned to the work of several literary scholars and historians who researched Velazquez's narrative, including Jesse Alemán, Richard Hall, Elizabeth Leonard, and Elizabeth Young. As Margaret Marshall explains in "Looking for Letters," "Secondary sources are . . . more than a way of contextualizing one's project; they may well offer essential clues to the location of manuscript collections and surviving archival records or at least provide researchers with other research strategies" (146). In reviewing the scholarship on *The Woman in Battle*, I was able to consider Velazquez's text from different disciplinary angles, but present in these works, too, were references to an exchange of letters Confederate General Jubal Early had with Velazquez. In his missives, he expressed concern with the veracity of her account. Following the lead of these noted scholars, I located these letters at the Wilson Library's Southern Historical Collection at the University of North Carolina, Chapel Hill. Subsumed within the Tucker Family Papers, the letters were made known to me only through these scholars' references. Read in full, these documents offered valuable insight into how Velazquez's shocking narrative was received at the time of its publication.

One of her more vitriolic critics, Early wrote to Arkansas representative William F. Slemons and Virginia congressman John Randolph Tucker in 1878 to protest the accuracy of her claims.[5] In his letter, Early took Velazquez to task for omitting names of several key players in her memoir, a move, he argued, that prevented readers from verifying her story. He continued his condemnation by pointing to what he believed were several factual inaccuracies. Velazquez, for example, wrote that her first husband went to Richmond, Virginia, in 1861, where he met General Robert E. Lee. Early explained to Slemons, however, that "Virginia had not succeeded at that time and was not expected to secede, and General Lee was still an officer in the US Army." Continuing his repudiation of her book, Early was also skeptical of Velazquez's claims of having raised and financed a battalion of 236 men to fight Union forces. He further disputed her discussions of traveling on a railroad that had yet to be built, taking charge of a company after the captain had been killed, walking extraordinarily long distances, and fighting with Confederate General Earl Van Dorn. "These," Early remarked, "are some of the points of her narrative which stuck out . . . There are many other statements which I could point out to show that the writer of the book is not telling the truth" (Letter to Slemons).

Included in Early's letter to Slemons is a copy of Velazquez's response to Early's accusations. This document is also discussed extensively in the scholarship of Alemán, Hall, Leonard, and Young. In my own review of this letter, I could see how determined Velazquez was to quash Early's criticisms. She explained that some of the inconsistencies Early observed were the result of the fact that she had written her account eleven years after the war without the benefit of notes. And, she continued, she purposefully chose to omit some names to "condense [her] manuscript" and avoid "offend[ing] the innocent" (quoted in Early Letter to Slemons). In a particularly emotional appeal, Velazquez also informed Early that the profits she earned from the sale of her book would help her support her young son. Her health, she commented, was "failing," and her "whole souls [sic] devotion [was] the education of him" (quoted in Early Letter to Slemons). It is clear from her letters that Velazquez did not want Early to pursue the issue further, fearing that his criticisms would impact the sale of her book.

These letters offered me the opportunity to review firsthand artifacts related to *The Woman in Battle*. From this research, I was able to better contextualize the publication of Velazquez's account and develop my own theories about her sensational rhetoric. Despite these initial successes with my archival research, I still hoped to uncover more about Velazquez.

TAKING THE NEXT STEPS: LORETA JANETA VELAZQUEZ

Having learned from my experience with the Early/Velazquez letters, I contacted archivists at several museums and libraries to see if they had any leads on Velazquez. Much to my dismay, the Museum of the Confederacy in Richmond, Virginia, sent me two letters Velazquez wrote that had not been previously discussed in the scholarship I reviewed. This experience illustrates how moments of serendipity can take place through cultivating human connections. Without reaching out to those who knew the collections best, I likely would not have found these letters. Initiating the correspondence, Velazquez contacted Reverend J. William Jones to express her concern with his review of her book that was published in *Southern History Society*. Although he acknowledged that her account "will be read by those who are fond of the marvelous," he questioned "how far it can be received as *history*" (Jones 208, original emphasis). Further, Jones wondered how Velazquez could "be at so many battles fought by different armies in different sections of the country . . . [and] manag[e] to accomplish various other physical impossibilities" (208). In her response, Velazquez insisted that her account was accurate, although "the book was not intended as a history of the late war between the States" (Letter to Jones, October 27, 1876). She further addressed Jones's criticisms by clarifying the time line of events she provided in her narrative. In concluding her letter, she offered Jones the names of several Confederate men who would verify her account. Concerned by Jones's lack of response to her first letter, Velazquez wrote him a second letter, reiterating that she believed his review to be "unfair and unjust" and imploring him to reread her narrative (Letter to Jones, November 12, 1876). She noted that she had included stamps so he might be more compelled to respond.

For my next steps, I turned to historical newspaper databases to see what I might uncover. Searching for "Loreta Janeta Velazquez," I located many book advertisements published in newspapers across the country. Hinting at the fame of her account, these adverts included information on the general plot, publishers, and purchase information. I also found advertisements for Ménie Muriel Dowie's collection titled *Women Adventurers* (1893). Excerpts from Velazquez's narrative were incorporated into Dowie's compilation, which detailed the lives of other cross-dressing women, including Hannah Snell, Christian Davies, and Mary Anne Talbot. *Women Adventurers* was published in England, giving Velazquez's narrative an international audience.

Although I primarily located reviews and advertisements in my search for "Loreta Janeta Velazquez," these artifacts speak to the attention Velazquez's narrative received. For my project this was important, as the familiarity of her book hinted at the possibility of additional existing archival documents. If her account was so widely circulated, I reasoned, there must be more information available on her life and text. As David Gold asserts, "We 'strike gold' . . . by having a strong sense of what we *should* find" ("On Keeping a Beginner's Mind" 43, original emphasis).

RESEARCHING ALIASES: HARRY T. BUFORD

Although Velazquez records an array of life experiences in her memoir, she devoted roughly the first half of her 600-page book to describing her experiences as cross-dressing solider Harry T. Buford. As Alemán observes, "Harry T. Buford" is a name that "most historians indefatigably track down" ("Crossing the Mason-Dixon Line" 112). They search the name "Harry T. Buford" or its variations—Henry Buford, H. T. Buford, Bensford, and Benford (Alemán "Introduction" xvi). But unlike the scholars Alemán references, I was less interested in confirming or disproving the events Velazquez describes in her narrative. Rather, my intention was to explore Velazquez's rhetorical approaches. Because of this, my search for "Harry T. Buford" entailed looking for documents related to her account.

Many of the findings from my search of "Harry Buford" in historical newspaper databases overlapped with reviews I encountered while looking for documents related to "Velazquez." These sources, too, often focused on the authenticity of Velazquez's experiences as a cross-dressing soldier. The *Dallas Daily Herald*, for example, reported that "some have refused to believe that there was such a person; but these are comparatively few in number, for Lieutenant Harry T. Buford, or Madame Loreta Juaneta Velasquez (which is her true name), is well known to thousands of officers and soldiers of the Confederate army; and there is the most abundant testimony of a kind that cannot be disputed" ("A Woman in Male Attire" 3). Similarly, an article in the Atlanta

Constitution maintained that Velazquez's account was "by no means a fictitious romance. The lady belonged to one of the best families of the south and after the war she published quite a handsome volume, giving a detailed account of her adventures" ("From Maid to Martyr" 16). Such reviews revealed that despite the controversy surrounding Velazquez's narrative, the book still had a loyal following.

But searching further for "Buford" also led to documents that reveal that Velazquez also went by Mrs. E. H. Bonner—a name she took from a previous marriage. This exciting bit of information led to documents pertaining to Velazquez's publicity strategies. Several articles, such as "A Confederate Amazon" found in South Carolina's *Orangeburg Times*, report that she announced her plans to publish the book almost two years in advance of its actual publication date. To further appeal to potential readers, Velazquez told several newspapers, including the Atlanta *Constitution*, the Louisville *Courier-Journal*, and the Mobile *Register*, that Mark Twain would be collaborating with her to write the book. Mark Twain's letters do indicate that Velazquez contacted him requesting that he "take hold of my Book," adding "if written up by you it will have a large sale in the South and West" (quoted in Twain 252). When Twain was asked about this partnership, he replied, "The woman is a fraud—her assertions are without any foundation whatever . . . I declined very positively" (254). Although some newspapers did print a retraction correcting her claims, the "Buford/Bonner" documents indicate that Velazquez succeeded in generating interest in her forthcoming book.

EXPLORING DIFFERENT SPELLINGS: MADAME L. J. VELASQUEZ

As I continued my search for information on Velazquez, I noticed that in several documents her name was spelled with an "s" instead of a "z." In his "Introduction," Alemán notes additional spellings of her name, including Loreta Juaneta Velasquez, Laureta Juaneta Velasquez, and L. J. Velasquez (xix). These observations encouraged me to search different variations of her first and last names, a move that generated several surprising finds.

One of the more exciting documents I discovered when searching World Cat was a pamphlet titled "Address to the American Congress on Cuba," located at both the New York Public Library and the Library of Congress. Although scholars, including Alemán and Hall, explore Velazquez's relationship with Cuba, they make no mention of her pamphlet. Composed by Madame L. J. Velasquez in 1877, this document urged the United States to intervene on behalf of Cuba, her native country, which had been engaged in the Guerra de los Diez Años, or the Ten Years' War, against Spain in a fight for its independence. She asked her American audience to use its "prestige among nations which commands both awe and respect . . . [to] speak out, and act if need be, so that the tottering through of barbaric Spain will heed the cry of humanity, and stay the slaughter and bloodshed among the patriots of Cuba" (2). Velazquez's pamphlet, the most staid document I discovered, draws more attention to the passages in her narrative that address Cuba. Although Coleman Hutchinson observes that "Velazquez's narrative does not spend much time in Cuba . . . the words 'Cuba' and 'Cuban' appear only 24 times in this capacious 230,000-plus word text" (199), her plea in the pamphlet on behalf of Cuban independence underscores the importance of this aspect of her text.

After searching World Cat, I returned to the newspaper databases; this time, though, I looked for various combinations of "Velasquez." Some of the articles I found focused on a counterfeit money scandal that took place during the Civil War. As she claimed in *The Woman in Battle*, she partnered with men of professed Northern allegiance to steal money from their own government. "Men high in public station, and occupying offices of the greatest responsibility," she explained in her narrative, "were engaged in robbing the government and swindling the public, to an extent that was absolutely startling" (*Woman in Battle* 466). While she discussed this event in her book, I had not seen these newspaper articles referenced in previous scholarship. In finding these documents, then, I felt a surge of excitement, as I was getting closer to a fuller picture of Velazquez and her sensational rhetorical strategies. In "Madame Velasquez: The Ridiculous Story Which Investigator Glover Swallowed," the reporter recounted that "with the assistance of officials in the Treasury Department, [Velazquez] . . . procured the abstraction from that Department of two steel-plates, each capable of [producing] four United States hundred notes at each impression" (9). She split the money acquired from the scheme with her co-conspirators to "bu[y] war vessels for the Confederacy" (9). She expressed the hope that by bringing more attention to the issue in both her memoir and the article, those involved might be brought to justice. The reporter speculated that Velazquez intended to "rui[n] the Republican party" with her accusations; he further maintained that her story was "too preposterous for consideration" (9). Although the reporter was skeptical of her claims, Velazquez's allegations were successful in sparking interest in her book.

CONSIDERING MARRIED NAMES:
L. J. VELAZQUEZ / VELASQUEZ BEARD

In her narrative, Velazquez revealed that she was married four times; however, she mentioned the name of only one husband: Captain DeCaulp. Tracking down her married names also proved fortunate to my research process. In addition to learning about her marriage to Bonner, I discovered that Velazquez was married to William Beard, a renowned geologist and mining expert. Through searching for "L. J. Velasquez Beard" in historical newspaper databases, I found several compelling articles that detailed her plans to build a railroad that would connect Mexico with the southern half of the United States. These articles highlight the importance of the second half of her narrative, which outlined her postwar adventures. When she returned to the United States after her international travels, Velazquez "found the financial and political situations, especially at the South, more deplorable than ever before" (*Woman in Battle* 570). In an effort to improve her financial situation, Velazquez wanted to "try [her] luck in the mining regions of the Pacific Slope" (570). This decision led her to travel west. In her discussion of the mines of New Mexico, she mentions the problem with transportation, but, as she remarks, "a railroad will aid immensely in developing this country, which is one of the richest in the world in minerals" (604). The *New York Times* reported that "she has been working on the project for seventeen years, and has been aided by the Mexican Consul General at San Francisco" ("Mrs. Beard's Big Scheme" 3). An article in the *Arizona Sentinel* further outlined her plans for the railroad, which was proposed to run from Banderas Bay in Mexico to Phoenix, Arizona ("Plans"). She also worked to develop a steamship that would run from Savannah, Georgia, to Mexico. The *Constitution* stated that "the object of the railroad and steamship line is to develop the south as these improvements will piece this section in direct communication with the orient, and will be the means of bringing goods here that are at present shipped to New York" ("Georgia Should Speak" 3). Through these articles, Velazquez attempted to corroborate her entrepreneurial efforts, particularly as discussed in her narrative, but they also speak to her media savvy. She used exciting and shocking stories to manipulate the press to her advantage.

Continuing to research her married name, I found additional articles—again, not referenced in previous scholarship on Velazquez—that discussed the death of her husband. As reported by the *Los Angeles Herald*, Beard was killed in Alaska in 1897 while on a mining expedition for North Star Mining Company ("Beard Is Found" 5). According to the article, he was killed in a snow slide. Although she was not with him at the time of his death, Velazquez insisted that he was murdered. As she explained, "When my husband's body was found there was not a penny on it and it lay six miles away from any glacier and six miles away from any possible snow slide" ("Beard Is Found" 5). Such a claim, not made by any other party involved, is consistent with the sensational approaches Velazquez utilized in previous encounters with the media.

Velazquez's many incredible stories added to her intrigue and fame, yet the circumstances of her own death are unknown. She was believed to have died in the late 1800s. Hall writes that after this time, she "literally fades from the pages of history, and no record has been found of her life after that, or of her death" (153). In searching for "L. J. Velasquez Beard" on the genealogy website Ancestry.com, however, I located the 1911 District of Columbia directory that listed "L. J. Velasquez Beard" as a resident; real estate was cited as her occupation (267). Continuing my research with the variation "L.J.V. Beard" on historical newspaper databases, I also uncovered an article from a 1912 *Washington Times* article titled "Woman Writer Here to Collect Data" that corroborates this finding. This piece reports that Velazquez was in Washington with the purpose of "rewriting her book, 'The Woman in Battle'" (5). Although there is no known record of the second book, this discussion of building on her infamous account only adds to her fascinating story.

CONCLUSION

As David Gold remarks in "The Accidental Archivist," "Accidents [that] come about only through painstaking research [are] no less miraculous. Chance may favor the prepared mind, but it is still chance. We never know where an archive will lead us" (18). Although "the name game" method helped me make several serendipitous finds, my success was really the result of the kind of doggedness that is required when conducting archival research. Each variation of Velazquez's name I searched had to be run through every museum, library, and database I consulted. This work was incredibly time-consuming and, at times, tedious. But my perseverance and persistence were rewarded. With each new discovery I made in this process, I was able to get a better sense of Velazquez and her sensational rhetorical activities. As my experience illustrates, luck can occur in archival research, but to truly court serendipity, scholars need to be thorough, systematic, and, most of all, unrelenting in their efforts.

Notes

1. Kirsch describes Ritter as "a physician, women's rights advocate, and civic leader active in California at the turn of the twentieth century" (20).
2. In my research, I have cataloged over 100 such accounts.
3. Many scholars have come to similar conclusions as Leonard: Velazquez's narrative "is a fantastic tale in many ways, but there is evidence as well that the narrative's contents—like the protagonist's reasons for joining the military—are rooted in real experience" (252). William Davis, however, argues that Velazquez's book is a complete fabrication: she never cross-dressed to fight in the Civil War.
4. Sarah Emma Edmonds's *Nurse and Spy in the Union Army* is the only other known personal narrative that publicly outlines the writer's own experiences as a cross-dressing nurse and spy in the American Civil War.
5. Seeking advice from Tucker on how to proceed with his concerns regarding Velazquez's book, Early sent him the letter he drafted to Slemons. This enclosure included a copy of the letter Velazquez sent to Early.

Works Cited

"A Confederate Amazon: Exploits on the Tented Field of Mrs. Bonner, Alias Lieut. Harry Buford." *Orangeburg Times* [SC]. 17 Sept. 1874. 3. Web. 10 Jan. 2018.

Alemán, Jesse. "Crossing the Mason-Dixon Line in Drag: The Narrative of Loreta Janeta Velazquez, Cuban Woman and Confederate Soldier." *Look Away: The US South in New World Studies*. Ed. Jon Smith and Deborah Cohn. Durham, NC: Duke UP, 2004. 110–29. Print.

Alemán, Jesse. "Introduction: Authenticity, Autobiography, and Identity: *The Woman in Battle* as a Civil War Narrative." *The Woman in Battle*. By Loreta Janeta Velazquez. Rpt. ed. Madison: U of Wisconsin P, 2003. ix–lxvi. Print.

"Beard Is Found." *Los Angeles Herald*, 14 Oct. 1898. 5. Web. 9 Jan. 2018.

Davis, William. *Inventing Loreta Velasquez: Confederate Soldier, Impersonator, Media Celebrity, and Con Artist*. Carbondale: Southern Illinois UP, 2016. Print.

District of Columbia Directory. *US City Directories, 1821–1989*. Web. 14 Sept. 2012.

Dowie, Ménie Muriel. *Women Adventurers: The Lives of Madame Velazquez, Hannah Snell, Mary Anne Talbot, and Mrs. Christian Davies*. London: T. F. Unwin, 1893. Print.

Early, Jubal. Letter to John Randolph Tucker. 26 May 1878. Tucker Family Papers, no. 2605. Southern Historical Collection, Louis Round Wilson Library, University of North Carolina, Chapel Hill. Archival source.

Early, Jubal. Letter to William F. Slemons. 22 May 1878. Tucker Family Papers, no. 2605. Southern Historical Collection, Louis Round Wilson Library, University of North Carolina, Chapel Hill. Archival source.

Edmonds, Sarah Emma. *Nurse and Spy in the Union Army: Comprising the Adventures and Experiences of a Woman in Hospitals, Camps, and Battle-Fields*. Philadelphia: W. S. Williams, 1865. Print.

"From Maid to Martyr." *Constitution* [Atlanta, GA]. 29 March 1896. 16. Web. 9 Jan. 2018.

"Georgia Should Speak." *Constitution* [Atlanta, GA]. 15 Jan. 1875. 3. Web. 9 Jan. 2018.

Gold, David. "The Accidental Archivist: Embracing Chance and Confusion in Historical Scholarship." *Beyond the Archives: Research as a Lived Process*. Ed. Gesa E. Kirsch and Liz Rohan. Carbondale: Southern Illinois UP, 2008. 13–19. Print.

Gold, David. "On Keeping a Beginner's Mind." Interview with Lori Ostergaard. *Working in the Archives*. Ed. Alexis E. Ramsey, Wendy B. Sharer, Barbara L'Eplattenier, and Lisa S. Mastrangelo. Carbondale: Southern Illinois UP, 2010. 42–44. Print.

Hall, Richard. *Patriots in Disguise: Women Warriors of the Civil War.* New York: Marlowe, 1994. Print.

Hutchinson, Coleman. *Apples and Ashes: Literature, Nationalism, and the Confederate States of the America.* Athens: U of Georgia P, 2012. Print.

Jones, J. William. *Southern Historical Society Papers.* Vol. II. Richmond, VA: Geo. W. Gary, 1876. Print.

Kirsch, Gesa. "Being on Location: Serendipity, Place, and Archival Research." *Beyond the Archives: Research as Lived Experience.* Ed. Gesa E. Kirsch and Liz Rohan. Carbondale: Southern Illinois UP, 2008. 20–27. Print.

Leonard, Elizabeth. *All the Daring of the Soldier: Women of the Civil War Armies.* New York: Norton, 1999. Print.

L'Eplattenier, Barbara. "An Argument for Archival Research Methods: Thinking beyond Methodology." *College English* 71.1 (2009): 67–79. Print.

"Madame Velasquez: The Ridiculous Story Which Investigator Glover Swallowed." *Chicago Tribune.* 23 Dec. 1879. 9. Web. 9 Jan. 2018.

Marshall, Margaret J. "Looking for Letters." *Working in the Archives.* Ed. Alexis E. Ramsey, Wendy B. Sharer, Barbara L'Eplattenier, and Lisa S. Mastrangelo. Carbondale: Southern Illinois UP, 2010. 135–48. Print.

"Mrs. Beard's Big Scheme." *New York Times.* 7 June 1900. 3. Web. 10 Jan. 2018.

"Plans for New Railroad." *Arizona Sentinel,* 13 June 1900. 1. Web. 9 Jan. 2018.

Twain, Mark. *Letters: 1874–1875.* Vol. 6. Ed. Michael B. Frank and Harriet Elinor Smith. Oakland: U of California P, 2002. Print.

Velazquez, Loreta Janeta. "Address to the American Congress on Cuba." N.p.: 1877? Call no. HOL p.v. 13. Stephen A. Schwarzman Building, New York Public Library. New York, NY. 22 Oct. 2012. Print.

Velazquez, Loreta Janeta. Letter to Reverend J. William Jones. 27 Oct. 1876. Museum of the Confederacy, Richmond, VA. Print.

Velazquez, Loreta Janeta. Letter to Reverend J. William Jones. 12 Nov. 1876. Museum of the Confederacy, Richmond, VA. Print.

Velazquez, Loreta Janeta. *The Woman in Battle: The Civil War Narrative of Loreta Velazquez, Cuban Woman and Confederate Soldier.* 1876. Madison: U of Wisconsin P, 2003. Print.

"A Woman in Male Attire: or, the Female Spy—the Most Remarkable Book of the Age." *Dallas Daily Herald.* 21 Sept. 1876. 3. Web. 10 Jan. 2018.

"Woman Writer Here to Collect Data." *Washington Times.* 4 June 1912. 5. Web. 10 Jan. 2018.

Young, Elizabeth. *Disarming the Nation: Women's Writing and the American Civil War.* Chicago: U of Chicago P, 1999. Print.

14
SERENDIPITY AND METHODOLOGICAL WILLINGNESS IN TEAM SCIENCE

Ellen Barton

Serendipity has long held an honored place in the history and sociology of science, first investigated in Robert Merton's definitive *Social Theory and Social Structure* (first edition in 1949) and then popularized in his lexical history *The Travels and Adventures of Serendipity* (written in 1958, intentionally not published in English until shortly after his death in 2003). Merton described the serendipity pattern as "the fairly common experience of observing an *unanticipated, anomalous,* and *strategic* datum which becomes the occasion for developing [or] extending theory, stimulating the investigator to 'make sense of the datum'" (*Social Theory* 158, original emphasis). Of the strategic nature of serendipity, Merton notes, "we are, of course, referring to what the observer brings to the datum . . . to detect the universal in the particular" (*Social Theory* 159). In a series of footnotes in their first edition of *The Discovery of Grounded Theory*, Barney Glaser and Anselm Strauss credit Merton's notion of unanticipated and anomalous data in the development of their constant comparative method, although they refused to endorse the term *serendipity* since its more humble focus is on contributing to or modifying theory rather than systematically developing grounded theory inductively from the data (2, n.1). Nevertheless, Glaser and Strauss centralized making sense of the data, including difficult-to-interpret data, as one of the bedrock principles of data-driven qualitative research and theory.

Qualitative approaches to research and data-driven theory have been vitally important in the research trajectory of writing studies, particularly in fieldwork-based workplace studies conducted by Technical/Professional Communication [TPC] researchers. Many landmark TPC studies, such as those by Clay Spinuzzi, Beverly Sauer, and Ann Blakeslee, used qualitative methods to analyze the communication of teams in business, engineering, and science. In medicine, TPC researchers have worked actively in fieldwork-based studies, also often focusing on teams, with early studies on drug development (Bernhardt and McCulley) and more recent studies of medical education (Kenny Fountain), medical materiality (Graham), medical identities (Lingard et al.), and medical deliberation in multidisciplinary clinic meetings (Teston). In these data-driven studies, TPC researchers typically take an observer's role in coming to understand, analyze, and theorize the communication and rhetoric of complex team ecologies.[1] Less often are TPC researchers full members of research teams in what is vernacularly called "team science," tasked with contributing significantly to the production of the team's research and its dissemination in the academic journals of science, engineering, or health and medicine.[2] Gregory Wilson's research during and after his career at the Los Alamos National Laboratory is an exemplar of team science with meaningful contributions from and to TPC: in 2007, two of his coauthored publications appeared in the journals *Reliability Engineering and System Safety* and the *Journal of Business and Technical Communication*. Wilson's early academic background was in psychology and his graduate training was in TPC, and what I most admire in his work is his facility with mixed methods, which I believe is an important direction for TPC as a field. I present here a narrative of my own migration toward mixed methods as a member of health and medical research teams, a migration that has been primarily experiential, more like Merton's rollicking account of serendipity in his *Adventures and Travels* than his sober definition of the serendipity pattern in *Social Theory and Social Structure*.

By any measure, my research career in medical communication and medical rhetoric has been nothing but serendipitous, actually beginning with a classic example of Merton's serendipity pattern. Around twenty-five years ago I became immersed in the language socially constructing a new lifeworld for me, to use Elliot Mishler's terms: my first observation of the use of language in the medical world came while visiting my brand-new daughter in the NICU (Neo-Natal Intensive Care Unit). There I listened to clinicians use both positive and evaluative role terms rather than names, greeting parents with the reinforcing role-descriptors "hi, Mom" and "hi, Dad" in the unit while overhearing talk about who was a "good mom" or a "bad mom" in the PICU team communication during shift changes. Thinking about this unanticipated and faintly anomalous observation strategically, as Merton described the serendipity pattern—in other words, bringing what I had to bear to make sense of the data, namely, my background in linguistics—became a serendipitous pivot for me, prompting a move in my research interests and methods into the discourse analysis of medical encounters.

Thus began a period of what I would call career serendipity, aided some years later by another serendipitous event: I was referred to a medical research team looking for a linguist as part of a project on end-of-life care and communication in the SICU (Surgical Intensive Care Unit). I had nothing to do with the referral: the medical anthropologist on the team asked her daughter, a linguist, if she knew anyone who could analyze a set of end-of-life discussions, and apparently my name popped up. Since then, I have had other serendipitous opportunities to work as a funded or unfunded researcher on NIH-funded health and medical research teams, analyzing fascinating data from telemedicine depression care and conducting interviews with bereaved parents who lost a child in the PICU (Pediatric Intensive Care Unit), as well as offers to participate in cancer clinical trials. In these projects I was essentially given a data set late in the process of the team's data analysis, usually motivated by a nagging question asked of the PI (principal investigator): as one put it doubtfully, "people have asked whether there's anything about the language," to which I responded with complete conviction and rising intonation, "well, yes" . . . From the post hoc analysis of these data sets, I first wrote and published articles more or less independently, primarily in my own journals in linguistics and TPC (e.g., *Communication and Medicine, Written Communication, Journal of Business and Technical Communication, Technical Communication Quarterly*).

Over the years, I slowly became more ambitious about publishing in my teams' journals of choice, which initially meant publishing discourse analysis studies in qualitative journals (e.g., *Qualitative Health Research*). However, publishing my research in the disciplinary journals of the teams meant coming to terms with basic quantitative research methods to develop mixed-methods studies. Given my complete lack of background in mathematics and statistics, this was excruciatingly difficult, as chronicled in years of Facebook posts. I compulsively read and reread sections of *Statistics without Tears: A Primer for Non-Mathematicians* (Rowntree) and other sources. More productively, I repetitively badgered my colleagues to explain the design and meaning of statistical analysis, not in mathematical terms but in practical terms given the language data at hand. With an incredible amount of scaffolding from my main coauthor, so much that I asked her to be first author, I wrote a mixed-methods article published in *Health Expectations*, a journal with a strong mixed-methods mission (Eggly et al.). Writing this article brought me to the clichéd position of being able to *talk to the statistician,* which I regarded as a hard-fought achievement. To adapt Merton's popular terms, serendipity pushed me to travel a short way down a road of quantitative adventures.

My career serendipity continued, and I had an opportunity to join a behavioral health team after the PI was told "get your own linguist to look at this" while she was organizing a team for a pilot study. For the first time, I was a member of a team from the beginning, actively involved in research design, specifically instrument development. I was acutely aware of my first-time role as a full team member, and I very much wanted to make a strong contribution to my team, again defined as publishing in their disciplinary journals of choice. However, I was immediately taken aback by the issues of methodological accountability I encountered, as I will narrate below. In the course of this project, centered upon an extended example of the serendipity pattern, it was turning to basic methods in TPC that created the affordances to develop a mixed-methods study within the disciplinary context of the team.

Led by an adolescent health psychologist (Naar-King "Interventionist"), the project was an investigation of the efficacy of Motivational Interviewing (MI) in increasing adherence to weight loss recommendations to obese African American adolescents and their caregivers, primarily mothers who were also obese. Obesity research on minority populations is crucially important in health and medicine: African Americans have the highest rates of obesity across race and ethnicity populations in the United States. In 2009–10, 23.7 percent of African American adolescents were obese, with a BMI for age > 95th percentile (Ogden et al.). African American girls are the population at highest risk for obesity and its lifelong health consequences (US Surgeon General), and previous weight loss interventions for minority youth, including the well-known Go Girl and Bright Bodies programs, have not been successful (Resnicow et al.; Savoy et al.).

Motivational Interviewing is a client-centered method of guided communication aimed at strengthening intrinsic motivation and self-efficacy for behavioral change (Naar-King and Suarez; Miller and Rellnick). Interestingly for this narrative, MI emerged as what its researchers call "an example of grounded theory . . . the method emerged from the data (session recordings), and only now is a theory beginning to be explicated" (Naar-King and Suarez 5). One key assumption within the theoretical framework of MI is that ambivalence about change is the primary barrier to change (Miller and Rose). The counseling method of MI is therefore centered on very specific linguistic sequences: counselors are trained to actively and consciously use open-ended questions, offers of information, reflections, and statements supporting client autonomy to explore ambivalence about change and to elicit and reflect what is called Change Talk and Commitment Language. In MI, a statement like "I need to eat breakfast every day" is Change Talk, and a statement like "I will eat breakfast tomorrow" is Commitment Language. Previous research has shown that when the counselor is correctly using MI methods, the amount and the strength of positive Change Talk and Commitment Language, especially at the end of a session, predict attitudinal and behavioral change and correlate with good outcomes (Armstrong et al.; Moyers et al.; Söderlund). The American Academy of Pediatrics has recommended the use of MI for clinicians talking to families about healthy eating and physical activity (Barlow et al.). However, the efficacy of MI interventions aimed at obese minority adolescents was as yet unknown.

Our pilot study data consisted of forty transcribed one-hour MI sessions aimed at increasing adherence to weight loss recommendations in three target behavior categories—nutrition, activity, and weight loss. The purpose of the pilot was to develop a coding instrument to capture the innovative features of this MI design, specifically the use of MI with minority adolescents and the incorporation of caregivers in the intervention. What I learned in the first meetings of the team was that despite its qualitative origins, the MI literature now employs a ferociously quantitative framework for interactional coding and data analysis. Our coding instrument was not to be developed from an inductive analysis of our own data, as I had expected, but in an incremental advance of MI instrumentation. This degree of methodological accountability surprised me considerably, probably because I had never worked in psychology before.

We thus started with the PI's strong expectation that the development of our instrument would be compatible with the reigning instrument in the MI literature for coding counselor-client talk, the MI-SCOPE (Motivational Interviewing Sequential Code for Observing Process Exchanges) (Martin et al.). Working from transcripts, we developed a specialized version of the MI-SCOPE, christened the MY-SCOPE (Minority Youth Sequential Coding for Observing Process Exchanges). As preliminary coding with the instrument started, however, the research assistants reported that they did not know how to code adolescent and caregiver statements that were both for and against change in the same turn, such as one adolescent saying about healthy eating "yeah, like tofu. People say it's good to eat tofu, but I'm not sure I'm going to eat tofu." Turns like these could not be coded straightforwardly as Change Talk

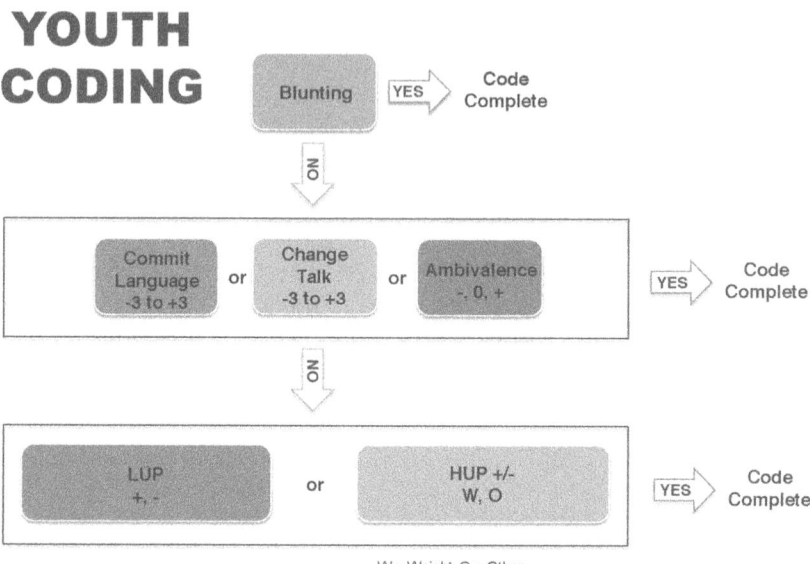

Figure 14.1. Youth coding.

or Commitment Language—the beginning of this extended example of Merton's serendipity pattern, although I didn't recognize it as such at the time. After much team discussion, we decided that the dual structure of these turns made them expressions of ambivalence, so we added a new code to the instrument called AMB, a code that was intended to capture these unanticipated and ambiguous data in terms of the theoretical framework of MI, specifically its assumption that ambivalence toward change is the primary barrier to change. Figure 14.1 presents the final version of the MY-SCOPE instrument for coding adolescent talk; there was a similar instrument for caregiver talk and a fidelity instrument for counselor talk. For the purposes of this narrative, the AMB code has a set of three strength valences, defined as positive/AMB^+, neutral/AMB^0, and negative/AMB^0 ambivalence. It took a full year to write the seventy-page MY-SCOPE coding manual so it could achieve the status of a validated and reliable instrument in the MI literature. The research assistants trained and trained with the instrument before independently coding the forty MI sessions, and the team was pleased (and perhaps relieved) that the final inter-rater reliability was good (k = 0.696), thereby validating the MY-SCOPE instrument.

It was now time for data analysis and dissemination of the results of the pilot study. Recall that I mentioned the ferociously quantitative framework of the MI literature. This was true for instrument development, and, predictably even for me by this time, it was true for the methods and methodologies in data analysis as well. Methodologically, data analysis in MI research uses the numbered codes as the primary data: the purpose of coding is to take a quantitative step away from the language. The statistical methods in the MI literature come from psychology, specifically a method called sequential analysis (Bakeman and Quera)—basically a Chi-square analysis on steroids that considers discourse a sequential process exchange (turn 1 to turn 2). A sequential analysis identifies the counselor statements (e.g., turn 1—an open-ended question or a reflection) most predictive of eliciting Change Talk and Commitment Language (e.g., turn 2—a statement like "I need to eat breakfast every day" or "I will eat breakfast tomorrow"). (You can imagine my discourse analyst's reaction to this strictly limited definition of discourse. But I got used to it.) The signature article from the pilot study (Idalski-Carcone et al. "Provider") described the coding instrument and reported that counselors' use of MI methods (reflections, open-ended questions, and statements emphasizing autonomy) were significantly predictive of adolescents' and caregivers' Change Talk and Commitment Language, consistent with the MI literature. I was fifth author of seven on this article, which was duly published in the *Journal of Developmental and Behavioral Pediatrics*.

The MI team moved on at this point, taking the MY-SCOPE instrument with them; they had a multi-arm clinical trial of the MI intervention to run. I, however, took what I thought would be a qualitative step back to the language, expecting to create my own methodological affordances by using discourse analysis to analyze the MI sessions in the pilot study. I confidently revved up my methods by reading and rereading the transcripts to see what I would find inductively in the discourse (Barton "Linguistic") while keeping an eye out for discourse features, patterns, and conventions relevant to the MI literature (Barton "Design"). Tellingly, I did not conceptualize my research in terms of a mixed-methods framework at this time, despite the fact that I had just finished writing a mixed-methods article for the clinical trials project (apparently serendipity can take a long time to kick in).

In my phase of getting to know the data, I was first struck by the many narratives in the data, some incredibly poignant accounts of the lived experience of obese adolescents and others surprisingly negative accounts of the lived experience of their caregivers, particularly in terms of the distribution of responsibility for adhering to recommendations in the target behaviors—nutrition, activity, and weight loss. I found competing narratives of family meals and shopping trips that would break your heart. But when I proposed an analysis of narratives in the MI sessions, the PI was politely unenthusiastic because the narratives concerned behavior in the past, not change or commitment to weight-related behaviors in the present and future. As she put it, "there's not enough of an MI component there." In other words, this study would not be a contribution to the MI literature; more concretely for me, it would not be a strong contribution to the team, by now my emotional audience.

After the meeting, the project manager continued the extended serendipity pattern for me: gently, she redirected me back to the coding instrument, pointing out that it would be interesting to know something about *the codes we added* to the MY-SCOPE. After a time-consuming but unproductive fling with the interactional codes (High and Low Uptake), I turned in some desperation to the AMB code, where I (finally) found my theoretical and methodological affordances. AMB was a code we added that was intended to capture more of the theoretical framework of MI in the MY-SCOPE instrument, and there were no empirical studies of expressions of ambivalence in the MI literature, either qualitative or quantitative. So an investigation of the AMB code could potentially turn the MI assumption that ambivalence is the key barrier to change into a fleshed-out theoretical and methodological construct. Best of all, an analysis of the AMB code was interesting to the team. When I pitched a qualitative analysis of AMB at the team's manuscript meeting, the PI was encouraging, saying "this is more in your wheelhouse" and setting a guiding research question: What are they ambivalent about? We know they're not ambivalent about losing weight. They want to lose weight. But they might be ambivalent about specific behaviors.

Having become obsessed with the idea of publishing in the MI literature, however, I still had much methodological work to do to answer this question. More specifically, I had to come to terms (again) with issues of methodological accountability in data coding and data analysis within the quantitative paradigm of MI. With many false starts and (again) an extraordinary amount of statistical scaffolding from my coauthors, I finally developed a mixed-methods study of the AMB code, summed up in the purpose statement for the article:

> In order to explore the ambivalence of African-American adolescents and their caregivers about adherence to weight-loss recommendations in more depth, the study reported here is a secondary analysis of the communication related to ambivalence during 40 single Motivational Interviewing weight-loss sessions. Specifically, the purpose of this mixed methods study was to analyze the frequency and content of the AMB codes in order to describe and compare what African-American adolescents and their caregivers were ambivalent about in terms of behaviors related to weight loss.

More specifically, we used quantitative methods to examine the frequency of ambivalence expressed by adolescents and their caregivers, which of the target behaviors of Nutrition, Activity, and Weight evoked adolescents' and caregivers' ambivalence, and whether the ambivalence expressed was weighted for or against change. We used qualitative methods to explore the specific content of adolescent and caregiver AMB codes. (Idalski-Carcone et al. "Exploring")

It took well over a year to get to this purpose statement, and I didn't even write the quantitative sentence. More relevant for this narrative, however, the process of researching and writing this article was largely one of figuring out how to develop two other coding instruments that, it turned out, allowed one of the less frequent moves in mixed-methods studies—a quantitative analysis setting up a qualitative analysis, the former legitimizing the latter for a literature not inclined toward ready acceptance of qualitative research on its own.

To do this, I first had to develop a validated and reliable coding instrument defining the target behaviors as category codes for a directed content analysis of the AMB turns. A directed content analysis derives its coding categories from previous research or theory (Hsieh and Shannon), in this case, the target behaviors of nutrition, activity, and weight loss. Note here the subtle change in methods: discourse analysis is out, content analysis is in, an example of my adopting methods more familiar to health and medical researchers (and peer reviewers for their journals). It was at this point that I found the affordances TPC contributed to the study: I used basic TPC methods for writing coding instructions and used TPC usability methods for testing the instrument, thinking of reliability as a function of usability. I developed a coding manual for the AMB code, and one of my coauthors and I independently coded the category of the 273 AMB codes into the nutrition, activity, and weight loss categories. The interreliability rate was outstanding (if I do say so myself): ($k = 0.907$), validating the instrument.

I then confidently turned to data analysis, which turned into a lengthy process of developing (and proofreading) data spreadsheets as I delved into the wrong statistical methods to analyze the frequency and distributions of the AMB codes. Each new attempt (every version of the t-test imaginable and a brief flirtation with a non-parametric method called the sign test) sent me back to Rowntree's *Statistics without Tears* and other sources (Creswell) for a painful conceptual review, followed by my more successful technique of insistently badgering the team statistician, again requiring so much scaffolding that I made her first author. After a horrifyingly embarrassing presentation at one of the team's manuscript meetings—the PI was not impressed at all with the choice of a sign test or its unimpressive results—we followed her suggestion to return to the trusty Chi-square, the foundation of the quantitative MI paradigm, yet another step in the serendipity pattern.

Using the right test did the trick. Briefly, we found that adolescents and caregivers had similar distributions of AMB codes across the target behaviors. In other words, adolescents and caregivers had similar proportions of AMB codes within the categories of nutrition, activity, and weight (for example, 44% of adolescents' AMB codes and 42% of caregivers' AMB codes were about activity). Analysis of the strength valence codes, however, told a more nuanced story. Adolescents' expressions of ambivalence were fairly evenly distributed across the valence categories (34% for AMB^+, 35% for AMB^0, and 32% for AMB^-), but the distribution for caregivers was not (19% for AMB^+, 22% for AMB^0, and a whopping 59% for AMB^-). In other words, caregivers were much more negatively ambivalent than adolescents, and statistically so ($p < 0.001$). To better understand this distribution of ambivalence, we then ran a combined analysis of the AMB^+ and AMB^0 codes compared to the AMB^- code, finding statistically significant differences in the frequency of adolescents' and caregivers' expressions of positive/neutral versus negative ambivalence. Adolescents were more favorably ambivalent (AMB^+ and AMB^0) than caregivers in the category of activity, whereas the caregivers were more favorably ambivalent in the category of nutrition ($p < 0.001$). Also, adolescents were more negatively ambivalent (AMB^-) than caregivers in the category of nutrition, whereas caregivers were more negatively ambivalent about making changes in activity ($p < 0.05$). In other words, adolescents and caregivers seemed to be at odds in their ambivalence: adolescents were favorable about making changes in activity, though caregivers were not; and caregivers were favorable about making changes in nutrition, though adolescents were not. This quantitative analysis was a legitimate contribution to the MI literature, and I posted Statistics Kitty on Facebook (figure 14.2).

When I say legitimate, I mean that this quantitative analysis of the AMB codes set up a qualitative analysis to describe and compare what specifically adolescents and caregivers were ambivalent about in terms of nutrition, activity, and weight loss. For this content analysis of the AMB codes, we used conventional content analysis, which derives its coding categories inductively from the data (Hsieh and Shannon). After recursively reading the data, the resulting instrument had three descriptive categories, intended to follow the significant differences found in the quantitative data: two categories of "things I could do" and "reasons I might do these things" were conceptually based on AMB^+ and AMB^0,

Figure 14.2. "Statistics Kitty." LOL Cats. *www.lolcats.com, n.d.*

and the third category, "reasons I might not do these things," was conceptually AMB⁻. We then coded to consensus the 273 AMB turns, inductively developing content-based subcodes. The content analysis then compared the most frequent subcodes to describe how adolescents and caregivers converged and diverged in their ambivalence. Consistent with the statistical analysis, we found that adolescents and caregivers diverged sharply upon perceived barriers to making changes in the target behaviors. In one example from the nutrition category, adolescents pointed first to family patterns (n = 11) of meal scheduling and family eating as their chief barrier; as one said, "it's kind of hard to eat healthier around others. It's like my main thing—how to eat around the other family members and stuff." Caregivers mentioned such family patterns only one time. The most frequent subcode caregivers mentioned as a barrier was their adolescents' unhealthy eating habits (n = 12): adolescents "eat the wrong foods, they like junk food," they "don't like healthy foods," and "they know how to eat healthy but won't." One caregiver said concisely, "It's completely up to her."

Analysis of examples like these revealed the complex distribution of responsibility for adhering to weight loss recommendations in these African American families, and the implications for MI counseling were important: counselors may have to explore competing and contrasting ambivalences in guiding family members to work together toward behaviors supportive of weight loss. The implications for the development of MI theory and methodology were also promising. The AMB code and the mixed-methods approach to unpacking it may well become part of the standard instrumentation in MI research, given the tight accountability within this literature: as we had to build our instrument on the existing instruments, so future MI teams will have to build their instruments on ours, especially if the projects are intended to address either obesity or minority and youth populations.

After two rounds of peer review in which one reader praised the quantitative to qualitative structure and the other demanded yet more statistical analysis, the study was accepted for publication in *Patient Education and Counseling* (*PEC*) (Idalski-Carcone et al. "Exploring"). Despite its awkward title, *PEC* is a top journal for medical communication studies aimed at an audience of medical communication researchers as well as practicing clinicians, in this case pediatricians and others trying to follow the American Academy of Pediatrics recommendation to use MI to talk about weight loss. Best of all, when the final acceptance email was sent to the authors, the PI responded "hurray for team science." The serendipity pattern had finally traveled to a happy ending, thanks to my adventures in mixed-methods design.

Robert Merton had this to say on the quotation that inspired this volume: "We also recall Pasteur's reverberating maxim that 'chance favors the prepared mind.' But apt and memorable though it may be, the psychological black box of the 'prepared mind' cannot itself explain the complexities of serendipitous discovery . . . At the least, the psychological perspective needs to be integrated with a sociological perspective. For if chance favors prepared minds, it particularly favors those at work in microenvironments that make for unanticipated socio-cognitive interactions between those prepared minds" (*Travels and Adventures* 259–60). In other words, transdisciplinary teams.

For me, serendipity has sometimes come from external events in my life and my career—a hospital visit, referrals to join research teams, this occasion of thinking about the role of serendipity in research. Merton's strategic serendipity, however, best describes my internal, evolving work on teams. More and more deliberately, I practice a methodological willingness to look and listen for ways to combine my methods with those of the teams because methods are concrete and transferable. I have learned a few other things about strategic serendipity over the years. The serendipity pattern can take a long time to work out—months and years, not moments—as it is often portrayed. It can be situated in intellectual and emotional fears and failures. It rewards paying attention to nagging questions, your own and those of others. My experience is that basic methods are sometimes the most transferable methods (recall that writing instructional manuals was the beginning of TPC). Talk to the statistician early and often. Reward your scaffolding colleagues with authorship if you can (for continued karma). Mixed methods are the way of the future in team science, especially in medicine, which is fundamentally communicative. TPC researchers bring important methods and methodologies to the table, and the team will see your mixed-methods studies as ones they would not have developed without you; in other words, you will have made a strong contribution. Good luck.

Notes

1. Space precludes a full review of the TPC literature on teams as well as the related literature in medical rhetoric (see, for example, Blake Scott's seminal *Risky Rhetoric: AIDS and the Cultural Practices of HIV Testing* and Judy Segal's recent collaborative work with medical teams researching migraine headaches [Young et al.] and sexual dysfunction ["The Sexualization of the Medical"]). The authors and citations here and above are ones that have been particularly influential in my own work.
2. Health and medical research teams often have members from communication science and medical communication, the quantitative and qualitative areas in the field of communication. Medical communication and medical rhetoric have a productive relationship, as evidenced by crossover research panels at the Rhetoric Society of America and the National Communication Association meetings. In this chapter, however, I focus more narrowly on TPC, which has a smaller presence in health and medicine as compared to communication scientists and health communicators.

Works Cited

Armstrong, M. J., et al. "Motivational Interviewing to Improve Weight Loss in Overweight and/or Obese Patients: A Systematic Review and Meta-Analysis of Randomized Clinical Trials." *Obesity Reviews* 12 (2011): 709–23. Print.

Bakeman, Roger, and Vicenc Quera. *Sequential Analysis and Observational Methods for the Behavioral Sciences*. New York: Cambridge UP, 2012. Print.

Barlow, Sarah, et al. "Expert Committee Recommendations Regarding the Prevention, Assessment, and Treatment of Child and Adolescent Overweight and Obesity: Summary Report." *Pediatrics* 120.Supplement 4 (2007): S164–S192. Print.

Barton, Ellen. "Design in Observational Research in Medicine: Toward Disciplined Interdisciplinarity." *Journal of Business and Technical Communication* 15 (2001): 309–32. Print.

Barton, Ellen. "Linguistic Discourse Analysis: How the Language in Texts Works." *What Writing Does and How It Does It: An Introduction to Analysis of Text and Textual Practice*. Ed. Charles Bazerman and Paul Prior. Mahwah, NJ: Lawrence Erlbaum, 2004. 57–82. Print.

Bernhardt, S. A., and G. A. McCulley. "Knowledge Management and Pharmaceutical Development Teams: Using Writing to Guide Science." *IEEE Transactions on Professional Communication* (February–March 2000): 22–34. Print.

Blakeslee, Ann. *Interacting with Audiences: Social Influences on the Production of Scientific Writing*. New York: Routledge, 2000. Print.

Creswell, John. *Research Design: Qualitative, Quantitative, and Mixed Methods Approaches*. 4th ed. Los Angeles: Sage, 2014. Print.

Eggly, Susan, et al. "A Disparity of Words: Racial Differences in Oncologist-Patient Communication about Clinical Trials." *Health Expectations* 15 (2015): 1316–26. Print.

Glaser, Barney G., and Anselm L. Strauss. *The Discovery of Grounded Theory: Strategies for Qualitative Research*. Chicago: Aldine, 1967. Print.

Graham, S. Scott. "Agency and the Rhetoric of Medicine: Biomedical Brain Scans and the Ontology of Fibromyalgia." *Technical Communication Quarterly* 18 (2009): 276–404. Print.

Hsieh, Hsiu-Fang, and Sarah E. Shannon. "Three Approaches to Qualitative Content Analysis." *Qualitative Health Research* 15 (2005): 1277–88. Print.

Idalski-Carcone, Annette, et al. "Exploring Ambivalence in Motivational Interviewing with Obese African American Adolescents and Their Caregivers: A Mixed Methods Analysis." *Patient Education and Counseling* (February 2016): Epub ahead of print. Web. 14 Jan. 2018.

Idalski-Carcone, Annette, et al. "Provider Communication Behaviors That Predict Motivation to Change in Black Adolescents with Obesity." *Journal of Developmental and Behavioral Pediatrics* 34 (2013): 599–608. Print.

Kenny Fountain, T. *Rhetoric in the Flesh: Trained Vision, Technical Expertise, and the Gross Anatomy Lab*. New York: Routledge, 2014. Print.

Lingard, Lorelei, et al. "Negotiating the Politics of Identity in an Interdisciplinary Research Team." *Qualitative Research* 7 (2007): 501–19. Print.

Martin, Tim, et al. "Motivational Interviewing Sequential Code for Observing Process Exchanges (MI-SCOPE) Coder's Manual." Albuquerque: Center on Alcoholism, Substance Abuse, and Addictions (CASAA), University of New Mexico, 2005. Web. 12 Jan. 2018.

Merton, Robert K. *Social Theory and Social Structure*. 1968 enlarged ed. New York: Free Press, 1949. Print.

Merton, Robert K., and Elinor Barber. *The Travels and Adventures of Serendipity: A Study in Sociological Semantics and the Sociology of Science*. Princeton, NJ: Princeton UP, 2004. Print.

Miller, William R., and Gary S. Rose. "Toward a Theory of Motivational Interviewing." *American Psychologist* 64 (2009): 527–37. Print.

Miller, William R., and Stephen Rellnick. *Motivational Interviewing: Helping People Change*. 3rd ed. New York: Guilford, 2012. Print.

Mishler, Elliot G. *The Discourse of Medicine: The Dialectics of Medical Interviewing*. Norwood, NJ: Ablex, 1984. Print.

Moyers, T. B., et al. "Client Language as a Mediator of Motivational Interviewing Efficacy: Where Is the Evidence?" *Alcoholism, Clinical and Experimental Research* 31.Supplement (2007): S40–S47. Print.

Naar-King, Sylvie, PI. "Interventionist Procedures for Adherence to Weight Loss Recommendations in Black Adolescents." NIH/NHLBI (1 U0HL097889–01). Detroit, MI: Wayne State University, 2009–13. Print.

Naar-King, Sylvie, et al. *MY-SCOPE [Minority Youth Adaptation of the Motivational Interviewing Sequential Code for Observing Process Exchanges] Coding Manual.* Division of Behavioral Sciences, Department of Family Medicine and Public Health Sciences, Wayne State University, Detroit, MI, 2013. Print.

Naar-King, Sylvie, and Marianne Suarez. *Motivational Interviewing with Adolescents and Young Adults.* New York: Guildford, 2011. Print.

Ogden, C. L., et al. "Prevalence of Obesity in the United States, 2009–2010." *National Center for Health Statistics (NCHS) Data Brief* 82 (2012): 1–7. Web. 14 Jan. 2018.

Resnicow, Ken, et al. "Results of Go Girls: A Weight Control Program for Overweight African-American Adolescent Females." *Obesity Research* 13 (2005): 1739–48. Print.

Rowntree, Derek. *Statistics without Tears: A Primer for Non-Mathematicians.* New York: Pearson, 2003. Print.

Sauer, Beverly. *The Rhetoric of Risk: Technical Documentation in Hazardous Environments.* New York: Routledge, 2002. Print.

Savoy, M., et al. "Effects of a Weight Management Program on Body Composition and Metabolic Parameters in Overweight Children: A Randomized Controlled Trial." *JAMA (Journal of the American Medical Association)* 297 (2007): 2697–2704. Print.

Scott, J. Blake. *Risky Rhetoric: AIDS and the Cultural Practices of HIV Testing.* Carbondale: Southern Illinois UP, 2003. Print.

Segal, J. Z. "The Sexualization of the Medical." *Journal of Sex Research* 49 (2012): 369–78. Print.

Söderlund, L. L., C. Nordqvist, M. Angbratt, and P. Nilsen. 2009. "Applying Motivational Interviewing to Counselling Overweight and Obese Children." *Health Education Research* 24.3 (2009): 442–49. Print.

Spinuzzi, Clay. *Tracing Genres through Organizations: A Sociocultural Approach to Information Design.* Boston: MIT Press, 2003. Print.

Teston, Christa B. "A Grounded Investigation of Genred Guidelines in Cancer Care Deliberations." *Written Communication* 26 (2009): 320–48. Print.

US Surgeon General. *The Surgeon General's Vision for a Healthy and Fit Nation.* Washington, DC: US Department of Health and Human Services, 2010. Web. 14 Jan. 2018.

Wilson, Alyson G., Laura A. McNamara, and Gregory D. Wilson. "Information Integration for Complex Systems." *Reliability Engineering and System Safety* 92 (2007): 121–30. Print.

Wilson, Greg, and Carl G. Herndl. "Boundary Objects as Rhetorical Exigence: Knowledge Mapping and Interdisciplinary Cooperation at Los Alamos National Laboratory." *Journal of Business and Technical Communication* 21 (2007): 129–54. Print.

Young, William, Joanna Kempner, Elizabeth W. Loder, Jason Roberts, Judy Z. Segal, Miriam Solomon, Roger K. Cady, Laura Janoff, Robert D. Sheeler, Teri Robert, Jennifer Yocum, and Fred D. Sheftell. "Naming Migraine and Those Who Have It." *Headache: The Journal of Head and Face Pain* 52 (2012): 283–91. Print.

15
THE SUNSHINE OF SERENDIPITY
Illuminating Scholarship of Genre (a New Canon) and Generosity (Yes You Can)

Lynn Z. Bloom

Serendipity is the scholar's generous ally. Serendipity can provide a shower of gifts to researchers at any age and any stage, sometimes in a steady stream, at other times in drips and drops, yet to the alert mind the possibilities never dry up. Even better, serendipity is indeed the gift that keeps on giving. Researchers can create a serendipitous climate for their colleagues and students without diminishing their own supply; in fact, the opportunities for serendipitous discoveries may even increase during the process. This chapter will demonstrate the many roles that serendipity, that powerful yet unacknowledged member of a researcher's team, plays in the research process.

Illuminating Scholarship of Genre: A New Canon. "What essays do people read" was my powerful, deceptively simple research question. The answer embedded another question, "Where do people find them?" I did not know that, in combination, the answers would serendipitously enable me to discover an entire literary canon, the essays reprinted in textbooks taught nationwide in America's only required college course, first-year composition, during the period 1946–96. Nor did I realize that in the process of locating these essays I would—surprise—create a 325-volume archive of canonical textbooks as well. This research project, extending during the years 1994–99, combined canon theory and quantitative research, leading to qualitative discoveries in literary analysis, with implications as well for understanding the publishing-industrial complex and its influence on textbook editing and pedagogy.

Serendipitous Generosity: Yes You Can. The conclusion of this chapter identifies issues central to research methodology, a blend of principles and pragmatism that can have serendipitous resonance for student researchers, new or more experienced, in their search for robust questions and the best ways to answer them. The brief case history of an honors student highlights the elements of a process, concurrently rigorous and improvisatory, that enables students to stop taking baby steps and to tap-dance up the walls and across the ceiling.

SERENDIPITY, THE SUSTENANCE OF PREPARED MINDS

Serendipity is universally acknowledged to be the unexpected discovery of a good thing or the faculty someone has for making such happy and surprising discoveries. Sociologists Robert Merton and Elinor Barber distinguish between luck and serendipity, concluding that "luck or chance . . . does not favor people at random; rather, it is prepared minds who are able to benefit from luck," especially when associated with "alertness, flexibility, courage, and assiduity. Only the able and virtuous are lucky in the field of discovery, just as on the battlefield fortune favors only the brave" (171).

Just what constitutes a prepared mind? The prepared mind is a focused mind, but with a latitudinarian perspective that opens wide on the subject rather than tunnel vision that closes it in. The researcher has to know the field in sufficient depth and breadth to understand the significance of what's out there—the available body of knowledge and normative ways of thinking about it. This knowledge should enable the researcher to go beyond the known parameters to recognize what's missing, where the gaps are, what an ideal solution (or solutions) might be. At that point the researcher—perhaps with a lot of help from colleagues, friends, and sophisticated students—must be able to engage in creative speculation on how to remedy the deficit, by either supplying or inventing what is necessary to fill the gaps. This may take many trials; not everything will pan out, and sometimes the researcher will be dead wrong. Serendipity thrives, too, in the resilient temperament that gets up after failure, dusts off its spirit, corrects the mistakes, revises the plan or the interpretation, and never loses sight of the goal. Thereby, unlike the manna of biblical legend, serendipity does not rain down on the populace at random, even though it might shower Isaac Newton under the apple tree at just the right moment to stimulate his further mathematical research.[1] Although the research matrix conducive to serendipity can be carefully prepared, the processes most conducive to serendipity in research can't be rushed. They take time, a highly elastic concept, and, as a rule, research support through a job, external funding, or both. Only after the critical elements are in (harmonious, yes) place can the "aha" moments occur.

In composition studies, for instance, some of the most insightful ways of thinking about the ways our teaching can make a difference are the "aha" moments often captured in the metaphors, slogans, and compelling titles of articles and books. The writing process paradigm, for instance, won the hearts and minds of English teachers and researchers in the 1970s and 1980s and today continues to undergird the teaching of writing, "post-process" concepts notwithstanding. Writing-as-process is epitomized in the serendipitous and inspiring key words of Donald Murray's "Teach Writing as a Process, Not a Product" and *zero draft*; Peter Elbow's *Writing without Teachers,* advocating freewheeling *freewriting*; Mike Rose's embracing concepts of *Lives on the Boundary* and America's *under-prepared* writers; and Nancy Atwell's exhortation for teachers to "come out from behind [the] big desk" (4) to turn their classes into writing workshops instead of skills-and-drills operations. We remember this inspiring terminology regardless of whether we recall either the underlying narratives or the research. Teacher lore continues to be inspired by the images of Murray, Elbow, Rose, and Atwell asking clear, succinct, key questions in simple, direct language that in a chain reaction of serendipitous discoveries has opened up whole worlds, brave and new, for generations.

MY RESEARCH PREPARATION

The short answer to "how long did it take you to do the research" is always "all my life." Indeed, to identify the essay canon, which is a pedagogical canon derived from textbooks, required a mind prepared by long experience as a writing teacher, an essayist, an insatiable reader, and a textbook editor to recognize the rhetorical robustness embedded in stimulating, exemplary models. I couldn't have done the research without the synergetic effect of these experiences, profound and enduring. In fact, if in the mid-1990s I had approached the project from the conventional perspective of a literary critic, I couldn't have done the work at all because except for occasional analyses of the essays of Joan Didion and George Orwell, until very recently there wasn't much critical commentary on essayists.[2]

WHAT'S AN ESSAY, ANYWAY?

Even before I started looking for essays, I had to decide what I was looking for. For over four centuries, ever since Montaigne defined the term, essays have been the louche genre of literature, a motley crew of authors' attempts (i.e., *essais*) to capture their topic in short, nonfiction prose. My long-term love affair with the genre informed my understanding that essays range from portraits, confessions, reportage, commentary, op-ed pieces, reviews, to a variety of types of what Elizabeth Hardwick calls "a condition of unexpressed hyphenation"—"the critical essay, the autobiographical essay, the travel essay, the political" (xiii), and I would add, essays about food, nature, spirituality, sports, science, or medicine for general readers—primarily in print, but with graphic elements. (Twenty-first-century technology makes it possible to consider mixed-media combinations online, incorporating sight and sound as well as print, podcasts, and video essays unavailable two decades earlier.)

WHERE DID I FIND THE ESSAYS TO STUDY? HOW DID I CHOOSE THEM?

My first impulse in answering my own question "what essays do people read" was to start by making a list of the essays by authors I knew and liked best. So there I was on my study floor, a capacious room full of natural light, surrounded by books—annual volumes of *The Best American Essays*; collections of Emerson, Darwin, Twain, Woolf, and my current favorites Scott Russell Sanders and Joan Didion and Annie Dillard. I quickly rejected that avenue, aware that Harold Bloom (to whom I am not and have never been related) created just such a canon of personal favorites, which with great fanfare he labeled *The Western Canon*. Today, two decades later, an internet search for *essay* provides a much wider range to choose among, with 235 million hits;[3] and essays themselves abound on websites of print periodicals (*New Yorker, Atlantic*) as well as hundreds of online publications (*Salon, Onion*) and innumerable blogs (such as *The Essay Daily* and *Brevity's Nonfiction Blog*). But in 1994 the first line of investigation meant looking at the actual materials in print: books and magazines articles—and especially anthologies, Readers intended for freshman composition courses.[4] There in the Readers were the essays, sitting around in plain sight waiting to be discovered, like purloined belles lettres. Indeed Readers, compilations of short nonfiction works and excerpts from longer ones—histories, memoirs, satires, social analyses—were the only places where essays were consistently reprinted. Readers kept essays alive and in front of a nationwide audience of millions of college students year after year after year. So I made a decision to identify and analyze essays that had a robust life in college Readers; this turned out to be critical to my research and to the serendipitous discovery of the canon that would follow. But which Readers?

RESEARCH METHOD

Quantitative Instead of Qualitative

After a frustrating perusal of the Readers lying about my study floor as too narrowly contemporary, I made a hugely significant decision. I would use a *scientific method* to identify the essays rather than depend on personal preference, an unsystematic poll of teachers, or an examination only of the Readers that came immediately to hand. I would *tabulate the results in a database* before analyzing them. If I hadn't had prior experience in applying a quantitative method to literary analysis (my doctoral dissertation "How Literary Biographers Use Their Subjects' Works, a Study of Biographical Method 1865–1962" [U Michigan 1963]), I wouldn't have realized that this type of research could be done in a literary field—where research is usually qualitative—let alone known how to do it: serendipitous preparation.

Time Span

This decision led to several others. (1) The study needed a long enough time span to yield meaningful evidence of what essays people actually read. I originally planned on a twenty-five-year span, but because so many of the Readers published in multiple editions began in the 1960s, I doubled its scope to fifty years. (2) Another incidental and serendipitous consequence of a good decision, this span proved to be an accurate existential *demarcation of post–World War II twentieth-century textbook publication* and its embedded pedagogy. Beginning in 1946, with the vast expansion of American colleges (serving a huge influx of veterans and, later, minorities), and extending to 1996, when the widespread use of the internet meant that teachers could bypass textbooks altogether by compiling their own materials online or printing them on demand, this time span encompassed the heyday of American commercial college textbook publication.[5]

Research Sample

A conservative estimate puts the fifty-year total at 1,750 Readers, reprinting 113,250 essays.[6] (3) A *sample*, collected according to consistent criteria, rigorously applied, was essential to make the data manageable and the results reliable. I decided to use a mathematical/frequency criterion. I would compile the entire tables of contents of all the nonfiction prose published in Readers of four or more editions during this time—another decision that led to serendipitous discoveries because it weighted the sample toward the most widely used Readers[7] (and thus their contents) most likely to be read. Moreover, this method kept the ubiquitous *Norton Reader*, with its potential for reprinting any given essay in all eighteen short and long editions, from allowing a single publication to dictate my research results.

This decision meant that I would sample approximately 20 percent of the total—58 titles in 325 volumes, with 21,000 reprints of 8,000 different essay titles[8] by 4,246 authors. My research team[9] located and compiled these works in a database sortable by author, essay title, textbook title, year of publication, and number of reprints.

The Essay Canon Emerges

As the numbers mounted into the thousands and we began to tally them, certain authors appeared with sufficient frequency and in a variety of Readers to be considered "aha" canonical—that is, in this case, perceived as essential components of a good freshman English course. Canon theory dictates that a given work/author has to have a significant place in the readers' culture so it will be read a great deal, very often during a compressed period of time (the nonce canon) after which it will drop out of sight, or that it will be read perhaps less widely but over a long(er) period of time, the more enduring canon, the "glacially changing core"—as Wendell Harris explains in "Canonicity" (113). A fifty-year period would thus encompass both nonce and core canonical works. Anyone can count the numbers, but it takes the expert eyes of someone who knows the works and authors and understands the conditions of when, where, and why they'll be read to interpret these numbers and their significance.

Authors Trump Individual Works

With few exceptions, it was the authors—from George Orwell to Gloria Steinem—who were canonical rather than individual works by these authors, which with some exceptions ("Once More to the Lake," "A Modest Proposal") were not reprinted with sufficient frequency to constitute a critical mass. I decided, again a professional judgment call, that in a canon any author reprinted 100 or more times over a fifty-year span was sufficiently influential to be considered canonical. From the tabulation emerged the 175 writers who comprised the upper 4 percent of all contributors. Their works constituted 42.1 percent of the Readers' total contents, close enough to 50 percent to warrant the authors' stellar status.

I divided the canonical Superstars into three categories, in descending order of reprint frequency: 18 Supernovas (over 500 reprints per author), 15 Stars (350–499 reprints per author), and 142 Luminaries (100–350 reprints). Among the Supernovas were George Orwell (1,795 reprints,[10] two-thirds of which were "Politics and the English Language" and "Shooting an Elephant"), E. B. White (1,355 reprints of 40 essays, dominated by "Once More to the Lake"), Joan Didion (1,090 reprints distributed among 31 essays), and Martin Luther King Jr., whose "I Have a Dream" and "Letter from Birmingham Jail" comprised most of the 830 reprints. The Stars' 252 titles ranged from Richard Rodriguez ("Aria") to Judy Syfers Brady ("I Want a Wife"). The Luminaries (Norman Cousins, "Who Killed Benny Paret?" to Gloria Steinem, "Why Young Women Are More Conservative") contributed 1,306 titles.

What Else I Needed to Know to Recognize the Essay Canon
Because the essays were reprinted in textbooks, this was a *pedagogical* canon. As a writing teacher I recognized that, first and foremost, to be chosen[11] an essay had to be teachable. That meant it had to be intellectually *accessible* and *engaging* to a wide range of both teachers and students, from novices to sophisticates. It had to be *short* enough (under 5,000 words) to be taught in one or two class periods. It had to *contribute to a dialogue about its subject* within the book and within the classroom, as well as in the larger world. An essay had to be a *good rhetorical model*—of, for instance, an argument or a narrative—although essays usually embed other techniques as well, such as definition, illustration, comparison, and contrast. It had to be *sufficiently well-written to serve as a good model* for style, organization, authorial persona, tone, and more. If the author was well-known, so much the better; the textbook could whet student appetites for future encounters. A serendipitous finding revealed that the essay canon represented the survival not only of the teachable but of major writers whose social conscience had the potential to influence millions of American students year after inspiring year, as the names above indicate. "The Essay Canon" was published in *College English* in 1999, a fitting demarcation of the century.

Who's next? A canon is not static. Scholars need to draw on their foundational understanding of canonicity to predict future developments. As might be expected, the Superstar core authors (Orwell, Didion, Thoreau, Woolf, Swift, and others) continue to be read widely in the early twenty-first century. In contrast, the nonce feminist authors, among them Judy Brady and Gloria Steinem, whose works were wildly popular at the height of the women's movement in the 1970s–80s, are even as I write being supplanted in the twenty-first century by human rights activists, such as Nobel Prize winner Malala Yousafzai, Sherman Alexie, and soon, Matthew Desmond. Other newer representative authors on currently significant topics include environmentalists such as Michael Pollan and Bill McKibben; medical writers with a social conscience, including Atul Gawande and Rebecca Skloot; and food writers M.F.K. Fisher and Adam Gopnik. Contemporary public intellectuals include Leslie Jamison, Jill Lepore, and William Deresiewicz. Of course, striking writers with engaging lives, including Cheryl Strayed (*Wild*), Elizabeth Gilbert (*Eat, Pray, Love*), and Roxanne Gay (*Bad Feminist*), appeal to the same types of youthful seekers of adventure and self-understanding who have been attracted to the canonical Orwell, Swift, and Thoreau for decades. Whether any or all of these authors will remain in the core canon or spin off as the paramount concerns of the moment change remains to be determined.

Nevertheless, researchers, like readers who immerse themselves in literature in the spirit in which Eudora Welty's mother dived into Dickens "in the spirit in which she would have eloped with him" (7), recognize a canonical author when they encounter that writer's exciting ideas, depth of field or human understanding, innovative thinking, memorable style, and other qualities engaging and enduring. Understanding canonicity in what William Butler Yeats called "the deep heart's core," they can identify works as canonical that are worth reading, rereading, and anthologizing no matter what diverse forms twenty-first-century anthologies take, even if they are collages, media mashups, or only "ten best lists" (767 million hits on February 22, 2016) or lists of lists.

IMPLICATIONS FOR STUDENT RESEARCHERS: MENTORS MATTER

As we've seen, many of the qualities that prepare one to make serendipitous discoveries require long-term immersion in the subject that novices simply haven't had time to develop. Yet every researcher and research project has to have a beginning and the sooner the better, certainly as a college undergraduate. Internships, research assistantships, supported research programs such as the University of Connecticut's IDEA Grants,[12] and honors programs that require a research project or a thesis are good places to begin (or to expand on prior knowledge and skills). All of these roles involve a strong working relationship between the student and a mentor—whether a professor or members of a research team—people who can transmit serendipity by osmosis and example.

Indeed, the successful students I've worked with over the years in these roles share many of the qualities that will make them good researchers, susceptible to serendipity from the outset.[13] They're intelligent, of course, but beyond that they love to learn and are willing to spend abundant time and energy to investigate a topic. Creative from the get-go, they inhabit a universe that they configure, reconfigure, and invent. Thus, they learn from the wide world around them in unconventional as well as more orthodox ways. As independent problem solvers, they love to defy conventional wisdom. They are not humble, but they are not always right. Most have the grace to admit this and ultimately, if not immediately, to scrap ideas that don't work and start all over again.[14] The entire process takes time—longer than a semester, it can and does stretch to a lifetime as the student becomes a skilled researcher. But that is the matrix that fosters serendipity, as illustrated Carla Hill's case history that concludes this chapter.

Mentors can help students address these make-or-break fundamental questions and adapt them to their own current and future research projects.

Starting Out: First, Get a Good Idea

What exactly is the question? Am I framing it in the best, most appropriate language? To answer this requires some knowledge of the essential resource materials in the field, as identified by the mentor at the outset to jump-start the project. Teachers can help students make an inventory of the essentials so they understand at the outset what they know and are comfortable with and what they need to find out—in the time available, for the semester's winged chariot never takes time out.

- Is the question new? If it's new only to me, can I present a new angle to consider so I won't just be repeating what the experts already know?
- Will the answer(s) to the question matter? In what ways?
- Is the question generalizable? Is it generative? Will this question/answer/discovery lead to more questions/answers/problems solved/discoveries?
- How much preliminary time and effort is it feasible to devote to this question before deciding whether it's worth pursuing?
- Do I care about the subject with enough passion to see it through?

Start Small but Think Big

These questions are impossible to answer in the abstract for either novice or experienced researchers; if prospective researchers—like people about to get married—waited until they understood all the implications of their work-in-progress before they began, they might never be able to start. But since research has to start somewhere, a student could begin by investigating a small segment of a larger question. Any large question will do, but a mentor's perspective can help in selecting a manageable slice. In literature, for instance, one could investigate whether a particular author (less likely, a single work) is likely to attain—or lose—canonical status, according to criteria the student might invent.

On the Viability of a New Student Research

Choosing a topic to investigate also depends on the student's ability to look at something unfamiliar or something familiar from a new angle and follow up on the questions above with some of these considerations.

- Can I understand the significance or potential of what I'm looking at?
- If so, what additional key reading, research do I need to pursue to make sense of what I want to discover?
- Are there particular theoretical, philosophical, methodological approaches to my topic that could prove especially useful? Any that I should stay away from?
- Do I need to enlist the help of others (teachers, known researchers, other students, essential literature) to help me interpret this matrix of materials? In what ways, and for what purposes?
- Where are the gaps in the information/evidence I have? Is there existing knowledge that will fill these gaps?
- Have I chosen the best (however defined) research method to answer my question?
- What kind of records do I need to keep so I or others can replicate what I've done and so there will be an unequivocal record or trail of the process as well as of the evidence?
- Will this research require funding? If so, how much? From what sources?
- Will this research require IRB (institutional review board) approval to ensure that it meets ethical guidelines?
- Do I have enough time to do the work?

As a reality check, I tell students to imagine the end result and anticipated date of completion (semester's end, graduation date, funding runs out) and calculate the amount of time each step will require to get there. (That is more efficient than starting at the beginning, which can lead to innumerable digressions before reaching the end.) Then double it. Add in a few extra days for unforeseen difficulties. Plot this on a calendar, and then modify your project to fit the time you have to do it, to have others scrutinize it, and to revise it.

SERENDIPITY IN CONTEXT: "HIGH STAKES GAMBLING IN THE MASTER CLASS"

"High Stakes," the case history of an honors student, art history major Carla Hill, demonstrates the happy outcome (despite a marriage that was tempestuous at times) of intense advance preparation, a supportive mentor insistent on quality, a willingness to start over, and the serendipitous consequences. In the middle of her junior year, Carla (whose status as a 4.0 GPA University Scholar gave her liberty to take any course in the university, graduate or undergraduate, with the instructor's consent) arrived at my office with an outrageously immodest proposal. Although she had never studied creative writing, she wanted to write a novella set in Florence, where she was to spend the spring semester learning the language, absorbing the art and history, and exploring the territory. "Sure," I said. "Why not?" No other creative writing professors would agree to work with such a novice, but—though not a gambling woman— I bet that she'd be able to figure it out.

Carla's writing the following fall emphasized the historical context she was accustomed to addressing in her art history papers. Her research in Florence enabled her to document and interpret the ancient art, venerable architecture, and layout of this walking city, as well as German occupation in World War II and the importance of hiding art treasures to prevent Nazi looting. Her art history perspective contributed lush descriptions brimming with sensory details—scenes, costumes, tapestries, textured walls, treats to the eye. But the characters were wooden. Their motivations were ill-defined, their dialogue (in pidgin Italian) stilted, their actions went nowhere, and they didn't connect with each other or the reader. I did what I usually do with novice but persevering writers. I didn't say much; I just asked a few pointed questions during every weekly tutorial session (What's going on? Who is this character? Why does he do that? Say this?). Although I believe that revision is the beating heart of writing, I asked for no revisions at this stage. Carla plugged away and at the semester's end turned in eighty pages of historical matrix from which shards of plot and glimmers of character were emerging. I gave her an incomplete, to be revised after the novella was completed in the spring, and good advice: "Don't write anything for a month. Read short novels about artists, such as *Girl with a Pearl Earring* and *Lady with a Lapdog*. Eat. Rest. Run."

When we met six weeks later, Carla had written seventy-five new pages, with only pentimento fragments of the original remaining. The work had a complicated double plot, action that was clearly motivated, fast-paced, engaging, with dialogue to match. "Just keep going," I said, smiling now, and a month later another hundred pages appeared that required only minimal tweaking, buttressed by a ten-page bibliography. A good deal of my mentoring had been to serve as a catalytic agent as Carla transformed the raw materials into a striking novella. Carla's comments illuminate the serendipitous nature of the process. We worked as colleagues:

> Dr. Bloom deferred to my knowledge of the historical facts . . . I took her advice in regard to my writing. She let my project develop at its own pace . . . She read the writing . . . without leaving it bleeding red pen. I always left her office feeling excited about writing . . . and energized to produce a new batch of writing for the next week . . .
>
> I scrapped the entire first semester's work because it was unreadable . . . My biggest problem the first semester was the romantic notion that the story would reveal itself to me if I just started stringing words together, [but] by the end of a semester of writing I had only created a series of disjointed vignettes that could never be a complete novella . . . The second semester I learned the value of writing nearly every day and working from beginning to end. I also learned that by observing people I knew well I could fashion my own characters . . . I also learned that deadlines . . . are a fantastic motivator. I set word goals for each week and month and kept a running tally of the number of words I had written . . .
>
> Dr. Bloom gave me the best piece of advice of all: to take a break from writing . . . I used the time to complete much-needed historical research, as part of my [earlier] difficulty stemmed from unanswered, but answerable, historical questions that Dr. Bloom had insisted on addressing. I also read some books on writing [which came at the right time, after I'd been struggling as a writer, when it] meant something to me . . . Reading analogous fiction, seeing professional writers do things that I was doing gave me confidence that I could complete my project . . . I wrote a complete summary of my novella in a page and a half and used this as a guide.
>
> Dr. Bloom allowed me to teach myself with the understanding that knowledge accumulated through trial and error is often the most potent and long-lasting. My writing from the first semester, which I regard as unreadable, was not an unmitigated failure but a much better teacher than a series of exercises from a creative writing book. If Dr. Bloom had heavily edited that writing, I know that I would have spent my time polishing something hopelessly tarnished instead of forging ahead with the learning process. Too much advice too soon would have made me doubt my ability to write at all. I would [have] felt attacked, become stubborn, and defended my earliest writing on principle. Instead, I was able to see its flaws myself and correct them. I think Dr. Bloom's style of advising was suited perfectly to me. If I had initiated my thesis with a strong creative writing background, earlier and more thorough critique would have been appropriate. Dr. Bloom understood that I was finding my way in writing as much as I was working towards a completed piece (Bloom and Hill "High Stakes Gambling" 4–10)

The completed piece constituted a nearly publishable work, in this proud adviser's eyes.

At this point I am resisting the urge to shout out "serendipity" at each critical juncture or to punctuate the narrative with hokey "ahas." By this stage of the discussion, readers familiar with the precarious process of nurturing the talents and ego of a novice writer-researcher should be able to recognize serendipity when they encounter it, arising in the climate of high energy and collegial trust that enables the best work to emerge from the ashes of the reject pile. I don't expect students to emulate my work, but they need to trust the coaching and the ethos. Beneath the relaxed surface of these transactions lies tough love, the ramrod core of research rigor enveloped in the shimmering cloak of serendipity.

After Carla graduated, with UConn's highest distinction, we collaborated on "High Stakes Gambling in the Master Class." We had fun.

Notes

1. Eve, though the first lady and thus perforce an innovator, had a different experimental use for this fruit.
2. Say, around 2010, when we could argue that essays finally came of age as a critical genre. Perhaps this was a consequence of the creative nonfiction tracks that began to flourish in MFA programs a decade earlier, leading to a flood of essays and places—often websites—that publish them and sometimes criticism as well. In addition to the online journal *Assay: A Journal of Nonfiction Studies* (first issue Fall 2014), see the host of possibilities identified on *The 25 Best Websites for Literature Lovers* (Flavorwire.com 23 Feb. 2016). Prior to that, Chris Anderson's *Style as Argument* was unusual, if not unique.
3. As of February 20, 2016, a 70 million increase from the year before and thereby a robust indicator of the essay's contemporary vigor.
4. Anthologization is the life preserver for an author's survival, enabling the work of many relatively unknown or mid-list authors to live far longer in textbooks (or other anthologies) than in its original venue. For instance, superstar author Edna St. Vincent Millay, winner of the 1923 Pulitzer Prize for poetry and a media darling because of her "mouth like a valentine" said Floyd Dell (one of her legion of lovers) and sexual escapades, forbade her work to be anthologized. She wanted people to buy her whole books; but the unintended consequence, after each volume's initial frisson of popularity, was that subsequent generations of general readers, who might as students have been introduced to her work in an anthology, didn't know her work at all. She was later eclipsed in student imagination by the robustly anthologized Sylvia Plath, a better poet as well as, because of "the suicide[,] a more romantic figure than the siren" (McClatchy).
5. I could not have foreseen at the time how absolutely right this demarcation of the predictable, commercial mainstream essay-publishing practices would be. It would take another decade for the mainstream to disperse into hundreds of microtributaries. By 2005 an enormous variety of individualized, customizable essay collections and other print-on-demand compilations had become widely available on the internet through mainstream publishers (*The Mercury Reader, The St. Martin's*

Custom Reader), custom printers, universities, and individual teachers. Because these sources are so specialized, variable, and ephemeral, the resulting essay compilations are much harder to categorize and analyze.

6. For an explanation of how I arrived at these figures, see "Essay Canon," 406–9.
7. As with any other type of publication, Readers with small sales are not usually reprinted. Except for books published by Bedford/St. Martin's, which always gives a book a second chance and thus a second edition, about 90 percent of Readers were published during this half century in only one edition. What a waste—of time, effort, permission fees, and especially lost pedagogical opportunities.
8. "Title" is not necessarily synonymous with an individual essay because editors often re-title the works they reprint. To make an accurate tally, I either had to see all the reprints or know the original well enough to recognize the editors' alternative titles. For instance, the editors of five different books supplied five different titles for excerpts from the opening chapter of Thoreau's *Walden*, titled "Economy" in the original. It was important for an accurate tally to recognize whether the different labels for these excerpts—including "The Fitness of a Man's Building His Own House," "How I Built My House," "To Build My House"—refer to the same portions of the same work.
9. How fortunate I was to have had a research assistant and a secretary and the funds to pay them. In the days before internet searches yielded much information, it took enormous effort and resourcefulness to locate the books because libraries don't buy them and many faculty members don't keep them. Even publishers pulp their darlings. Sleuthing, pleading, cajoling, and occasional whining yielded hard copies of about half the total; and my ingenious research assistant Valerie Smith acquired Xeroxes of the remaining tables of contents. Secretary Lori Nelson spent hundreds of hours compiling, checking, and re-checking the database.
10. The reprint numbers given here reflect a multiplier of five, based on a 20 percent sample.
11. This is one reason editors refer to the works as *selections* rather than *essays*; editors *select* them. It's an odd term, however, because no author in any genre, to my knowledge, has ever written a "selection." Real authors write essays, memoirs, manifestos, satires, editorials, reviews, and other forms of nonfiction (on travel, food, medicine . . .). But using "selections" exempts editors from employing more nuanced labels and thus identifying genres.
12. The University of Connecticut, where I conducted my essay canon research, has in recent years established an Office of Undergraduate Research with a variety of programs and mentorships to enhance student research. The University of Rhode Island aims to prepare undergraduates to contribute to their fields—locally, nationally, and worldwide—and in the process to "test out career and/or academic options, build a network of like-minded peers," and become competitive applicants for graduate schools and research funding. With funding of up to $4,000 per well-prepared mind, the IDEA (imagine/develop/engage/apply) Grant program, for example, recruits student researchers, who can apply as individuals or members of small groups, by asking: "Is there a creative endeavor you want to engage in, or an original research project you would like to conduct? Do you have an idea for a product you would like to develop, an entrepreneurial venture you want to launch, or a service initiative you would like to implement? This is your chance to flex your creative muscles, innovate, and explore . . . The UConn IDEA Grant is an opportunity for creativity, innovation, original research, and service. The project should be personally meaningful, relevant, and engaging. The project does not need to be tied to a student's major or minor, but it should be guided by a student's academic goals and future plans."

Successful applicants, the website continues, need to have strong academic records, a passion for their project, and a mentor onboard. Their research has to investigate "creative, innovative, original ideas" through a realistic, well-designed research plan with "a feasible timeline, and a reasonable and justified budget." Moreover, applicants should be able to "articulate the impact of the work proposed—both for them as individual learners and for the field—in compelling, but realistic, terms" and to "design project outcomes (products, outputs, reports, presentations, or performances) that will engage or serve an audience that is large or significant" (UConn Idea Grant Program). Projects funded in 2014–15 ranged from "3D Printed Prosthetic Hand" (mechanical engineering) to "Synthesis of Novel Compounds That Target Death Receptor Trafficking Defects in Colon Cancer Cells" (molecular and cell biology) to "They Called Me Osama," a short film that shares "the stories of Sikh Americans who have been victims of hate crimes" to address various initiatives to combat mistaken identity (business administration and digital media and design).

13. Information in this paragraph is adapted from Bloom and Hill and derived in part from my own family history—as daughter, child, wife, parent, and grandparent of high-achieving honors students and academic researchers. See also Fritz Grobe, "I Don't Believe in Genius," TEDx Talk (11 Jan. 2013, web access 24 Feb. 2016), which explains how he left studying math at Yale University to join Cirque de Soleil and win five gold medals in international juggling competitions.

14. This willingness to scrap one's work, start over, revise and revise and yet again revise separates professional writers (for whom this is the norm) from amateurs, reluctant to change even a word of their sensitive first and only drafts.

Works Cited

Anderson, Chris. *Style as Argument: Contemporary American Nonfiction.* Carbondale: Southern Illinois, UP, 1987. Print.

Atwell, Nancy. *In the Middle: Reading, Writing, and Learning with Adolescents.* Portsmouth, NH: Heinemann, 1987. Print.

Bloom, Lynn Z. "The Essay Canon." *College English* 61.4 (March 1999): 401–30. Print.

Bloom, Lynn Z., and Carla Hill. "High Stakes Gambling in the Master Class." *JAEPL: Journal of the Assembly for Expanded Perspectives on Learning* 12 (2006–7): 1–13. Print.

Elbow, Peter. *Writing without Teachers.* New York: Oxford UP, 1973. Print.

Hardwick, Elizabeth. "Introduction." *Best American Essays 1986.* Ed. Robert Atwan. Boston: Houghton Mifflin, 1986. xiii–xxi. Print.

Harris, Wendell V. "Canonicity." *PMLA* 106.1 (Jan. 1991): 110–21. Print.

McClatchy, J. D. *"Edna St. Vincent Millay: A Life." New York Times Book Review.* 16 Sept. 2001. Web. 19 Feb. 2016.

Merton, Robert K., and Elinor Barber. *The Travels and Adventures of Serendipity: A Study in Sociological Semantics and the Sociology of Science.* Princeton, NJ: Princeton UP, 2004. Print.

Murray, Donald M. "Teach Writing as a Process, Not a Product." 1972. Rpt. *The Essential Don Murray: America's Greatest Writing Teacher.* Ed. Thomas Newkirk and Laura C. Miller. Portsmouth, NH: Boynton-Cook/Heinemann, 2009. 1–5. Web. 20 Feb. 2016.

Rose, Mike. *Lives on the Boundary: The Struggles and Achievements of America's Underprepared.* New York: Free Press, 1989. Print.

UConn IDEA Grant Program. Office of Undergraduate Research. U of Connecticut. Web. 18 Feb. 2015.

Welty, Eudora. *One Writer's Beginnings.* Cambridge, MA: Harvard UP, 1984. Print.

16
SERENDOLOGY, METHODIPITY
Research, Invention, and the Choric Rhetorician

Jennifer Clary-Lemon

Like other stories of research, the narratives that appear here won't be the ones you can read in the methods sections of published research. Yet they are nonetheless fundamental to the way researchers dwell in their subjects. We often think about methods as the dry stuff of research manuals rather than those entryways into what allows us to change and be changed by what it is we study. In this piece on moments of serendipity and methodological choices, I tend to the Heideggerian notion of dwelling as "a mode of thriving—knowing, doing, and making—attuned to what an environment affords" (Rickert *Ambient Rhetoric* 15). I think about Rickert's notion of choric invention, how methods give place to ideas, how to be a choric researcher is to move beyond "static heuristics" of how-to-know (Santos et al.). I hope here to give weight in research methods to "emotions, sensations . . . and traces of psychical and material experience" (Rickert *Ambient Rhetoric* 57), to "memory, networks, technologies, intuitions, and environments" (67) as complementary to, and constitutive of, meaning making. To connect chance and the prepared mind (that is, to embrace serendipity) is also to imagine the *chōra*, both a "place" and a "proper positioning," a "land," a "ground," a boundaried territory (47–49) of each methodological moment—in other words, to allow for the moment of chance, the body as speaker, the affect as leading, the memory as salient, the network as meaningful. In what follows, I identify moments of serendipity in four different methodological frames as *ways of being*, in homage to Rickert's notion of *rhetorical being*, to "construe systemicity not as directly following a method, in some linear fashion, but rather as being immersed in, negotiating, and harnessing complex ecologies," and to work toward his assertion of the *chōra* that "suggests that no clear demarcation separates 'in here' from 'out there'" (46–47). I argue that as we make a scholarly life, we would do well to imagine "the discipline as concerned with more than—and often something entirely other than—reason, rationality, or the symbolic work of language" (Hawhee "Rhetoric's Sensorium" 3).

BEING TOUCHED: ORAL HISTORY AND THE BODY

In "Toward the *Chōra*: Kristeva, Derrida, and Ulmer on Emplaced Invention," Rickert suggests that if we took the idea of *chōra* seriously, "mood, feeling, situation, sensation, accident, environment, memory, and sociopolitical negotiation . . . would then need to be factored into any accounting of beginning" (262). This is the beginning (is this the beginning?), a serendipitous anecdote that has framed over seven years of research, a story of a beginning that "fall[s] out of systematized inventional method" (262) and destabilizes methods as entirely coherent and linear systems. In many ways, our methods are both our middles and beginnings (see Hawhee "Kairotic" 17). As scholars like Ritter have argued and as I have argued elsewhere, our methods are not untroubled and often do not reflect the rational idea of systemicity (see Clary-Lemon "Archival"; Rickert "Toward" 262). We may establish them by accident, by familiarity, or by targeted expertise. Or we may establish methods by dwelling—by matching up what we know with what we make, in this case. In what follows, I take up the notion that inventional work—even methodological work—often begins with the body and its attentions, embracing Hawhee's notion of a *rhetorical sensorium* in which "a host of bodily processes are enlisted in a speaker-audience exchange, most of them sensuous" ("Rhetoric's Sensorium" 3).

In the summer of 2007 I was getting newly acquainted with my surroundings in Winnipeg, Manitoba, where I had moved to take a position at the University of Winnipeg. I was armed with vague plans of research but exhausted from the thought of getting any more than one article out of my dissertation, still learning the geography of the city, still lonely from the shocks of moving 1,800 miles and across an international border to embrace an academic job offer. It was through chance and the symbiotic factors of summer, free time, exhaustion, and loneliness that I entered into a conversation with a colleague about where to find a good massage therapist and thus found myself on a massage table with an affable Newfoundlander working on the tension in my lower back. But as I was to learn about being in my small city, you're never quite as alone as you'd like to think: this massage therapist was chatty, taking dual time to both massage and query, tell me about her life, inquire about my relationship with the colleague who referred me to her, and tell me about how they had connected by being Newfoundlanders and having done volunteer work for the Irish Association of Manitoba. I was slipping into that deep and agreeable place of relaxation during the massage when the therapist began talking about the founding members of the association, their ages and declining health, how their stories of emigration to Canada would soon be unrecoverable, and how she wished there was someone to take down their stories before a generation of Irish septuagenarians who founded the association was gone. It was something about that state of being, of listening sympathetically to her meandering chatter, that reached me enough to open my mouth and say, in a moment that would impact me for the next seven years and into the now, "I can do that."

What I claimed I could do was to begin an oral history project as a volunteer effort for the Irish Association. What it morphed into was a career-altering research agenda that had me later developing expertise in both sociolinguistics and archival research. Yet it is that moment of "I can do that" in which I wish to dwell before moving on, a moment of serendipity in which chance favors the prepared mind, yes, but also the prepared body, the world of being and being touched. As Davis reminds us, " 'Rhetoric' is itself dependent on an always prior rhetoricity, an affect*ability* or persuad*ability* that is due not to any creature's specific genetic makeup but to corporality more generally, to the *exposedness* of corporeal existence. To be affectable, persuadable, is to be always already affected, persuaded, which means: always already *responsive*" (89, emphasis added).

While the double entendre of exposedness does dual work in this particular vignette, I don't mean to use Davis's work flippantly here. Rather, the notion of corporeality is central to considering serendipitous moments of *yes*, moments like the one I have described as being poised as a body-in-place to receive, to respond, to feel, to connect matter and meaning. My body in a low-lit room, the tactile sensation of the laying on of hands, the bone-weariness of the strangeness of a new city, a new place, and directionless scholarly agenda—all of these affective and corporeal details arguably created a perfect and sensuous space to open to something new, to be amenable to the unknown, to say yes to a research experience that would require far more relational work with others than I had ever undertaken (and truthfully, un*reasonable* expertise in a range of research areas than I actually had—in other words, I couldn't really "do that" at the time). I look back on that barely-in-my-mind moment of "I can do that" and what it turned into—navigating human ethics and institutional review board (IRB) processes and oral history best practices; getting approval of the process by working with a community organization; traveling to different parts of the city to meet association members for interviews in their homes, at the club, or in their places of business; writing grants and navigating institutional processes to find equipment and transcribers; researching my way into oral history and discourse analysis—and I am struck always by how "language is not the only medium or material that speaks" (Selzer 8). No matter how much we wish to ascribe developing methodological expertise to a simple narrative of successful learning/knowing, we always begin in a space of human relations and networks, in the touches of everyday life, outside of reason and rationality, in the exposedness of corporeal existence which clearly speaks to researchers that "the body is not so easily left behind" (Consalvo 359).

BEING HEARD: CDA AND NETWORKS OF SCHOLARS

While the sumptuous methodological combination of oral history, serendipitous moment, and the body offered above makes the case, in part, for inventional *chōra* that pays attention to the boundaried territory of the body, here I turn to the network, a kind of choric "proper positioning" in place that allows for methodological movement, growth, and discovery. I link research methodology with Viém Flusser's notion of the network: "We must imagine," he writes, "a net of relations among human beings, an 'intersubjective field of relations.' The threads of this net should be seen as channels through which information flows" (quoted in Gochenour 4). Seeing methodologies as channels connecting other research, ways of knowing, and ways of being fundamentally changes one's own positioning toward research; as Edbauer notes, "we find that networks involve a different kind of habitation in the social field. To say that we are connected is another way of saying that we are never outside the networked interconnection of forces, energies, rhetorics, moods, and experiences" (10). Imagining our research and chosen methodologies as part of a network of intersubjective human relations (rather than a static and systematic hosting of knowledge work) opens them and connects them to other flows of information, complementary ways of knowing, and interrelationships.

In the fall of 2010, three years after the "I can do that" moment described in the prior section, I had published an article in *Discourse and Society* that combined oral history methodology with critical discourse analysis (see Clary-Lemon "We're Not Ethnic"). As a result of that publication, at the end of 2010 I was invited by Thomas Huckin and Jennifer

Andrus to speak at A Conference on North American Critical Discourse Analysis, to be held in May 2011 in Salt Lake City, Utah. Let me add that three years into my "official" scholarly career post-PhD, I had never been invited to speak at anything in my life; having only the knowledge of critical discourse analysis (CDA) that I had cultivated in the three-year period of working with oral history interviews (complemented by sociolinguistic work in my PhD program), I was almost positive that the organizers had made some kind of mistake in contacting me. Although I recognized that by virtue of publication in any field I was to some degree "membershipped" within it—and certainly as an ongoing attendee and participant in College Composition and Communication (CCCC) and other conferences I worked diligently at seeing myself as a member of the field of rhetoric and composition—the way the publication of the *Discourse and Society* piece (with CDA as its methodological framework) was taken up remains both a serendipitous moment and one that bears consideration in terms of examining methodologies in terms of networks of scholars.

The metaphor of the network embraces serendipity; as Hayles suggests, "networks operate through a dialectic of pattern and randomness, rather than one of presence and absence" (285, quoted in Shaviro 10). To think about the ways the scholarship we produce and the methods we use are taken up and moved through information channels in ways we are not privy to is to think about both network and methodology in generative ways. While we follow, observe, and create methodological guidelines to create knowledge that is generalizable, transparent, and systematic, in so doing we often miss or purposefully elide connective *heuresis*—the "finding and creating" (Simonson 312)—that emerge from our methods. Networks remind us that "what matters is not the hardware, but the software; not what the network is actually made of, but only the way it is connected and the information that gets transmitted through it" (Shaviro 11). The network allows for creation of group knowledge through textual transactions (Barker and Kemp 15), and the "spatial qualities of networks" (Swarts 122) mean the information that we publish in one venue will be taken up, channeled, and placed in entirely different ways than we imagine, both with us (as is indicated by bodies-in-place at the Utah conference) and without us (through technological infrastructure).

The aim of the Utah conference was to highlight the "developments and innovations . . . unique to North American uses of CDA," and it included speakers who used CDA as a methodology to examine a range of topics: contemporary discourse on sports broadcasting, newspapers, greeting cards, satirical news, mediated construction of disaster events, classroom and administrative discourse, and legalistic and religious discourse (*A Conference* n.p.). Two items are worth noting here. The first is the measured and purposive approach of the conference organizers to create a scholarly network of researchers who shared a methodological approach separate from contemporary European CDA researchers, emphasizing North American concerns with multiple texts, multiple methods, rhetoric, non-elite discourse, digital media, interdisciplinarity, and pedagogical application. The second item of note is that other than setting up infrastructure and inviting scholars, the possibilities for this network-around-a-methodology were otherwise unknown, uncharted, and relatively uncontrollable. My participation as a "North American CDA" scholar was a serendipitous moment of published scholarship *being heard* by others, taken up and recontextualized in a network of scholars, and later reshaped into a collaboratively produced article for *College Composition and Communication* (see Huckin, Andrus, and Clary-Lemon). Unlike agentive listening (see Ratcliffe), we cannot control the network, how we are heard, how we are taken up—yet both being heard and listening contribute to the sense of what Glenn and Ratcliffe call "interpretive invention" (7), placing networks of scholars, their methods, and chance firmly in their "proper positioning," in the realm of the *chōra*.

BEING PLACED: ARCHIVAL RESEARCH AND AFFECT

Affect and emotion are often seen as contrary to research, reflecting empirical values that contrast emotion and passion with reason (Gross 19; see also Miller x). In what follows, I make the case that methodological choices are shaped by serendipitous moments that connect place to memory and emotion; in other words, that paying attention to affect is also being attuned to what a particular research environment affords in ways that can fundamentally invent, change, or dismantle research stories. Here I focus on *dwelling* in research, with Reynolds's assertion that "writers dwell in ideas to make them their own" (141) at the forefront of my mind. Making, questioning, or inventing methodological choices while considering the roles of memory, place, affect, and the material world positions emotions as generative, as "a performative that produces effects" (Micciche 1), effects that offer a fuller understanding of the messiness of methodology and its rhetorical, choric nature.

This is the story behind a story of methods and methodology. Although part of this story and the argument guiding it appear in the published outcome of an archival research project (see Clary-Lemon "Archival"), embedded in this version is the role of memory, travel, and notions of place that in themselves make up their own archive (Kirsch and Rohan 5). As our methods account for our positionality, so should they acknowledge the "*stickiness* [or . . .] the accumulation of affective value" (Ahmed quoted in Micciche 27, emphasis added) on our research objects and subjects. Here I argue that archival research is perhaps the "stickiest" method of them all, so often requiring travel to virtual or imagined records, to visit geographic locations, to recover family histories, to contend with personal memories, to grapple with death, or to touch material objects (Kirsch and Rohan 3–7).

The visit to Ireland following the publication of the *Discourse and Society* oral history project followed as a "natural" progression of a chosen methodological triangulation of data using the discourse-historical approach after analyzing historical data in Canadian newspapers (see Clary-Lemon "Irish Diaspora"). Yet a sentence such as that masks stickiness that leads to inventive moments; specifically, it masks the fact that as a researcher I was juggling a particular affective state, social network, and ambient environment (Rickert *Ambient Rhetoric* 61). As Kirsch and Rohan suggest, traveling to on-site locations of archival subjects represents in itself "another important, undertheorized research method" (5). Travel, visitation, dwelling *do* something to us and to our research. In this case, travel to Ireland was not only a simple research trip. Ireland is not just another place. It is perhaps the most storied, sticky, *invented* place for most westerners; the enchanted motherland Eire; the magical, green, enchanted land of the fay, blarney, and *craic*. Testaments to Ireland, "because it feels like home & smells like a bit of heaven on earth" (Walsh), saturate contemporary media, leaving non-Irish visitors with an imprint of the land that accretes far before they ever step foot on it. Emotional and visceral response to place—that is, how we *feel* about it—is built up over time and often, as Reynolds contends, stems from "hearsay, family stories, 'common knowledge' or media images" (145).

In my case, the affect of Ireland—specifically, Northern Ireland—and its habitus linked inhabiting, dwelling, with research. While I don't claim Irish heritage, my partner's grandfather, Moore Lemon (the family patriarch), was born in Belfast. Although my archival gathering of materials was done first in Dublin, I can't divorce the messiness of emotion (that is, the way I felt about the place) from the fact that my partner and small child accompanied me to Belfast in the first half of the research trip, as a kind of family pilgrimage—the first of any of Moore's grandchildren and great-grandchildren—to visit the house Moore grew up in. My interest in place, in the archive of the Public Records Office of Northern Ireland (PRONI), was influenced as much by an archival research project as it was by emotion, genealogy, and an imagined nation. In fact, it was taking note of how place shaped methods that resulted in a publication about methods themselves that far outweighed the original scope of the project, which reflected an analysis of discursive materials (see Clary-Lemon "Analyzing Discourses"). That project ("Archival") became the far more revealing project of the two.

My original methodological intention was to focus on the more easily accessible archives, located in Dublin. But it was during travel to Belfast for my family, taking the train across the countryside, crossing an unclear border between the Republic and the United Kingdom, and driving through Shankill and Falls Roads (Protestant-only and Catholic-only neighborhoods in Belfast) when my research became present, when PRONI became an invaluable part of both the project and methodological inquiry. I'm not Catholic and I'm not Protestant, though I was not without awareness in visiting Moore's Ravenhill Road flat that Protestant sentiment runs in my daughter's blood and that my mother was raised Catholic. It was not without awareness that such connection, by virtue of family residue and the powerful ways in which decades of eavesdropping on conversations about extended family connections with Belfast, brought the Irish Troubles, the subject of my research, much closer—uncomfortably so. I was reading about history that became affectively more proximate, to borrow from Solberg, by virtue of the stickiness of emotion: a long-held interest in my subject, deep sorrow for lives lost in thankless and deep-wounding sectarianism, gratitude to connect parts of my future and my past, shame at connecting my Catholic family's past with my partner's Protestant one, fear for my safety over the Union Flag Disputes, desire to know more, feel more.

As Derrida suggests, the *arkhe* is where things begin (9) and "archives take place" (10). But an approach to the archives, the visit, the travel, our dwelling in the places we dwell, *place us* as we do research. It is part "getting in touch" (Sutherland 29) with our research projects, part of "want[ing] more than just knowledge of the facts" (Wider 69) that place gives us. The archive itself is a place where we struggle with the ways we can construct completeness out of imperfect records, augmenting their "ordinariness" (Osborne; see also Steedman) with our own sense of history, memory, and emotion. Yet archives are also re-made as we dwell in them and around them (Rickert *Ambient Rhetoric* xiii). Visiting Belfast beyond just the archives—walking past St. George's Market, taking pictures of my daughter climbing the Bigfish statue at Donegall Quay, exploring the Titanic Quarter—was a planned chance, done for reasons outside of my immediate scholarly search for information. But such a chance and its connection to moments of insight suggests that archives-as-places are both a place where things begin and a "beginning-in-the middle" (Hawhee "Kairotic" 17) that circulate with us, within us, and around us as we connect knowing and being.

BEING KNOWN: CASE STUDIES AND RELATIONSHIPS

Thus far, I've touched on choric moments that suggest within every chosen method-methodology there is a struck balance between what has come before as a systematic approach to knowledge dependent on a particular kind of repetition and moments of intuition, interaction with materials and people, feeling, connection, and emotion that take methodological processes, at least in part, out of the realm of the *topos* and into the *chōra*. If we consider our methodological processes as fundamentally rhetorical, our material environment and the affective world in which we dwell become, as Rickert suggests, not only complementary to our ways of thinking but integral (*Ambient Rhetoric* xiii).

Let me say that given my fifteen-odd years as a member of our field, I don't consider myself "known," a big name that excites graduate students into sparkle pony moments. I've written before about the role of mentoring in my life and how central it has been to acknowledging my felt place—that is, where I belong in relation to others working in the field, sharing a discipline, being curious about what I am curious about (see Clary-Lemon and Roen). Yet it wasn't until I sat down to write this piece that I looked back on the 2008 publication with Duane Roen and realized that I invoked, then as now, moments of "being in the right place at the right time," or serendipity, and how it has shaped my place in the field (181). Since I wrote that piece with Duane in 2006, the role of peer mentoring in my life has also changed—my graduate student "peers" are now colleagues at universities around the nation, most of them tenured professors, most of them becoming the next "big names" in the field. But I know them as friends; I've gone to their weddings or celebrated the births of their children or counseled them through heartache or acted as a reader of their tenure files. I've met new folks at annual conventions who still dazzle me because of those very same relationships. Every story of collaborative authorship I've ever had begins with those relationships. This story of writing my way into a case study—how the method of a case may be framed by serendipitous "interactions, relationships, roles, social identities" (Simonson 314)—more than does the same.

In this story, I place research temporally and relationally; that is, this is not the story of a quick analysis of a phenomenon of interest. Instead, it is a time-trace of a project tied into my location, back into the moment of "I can do that," into my first tenure-track job, into my movement across an international border, into my making sense of my new-where. In 2009, as a result of trying to do this "making sense" work, I published a piece in which I tried to classify Canadian writing research. In doing so, I read Canadian scholarship widely, reconnected with a graduate school professor and mentor Roger Graves, and read work that placed my own institution in a historical and cultural context. At the same time, I was on departmental committees wondering about the appropriateness of graduate studies for our small department and was in the middle of writing a collaborative article with Pete Vandenberg about the place of the MA in writing studies. As a result, I happened to be in the "right place at the right time" when Louise Wetherbee Phelps attended a meeting of the MA consortium at CCCC that I also attended, as Pete and I were working on that publication and as Louise was working on the Visibility Project with John Ackerman.

As a result of those converging projects and relationships, I invited Louise to be a Fulbright Specialist at the University of Winnipeg for the purpose of institutional review. We successfully applied for a Fulbright grant, and she spent six weeks in Winnipeg in a curricular consultation. As a result, I not only got to know Louise more closely but also grew my own curiosity through the consultative process. This resulted in conference presentations with Louise and departmental colleagues about the Fulbright project, as well as the inklings of a larger project that drew on my own positioning as a dual-national scholar working in a unique Canadian department of writing and rhetoric. As my relationship with Louise grew through reading her work, having long conversations, and presenting at conferences, my interest in seeing Winnipeg as a case study also grew. In addition, our interests converged around cross-border interconnections of the discipline. At the 2013 CCCC, Louise introduced me to two other scholars interested in this work, Andrea Williams (at the University of Toronto) and Derek Mueller (Eastern Michigan University). Together, we conceived of a collaborative conference panel that examined cross-border interdependencies from a range of different methodological perspectives, which we presented together at the 2014 Writing Research across Borders conference. My preliminary work for that presentation traced contemporary updates on the University of Winnipeg and developed into a methodological "close look" at the case of the department as it has moved from a position of both particular and ordinary on the Canadian landscape to one that is now of interest in offering insight for redrawing generalizations about writing studies in Canada. In the audience at our presentation, among a small group of others (during the last time slot on the last day), were Roger Graves and Andrea Lunsford. At the end of the day, we had an invitation to submit our panel as a book to a scholarly press and have since confirmed Andrea's commitment to act as a respondent on that manuscript.

In writing this happy story of scholarship, I'm drawn back not only into moments of serendipity but into moments that make the case for method—in this instance, case study—for being seen in relationship to time and to people. I would not have been able to write a case study, been draw to this method, if not for my national location, if not for my interest in understanding a new-where, if not for seven years of trying to understand the institution in which I worked, if not for cultivating old relationships and drawing on new ones. My interest in the method stemmed out of my experience, out of paying attention to my location in new and different ways, in recognizing that my interest in the project was "both situated and dispersed" (Simonson 311) by place making in Winnipeg; the required travel to conferences to meet with both Canadian and American colleagues; the interactions I've had with mentoring networks regionally, nationally, and internationally. I draw upon the concept of *being known* here not only because of its gesture to ontology but also because, in reflecting back on serendipitous moments of mentoring in graduate school, being known is what strikes me as the critical temporal difference between then and now, even as the thematic of serendipity has remained the same.

BEGINNING AGAIN

In drawing distinctions between choric invention and the *topoi*, Rickert suggests that the *chōra* is "fundamentally indeterminate, that [it] mirrors an ambiguity concerning ideas of beginning and creation, genesis . . . And, in order to begin—in order to go forward—the conversation must first go back, which raises the issue of memory" ("Towards" 256–57). While I don't claim here that the serendipity of our methods echoes or twins choric inventional or ambient approaches to invention, I do wish to move methodological considerations from their oft-relegated place as either strict algorithmic rules or more flexible heuristic guidelines. Instead, I suggest that our methods—rhetorical choices, to be sure—often go back, into our memories, into our movement through environments, into our senses, into our relationships with people and things; in other words, that methods, too, "emerg[e] from the ambient environs, the in which and from which that give [them their] bearings and thrust [them] forward" (*Ambient Rhetoric* 254). Writing this piece—and its narrative curriculum vitae of mine that has emerged from it—has itself been an act of memory and a recall of the lifespan of research projects that demonstrate both an inseparability from one another and a continuation into the present.

What a reader should take from serendipitous methodology (serendology? methodipity?) is to recognize the ways our methodological choices bleed into one another, inform our next choice, get mixed in with our bodies and networks and places and people. As I wrote this piece, it was impossible to pinpoint a beginning of a method from how I inhabited the spaces I was in at the time I was making methodological choices. As I wrote on, too, it became clear that I couldn't recognize when one method ended and another began—should this be read as triangulation, a marker of "good research," or an ecology of methods, which is considerably more dangerous (and in some ways lucrative)? When we research, we know, we do, and we make. We tangle our bodies up with things; we mark knowing with intangible conversations and feelings about place; we listen differently and attune ourselves to people, objects, media, and geographies. Our methods are often guided by rules that mark the "beginnings" of our research, but as Rickert suggests, "the *chōra* helps us understand that rhetorical concepts such as 'beginning,' 'invention,' and 'place' are not in fact clear" (*Ambient Rhetoric* 47). As we open ourselves to serendipitous moments in research, positioning ourselves chorically means a different attunement to the possibilities available to us and allows us to think about method-methodology in richer, more human ways.

Works Cited

A Conference on North American Critical Discourse Analysis. Conference Program. Salt Lake City: University of Utah, 2011. Print.

Barker, Thomas, and Fred Kemp. "Network Theory: A Postmodern Pedagogy for the Writing Classroom." *Computers and Community: Teaching Composition in the Twenty-First Century.* Ed. Carolyn Handa. Portsmouth, NH: Boynton Cook, 1990. 1–27. Print.

Clary-Lemon, Jennifer. "Analyzing Discourses of Political Elites: Discourse of Irish Emigration in the 1970s." *Discourse and Society* 25.5 (2014): 619–39. Print.

Clary-Lemon, Jennifer. "Archival Research Processes: A Case for Material Methods." *Rhetoric Review* 33.4 (2014): 381–402. Print.

Clary-Lemon, Jennifer. "Irish Diaspora and National Identity: Circulations of Public and Private Discourse in a Discourse-Historical Analysis of the *Toronto Globe and Mail.*" *ISLS Readings in Language Studies*, vol. 3: *Language and Identity.* Ed. Paul Chamness Miller, John L. Watzke, and Miguel Mantero. Grandville, MI: International Society for Language Studies, 2012. 21–40. Print.

Clary-Lemon, Jennifer. "Shifting Tradition: Writing Research in Canada." *American Review of Canadian Studies* 39.2 (June 2009): 94–111. Print.

Clary-Lemon, Jennifer. "'We're Not Ethnic, We're Irish!' Oral Histories and the Discursive Construction of Immigrant Identity." *Discourse and Society* 21.1 (2010): 5–25. Print.

Clary-Lemon, Jennifer, and Duane Roen. "Webs of Mentoring in Graduate School." *Stories of Mentoring: Theory and Praxis.* Ed. Michelle Eble and Lynèe Gaillet. Anderson, SC: Parlor Press, Lauer Series, 2008. 178–92. Print.

Consalvo, Mia. "Gender and New Media." *The Sage Handbook of Gender and Communication.* Ed. Bonnie J. Dow and Julia T. Wood. Thousand Oaks, CA: Sage, 2006. 355–70. Print.

Davis, Diane. "Creaturely Rhetorics." *Philosophy and Rhetoric* 44.1 (2011): 88–94. Print.

Derrida, Jacques. "Archive Fever: A Freudian Impression." *Diacritics* 25.2 (1995): 9–63. Print.

Edbauer, Jenny. "Unframing Models of Public Distribution: From Rhetorical Situation to Rhetorical Ecologies." *Rhetoric Society Quarterly* 35.4 (Fall 2005): 5–24. Print.

Glenn, Cheryl, and Krista Ratcliffe, eds. *Silence and Listening as Rhetorical Arts.* Carbondale: Southern Illinois UP, 2011. Print.

Gochenour, Philip H. "Nodalism." *DHQ: Digital Humanities Quarterly* 5.3 (2011). Web. 2 Feb. 2015.

Gross, Daniel. *The Secret History of Emotion: From Aristotle's Rhetoric to Modern Brain Science.* Chicago: U of Chicago P, 2007. Print.

Hawhee, Debra. "Kairotic Encounters." *Perspectives on Rhetorical Invention.* Ed. Janet M. Atwill and Janice M. Lauer. Knoxville: U of Tennessee P, 2002. 16–35. Print.

Hawhee, Debra. "Rhetoric's Sensorium." *Quarterly Journal of Speech* 101.1 (Feb. 2015): 2–17. Print.

Hayles, Katherine. *How We Became Posthuman: Virtual Bodies in Cybernetics, Literature, and Informatics.* Chicago: U of Chicago P, 1999. Print.

Huckin, Thomas, Jennifer Andrus, and Jennifer Clary-Lemon. "Critical Discourse Analysis and Rhetoric and Composition." *College Composition and Communication* 64.1 (Sept. 2012): 107–29. Print.

Kirsch, Gesa E., and Liz Rohan. "The Role of Serendipity, Family Connections, and Cultural Memory in Historical Research." *Beyond the Archives: Research as a Lived Process.* Ed. Gesa E. Kirsch and Liz Rohan. Carbondale: Southern Illinois UP, 2008. 1–9. Print.

Micciche, Laura. *Doing Emotion: Rhetoric, Writing, Teaching.* Portsmouth, NH: Boynton/Cook Heinemann, 2007. Print.

Miller, Richard E. "Foreward." *Doing Emotion: Rhetoric, Writing, Teaching.* Portsmouth, NH: Boynton/Cook Heinemann, 2007. ix–xiv. Print.

Osborne, Tom. "The Ordinariness of the Archive." *History of the Human Sciences* 12.2 (1999): 51–64. Print.

Phelps, Louise, and John M. Ackerman. "Making the Case for Disciplinarity in Rhetoric, Composition, and Writing Studies: The Visibility Project." *College Composition and Communication* 62.1 (Sept. 2010): 180–215. Print.

Ratcliffe, Krista. *Rhetorical Listening: Identification, Gender, Whiteness.* Carbondale: Southern Illinois UP, 2006. Print.

Reynolds, Nedra. *Geographies of Writing: Inhabiting Places and Encountering Difference.* Carbondale: Southern Illinois UP, 2004. Print.

Rickert, Thomas. *Ambient Rhetoric: The Attunements of Rhetorical Being.* Pittsburgh: U of Pittsburgh P, 2013. Print.

Rickert, Thomas. "Toward the *Chōra*: Kristeva, Derrida, and Ulmer on Emplaced Invention." *Philosophy and Rhetoric* 40.3 (2007): 251–73. Print.

Ritter, Kelly. "Archival Research in Composition Studies: Re-Imagining the Historian's Role." *Rhetoric Review* 31.4 (2012): 461–78. Print.

Santos, Marc C., et al. "Our Electrate Stories: Explicating Ulmer's Mystory Genre." *Kairos* 18.2 (2014). Web. 15 Jan. 2018.

Selzer, Jack. "Habeas Corpus: An Introduction." *Rhetorical Bodies*. Ed. Jack Selzer and Sharon Crowley. Madison: U of Wisconsin P, 1999. 3–15. Print.

Shaviro, Steven. *Connected, or, What It Means to Live in the Network Society*. Minneapolis: U of Minnesota P, 2003. Print.

Simonson, Peter. "Re-Inventing Invention, Again." *Rhetoric Society Quarterly* 44.4 (2014): 299–322. Print.

Solberg, Janine. "Googling the Archive: Digital Tools and the Practice of History." *Advances in the History of Rhetoric* 15.1 (2012): 53–76. Print.

Steedman, Carolyn. *Dust: The Archive and Cultural History*. New Brunswick, NJ: Rutgers UP, 2002. Print.

Sutherland, Christine Mason. "Getting to Know Them: Concerning Research into Four Early Women Writers." *Beyond the Archives: Research as a Lived Process*. Ed. Gesa E. Kirsch and Liz Rohan. Carbondale: Southern Illinois UP, 2008. 28–36. Print.

Swarts, Jason. "Network." *Keywords in Writing Studies*. Ed. Peter Vandenberg and Paul Heilker. Logan: Utah State UP, 2015. 120–24. Print.

Vandenberg, Peter, and Jennifer Clary-Lemon. "Advancing by Degree: Placing the MA in Writing Studies." *College Composition and Communication* 62.2 (Dec. 2010): 257–82. Print.

Walsh, Jane. "'I Love Ireland Because': Americans Explain Why Ireland Is Magic." 19 Dec. 2014. Web. 6 March 2015.

Wider, Kathleen. "In a Treeless Landscape: A Research Narrative." *Beyond the Archives: Research as a Lived Process*. Ed. Gesa E. Kirsch and Liz Rohan. Carbondale: Southern Illinois UP, 2008. 66–72. Print.

PART V

Trusting the Process

17

THE ETHICS OF SERENDIPITY
Rare Events and a Need to Act

Bill Endres

Before earning tenure, I never planned to digitize an early medieval manuscript. My plan had been to do the necessary research to turn my dissertation into a book. However, this required that I visit Lichfield Cathedral, England, and examine the St. Chad Gospels, an eighth-century illuminated manuscript for which a facsimile had never been produced. As a visual rhetorician, I research manuscripts made from roughly 600–850 CE in the British Isles, a period known as Insular. Insular manuscripts present a rich 250-year tradition of portraying knowledge with images and words, a tradition whose practices are little understood.

At best, my likelihood of digitizing an Insular manuscript was slim, let alone the St. Chad Gospels, one of the oldest and most important illuminated manuscripts in England. Six years prior to my arrival in Lichfield, scholars had failed to make images of the complete St. Chad Gospels available online, able only to produce a sampling of folios in a British Library "Turning the Pages" version.[1] The use of photographs for major manuscripts is generally restricted and guarded as a potential source of revenue, especially for a cathedral such as Lichfield, located in a small city away from major tourist routes and their ensuing revenue streams—all but forgotten in the English Midlands. However, I remained optimistic. Through my research I hoped to establish a relationship with the cathedral, secure an NEH startup grant, and work toward the digitization—a six- to eight-year process. But oh, serendipity . . .

In a series of serendipitous events, perhaps the most unlikely occurred three months prior to my arrival in Lichfield. Four miles from the cathedral, a metal-detector enthusiast discovered the largest Anglo-Saxon hoard of silver, gold, and other treasures ever found.[2] The hoard's wealth reminded the world of Lichfield's past prominence as an ecclesiastical center in the kingdom of Mercia that once controlled London. Therefore, when I arrived, favorable events were in motion. These events would later include an opportunity generated by an untimely death. Serendipitous events are as likely to emerge from tragedy as from happy accidents.

But serendipity can also generate adversity and difficulty. In spite of its grace, the research serendipity engenders must live in the academic "world of men." I choose the word "men" to emphasize the structures of academe that feminists scholars have justifiably critiqued: a world of rigid hierarchies and structures of power, of exclusions and limited reflexivity about its own practices.[3] For scholars, serendipitous events can open possibilities that demand diverting from a carefully thought-out research agenda, that can pull a scholar out of his or her comfort zone (requiring collaborations and scholarship in complimentary fields), and that sometimes place a scholar's tenure or promotion at risk.

Therefore, I write this narrative accompanied by a question: Do scholars have an ethical responsibility to pursue scholarship made possible by serendipity? For certain types of scholarship, having the necessary alignment of events can be rare and fleeting. An ignored or missed opportunity can have profound implications for what can and cannot be known.

THE SERENDIPITY OF SURVIVAL

In and of itself, the survival of a 1,300-year-old manuscript is a celebration of serendipity. Invasions, natural disasters, wars, and thieveries make the likelihood of a manuscript's survival slim. The early medieval period was an unstable and destructive time; however, the modern world has been equally unstable and destructive, evidenced by two world wars, economic depressions, and the current targeted destruction of cultural heritage in the Middle East. But even with persistent threats, good fortune can prevail.

The St. Chad Gospels had its share of good fortune and bad. While it survives, the manuscript suffered losses. This is typical of early medieval manuscripts: rarely have they survived intact. In the first half of the ninth century, bad fortune first struck. Viking or Welsh raiders likely stole the St. Chad Gospels, targeting the manuscript for its cover, adorned with precious metals and jewels (James 52). For Insular deluxe gospel books, while such riches provide a stunning and glorious celebration of faith, they motivated thieves who discarded a manuscript once they pried off the cover (Brown 64–65). Such a fate likewise befell the ninth-century Book of Kells. The Annals of Ulster reports that thieves stole this great gospel book and discarded it after removing its cover, with the bulk of the manuscript retrieved when found three months later, covered in sod (Bambury and Beechinor U1007.11). For the St. Chad Gospels, theft explains its missing preliminary materials, plausibly lost when the cover was pried off. Also, theft explains the reason for the first surviving page being the opening of Matthew's Gospel—the page worn in such a manner as to suggest that it served as the manuscript's front cover for a substantial time (Brown 64).

On the good side of fortune, someone picked up the St. Chad Gospels and carried it off to Wales. From its time in Wales, the St. Chad Gospels contains marginalia written in Old Welsh, the earliest surviving examples of Old Welsh writing. One entry reports the serendipitous events that led to the manuscript's survival: a Welshman named Gelhi traded his best horse for the manuscript and presented it, for the good of his soul, to the church of St. Telio in Llandeilo Fawr, Wales (Alexander 49; Jenkins and Owen 48–51). Such a transaction provides further evidence of thievery: a manuscript such as the St. Chad Gospels is worth much more than a horse—the calfskin for its pages would have required 100–120 cattle (Powell 261). However, for a stolen manuscript missing its jeweled cover, trading it for a horse would represent a good profit. Luckily for the St. Chad Gospels, such a trade was made.

While in Wales, the St. Chad Gospels likely escaped further tragedies, but no evidence remains to reveal them. The other Old Welsh marginalia report land transactions and the settlement of disputes, but they are silent about raids, wars, and natural disasters. In the tenth century the St. Chad Gospels mysteriously reappears in Lichfield, evidenced by the signature of Wynsige (a tenth-century bishop of Lichfield) on the first page of Matthew's Gospel, perhaps declaring ownership. Some scholars speculate that relations between Wales and Mercia improved, perhaps leading to the manuscript's return, or that it returned during a Mercian raid (Savage 10–12).

For the next 600 years, little is known about the challenges the St. Chad Gospels faced—until the seventeenth-century English Civil War. During this war, good and bad fortune befell the manuscript. On the good side, Precentor Higgins recognized the threat of Oliver Cromwell's approaching forces and secreted away one volume, delivering it to Lady Somerset in Oxford for safekeeping (Savage 13–14). On the bad side, the second volume was lost—although it might have been lost slightly earlier, during the sixteenth-century Reformation. Consequently, today's extant pages include the Gospels of Matthew, Mark, and part of Luke, ending in the middle of Luke 3:9.

While the entire St. Chad Gospels is not extant, its survival is a remarkable feat: stolen, taken to Wales, traded for a horse, donated to a Welsh church, returned to Lichfield, and secreted away during the

English Civil War. The manuscript has suffered water damage but, fortunately, no fire damage. Regrettably, details of all serendipitous events leading to the St. Chad Gospels' survival are beyond knowing. However, the known details speak volumes about the impact of good fortune on the survival of an Insular gospel book, serendipitous events that provide scholars with a rare glimpse into the early medieval world.

WHY RHETORICIANS AND SCHOLARS OF COMPOSITION SHOULD CARE ABOUT THE ST. CHAD GOSPELS

Insular manuscripts such as the St. Chad Gospels return scholars to the origins of today's textual practice. Such practices include space between words and punctuation, conventions attributable to the Irish. While Thomas Cahill's *How the Irish Saved Civilization: The Untold Story of Ireland's Heroic Role from the Fall of Rome to the Rise of Medieval Europe* overstates the claim, much truth exists regarding Ireland's irreplaceable role in preserving, inventing, and rebuilding culture in Europe. But a noteworthy aspect of these events is Ireland's wholesale and relatively quick transition from an oral Celtic culture to a literate Christian one. This wholesale conversion began in the fifth century and concluded in the sixth century, after the fall of Rome. Rome had never conquered Ireland; therefore, the Irish had maintained their long-standing oral tradition until their Christian conversion. Inventions such as space between words and punctuation were designed to ease the difficulty of reading and apprehending Latin, a foreign tongue to the Irish, one they generally learned through the written word.

Yet Insular manuscripts do far more than return scholars to the origins of today's textual practices: they also return scholars to an originating spark for *mise en page*. This unique spark was fueled by Irish scribes and artists viewing written text and imagery as one and the same: visual expression. For these scribes and artists, neither word nor image had hierarchical dominance over the other. Therefore, the Irish developed conventions to facilitate the sharing of a page's space between text and imagery, a sharing eminent art historian Françoise Henry describes as a "constant accompaniment," imagery mixing freely with the script (163). Such conventions include what became known to later Irish scribes as *cor fa carsan* (turn-in-the-path) or *ceann fa eitil* (head-under-wing). These conventions allow scribes to systematically displace text and still make its sequential order discoverable by readers, all the while accomplishing a larger goal: generating space for imagery so it can portray or interact with text to produce meaning.

By the ninth-century making of the Book of Kells, Insular scribes displaced text so frequently that it appears random. This encouraged Henry to view the practice as "a sort of game, a feat of ingenuity" (157). However, the monastic tradition neither tolerated nor celebrated individual ingenuity—any hint of such personal expression would suggest pride, which as one of the deadly sins was feared and guarded against. Instead, scribes employed turn-in-the-path for reasons other than a game or show of virtuosity. Understanding the St. Chad Gospels and its uses of this technique provides a means for apprehending the meaningful displacement of text in the later Book of Kells and regaining a lost practice of *mise en page* for modern composers.

The Book of Kells has lingered at the edges of rhetoric and composition scholarship. Jay David Bolter briefly references this great gospel book, using its *chi-rho* page as an example of how "pictorial and verbal spaces interpenetrate" (65); that is, letters functioning simultaneously as text and picture (a *chi-rho* page ornamentally presents the first three letters of the Greek word for Christ: *chi*, *rho*, and *ito* [*xpi*]). Anne Wysocki likewise briefly mentions this page, quoting noted medievalist Mary Carruthers who describes Kells's *chi-rho* as a visual model for meditative reading, encouraging thought and structuring memory ("Seeing the Screen" 601). However, these inclusions say little about the concepts of design and supportive conventions that allow such meditative readings and structuring of memory to emerge. Instead, they merely point to a rich 250-year tradition of Insular practices that need to be explored.

During what scholars have termed a "turn" to multi-modal composing, Insular manuscripts provide a tradition of practices to borrow and learn from. Emerging from 500 years dominated by print, present-day composers must invent structures and practices to organize visual expression and work out complications for combining text and imagery. This lack of structures and practices has been described by Wysocki as "unavailable designs," a deficit of resources faced by composers in shaping the interplay of words and images and stretching beyond current limitations conditioned by print (away 56–59). Insular manuscripts provide one way to begin to fill this void, supplying scholars of rhetoric and composition with a lengthy and rich tradition of lost practices.

However, the benefits of Insular manuscripts go well beyond Insular solutions for organizing visual expression. Insular manuscripts provide a contrasting and potentially complementary tradition from which to view contemporary multi-modal composing. In the case of the Insular, its multi-modal practices emerged from a lengthy oral tradition, whereas current digital practices emerged from a tradition profoundly invested in the written word. These different historical circumstances lend themselves to differing views about various modes and available designs for visual expression. As Damian Baca reminds scholars, studying alternative traditions "calls for new ways to think about communicative practices" (5).

A RELATIONSHIP FORGED BY A HARDWOOD CHAIR

The library at Lichfield Cathedral is one of my favorite places to do research. Built in the first half of the thirteenth century, it is located immediately above the Chapter House, the space that likely served as the early treasury. Before the English Civil War, the library occupied a separate building. However, Cromwell's forces gutted it. When the Duchess of Somerset returned the St. Chad Gospels, she donated 1,000 books from her husband's collection to help rebuild the library. Her donation included many significant manuscripts and incunabula, including an impressively decorated *Canterbury Tales*.

The library is small, as are most of the peripheral spaces in the cathedral, whether the servers' vestry or St. Michael's Chapel. Lighting is poor and desk space is limited. A few hardwood chairs discourage sitting. However, the library is a spectacular space: thirteenth-century encaustic tile floor, stained glass windows, pointed arches, and a vaulted gothic ceiling. The beauty of the library defies the notion of "gothic" as a pejorative term, coined during the Renaissance to express disdain for this style of architecture, which that period viewed as unrefined. When working, I need to resist the temptation to look endlessly at the lines of the vaulted ceiling, following them up from the pillars, along the arches, and back down again.

During my first visit to the cathedral and because of conservatory practices, I did not have access to the full St. Chad Gospels. Instead, I had access to a complete set of 6 inch × 8 inch black-and-white photographs. These photographs were taken during the 1962 rebinding, when the pages were separated. A complete set of color images did not exist. Therefore, scholarly inquiry was limited. For instance, much of the expression through color is lost: bright colors, like the St. Chad Gospels' golden yellow, appear as smudges on the vellum (calfskin) pages. For a limited number of pages, I was able to consult the manuscript; however, scholarship desperately needed a complete set of color images.

Sitting for hours on a hardwood chair, looking at reduced-sized black-and-white photographs (the St. Chad Gospels' pages are slightly larger than 12.5 inches × 9.5 inches), and relying on a magnifying glass—these less than ideal circumstances suggest anything but a serendipitous moment in research. However, that hardwood chair spoke volumes. It attested to my willingness to brush aside inconveniences and push forward with my research agenda. It attested to my research agenda's need for a systematic and thorough study of that which survives of the St. Chad Gospels. But most important, it attested to my commitment to Lichfield Cathedral's treasured manuscript. Unrecognized by me at the time, I was interviewing for my later digital work: Why would the cathedral agree to allow a scholar to digitize the St. Chad Gospels without that scholar demonstrating a strong commitment to the cathedral's most treasured manuscript?

My commitment and careful, thorough study did not go unnoticed. Without me asking, Pat Bancroft, the librarian, sent me photocopies of the last group of photographs, which I had time to examine only briefly. In an article about my digital project that later appeared in the *Chronicle of Higher Education*, the canon chancellor, the Rev. Dr. Pete Wilcox, comments positively about my initial time at the cathedral (quoted in Howard A8). In private, he mentioned that he was excited to see a scholar examining features of the St. Chad Gospels so carefully and systematically, something he had hoped for but not witnessed since becoming canon chancellor at Lichfield Cathedral. He felt that my research could inspire further scholarly attention to the cathedral's treasured gospel book, attention he viewed as long overdue.

My time in that hardwood chair turned out to be time well spent, for both my scholarship and what was to follow. But the discovery of the hoard four miles from the cathedral was already generating interest in the St. Chad Gospels and the need for color images. Inquiries had increased, and the cathedral was beginning to see a rise in the number of visitors. Scholars dated the hoard as buried during a period that included the time in which St. Chad, the gospel's namesake, was Bishop of Mercia—slightly before, during, or within seventy-five years after his death. St. Chad died in 672; monks made the St. Chad Gospels around 730.

Also during my visit, Dr. Wilcox noticed my digital camera and its professional lens. Because of the increase in visitors and expectation for this number to grow, Dr. Wilcox asked if I would take a few photographs of the St. Chad Gospels for his use in training additional cathedral guides—a promising sign for my later digitization.

TRAGEDY AND SERENDIPITY

The unearthing of the Anglo-Saxon hoard caused quite a stir in England—the story is compelling. Longtime metal-detector enthusiast Terry

Herbert discovered the artifacts of gold and silver while detecting on private farmland near Watling Street, the site of a major Roman thoroughfare. Previously, others had searched this site, to no avail. The discovery contains a variety of items, including crosses and zoomorphic mounts made of gold; however, the majority of items are objects of war, including the largest discovery in history of Anglo-Saxon sword fittings, many with elaborate filigree and inlaid garnets. These fittings and other items contain over 3,500 garnets. The find is the largest unearthing in history of Anglo-Saxon silver and gold. Nothing of its quantity and quality had previously been found in Britain or Europe.

When I arrived at Lichfield in the fall of 2009, archaeologists were still busy cleaning soil and clay from the items and determining what had been unearthed. In my wildest dreams I could have never pictured my return to Lichfield less than two years later, in August 2011, to deliver talks about my findings from digitizing the St. Chad Gospels and to participate in an exhibit of the hoard's star pieces, facilitating a VIP tour that included the queen's representative, Lord-Lieutenant Sir Algernon Heber-Percy. Significant for my research, items found in the hoard echo decorative features in the St. Chad Gospels. Insular artists, whether metalsmiths, stone carvers, or illuminators, borrowed inspiration from one another. For instance, the St. Chad Gospels' cross-carpet page appears to be inspired by the metalwork of inlaid garnets. These garnets are uncommonly dazzling because the metalsmiths placed a thinly pounded layer of gold foil beneath them, increasing the amount of reflected light. Such a technique might have inspired the artists of the St. Chad Gospels to layer pigment, the earliest surviving Insular manuscript to extensively do so. On the cross-carpet page, a combination of folium (translucent reddish-brown pigment) and white lead over-painted with folium generates a dazzling play of light, resonating with the effect of inlaid garnets.

However, my route to digitizing the St. Chad Gospels was anything but simple. In December 2009 a computer scientist at my university contacted me. He was involved in a large, multidisciplinary grant from the National Science Foundation called EDUCE, Enhanced Digital Unwrapping for Conservation and Exploration (IIS–0535003). Tragically, the only humanities scholar involved in the grant, Ross Scaife, unexpectedly passed away. Ross, a classicist and well-known digital humanist, had wanted to digitally unroll Herculaneum scrolls reduced to near ash when Mount Vesuvius erupted. The computer scientist had become stuck on the unwrapping and was trying to find a way to spend the remaining money so as not to lose it. He thought digitizing a manuscript might be a good plan. But without Ross, he needed a scholar who had knowledge of manuscripts and who could put together a digital project. The computer scientist had partnered with a classicist from another university, but the classicist was having difficulty gaining permission to digitize two different manuscripts. The computer scientist approached me, needing a backup plan.

A possible manuscript did exist. While I was at Lichfield, the Rev. Dr. Wilcox had shown me the cathedral's fifteenth-century Wycliffe New Testament, bequeathed to the cathedral in the 1940s. Dr. Wilcox was interested in having it digitized. In private hands, the manuscript had gone unnoticed by scholars, only recently included in a listing of Wycliffe Bibles by Mary Dove. In January, once Dr. Wilcox had finished with the cathedral's demanding Christmas schedule, we began sorting out details for the Wycliffe New Testament as a backup digital project.

At the end of January, serendipity struck again: unable to complete the work for the grant, a subcontractor returned funds. Suddenly, sufficient funds were available, counting my own funding sources. The project no longer depended upon what happened with the classicist and his potential project. One of the major expenses for imaging was shipping equipment and technical staff across the Atlantic. Once across, traveling and moving equipment and people between sites was relatively inexpensive. Furthermore, my project turned out to be serendipitous for the classics professor. He had been unable to gain permission to digitize two manuscripts in which he was interested. After I completed digitizing at Lichfield Cathedral, my project afforded him the luxury of having the imaging team travel to his potential site and help him secure an agreement.

But for me, the returned funds generated an intriguing possibility: digitizing the St. Chad Gospels. This would not be easy. Time was against us. Working through the details for digitizing a manuscript of the stature of the St. Chad Gospels generally takes better than a year. I had under six months. For the possible imaging of the Wycliffe New Testament, Dr. Wilcox and I had already identified the only available time: the second half of June. We had also identified a possible imaging space, the server's vestry, one of the few available spaces in the cathedral for which light could be blocked out for multi-spectral imaging. Multi-spectral imaging captures photographs using different frequencies of light, from ultraviolet to infrared. Ultraviolet and infrared are adept at revealing visual information unable to be seen by the unaided human eye. For early medieval manuscripts, such imaging helps recover worn and water-damaged text and imagery.

However, a number of questions needed to be answered about the St. Chad Gospels and the stress digitizing would place on the manuscript.

For this, a conservator needed to conduct a condition report, assessing the state of the binding, pigments, and vellum. For example, pigments are especially vulnerable: they are relatively rigid and adhere to vellum, not dying it like ink does. Turning a page places stress on the adhesion, with vellum flexibly bending and arching as it turns.

But the most difficult issue for a digital project is receiving permission. At Lichfield, the canon chancellor has responsibility for the library and its holdings, generally controlling what happens with the books and manuscripts. The Chapter, the governing body of the cathedral, commonly approves the canon chancellor's requests without much debate. For a manuscript like the Wycliffe New Testament—a valuable and significant manuscript, but one bequeathed to the cathedral and not intimately connected to its past—permission is generally left to the canon chancellor. The St. Chad Gospels is a different matter. Its value to the Cathedral is unmatched. As Dr. Wilcox explains, the St. Chad Gospels links the community to its origins within a generation of St. Chad, who is the reason a cathedral exists at Lichfield (Howard A8). Therefore, Chapter members had much to debate about digitizing their treasured manuscript, including issues such as copyright, internet access, insurance, the impact of imaging on the manuscript, and the effect on the cathedral's bottom line.

Sorting out these complexities through email and telephone proved far too difficult. So during spring break, I decided against presenting a paper at the College Composition and Communication Conference (CCCC) and flew to Lichfield. My time at Lichfield was productive beyond my hopes. Dr. Wilcox and I worked through a great deal of material. In addition to digitizing the manuscript, I also proposed digitizing past historical images, such as the black-and-white photographs I had labored over. Digitizing these photographs would allow comparisons for assessing issues of aging, such as pigment loss, alerting the cathedral to areas of the manuscript that needed special care. Pigment loss is difficult to identify and track: it occurs gradually, over decades, and the chips that break free generally measure a fraction of a millimeter in length. Therefore, tracing these losses requires photographs. Fortunately, the artistry and significance of the St. Chad Gospels have inspired much photography through the years, including a few pages reproduced in an 1887 book, a 1929 Photostat copy, and 1956 color slides (which I discovered later in the cathedral's archive).

While controlling temperature and humidity eliminates much of the risk, travel and turning pages can also have adverse effects. For example, in 2000 the Book of Kells suffered pigment loss during an exhibition in

Australia. Because the St. Chad Gospels is the oldest known gospel book still serving its original purpose (albeit in extremely limited roles), Dr. Wilcox was interested in my suggestion of comparative analysis. He did not want these limited roles, such as carrying the St. Chad Gospels in the procession during Christmas Day mass, to potentially harm the manuscript. For my analysis, I wanted to digitize, align, and overlay historical images, adjusting the transparency of the top image for comparisons. To my knowledge, this work had not previously been done on an early medieval manuscript. Therefore, I could supply the cathedral with a new tool for understanding and preserving its manuscript, providing reciprocity for its risk and willingness to allow my digital efforts (Endres 57–60).

Even with my productive visit, in what now was down to three months, much still needed to happen. I had formed a strong working relationship with Dr. Wilcox, and he ably guided the discussions and debates that occurred among members of the Chapter. Somehow, permission was granted, copyright agreed upon, and a schedule set, with my university sending the signed contract overnight to Lichfield because all of the signatures could not be collected before I had to leave for the cathedral and begin imaging.

Accomplishing everything in less than six months was epic. It took a hardwood chair, a devoted and skilled canon chancellor, a substantial piece of funding through an untimely death, my securing additional funds, an eighth-century manuscript that had been neglected by scholars, and discovery of the largest Anglo-Saxon hoard ever found. During all my conversations and correspondence with Dr. Wilcox, the hoard remained ever-present in the background. Its effect on the cathedral would be felt in one year, when the star pieces of the hoard were exhibited with the St. Chad Gospels in Lichfield. The three-week exhibit was successful beyond expectations: tickets sold out before the first visitor laid eyes on a single garnet, gold cross, or glorious pigment in the St. Chad Gospels.

But the attention was only beginning. The hoard's star pieces would travel to Washington, DC. To include the St. Chad Gospels (because such travels would stress the manuscript), my images were incorporated into the exhibit. Furthermore, before I began imaging, the hoard had captured the attention of the National Geographic Channel (NGC). It planned a two-part series, one about the hoard and the other about the Anglo-Saxon context in the area, including Lichfield Cathedral and the St. Chad Gospels. When Dr. Wilcox told NGC about my project, they wanted to interview me and film the digitizing process, making the series a three-part series instead. To tell the story, they set up a camera crane and taught me how to walk for a camera, planning to open the segment with a clip of me approaching and entering the cathedral. Unfortunately, executives decided that the market was not substantial enough for a three-part series. They aired only the first part. However, a stronger-than-expected audience encouraged NGC to air the second part about the Anglo-Saxon context, so there is still hope for my segment.

SERENDIPITY AS A CRISIS IN SCHOLARSHIP

Do scholars have an ethical responsibility to pursue scholarship made possible by serendipity? The ethical dimension of serendipity depends upon how "scholar" is constructed and how "serendipity" is understood. In rhetorical scholarship, a concept akin to serendipity is *kairos*, the opportune moment. Serendipity opens such opportune moments and makes scholarly activity possible, such as my digitizing the St. Chad Gospels. For a rhetorician, the question of *kairos* is whether she or he can rise to the occasion the moment demands; thus, good rhetorical training is necessary, as promoted in ancient and classical times. The significance but also the rarity of the opportune moment is made explicit by Eric Charles White. He explains, "*Kairos* regards the present as unprecedented, as a moment of decision, a moment of crisis" (14). As a happy accident, serendipity is not generally considered a crisis. However, the opportunity would not be serendipitous if the scholarship made possible were not needed. This scholarship is both fortunate and unprecedented, the opportunity likely fleeting. Therefore, serendipity presents scholarship in a moment of crisis.

My experience digitizing the St. Chad Gospels exemplifies such a moment of crisis in scholarship. The St. Chad Gospels' lack of a facsimile or color photographs attests to the need for favorable circumstances if such scholarly activity is to happen. Otherwise, a facsimile would have been produced or scholars would have digitized the entire St. Chad Gospels in 2003. Circumstances matter. Many times, a number of events and circumstances must align—some remarkably rare, such as the improbable aligning of my research agenda, an untimely death, and the discovery of an Anglo-Saxon hoard. If the opportunity presented by these events goes unmet, irreplaceable information for conserving the St. Chad Gospels is lost and scholarship about this illuminated manuscript and its larger influences remains limited.

However, does serendipity generate an ethical responsibility for a scholar to act? At first thought, academic freedom appears to imply that scholars have little ethical responsibility to respond to serendipity and the research it engenders. However, academic freedom is not based on the individual or the individual's needs. Instead, academic freedom and its guarantor, tenure, are based on the larger social good. The statement on which modern-day tenure is based, the "1940 Statement of Principles on Academic Freedom and Tenure," declares that "institutions of higher education are conducted for the common good and not to further the interest of either the individual teacher or the institution as a whole" (AAUP 14).[4] Such a statement constructs a tenured position as a social trust.

What type of scholarship should faculty members engage in if their positions are viewed as social trusts? Can they ignore research made possible by serendipity? Does ignoring serendipitous events constitute an ethical breach? I find these questions intriguing, especially within the context of my digitizing a cultural heritage artifact to which scholars and people generally had limited access, limited access had caused limited scholarship, and trends in aging had been little studied for lack of access and means.

Scholars work within vastly different circumstances, contexts, and material conditions. Therefore, serendipitous events affect scholars, their research, and disciplines differently. However, the question remains: Does a scholar have an ethical responsibility to respond to the unprecedented moment and meet the crisis in scholarship revealed by serendipity?

CONCLUDING THOUGHTS

> Bureaucratization of the Imaginative: "the vexing things that happen when men try to translate some pure aim or vision into terms of its corresponding material embodiment, thus necessarily involving elements alien to the original."
>
> —Kenneth Burke

My story may not have a happy ending. I digitized the St. Chad Gospels when my tenure line was in an English department. Digital scholarship was not included in the department's tenure and promotion guidelines. However, motivated in part by the Modern Language Association having declared the digital humanities "the next big thing," the department flirted with changing its guidelines; the faculty lost interest, however, never generating a vote on possibly including digital scholarly activities. However, through serendipity, the writing program at my institution split from the English department and formed its own unit. In putting documents in place for departmental status, the faculty approved guidelines that included a digital project as a viable centerpiece for tenure and promotion, similar to a monograph or a collection of articles. These guidelines were based on best practices in the digital humanities, such as those described in the fall 2012 issue of the *Journal of Digital Humanities*, which examines multiple ways to approach peer review for digital work.

When departmental status was granted, I was blessed once more by serendipity. However, during the first steering committee meeting after the new department was created, one of my senior colleagues announced that he was biased against the book for tenure and that two of my other tenured colleagues likely felt the same way. Only four faculty members would vote on my tenure case; therefore, odds were stacking up against me.[5] I met with him to discuss his position, but as I was untenured, I had little sway over his feelings and how his experience in gaining tenure motivated him. As human beings, scholars are not exempt from their prejudices and what Kenneth Burke describes as the bureaucratization of the imagination. Let me explain.

Scholarship becomes bureaucratized when scholarly activity becomes measurable in one major acceptable manner: text. In this *material embodiment* of scholarship, the *pure aim or vision* of scholarship becomes recognizable and rewarded solely through its *corresponding embodied* and *alien form*: a quota of text. In the publish-or-perish atmosphere of academe, any sense of the common good is lost. Writing articles and books does not necessarily align scholarly activity with the common good—or even good scholarship. It can do so, and when it does, academic writing still need not be exclusionary. I value the written word. I wrote this essay recognizing the importance of academic writing for scholarship. I began my journey toward a PhD in rhetoric, composition, and linguistics with a master's degree in writing poetry. I publish academic articles and have two books in progress, one with interest from an international medieval series. But in a digital age, scholarly production as bureaucratized in monographs and articles is detrimental to and dangerous for future scholarship. All scholarship builds upon what came before. Limiting scholarly production in the area of digital materials, tools, and data obstructs the building of a dynamic and expansive digital base for future scholars.

Ironically, Insular monks did not bureaucratize text in the manner of contemporary academia. As mentioned earlier, they viewed text and imagery as non-hierarchical visual expression. They, like Burke, provide a response to a bureaucratized sense of scholarly production.

The events that occurred to allow the St. Chad Gospels to survive and to make my digital project happen are beyond explanation and simply need to be celebrated. However, the common good from digital scholarship is quantifiable. In slightly over three years, my website for the St. Chad Gospels and Lichfield Cathedral's Wycliffe New Testament,

Manuscripts of Lichfield Cathedral (https://lichfield.ou.edu),[6] has had over 11,000 visits from people from 106 countries (20 more than participated in the Sochi Olympic games) and over 450 universities, libraries, and museums. The website has been referenced in scholarly books, provided a base for articles, and been used worldwide in graduate seminars and undergraduate courses. It is listed in all major scholarly medieval databases for manuscripts online.

The historical images have shown themselves to be of particular benefit. They have provided insight into trends of pigment loss and helped identify pages where pigments and inks are at risk. Comparing historical images has facilitated decisions about loaning the St. Chad Gospels for exhibits and determining best methods for the manuscript to travel.

Regardless of whether scholars who have gained status and power through text can come to value and reward digital scholarly activity is yet to be seen. But scholarship benefits from a convergence of fortunate happenings in irreplaceable ways, whether digital or traditional. Such events provide openings for knowing that were previously unconceived of or blocked. However, these events are fleeting. They are *kairotic* moments that have implications in the world. In this, they place scholarship in a moment of crisis. Determining how to respond should not be measured by guidelines for tenure and promotion but by questions about the social trust invested in academic positions. If this is the measure for serendipitous openings, these openings provide an additional happy accident: they reconnect scholars to the roots of scholarly activity—the common good.

Notes

1. The British Library developed "Turning the Pages" software to emulate the look of a page turning for online presentation. It enables other features as well, such as magnification and brief commentary.
2. The Staffordshire Hoard website provides extensive information about the discovery of the hoard, images, and the latest information about the progress of research; http://www.staffordshirehoard.org.uk.
3. For one of the most complete feminist critiques of academe, which also significantly addresses race, see Royster.
4. The 1940 statement footnotes *teacher*, explaining that the word refers as well to a researcher employed by an academic institution without teaching responsibilities.
5. I have since been recruited and hired by another university. After I left, this faculty member who is biased against the book and is now the department chair successfully worked to remove the possibility of a digital project counting as a centerpiece for tenure and promotion. It now counts solely as an "enhancement."
6. When I moved to my new university, I transitioned my website to one of its servers. This is the new URL.

Works Cited

Alexander, J.J.G. *Insular Manuscripts 6th –9th Century*. London: Harvey Miller, 1978. Print.

American Association of University Professors (AAUP). "1940 Statement of Principles on Academic Freedom and Tenure." Web. 18 Feb. 2015.

Baca, Damian. *Mestiz@ Scripts, Digital Migrations, and the Territories of Writing*. New York: Palgrave Macmillan, 2008. Print.

Bambury, Pádraig, and Stephen Beechinor, comp. and ed. *The Annals of Ulster*. Web. 1 March 2015.

Bolter, Jay David. *Writing Space*. New York: Lawrence Erlbaum, 2001. Print.

Brown, Michelle P. "The Lichfield/Llandeilo Gospels Reinterpreted." 2008. *Authority and Subjugation in Writing of Medieval Wales*. Ed. Ruth Kennedy and Simon Meecham-Jones. New York: Palgrave Macmillan, 2008. 57–70. Print.

Burke, Kenneth. *Attitudes toward History*. Berkeley: U of California P, 1984. Print.

Cahill, Thomas. *How the Irish Saved Civilization: The Untold Story of Ireland's Heroic Role from the Fall of Rome to the Rise of Medieval Europe*. New York: Anchor, 1996. Print.

Endres, William. "Imaging Sacred Artifacts: Ethics and the Digitizing of Lichfield Cathedral's St. Chad Gospels." *Journal of Religion, Media, and Digital Culture* 3.3 (2014): 39–73. Web. 18 May 2016.

Henry, Françoise. *The Book of Kells: Reproductions from the Manuscript in Trinity College Dublin*. New York: Alfred A. Knopf, 1974. Print.

Howard, Jennifer. "21st-Century Imaging Helps Scholars Reveal Rare 8th-Century Manuscript." *Chronicle of Higher Education* (Dec. 5, 2010): A8, A10. Print.

James, Pamela. "The Lichfield Gospels: The Question of Provenance." *Parergon* 13:2 (1996): 51–61. Print.

Jenkins, Dafydd, and Morfydd Owen. "The Welsh Marginalia in the Lichfield Gospels, Part I." *Cambridge Medieval Celtic Studies* 5 (Summer 1983): 37–66. Print.

Royster, Jacqueline Jones. "When the First Voice You Hear Is Not Your Own." *College Composition and Communication* 47.1 (1996): 29–40. Print.

Savage, Henry E. *The St. Chad Gospels*. Lichfield: Bull and Wiseman, 1931. Print.

White, Eric Charles. *Kaironomia: On the Will-to-Invent*. Ithaca, NY: Cornell UP, 1987. Print.

Wysocki, Anne. "awaywithwords: On the Possibilities in Unavailable Designs." *Computers and Composition* 22 (2005): 55–62. Print.

Wysocki, Anne. "Seeing the Screen: Research into Visual and Digital Writing Practices." *Handbook of Research on Writing*. Ed. Charles Bazerman. New York: Lawrence Erlbaum, 2008. 599–612. Print.

18

CREATING KISMET
What Artists Can Teach Academics about Serendipity

Brad Gyori

Jackson Pollock famously said, "I deny the accident" (Wright). Although he was often accused of haphazardly splashing paint on canvas, he insisted that there was a method to his madness, intention behind each seemingly random gesture. Pollock may also have been making a larger point about the relationship between art and the serendipitous. While everyday life marches to a monotonously predictable drumbeat, art thrives on the unexpected. It flourishes in liminal spaces where mundane events are transformed into myths and legends (Turner). This alchemical process defies expectation and thus thrives on the unforeseen and, in some respects, the unknowable. When artists seek inspiration, happenstance is not just acceptable; it is compulsory. Thus, when Pollock denied the accident, he was not suggesting that each of his paintings was carefully mapped out in advance. Instead, he was explaining that the impulse to resist such pre-mediation is itself a deliberate choice. Pollock's work is entirely non-representational, referring only to his interior world. The expressionist element in abstract expressionism involves the artist experiencing an emotional state at the moment of creation and spontaneously articulating this through the painting process. By insisting that his actions were intentional without being premediated, Pollock was calling into question the standard definition of "accident," which Merriam-Webster describes as "an unfortunate event that is the result of carelessness." He was suggesting that an act could be *both* spontaneous and intended.

Serendipity occurs when a seemingly random event results in a positive outcome that feels predestined. This resonates with another term of Near Eastern origin, the Turkish word "kismet," meaning "fate" or "destiny" (Merriam-Webster.com). Operating at the intersection of chance and destiny, where the accident is transcended and providence is achieved, serendipity is the pathway leading to this happy outcome. Artists are kismet-hunters, actively seeking patterns of harmonic convergence. Filmmakers, writers, musicians, and painters often value these chance occurrences too much to leave them entirely to chance. So, somewhat paradoxically, they develop strategies for creating kismet on demand.

While artists celebrate serendipity, academics may be less inclined to acknowledge that their carefully crafted arguments are influenced by mere chance. Still, scholarly innovation and artistic creation have a great deal in common. The supposed artist/academic binary is unstable at best, composed as it is of two culturally contingent and mutually influential categories. The bleak philosophical musings of Søren Kierkegaard informed Franz Kafka's dark absurdist prose, which, in turn, informed Jean Paul Sartre's existential philosophy. When Le Corbusier began to design buildings that were a pastiche of classical and modern styles, he inaugurated postmodern architecture. He also presaged the theories of Jean-François Lyotard. And the work of postcolonial theorists such as Edward Said and Gayatri Spivak is certainly indebted to Chinua Achebe's *Things Fall Apart*, a novel that challenges the cultural hegemony of the West by focusing on a native Nigerian protagonist.

Artists and academics are engaged in an ancient reciprocally advantageous dialogue. When artists learn from academics, they come to see their work in relation to larger cultural trends and traditions. When academics learn from artists, they welcome the serendipitous rupture that occurs when premeditation is shattered and new insights emerge. While scholarly methods are carefully explicated at the outset of each research project, artistic methods are often veiled by a quasi-religious mystique. The artist as magical conjurer, answering only to an ethereal muse, is a long-standing and in some respects an alluring myth, but artistic methods are not as mysterious as they may appear at first glance. Because artists value spontaneity, they often employ methods that deliberately disrupt old habits of mind, forcing them to improvise and adapt. I call these techniques "disjunctive strategies."

The act of disjunction involves breaking and reordering continuity. This can allow audiences to make new and interesting associations through intuitive pattern recognition. Of course, extreme disjunction, as with a hyper-cut film montage, can lead to a sensation of pattern blindness in which the audience is bewildered by an onslaught of disjointed information. This may be precisely the effect an artist is seeking, but for longer works, it can sap interest and strain attention. The promise and the risk of disjunctive strategies reside in their capacity to shatter expectations. They do so in a variety of ways. Temporal disjunction involves a sudden leap forward in time, as when a bit of footage is removed from a single shot of film so that a jump cut occurs. With spatial disjunction, the continuity of time is preserved, but the viewer's perspective shifts to a new location, for instance, cutting between two cameras filming the same scene from different angles. Spatiotemporal disjunction involves a shift between both space and time, as when an epistolary novel shifts from a diary entry written in the morning in the countryside to a letter written in the evening in the city. Syntactic disjunction involves shattering symbolic continuity, as with the cut-up novels of William S. Burroughs, pages of linear prose sliced into sections and reassembled in a nonlinear fashion. Authorial disjunction involves shifting between authorial perspectives, as with the "exquisite corpse" experiments of the surrealists, in which multiple artists created collaborative drawings and poems.

Each of these disjunctive types can by created through three disjunctive strategies: remixing, rebooting, and deconstructing. Operating as disjunction generators, these methods deliberately shatter and reassemble continuity in a variety of ways. The mere act of naming these tactics suggests that they are in some respect stable and coherent categories, but this is misleading. The taxonomy is porous. Characteristics overlap and bleed into each other, often in interesting and productive ways. Still, this chapter identifies some general features of these techniques to suggest ways in which both artists and scholars can successfully deploy them. The common thread linking these diverse signifying practices is serendipity. Each approach conjures intriguing new juxtapositions of content and form, challenging expectations, consciously denying the accident, and actively creating kismet.

REMIX

At times, academic discourse can seem oddly antagonistic. Scholars construct "arguments," raise "objections," and "defend positions." But research is more than a zero-sum game in which self-interested individuals arrive at a fixed position and refute any ideas that complicate or contradict it. Actually, the most productive modes of inquiry are far more fluid and exploratory, and the most productive scholars are talented remix artists contemplating a set of core concepts while constantly adding and subtracting elements and altering emphasis. Karl Marx is a prime example. Throughout a long and highly prolific career, his thought was anything but static, hence the necessary distinction between classic early Marxism (Marx and Engels) and the more nuanced later work (Marx). Marx was so resistant to the idea of being pinned down and narrowly defined that he once told his son-in-law Paul Lafargue, "If anything is certain, it is that I myself am not a Marxist" (*Karl Marx Friedrich Engels*, 229). This tendency to eschew self-imposed ideological constraints is the remix artist's default position. Her worldview is a shifting constellation rather than a codified whole. By constantly breaking the mold while combining and recombining ideas, she creates ample opportunities for new insights to emerge.

Russian formalist filmmaker Sergei Eisenstein believed that when two independent strips of film are edited together, a "tertium quid," or third meaning, is created. In this respect, the art of cinematic montage is similar to the gestalt of the fine art collage, which combines disparate elements that, in turn, suggest various subliminal associations. Whether organized in terms of montage or collage, the power of the remix primarily resides not in element A or element B but in the *relationship* of A to B. Fine art studios and film edit bays are hotbeds for creating this type of kismet, as diverse elements are conjoined, cut, and re-linked in all sorts of different ways, allowing artists to suggest moments of powerful synergy. Screenwriters do something similar quite early in their creative process, jotting scene summaries on index cards, then experimenting with different narrative sequences.

As historian and literary theorist Hayden White points out, rhetorical tropes organize information in a manner that privileges certain modes of interpretation. Because disjunctive strategies can potentially influence perceived values and meanings, proponents of remix theory view the remix as a political act affording opportunities to disrupt and reimagine the status quo (Lessig; Navas; Sonvilla-Weiss). Thus, scholars organizing book chapters, literature reviews, journal collections, or article sections can and do challenge entrenched views by simply considering multiple remix combinations and organizational structures. Shuffling the deck in this manner is a way of seeing the larger structure with fresh eyes and looking for interesting and unexpected patterns and associations.

Scholars can also remix by cross-pollinating entire disciplines and juxtaposing the perspectives of diverse collaborators. The Santa Fe Institute in New Mexico is a remix of the entire notion of a traditional research culture (Bonabeau, Theraulaz, and Dorigo). There are no disciplinary silos, and think tanks are composed of scholars from apparently unrelated fields. These somewhat unlikely colleagues search for fresh insights related to highly complex issues. Thus, a group consisting of a physicist, a novelist, a botanist, and a computer programmer might discuss topics as diverse as climate change, terrorism, and drug trafficking.

The scholars interacting at the Santa Fe Institute reject specialized jargon and methodologies and actively seek out unexpected and highly fruitful patterns of conjunction, the hallmark of the serendipitous.

REBOOT

Like works of art, scholarly creations are never wholly original. It is exciting to think of a new theory bursting forth like Athena from the head of Zeus, fully formed and with no historical precedent, but academics are always in debt to their predecessors, even those they disagree with. The evolution of any scholarly enterprise is not a teleological progression or a random free-for-all. It does not automatically refine or reject established trends; it does both at once. Schools of thought are fractal patterns, distorted echoes, retaining much of their original form, yet changing a bit with each iteration as new local and historical particulars inflect their unfolding evolution.

In the world of comic books, story sequences have a limited shelf life. After several years, when a narrative pattern appears to have run its course, it is overridden by a new approach, one that interrupts the continuity of its predecessor, returning readers to the origin of the tale and proceeding to impart a reimagined version of the previous story. This type of radical reinvention is known as a "reboot" (Proctor). It occurs when an entire franchise, or sequence of stories, is reimagined from beginning to end. While a remake reinvents a single stand-alone work, a reboot reinvents an entire *body of work*. Unlike the remix, which reconfigures the original source material, the reboot wipes the slate clean, creating a new origin story with new foundational concepts to build upon. When a comic book franchise is rebooted, it may even switch to a new genre. At the very least, the tone is substantively altered. Tropes derived from the original text are appropriated and incorporated into this retelling, but they are *not* sampled directly from the source material. In other words, a reboot is not the deck reshuffled; it is a new deck altogether, albeit with some clear similarities to the early model.

In an academic context, a reboot can involve the reinvention of an entire discipline or school of thought. Likely reboot targets include any body of work that has become so canonical that a sort of intellectual paralysis has set in, inhibiting its ability to generate fresh insights. When this occurs, classicism is rebooted as neoclassicism and Marxism is rebooted as Neo-Marxism. Some scholars are more in debt to the reboot than others. While Sigmund Freud's theories draw on a variety of influences with no single dominant precursor, French psychoanalyst Jacques

Lacan spent much of his career rebooting Freud in relation to structural and post-structural theory. Lacan took many liberties with Freud's thought; nonetheless, he felt so indebted to the master that he rejected the idea that he had spawned his own unique school of thought, telling followers "you can be Lacanians, if you want. As for me, I'm a Freudian" (Clifton, xvi). Rebooting involves equal parts irreverence and fidelity. While it affords ample opportunities for disrupting familiar patterns and exposing novel insights, it also requires a degree of devotion to the source material it means to reinvent.

DECONSTRUCTION

In popular parlance, the word "deconstruction" is used interchangeably with remix. According to this perspective, the process of deconstructing a text involves nothing more than taking it apart and reassembling it in some new form. But the original concept of deconstruction proposed by Jacques Derrida operates in a more complex and indirect way (*Of Grammatology*). Deconstruction in this sense is the act of looking past the structure of a text to discover what it conceals. Like the surrealist technique known as grattage, in which an artist flips her brush and uses the handle to scrape paint from a canvas, deconstruction strives to uncover a text's hidden potential. Just as there are endless ways to scrape off paint, there are endless ways to deconstruct a text. This led Derrida to explain that deconstruction is not a strategy in the traditional sense, capable of yielding predictable results, "a final goal, a telos" (*Margins*). Instead, it proceeds by the strange anti-logic of "blind tactics" and "empirical wandering" (*Margins*). Any text can be deconstructed in this manner, often with interesting results.

The book *Wicked* is a Derridean deconstruction of *The Wizard of Oz* because it gives voice to the so-called Wicked Witch of the West, a character marginalized and vilified in the original text. *Wicked*'s author, Gregory Maguire, has written three other revisionist novels based on L. Frank Baum's *The Wonderful Wizard of Oz*, focusing on characters from the original text such as the cowardly lion, *A Lion among Men*, as well as characters of his own invention, *Son of a Witch* and *Out of Oz*.

A fan edit is a cinematic scene or trailer recut to create a genre-jumping deconstruction. The horror film *The Shining* becomes the feel-good family romp, *Shining*. *The 40-Year-Old Virgin* shifts from a farce to dark psychological thriller. The mediating practices that allow artists to create cinematic fan edits afford scholars similar opportunities to restructure and reimagine canonical scholarly works. For instance,

Jacques Derrida's deconstruction of Plato's *Phaedrus*, titled "Plato's Pharmacy" (*Dissemination*), is in some respects a scholarly fan edit. Throughout the text, deconstructive tactics challenge philosophical assumptions. In this instance, deconstruction serves to destabilize an ancient text, yet this disjunctive strategy can also be deployed to critique more recent works. What would a fan edit of an article by Judith Butler, Henry Jenkins, or Derrida himself look like? What hidden potentials might be realized and what unstated biases might be exposed?

Deconstruction is the most radical disjunctive strategy because it does not merely remix or even entirely reboot; instead, it creates a compelling counter-narrative, a perspective framed in opposition to the source it means to dismantle. It is the anti-establishment impulse, the attempt to invert hierarchies, to reject normative biases and cultural commonplaces, to give voice to the voiceless, and to unseat the ruling class. In ancient Rome this impulse found expression in the Saturnalia, an eight-day festival in which cultural norms were upended. Masters and servants traded places. Women dressed like men, and vice versa (Delanty, Giorgi, and Sassatelli). This yearly rite dramatically redrew social distinctions, but only temporarily. Scholars have debated whether this had some kind of cathartic effect or if it was merely a cultural anomaly that served no verifiable function. Whatever the case, the phenomenon known as the "counterculture" is a type of open-ended Saturnalia in which cultural norms are inverted in a far more sustained fashion. Inversion begets inversion as these deconstructions radically disrupt the status quo. When white male musicians grow long hair and sing the blues, they claim a kind of alternative subject position. By emulating women and people of color, they retain their privileged white male status while gaining the sense of exoticism often associated with specific oppressed groups. If this identification with marginalized others is viewed as successful, it can, paradoxically, raise their cultural status. At the same time, this type of boundary crossing can unsettle entrenched hierarchies and create opportunities for oppressed people to avail themselves of cultural advantages usually monopolized by social elites. For instance, at the height of Beatlemania, young girls aggressively chased after and screamed for the attention of their feminized idols. This behavior was far from "ladylike," hence its subversive appeal.

The deconstructive move allows for cultural innovation that is spontaneous and in some respects unpredictable. It invites serendipity by flipping the script in a particular way. Outcasts become heroes and oppressed groups step into the critical spotlight. The process of deconstruction can be applied to the emergence of entire aesthetic and intellectual counter-movements; thus, impressionism, colonialism, modernism, and structuralism become post-impressionism, post-colonialism, postmodernism, and post-structuralism. Like the reversals that advance a dramatic narrative, these dynamic transpositions propel culture forward along unfamiliar pathways.

CODA

In our hyper-mediated digital age, artists are remixing, rebooting, and deconstructing in all sorts of playful and intriguing ways. They are creating transmedia story worlds distributed across multiple high-tech platforms, gamifying real world settings, creating flash mobs, lip dubs, mashups, fan edits, diaporamas, podcasts, vodcasts, mobcasts, and live-streamed events with increasing frequency and fluidity. While it is impossible to predict exact what scholarly innovations will emerge in relation to this riot of creative experimentation, we may at least begin to glimpse the contours of some nascent methodological practices.

The three disjunctive strategies I have described are powerful catalysts of cultural innovation, highly nuanced and necessarily unstable. So rather than attempt to corral them, this final section gives them free rein, complicating and complexifying what has so far been said about these unsettling and unsettled tactics.

Digital artists not only manipulate media forms with impressive proficiency; they also mix and match disjunctive practices in all sorts of surprising ways. The always porous categories of remix, reboot, and deconstruction have grown increasingly permeable, and this has been a boon to artistic expression. This trend has implications for scholarly research as well. As the stranglehold on intellectual property continues to slacken, more and more scholarly articles are migrating to online forums. The shift from material to virtual venue affords new opportunities for multi-modal experimentation, but to what end and by what means? If the primary goal of scholarly research is intellectual illumination, could there be an advantage to consciously deploying sophisticated disjunctive practices in the hope of attracting serendipity's lightning-bolt insights?

Disjunctive strategies do more than challenge audiences; they also challenge authors. This is not a violation of authorial intent, provided the author has intended to systematically unsettle her initial assumptions, to deny the accident. In contrast, researchers who carefully avoid disjunctive strategies risk becoming data miners, finding only what they seek as they cull thorough unmediated information, focusing primarily on evidence that supports their argument du jour. If research is to become a legitimate process of discovery, researchers *must* consciously adopt methodological strategies likely to complicate and even confound the intuitions undergirding their proposed agendas.

Few scholars in our post-postmodern era would claim an ability to locate anything they might confidently label "the truth," a statement of irrefutable fact, pure and unalloyed by ideological bias. We have learned to content ourselves with the quest for a far more modest goal, a search for contingent, context-dependent significance, yet even this may not be perfectly attainable. After all, notions such as determinism, relativism, postmodernism, and modernism only make sense in relation to each other. Meaning is never located in a single fixed place or everywhere at once or nowhere at all. We can only glimpse it at the moment when two perspectives collide and a third insight emerges, a spark of illumination: kismet.

Works Cited

Achebe, Chinua. *Things Fall Apart*. New York: Penguin Classics, 2006. Print.
Bonabeau, Eric, Guy Theraulaz, and Marco Dorigo. *Swarm Intelligence: From Natural to Artificial Systems*. Oxford: Oxford UP, 1999. Print.
Clifton, Linda, ed. *Invention in the Real: Papers of the Freudian School of Melbourne*. London: Karnac Books, 2012. Print.
Delanty, Gerard, Liana Giorgi, and Monica Sassatelli, eds. *Festivals and the Cultural Public Sphere*. London: Routledge, 2013. Print.
Derrida, Jacques. *Dissemination*. Trans. Barbara Johnson. Chicago: U of Chicago P, 1983. Print.
Derrida, Jacques. *Margins of Philosophy*. Trans. Alan Bass. Belfast: Prentice Hall/Harvester Wheatsheaf, 1982. Print.
Derrida, Jacques. *Of Grammatology*. Trans. Gayatri Chakravorty Spivak. Baltimore, MD: Johns Hopkins UP, 1998. Print.
Eisenstein, Sergei. *Film Form: Essays in Film Theory by Sergei Eisenstein*. New York: Harcourt, 1969. Print.
Kafka, Franz. *Selected Stories*. London: W. W. Norton, 2006. Print.
Karl Marx Friedrich Engels Selected Letters. Ed. J. Fritz. New York: Little, Brown, 1980. Print.
Kierkegaard, Søren. *Fear and Trembling*. New York: Penguin, 1986. Print.
Lacan, Jacques. *Ecrits: The First Complete Edition*. London: W. W. Norton, 2007. Print.
Le Corbusier. *Towards a New Architecture*. Eastford, CT: Martino Fine, 2014. Print.
Lessig, Lawrence. *Remix: Making Art and Commerce Thrive in the Hybrid Economy*. New York: Bloomsbury Academic, 2008. Print.
Lyotard, Jean-François. *The Postmodern Condition: A Report on Knowledge*. Manchester: Manchester UP, 1984. Print.
Marx, Karl. *Das Capital: A Critique of Political Economy*. Washington, DC: Regnery, 2009. Print.
Marx, Karl, and Freidrich Engels. *The German Ideology*. Amherst, NY: Prometheus, 1998. Print.
Navas, Eduardo, Owen Gallagher, and xtine burrough, eds. *The Routledge Companion to Remix Studies*. London: Routledge, 2014. Print.

Plato. *Phaedrus.* New York: Penguin Classics, 2005. Print.
Procter, William. "What Is a Reboot?" *Pencil, Panel, Page* (2012). Web. 4 April 2015.
Said, Edward. *Orientalism.* New York: Penguin, 2003. Print.
Sartre, Jean Paul. *Existentialism Is a Humanism.* New Haven, CT: Yale UP, 2007. Print.
Sonvilla-Weiss, Stefan, ed. *Mashup Cultures.* New York: Springer Vienna Architecture, 2010. Print.
Spivak, Gayatri Chakravorty. *In Other Worlds: Essays in Cultural Politics.* London: Routledge, 2006. Print.
Turner, Victor. *The Ritual Process: Structure and Anti-Structure.* Chicago: Aldine, 1969. Print.
White, Hayden. *Tropics of Discourse: Essays in Cultural Criticism.* Baltimore, MD: Johns Hopkins UP, 1985. Print.
Wright, William S., interviewer. "Jackson Pollock." *Abstract Expressionism: Creators and Critics.* Ed. Clifford Ross. New York: Abrahams, 1990. 47–52. Print.

19
COORDINATING CHAOS AND BEFRIENDING A FUZZY FOCUS
Reflections of a Serendipitist

Judy Holiday

As has been the case with many authors and scholars, Lillian Smith entered my life serendipitously, by way of a book held in my mother's outstretched hand. She and I were discussing banned books, and she had excused herself and returned with an old hardcover book. "Here's one of my favorite banned books, one you may not be familiar with," she said as she handed me a copy of *Strange Fruit* by Lillian Smith (1897–1966). First published in 1944, *Strange Fruit* sold more than 2 million copies that year, catapulting Smith onto the national literary scene. *Strange Fruit* tells the story of a World War I–era interracial love affair between the white son of a prominent southern family and a black woman in Jim Crow Georgia. The book was banned in Boston for "lewdness." It was also banned for several days under the same charge by the US Postal Service until Eleanor Roosevelt talked her husband, Franklin Delano Roosevelt, into lifting the ban.[1] The novel is a page turner, and I read it with pleasure during a summer visit with my parents. I had just finished my first year in a master's program in composition studies and was so new to the field of rhetoric and composition that the term "rhetoric" held little nuanced meaning for me. Writing studies provided a bit more traction but was still narrowly situated in my mind as largely the study of expository and transactional writing. That explains why, when I read *Strange Fruit* through the lens of fiction, I associated the work with literary studies, not composition, and thus dismissed it as a diversion from my "real" studies, despite having noticed places in the book where Smith presciently took on issues of race, class, and gender—all topics of deep interest to me.

Eight years later Smith would be the subject of my dissertation research, and her work would help me better understand myself and others, as well as impel me to articulate ways to address questions with which I'd been consumed since childhood: Why is the human world such a violent mess? And what can be done about it? The fact that Smith would serve as my guide on a journey that would help me provide some answers to these questions never occurred to me during my first reading of *Strange Fruit*. Nor did I think it was even possible to postulate cogent resolutions to such a complex, wicked cross-cultural problem as the etiology of violence. Yet thanks to Smith, feminist rhetorical studies, and a burning question, I like to think my research has carved out a way for humans to approach the problem of violence and to see intrapersonal, interpersonal, and group violence as stemming from the same source: a cross-cultural episteme that is socially constructed, learned, and internalized during childhood, prior to the maturation of meta-cognition and self-reflection.

I'm convinced, however, that I could not have accomplished the work I did without adopting an interdisciplinary and transdisciplinary approach,[2] one underwritten by a philosophy I think of as "maintaining chaos," a term Irene Clark uses in the context of writing center work but which easily transfers to any knowledge-making enterprise. Clark defines "chaos" as "a willingness to entertain multiple perspectives on critical issues, an ability to tolerate contradictions and contraries" so as "not to become so dogmatic, so set in our ways, so fossilized, so sure that we know how to do [something] 'right' that we stop growing and developing" (82). Because the etiology of violence is a topic that traverses most, if not all, human activities and cultures, my willingness to "maintain" the uncertainty chaos brings was vital to my developing multiple perspectives on the topic of violence.[3] Despite my having acquired that willingness years ago, I realize now that until more recently, I had not yet unpacked many of the epistemological assumptions inherent in a "maintaining chaos" approach, even though I had embraced the idea that, as a researcher, I should suspend the idea of control and surrender myself to the serendipitous—that is, to whatever came my way.

Everyone who has taken on an extended research project probably knows that it's impossible to know precisely where that research will ultimately lead. "Maintaining chaos" alludes in part to the idea that research projects have lives of their own. This is one of the great rewards of research: becoming friends with uncertainty and immersing oneself in a project that develops in ways that cannot be anticipated. Taking a purposely chaotic approach heightens that aspect of research by inviting the unexpected. At least two assumptions underlie such an approach: (1) Knowledge construction is an associative and synergistic endeavor whereby humans synthesize information in ways that are impossible to foresee at the outset of a research project; and (2) the unexpected is subject to serendipity, which involves both *chronos* and *kairos*.

Thinking about the first premise encouraged me to accept the second, and once I did, serendipity played a part in every stage of my research. As soon as I began to attune my attention to serendipity as an intrinsic and critical part of research, paying attention to when, why, and how serendipitous moments happened, the way I thought about serendipity changed. Instead of perceiving serendipity as a random instance of good luck, subject to chance, I began to focus on what I now know as its secondary definition, that is, the "faculty of" or "aptitude for" making fortunate discoveries. Obviously, faculties and aptitudes can be developed, so one goal of this chapter is to use my graduate research story to demonstrate how serendipity can be cultivated and consciously and strategically utilized at various stages of the research process.

I'm often reminded that a first step in learning anything is noticing the existence of that thing, what Judith Butler calls "intelligibility" (3). Consciousness-raising sessions of the 1960s, wherein participants came to realize that "the personal is political," exemplify the concept of "intelligibility." The process by which I came to recognize serendipity as a cultivable faculty was no less consciousness raising. I even experienced a "click" moment.[4] In retrospect, I feel as though I could have "awakened" much sooner to what seems so obvious to me now that I am attuned to the concept of serendipity—I would have known that attunement to our own passions is key to topical invention.

Had I understood the importance of listening to personal interest as an invention strategy, finding a dissertation topic during the first few years of my doctoral program would not have been such a grappling match, since a topic area had practically fallen into my lap when I first read *Strange Fruit* during my master's program. At the time of that first reading, however, my self-limiting conceptions of what constitutes research predisposed me to block my intuitions. What transpired in the week following that first reading of *Strange Fruit* would have otherwise signaled to me the richness of a project in the making. During that week I was thirty-eight and new to scholarship, a first-year student in a master's program. I remember liking the novel so much that I spent several hours scouring the internet for more information about it. I learned that the title of the novel alludes to a song by the same name, made famous by Billie Holiday. The song "Strange Fruit," with which I was unfamiliar at the time, graphically and horrifically depicts the bodies of lynched human beings hanging from trees. As I continued to surf the web, I became enthralled with the interconnectedness and strangeness of life as I learned that Abel Meeropol (whose penname is Lewis Allan) wrote and composed the song—the same Abel Meeropol who, as a communist and social activist, adopted Robert and Michael Rosenberg, the orphaned children of Ethel and Julius Rosenberg who were convicted of being communist spies and executed in New York City in 1953.

I learned much that week and remember feeling the headiness of new knowledge learned in a short time period because a day or two after I had searched for more information about Smith and *Strange Fruit*, I became introduced to the idea of historiography—in the waiting room of a dentist's office. Awaiting my appointment, I picked up a copy of the *Smithsonian* and opened it to an article about Ida B. Wells. I felt outraged that I hadn't learned during high school or college about a figure as important to US history as Wells. I spent the remainder of my wait fuming over what I perceived as the "whiteness" of K–12 education in the United States, angered that I hadn't received the comprehensive overview of American history I should have received. The following day, when I expressed my outrage to one of my master's professors, she introduced me to the terms "historiography" and "whiteness studies" and suggested some readings.

Without knowing it, I was already on a research path. While Smith is, in my opinion, the mother of whiteness studies, that's not the angle I later took in my dissertation, despite my work being essentially a feminist historiography of Smith. Rather, my dissertation ultimately argues that throughout Smith's corpus, which is extensive (she published seven books; corresponded widely; and wrote regular columns in various journals, including one she founded and edited), Smith articulates a coherent if implicit rhetorical theory on Othering as an episteme underwriting violence. Yet hindsight reveals that I had already been spirited away by Smith. I spoke about her to everyone I could—which I now know to be a sign of a good research topic. For instance, while speaking with my father on the phone during that memorable week, I recall him telling me that "*everyone* read *Strange Fruit* when it came out" and that he remembered it being "off-color" ("on-color" would have been more race- and gender-conscious).

Later that night I spoke about *Strange Fruit* with Larry, the maître d' of the fine-dining restaurant that employed me as a food server. When I began to speak about the song "Strange Fruit," Larry registered surprise at the fact that I was unfamiliar with the song, and he pointedly directed me to go home and listen to Nina Simone's version of it, his favorite. I could scarcely forget what happened next. I went home, turned on the television, and stared at the screen in astonishment as I watched the lyrics of "Strange Fruit" scroll across the screen—transposed over a black-and-white silhouette of Nina Simone's face. The program being aired was about the history of the song, and I was catching the final few minutes of the program, including Simone's version of the song and a list of more than a dozen artists who had recorded it. The memory of that strange sequence of events still raises hairs on the back of my neck and fills me grateful excitement, feelings I have now become familiar with whenever I experience the serendipitous. I share these incidents to illustrate that had I been attuned to the idea of serendipity during that memorable week amid my master's studies, I would have realized that I was somehow being "presented" with a topical area for a research project.

At the time, however, I didn't know that research is personal and that it engages the "I." Composition studies had taught me that "I Writing" refers to personal narratives, but my later feminist and rhetorical studies helped me see that theoretically, the "social turn" suggests that all writing is "I Writing"—the self is always in conversation with others. An important aspect of topical invention, then, is to pay attention to one's affective response to just about anything. I certainly paid attention to my affective response to Smith the next time I ran into her, during my doctoral coursework. Looking for some diversion one weekend, I reread *Strange Fruit* and found myself excited—very excited—because I could now see Smith as both a rhetor and a rhetorician with proto-feminist and proto-postmodern understandings of Othering. While Smith's writing had previously enthralled me, I had not been able to conceive of ways to utilize her work, to make meaning with it. Had I been *attuned*, however, to a conception of research as an endeavor in which the researcher is materially centered *inside* the research, I would have immediately recognized Smith's work as research-worthy. Debra Hawhee describes what such a bodily move entails:

> Bodies, for [Kenneth] Burke, enable critical reflection on meaning-making from an anti-Cartesian, noncognitive, nonrational perspective—that is, from a perspective that does not begin by privileging reason or conscious thought. It would be a mistake, however, to believe (as I did when I began writing this book) that Burke moves to the body as reason's binary other, the sole answer to a Cartesianism that privileges mind and reason. Instead a focus on the body as more than just the obverse of the mind can enable a productive theoretical move to the thought-work of rhythm, energy, material, and movement. Such a move to the body thereby complicates an easy separation between mind and body, body and culture, and, as this book will show, body and language. (2)

In effect, Hawhee here describes the research methodology I developed after I heeded the excitement I felt, a methodology that acknowledges the importance of my body and the validity of my "self" as part of the research process. Listening to the self, however, necessitated a theoretical move on my part, a move to value my gut feelings and to see research as thought-work centered *within* the researcher.

Once I made that theoretical move, my research methods changed dramatically. Because I had taken on such a complex problem, I realized that I needed to take an inter/transdisciplinary approach, which necessitates reading widely, so the ways I read changed correspondingly. Once I understood that, as William H. Newell puts it, "interdisciplinarity is, at root, concerned with the behavior of complex systems" (4), I surrendered to *kairos* and read most of what came my way, whether that entailed reading Facebook posts, book reviews on any sort of topic, or journal articles. Because violence is such a complex system (which explains why Smith wasn't recognized for having a coherent theory, as she *seemed* to write about disparate topics), I knew I had to expand my available means by opening myself to as many sources as possible. Most of the deeply influential sources I used in my writing came from this approach and not, as one might think, from searching keywords and subjects in academic databases. As soon as I realized that the sources that were fundamentally shaping my project seemed to come out of the blue, I attuned myself to that fact and foreswore that I wouldn't foreclose any possibility by refusing to listen to or read something that came my way.

Serendipity (and its counterpart, synchronicity), for whatever reason(s), exists. When I was thinking about writing the first draft of this chapter, for example, two serendipitous events took place within days of each other, which ultimately informed the writing of this piece. First, for the first time in years I met informally with the director of the writing center in which I worked during my master's. As I was telling her about my idea for this collection, she told me my idea reminded her of Irene Clark's phrase "maintaining chaos,"[5] so I read Clark's piece and found it helpful for thinking about this one. Second, later that same week as I was standing next to a shared printer in the humanities office of the university where I'm employed, out shot a page with an excerpt from *SAT Perfect Score: 7 Secrets to Raise Your Score* by Tom Fischgrund, so I took a look at it. According to the page, "The brightest of the bright students have common personality traits and lifestyle habits that made it possible for them to score a perfect score." Not surprisingly, the brightest students "pursue their passions," "create their own luck," and "read quickly and voraciously, following their interests wherever they lead" (53–54).

All three of these practices eventually become habits and place students (or any other researchers) in the center of their own learning. This research method may be likened to a dancer who surrenders to the moment and the music to produce an un-choreographed dance. A researcher-as-dancer metaphor suggests the "thought-work of rhythm, energy, material, and movement" (2) that Hawhee describes as a Burkean perspective on bodies. The music *guides* the dance without overdetermining it, much as sources in a transdisciplinary research project effectively shape (without predetermining and restricting) the knowledge a researcher constructs. The image of an un-choreographed dance, enacted in time and space by a dancer, acknowledges time and chance (both *chronos and kairos*) in research yet moves a discussion of "maintaining chaos" to include the existence of occurrences that arise outside the realm of chance and random coincidence and beyond the vague idea of projects having "lives" of their own. While rhythm, energy, and material are vital variables that represent "chaos" in a researcher-as-dancer model, "maintaining" injects the dancer as the locus where maintenance presides. "Maintaining chaos" serves, then, to establish a vital relationship between the dancer and everything else involved in the dance. In "maintaining chaos," the dancer cannot precisely replicate the dance, which is subject to the vagaries and variables of time, music, energy, and the dancer herself. The aggregate dance therefore can never be precisely choreographed, which is an important caveat for the researcher-as-dancer, an advisory to eschew the "fossilization" of which Clark warns: "not to become so dogmatic, so set in our ways, so fossilized, so sure that we know how to do [something] 'right' that we stop growing and developing" (82). Research-as-dance calls for the "wonder and curiosity" and the "questioning of tradition" that Clark advocates (82), all of which comprise a research strategy that reflects an animus of learning, as evidenced by those successful students who "follow . . . their interests wherever they lead" (Fischgrund 54).

Moreover, a research-as-dance metaphor highlights the belief in self that a researcher needs when undertaking a trans/interdisciplinary research project, which generally requires some creative thought-work with respect to the construction of knowledge. Just as successful students know that they "create their own luck" and are the makers, the producers, of whatever endeavors they undertake (including themselves and their own subjective experiences), dancers know that to perform a dance, they must listen to their bodies as well as their minds. As with many scholars, I am a product of a culture that taught me binary thinking with respect to mind and body in which the mind is disproportionately privileged, especially in cognitive and labor-intensive activities such as intellectual research. This is why listening to our guts as an epistemological endeavor is something we all have to learn by our own efforts.

A couple of experiences during my dissertation research impressed upon me the ways in which listening to the body and trusting one's "gut" are integral to the process of making knowledge. While attunement to affective response is key during topical invention, it is equally important when developing ideas. Idea development is a never-ending process that persists during and beyond the writing up of research. If topical invention were viewed as the subject of a sentence, idea development would be the predicate—everything that comes after nominalization, that is, the "dance" of the verb onward. As a cognitive, bodily, and collective endeavor, such knowledge construction is self-perpetuating and boundless. During my dissertation research, as a "dancer" immersed in the "music" of any number of sources, I discovered the importance of paying attention to the spaces between notes, not just to the notes themselves. That is, relaxation played as significant a role in the construction of knowledge as attentive focus did, which is readily understandable given the nature of transdisciplinary research. "Transdiciplinarity," Hawhee explains, "is marked by shared interest in a particular matter or problem but often draws together radically different approaches" (3). Because transdisicplinarity entails synthesizing disparate approaches, the connections between those approaches often elude notice.

During my research on the etiology of violence, what I found to happen is that, given my approach of reading widely and messily, I would often be exposed to seemingly unrelated yet interesting sources that struck me as irrelevant to my project—until, that is, some later time when I wasn't thinking about the project at all. In fact, epiphanic connections virtually *always* happened when my intellectual focus was directed toward something else, for instance, drifting off to sleep, taking a walk, driving, or showering. I have learned that the our cerebral activities never cease even when we are resting or sleeping. In fact, research suggests that "a relaxed mind is a productive mind" (Goleman) and that relaxing breaks "increase productivity, replenish attention, solidify memories and encourage creativity" (Jabr). Time off turned out to be just as serendipitous as a messy reading strategy, talking with everyone, and listening to whatever came my way.

Suspending my preconceived notions of how I would or should utilize information that came my way is one of the most valuable lessons I learned from adopting a methodology of "maintaining chaos." Epistemologically, I came to see that by placing myself in the center of the research process as "researcher-as-dancer," I had serendipitously come upon a methodology that permitted me to enact an ethic-of-care (Foucault "Ethics," "Genealogy"; Gilligan) with respect to myself. Rather than beat myself up during times of inactivity (either during my own willful downtime or during periods of stasis when it seemed I wasn't making any headway toward developing my ideas and contributing to knowledge construction), I forgave myself for "wasting time," choosing instead to perceive those moments as unavoidable constitutive elements of *any* research project. All projects have stages, and often, for many (myself among them), there are slumps between those stages, when a researcher doesn't know where to go next.

While one must have patience when stuck, expanding one's "available means" through uncensored reading and listening combined with an ethic-of-care that minimizes anxiety can and does, as in my case, move a project along and help bring it to fruition. For many neophyte researchers, the research process can be dispiriting and enervating. However, an "eye-off-the-prize" long view of research can counter such affective tendencies. Adopting a methodology of "maintaining chaos," as underwritten by the concept of researcher-as-dancer and in recognition of research as a form of "I Writing," helped me develop this kind of a long view of research. Cultivating the faculty for serendipity has thus not only accelerated and enriched my research process but has also served as an ideological palliative, often making research an electrifying endeavor and a much more palatable one when not.

Notes

1. It was illegal for the US Post Office to deliver "pornography." Officially, according to Erin Z. Bass, the book remained banned in Boston until 1990.
2. In *Moving Bodies* Debra Hawhee offers this explanation to distinguish interdisciplinarity and transdiciplinarity: "Interdisciplinarity is marked by disciplinary affinity—closely allied fields such as history and literary studies or gender studies and rhetorical studies sharing methods and cross-listing courses—whereas transdiciplinarity is marked by shared interest in a particular matter or problem but often draws together radically different approaches" (3).
3. To that end, I deliberately took a wide variety of classes and completed a graduate certificate in women and gender studies with the aim of expanding the invention process.
4. In conciousness-raising (CR) sessions of the 1960s, denoting both the moment of realization that the "personal is political" and an epistemic change. Here, "click" refers to the latter.
5. Thank you, Carol Haviland, one of my first of many mentors who showed me in numerous and abundant ways that conversation is indeed how knowledge is constructed. A conversational perspective I acquired later, one equally important, suggests that conversation constructs limits of knowledge by delimiting our "available means."

Works Cited

Bass, Erin Z. "The Strange Life of *Strange Fruit*." *Deep South Magazine* (12 Dec. 2012). Web. 22 July 2016.

Butler, Judith. *Excitable Speech: A Politics of the Performative*. New York: Routledge, 1997. Print.

Clark, Irene Lurkis. "Maintaining Chaos in the Writing Center: A Critical Perspective on Writing Center Dogma." *Writing Center Journal* 11.1 (1990): 81–93. Print.

Fischgrund, Tom. *SAT Perfect Score: 7 Secrets to Raise Your Score*. New York: HarperCollins, 2004. Print.

Foucault, Michel. "The Ethics of the Concern of the Self as a Practice of Freedom." *Ethics: Subjectivity and Truth*. Ed. Paul Rabinow. New York: New Press, 1997. 281–301. Print.

Foucault, Michel. "On the Genealogy of Ethics." *Ethics: Subjectivity and Truth*. Ed. Paul Rabinow. New York: New Press, 1997. 253–80. Print.

Gilligan, Carol. "Moral Orientation and Moral Development." *Feminist Ethical Theory*. Ed. Alison Bailey and Chris Cuomo. Boston: McGraw-Hill Higher Education, 2008. 467–77. Print.

Goleman, Daniel. "A Relaxed Mind Is a Productive Mind." *Mindful*. 10 Sept. 2015. Web. 15 Jan. 2018.

Hawhee, Debra. *Moving Bodies: Kenneth Burke at the Edges of Language*. Columbia: U of South Carolina P, 2009. Print.

Jabr, Ferris. "Why Your Brain Needs More Downtime." *Scientific American*. 15 Oct. 2013. Web. 15 Jan. 2018.

Newell, William H. "A Theory of Interdisciplinary Studies." *Issues in Integrative Studies* 19 (2001): 1–25. Print.

Smith, Lillian. *Strange Fruit*. New York: Reynal and Hitchcock, 1944. Print.

20
THE STRANGE PRACTICES OF SERENDIPITOUS FAILURE
Considering Metanoia *as an Alternative to* Kairos

Zachary Beare

> *Under certain circumstances failing, losing, forgetting, unmaking, undoing, unbecoming, not knowing may in fact offer more creative, more cooperative, more surprising ways of being in the world.*
> —Judith Halberstam

In the spring of 2010, just as I was finishing my master's thesis, I was rejected by seven PhD programs. By some mail-merge fluke (or cosmic joke), the University of Minnesota sent me three rejection letters on the same day, bringing my sad collection of letterheaded sheets of paper up to nine. This is, of course, one of those stories we are not supposed to tell in the academy. Higher education is a business in which we chart success, listing degrees, awards, publications, grants, and other markers of achievement. In this hyper-competitive space, as the job market continues to narrow, failure is not something to be shared out loud; it is a secret shame, the kind shared behind closed doors with only the most trusted colleagues. Even now, seven years later, I feel a great deal of anxiety in sharing this truth about myself. I can feel my face flush and my throat tighten. I struggle with the urge to defend my application file to the readers of this chapter, to share GPAs and honors and all the relevant CV data to explain why I should have been admitted. I want to present testimonials from the professors who assured me I would be accepted and funded. But the fact is, I wasn't. I was rejected by all the programs I applied to. The dream of getting a PhD in literature was, at least for the moment, gone.

It is difficult to describe the identity crisis I experienced in 2010. I had always been the "good student," and suddenly that identity marker—the one I had considered so essential to my conception of self—was going to be out of reach. As the type of neurotic student who thought in five-year plans, I suddenly found myself without a future. Like someone discovering that half of the map had been erased, I felt disoriented and confused; all the information had been right there in front of me a second ago, but now it was inexplicably gone. At the same time, I was also faced with the horrifying realization that my not being in school meant that my mounting student loans would transition into repayment within six months. This meant two things: I needed to get a job (and fast), and I needed a job that would pay consistently because I was going to have a much more complicated budget.

This second requirement was trickier. While most of my friends were looking at jobs as adjuncts at multiple institutions, I knew that that the inconsistency of adjunct work wasn't a wise option for me with the amount of debt I had; I wouldn't be able to handle having my salary drop by half at the end of an academic term. But as a newly minted MA, a tenure-track community college position in the Puget Sound region was basically out of the question. The market was too saturated with applicants with more teaching experience. This meant I had to look for non-teaching jobs. This reality was the second blow. Throughout my master's program, teaching was what I had come to love most. Though I enjoyed and excelled at my work studying and writing about literature, it was the time I spent working in the classroom with writers that I found most energizing. It broke my heart to realize that I would likely have to be outside that classroom space for a while. Feeling somewhat defeated, I started applying for various staff jobs at different institutions, mainly in advising, but I also applied for a job as the coordinator of a writing center at the University of Washington, Tacoma, and this was the job that, to use the inescapable cliché, "changed my life."

Typically, when one thinks about serendipity, one associates it with positive affect. One usually imagines those moments when the stars align and all the pieces fall into place, those moments when everything works out. But, of course, stars align in all sorts of ways, many of which do not feel as fortunate and some of which feel devastating. In this short chapter, I want to consider those moments when serendipity doesn't feel serendipitous, those moments when serendipity is accompanied by the negative affects of disappointment, frustration, depression, and anxiety. I want to explore those moments when serendipity involves everything going wrong, or at least when it is born out of moments perceived as tragic or evidence of failure.

Rather than the typical association of serendipity with *kairos* (opportunity), in this chapter I consider how events from my own academic life of research and teaching showcase how *metanoia* (missed opportunity) should also be considered for its serendipitous possibilities. Kelly Myers has provided perhaps the most extensive discussion and theorization of *metanoia* in "*Metanoia* and the Transformation of Opportunity." In distinguishing *kairos* from *metanoia*, Myers explains that "if *kairos* is seized, a person is carried down the path of that particular opportunity, but if the moment is missed, the path(s) of *metanoia* remain—paths that bring opportunities richly variegated with reflection, regret, transformation, and repentance. In this revitalized space, the missed moment can be reconceptualized as a rhetorical and reflective tool" (11). In this way, then, the removal of one route of opportunity makes room for the consideration of multiple alternative options. To think about this in terms of the anecdote with which I began this chapter, while it might have been easy in the moment to see my rejection from PhD programs as an erasure of opportunity, as the least serendipitous experience of my academic life (and indeed I did think about it in this way at the time), considering the situation in light of *metanoia* showcases the ways this missed opportunity afforded alternate paths that might (and indeed *did*) lead to discovery. In some ways, this makes missed opportunity potentially even more generative of serendipitous possibilities.

But more than just illustrating newly available routes for action, Myers provides a thoughtful discussion of the ways missed opportunity affords individuals time to reflect on their current state of being, to process experiences, and to prepare themselves for the future. As she argues, "*Metanoia* offers an important form of reflection in which the emotional impact of a missed opportunity motivates a transformation of thought, advancing a rhetor's understanding of the situation. Thus through such a learning process, painful as it may be, a rhetor becomes better prepared for the next moment of opportunity" (11). In a similar vein, this chapter tries to illustrate the way my own experiences of disappointment, missed opportunity, and dislocation have afforded the space and time to think about my career and academic trajectory and to discover and complicate my research in the field, the way moments of incredible discomfort have, in fact, been most serendipitous.

STRANGER IN A STRANGE LAND

When I first accepted my position coordinating the writing center at the University of Washington, Tacoma (UWT), I knew that I was stepping into new and alien terrain because I would be transitioning from the position of a teacher to a position as an administrator responsible for overseeing and training a staff of writing tutors, preparing budget information, and developing and utilizing qualitative and quantitative measures of assessment. I would also have to dedicate a great deal of time to one-on-one consultations with students and faculty about writing pedagogy and writing assignment design and assessment. Though it may seem like the business end of the administrative position would have been the most difficult adjustment for me, and, indeed, I assumed it would be, I was surprised to find out very quickly that the most difficult part of navigating this new environment would come at the conference table working one-on-one with student writers.

This was partly because of the makeup of the student body at UWT. UWT was initially conceived of as an upper-division and graduate institution designed to serve the South Puget Sound. During my time there, the majority of students I consulted with were graduate students in professional programs, specifically social work and nursing. UWT is still relatively small, but at the time I was there, the writing center had approximately 3,300 appointments per academic year—a number greater than the full-time enrollment, a ratio that is impressive in the writing center world. Approximately 25 percent of these appointments were with graduate students in the two professional programs, who made up over 75 percent of the students I saw during my time there.

While I was skilled at and trained to write about contemporary American literature and popular culture and I had some training and experience teaching first-year composition, I entered this position with almost no knowledge of the writing practices and research methodologies utilized in professional programs like nursing and social work. I quickly found myself in a position where I was asked to tutor students in disciplines very alien to my own; not only was I tasked with this, I was also tasked with the job of preparing others to tutor this population.

Both of these tasks created a great deal of anxiety for me and brought up issues related to power, authority, and the assumption of expertise because despite my own knowledge and how ill-prepared I was, both my tutors and my students assumed and expected me to be an authority. Nancy Grimm provides one of the best discussions of the complex power relations and negotiations that take place at the conference table in her book *Good Intentions: Writing Center Work for Postmodern Times*. Grimm explains that "whether or not a writing tutor feels she is in a position of institutional power, the students who walk into a room institutionally labeled 'Writing Center' automatically construct [those] sitting inside the room as having institutional authority . . . [and have an] expectation that they have some sort of expertise" (113). Grimm is discussing institutional authority and expectations of expertise to dispel the myth that undergraduate tutors can be conceived of as "peers" with the students they are working with, but I think her argument is also useful to think about when one considers the frustrations writing tutors and tutees have when working in disciplines alien to our own. Students see tutors as authorities who must possess some form of expertise, and tutors know they are being constructed in this way. This is the situation in which I found myself almost immediately; despite being a stranger in a strange land, I was expected to perform as a guide. Students' expectations of my expertise created numerous ethical dilemmas and forced me to wrestle with my ego, my desire to appear as an authority, and my commitment to a critical pedagogy that embraces transparency. At the same time, this discrepancy between expectation and reality established the exigency that pushed me to learn as much as I could about writing in these alien disciplines.

This experience of dislocation and anxiety is what led me to the field of composition and rhetoric, first out of necessity and then, later, out of excitement. In struggling to understand how to communicate with these students in social work and nursing, I remember reading Charles Bazerman's "The Life of Genre, the Life in the Classroom" and his argument that "genres are not just forms. Genres are forms of life, ways of being. They are frames for social action. They are environments for learning . . . and guideposts we use to explore the unfamiliar" (19). These last two sentences are for me two of the most interesting and important insights of genre theory, for they speak to the ways we *do genres* and the ways genres provide a frame and roadmap to explore and comprehend the unfamiliar. These social and structural insights became very important to me as I learned more about these disciplines because they also provided insights into their social, epistemological, and ontological dimensions. In addition, my growing understanding of the importance of examining genre led me to another tool of composition and rhetoric—discourse analysis. I pored over published journal articles in these disciplines, dissecting and labeling the rhetorical moves found to identify the features of the genres to determine what Carolyn Miller describes as "typified rhetorical responses based in recurrent situations" (31). I emailed countless faculty members to ask for assignment sheets to construct rhetorical outlines and gain insight into the rationales behind such work. This ability to identify and articulate the structure of writing in these disciplines became incredibly useful in conversations with students and faculty, and for me it emphasized Grimm's insistence that "meta-discursive fluency—the ability to recognize and articulate the different values, expectations, and habits of mind that underlie competing cultural notions of literacy—is a skill that the most effective writing center workers develop without conscious awareness" (52).

Though I developed some means for navigating these alien disciplines, means that deepened with every new consultation I had with a student, it is important for me to note that this development as a professional would not have been possible or realized without the initial experience of not knowing, of recognizing my position as an outsider, of being clueless in this space where I was supposed to be an expert. David Gold argues that cluelessness is "a feeling . . . at the heart of the scholarly process" (15). He writes that at any given point, "your growing body of expertise simply mark[s] the expanding edge of your ignorance" (15). And, of course, there is work to be done at these edges of ignorance; these edges inspire the new research questions. My experience of not knowing how to work with this group of students created, to use a phrase from Gayatri Spivak, a "productive crisis." I think such moments of crisis are one of the beauties of writing center work (and of scholarly work more broadly). One never knows what the next conference session will bring.

This element of uncertainty can afford us as educators and writers the opportunity to reflect on the situated and limited natures of our knowledge and can help us empower and inspire the work of our students. Nancy Welch discusses this rather beautifully in "Migrant Rationalities: Graduate Students and the Idea of Authority in the Writing Center." Welch explains that "we need to continually remind ourselves and our students that incompleteness and uncertainty are not tragedies to be covered up with authoritative statements. Instead, incompleteness . . . is an opportunity to talk, to write, to imagine what else [one] might say, what [one] needs to learn. Likewise, a teacher's uncertainty—a moment that exiles us from our usual advice and forces us to recognize the limits of what we know—can also be a rich site for learning, if we acknowledge those limits, voice our uncertainty" (19). I read Welch's essay when I was first beginning to recover from my own feelings of depression and displacement in my new job, and I was moved by her use of the word "exile." Her ability to see its critical and pedagogical potential, to see the ways that being an outsider can motivate thought and reflection, is impressive, and it is a view of writing center work that has significantly impacted my ideas of the profession and the space of the center. It speaks to both the complexity and fraught nature of writing center work within the university and its incredible potential. I think this conceptualization of exile also connects nicely to the serendipitous possibilities of missed opportunities, of seeing opportunities for learning and growth and discovery in spaces that seem scary and treacherous.

WALKING INTO RESEARCH PROJECTS

At the same time I have been using this chapter to discuss the ways experiences of crisis, dislocation, and perceived failure necessitated and inspired learning and my own disciplinary reorientation within English studies, I also want to showcase the ways these types of experiences have inspired and complicated more specific research projects. In fall of 2011, after a long campaign advocating for the creation of a course on Writing Center Theory and Practice to train new tutors, I was able to teach the course for the first time. This first incarnation in 2011 was somewhat unusual because the majority of my students were tutors with significant tutoring experience rather than the new tutors or students who might someday want to be tutors who normally populate such courses. Perhaps because I was teaching a group of veteran writing center tutors, I, perhaps foolishly, predicted a relatively smooth reception of course readings. This assumption was destroyed almost immediately, but it was on the fourth day of class, the day we sat down to discuss Andrea Lunsford's "Collaboration, Control, and the Idea of a Writing Center," that I was most struck by a tension between my vision of writing center work and the one possessed by my team of smart and capable tutors.

Lunsford's often-taught landmark essay describes three conceptualizations of the writing center: (1) as a storehouse of information, an idea emerging from the banking model of education; (2) as a garret center, which follows a sort of Romantic idealization of the individual author as a singular source of knowledge; and (3) as the Burkean parlor, a space of necessary and important dialogue and collaboration, which Lunsford champions. As I was preparing for the class discussion on Lunsford's essay, I assumed we would discuss the problems with the storehouse and garret house models and then move into sort of a celebration of the radical re-envisioning of education represented by the Burkean parlor model of writing center work.

That is not what happened, though.

Even before class began, Stefan, a tutor who had worked at writing centers at multiple institutions, raised his hand and, with obvious frustration, asked, "Why is Lunsford so against helping writers be independent? Don't we want it to be all *their* work?"

On the one hand, Stefan's confusion seemed to be centered around a disconnect between the "hands-off" policy commonly adopted by many centers (including ours) that is designed to locate the locus of agency within the individual writer and to avoid imposing the tutor's ideas, vision, or logic onto the piece of writing. Stefan seemed very committed to such a perspective. In a strange but understandable way, he didn't want to see himself as essential to the learning that takes place inside the center. Beyond Stefan, it quickly became clear that I faced a class of tutors who very much wanted to defend the garret house model, who were invested in and convinced that the mission of writing centers should be to celebrate the individual author and foster the writer's independence, that the ultimate goal of the writing center is to help the writer be as self-sufficient as possible.

This tension that manifested itself within my classroom is representative of a larger disciplinary debate, and a reminder of that came only two days after this class discussion of Lunsford. That weekend I was at a regional Two-Year College English Association conference, attending a presentation on the value of collaboration in writing center work. The presenters began by projecting the mission statement of their center, which ended with this line: "Our goal is to help students develop skills to foster their independence as writers." The mission statement, juxtaposed with the presentation's insistence on the value of collaboration, showcased a dissonance that I found fascinating, and I immediately wanted to study it.

This moment in teaching, then, a moment where nothing went as I had hoped, inspired a research project I continue to work on today. To begin to answer this question, I decided to start collecting mission statements to engage in a more organized study of them. I initially had two research questions: (1) Given the amount of scholarship that details both individual and institutional misunderstandings of the missions of writing centers, what do our own words tell us about how we envision our work? And more specifically, (2) Do writing center mission statements (a) emphasize a goal of creating/fostering independent writers, or (b) do they articulate a vision of writing and learning that sees these activities as inherently collaborative? Throughout the process of analysis, multiple other research questions have emerged and sent me back to reinvestigate the data I have collected.

I had two main goals to help accomplish this—institutional variation and geographic diversity—and with those goals, I worked to construct a structured sample of 150 online, publicly accessible mission statements, three from each state. Because I wanted to have some sort of institutional comparison, I decided to create my sample by locating a mission statement from one public research institution, one private liberal arts institution, and one two-year community college from each of the fifty states.

The findings from this study have revealed fascinating trends about the ways different institution types privilege independence versus collaboration (and the ways these respective emphases are likely a result of the budgetary restrictions of histories of certain institution types). I have also been fortunate that numerous serendipitous events have inspired me to reexamine my data set through new lenses and discover even more intriguing findings. For instance, presenting on a panel about the ways writing center tutor alumni have been impacted by their tutoring experience led me to discover the almost complete absence of references to tutors in mission statements (which also is connected to conceptualizations of writing center work as either collaborative or fostering the independence of writers), and participating in a roundtable on writing centers and social justice work sent me back to the data set to discover the surprising absence of references to the social justice work of writing centers in our missions.

This project, which has continued to be generative, was born out of multiple layers of perceived failure, of things not going right—the class period that didn't go as I had planned and, perhaps more significant, the job and field I found myself in when Plan A didn't work out. But again, isn't that what serendipity is?

FAILURE FUTURES

While it might be tempting for me to look at (and explain) my current happiness in the field of composition and rhetoric and the continued evolution of various research projects as evidence of success, as everything going right and falling into place, I think it is important on both a political and an epistemological level to both remember and narrate the feelings of failure these successes emerged from. The way failure is taboo in the academy is disturbing to me because, personally speaking, my most learningful experiences as a student, as a teacher, and as an administrator have involved failure and interrogation of the *felt* realities of those experiences.

I would also urge us to remember that despite being a taboo, failure is strangely (and beautifully) central to the nature of academic work. We need to remember that the process of continually working on the edges of our knowledge and understanding, which I would argue is what we are supposed to be doing, involves navigating strange and alien terrain and will surely involve missteps. Though uncomfortable to say and realize, I would argue that our work continually fails. The whole enterprise of academic work and publishing relies on this fact. Our projects never fully succeed, our arguments are forever incomplete, resolutions are continually deferred. There is always more work to be done.

In my classroom, I frequently remind students about the etymology of the word "essay," its origins in the French *essayer*, meaning "to attempt, to try." I explain to them that the genre itself foresees its own failure, and yet we continue on ahead in spite of this. To me, this idea is key. When I talk about my interest in embracing failure with colleagues, too often individuals assume that I am adopting or advocating for some sort of defeatist position. This is not so. Rather, I argue that the skill of recognizing and interrogating the always existing failures of our attempts is central to our work as academics, as teachers, and as program administrators. There is opportunity in that work. Serendipity is housed there.

Works Cited

Bazerman, Charles. "The Life of Genre, the Life in the Classroom." *Genre and Writing: Issues, Arguments, Alternatives*. Ed. Wendy Bishop and Hans Ostrom. Portsmouth, NH: Boyton/Cook, 1997. 19–26. Print.

Gold, David. "The Accidental Archivist: Embracing Chance and Confusion in Historical Scholarship." *Beyond the Archives: Research as a Lived Process*. Ed. Gesa E. Kirsch and Liz Rohan. Carbondale: Southern Illinois UP, 2008. 13–19. Print.

Grimm, Nancy. *Good Intentions: Writing Center Work for Postmodern Times*. Portsmouth, NH: Boyton/Cook, 1999. Print.

Halberstam, Judith. *The Queer Art of Failure*. Durham, NC: Duke UP, 2011. Print.

Lunsford, Andrea. "Collaboration, Control, and the Idea of a Writing Center." *Writing Center Journal* 12.1 (1991): 3–10. Print.

Miller, Carolyn. "Genres as Social Action." *Genre and the New Rhetoric*. Ed. Aviva Freedman and Peter Medway. Bristol: Taylor and Francis, 1994. 23–42. Print.

Myers, Kelly. "*Metanoia* and the Transformation of Opportunity." *Rhetoric Society Quarterly* 41.1 (2011): 1–18. Print.

Spivak, Gayatri. *The Post-Colonial Critic: Interviews, Strategies, Dialogues*. New York: Routledge, 1990. Print.

Welch, Nancy. "Migrant Rationalities: Graduate Students and the Idea of Authority in the Writing Center." *Writing Center Journal* 16.1 (1995): 5–23. Print.

AFTERWORD
Serendipity and Ethics in Rhetoric, Writing, and Literacy Research

Gesa E. Kirsch

The vivid stories assembled in *Serendipity in Rhetoric, Writing, and Literacy Research* illustrate powerfully the importance of researchers' curiosity, surprise, and flexibility—facets that can lead researchers down unexpected paths, reveal surprising insights, shape their choice of research methodologies, and influence their engagement with the community. This fine collection of essays continues the tradition of collecting researchers' encounters with serendipity that were begun in such volumes as *Working in the Archives* (Ramsey et al.) and *Beyond the Archives* (Kirsch and Rohan). While these earlier volumes focus on archival research, the editors of this collection, Maureen Daly Goggin and Peter Goggin, offer a timely, rich expansion of studies of serendipity by highlighting a broad range of research topics—all of which, we learn here, also depend on chance discoveries, an open and prepared mind, and a willingness to be surprised. We encounter scholars who discover that they need to invent or adapt research methodologies that speak to the moment (a disaster), the location (New Orleans), and the community that attempts to cope with and mobilize after disaster hits (Piano, this volume). We meet scholars who chance upon great opportunities (unexpected access to grant funding, a rare manuscript, the opportunity to digitize historical materials) and equally great challenges (coping with the loss of a colleague, assessing the risk of pursuing an unconventional research project before being tenured; Endres, this volume). We also learn of scholars who use the occasion of a chance phone call to a former colleague as the basis for a new research project, investigating the rhetorical practices (and failures) of pre-sentencing reports that are mandated in the criminal justice system (Converse, this volume).

When Liz Rohan and I first began collecting stories of "archival adventures" (as I have come to think of them) for *Beyond the Archives: Research as a Lived Process*, we learned of the origins of our contributors' research projects—often highly personal, deeply meaningful, and intimately connected to some part of the scholar's identity, history, community, culture, or lived experience. Further, we learned that the archival experience can be transformative: the researcher enters the archives as one person and leaves as another, transformed in some way by having discovered a little "nugget of gold"—a quote, a letter, a photograph, a handwritten note, a medical record, a conference program, or a historical artifact. When researchers explore, touch, and handle historical artifacts, their responses can be strong, visceral, and embodied; archival encounters almost always evoke passion, intrigue, and excitement.

What Liz and I did *not* know was how many of our colleagues would want to share stories of serendipity, sagacity, and chance discoveries; nor did we anticipate how much intrigue and mystery can be involved during field trips, site visits, or jaunts to the attic, the basement, or the kitchen pantry. We also did not realize the full extent to which the archives themselves can serve either as formidable gatekeepers—foreboding, even ominous—or as inviting gateways—promising, thrilling starting points for treasure hunts. Once *Beyond the Archives* was published, we were surprised once again—and pleased—by the great response the book received and by the number of colleagues and students who reached out to tell us "I have a story, too. I wish I could have written a chapter for your book."

For this reason alone, I am particularly delighted to see this volume come to fruition, as it offers a valuable contribution to our understanding of sagacity and serendipity in rhetoric, writing, and literacy research. With this book in hand, writing studies scholars from now on will be able to teach students—as a matter of fact—that the research process can be exciting, surprising, and challenging; that it involves passion, a sense of curiosity, and a sense of place; and that it can reveal delightful surprises as well as painful secrets (more on this below).

HOW DO WE INVITE SERENDIPITY INTO OUR LIVES?

Much has been said about the fact that "chance favors the prepared mind." By now, it has become apparent, even self-evident, that researchers who are poised to invoke serendipitous encounters tend to be creative, flexible, willing to adjust on the fly, to step outside their comfort zone, live with ambiguity, and read widely across fields, across domains, and beyond their areas of expertise (e.g., Holiday, this volume; Ostergaard, this volume).[1] In the excellent literature review on serendipity that Goggin and Goggin offer in the introduction to this volume, they cite, among others, the work of Isabelle Rivoal and Noel Salazar, two authors who list four salient characteristics that can enable serendipity: "sufficient background knowledge, an inquisitive mind, creative thinking, and good timing" (Goggin and Goggin, this volume, 6). To these characteristics I would add the importance of *embodiment, a sense of place*, and *being mindful*. Here I draw from the notion of *strategic contemplation*, a concept Jacqueline Jones Royster and I developed in *Feminist Rhetorical Practices: New Horizons for Rhetoric, Composition, and Literacy Studies*. We propose:

> Ultimately, with the term *strategic contemplation*, we want to reclaim a genre of research and scholarship traditionally associated with processes of meditation, introspection, and reflection. We suggest that using a meditative/contemplative approach allows researchers to access another, often underutilized dimension of the research process . . .
>
> This process of paying attention, of being mindful, of attending to the subtle, intuitive, not-so-obvious parts of research has the capacity to yield rich rewards. It allows scholars to observe and notice, to listen and to hear voices often neglected or silenced, and to notice more overtly their own responses to what they are seeing, reading, reflecting on, and encountering during their research processes. Strategic contemplation asks us to take as much into account as possible but to withhold judgment for a time and resist coming to closure too soon in order to make the time to invite creativity, wonder, and inspiration into the research process. (84–85)

In short, setting aside time for reflection, introspection, and contemplation allows researchers to be attuned to embodied experiences, to speculate about possibilities, and to cultivate mindfulness. Numerous authors in this collection speak to this process; particularly vivid is Jennifer Clary-Lemon's description of her sense of place, embodiment, intuition, and geography as she moves across an international border for a job opportunity and, in the process, stumbles upon an unexpected research project that requires further international travel. She suggests—and clearly illustrates—how "we tangle our bodies up with things, we mark knowing with intangible conversations and feelings about place, we listen differently and attune ourselves to people, objects, media, and geographies" (Clary-Lemon, this volume, 216). In her chapter as well as several others (e.g., Rohan, this volume; Wilde, this volume), we learn how mindfulness, introspection, and a sense of place can contribute to new insights, pathways, and research projects.

When we reclaim "meditation" as a scholarly practice, as Royster and I propose we do, we need to resist the impulse to make quick judgments: to sort, categorize, analyze, and evaluate immediately the research materials we encounter. Our training as scholars and academics has prepared us well for this later process—making judgments—and much less for the open-ended, exploratory process required of strategic contemplation: to invite our whole selves into the research process—body, mind, and spirit—and to make time to notice, observe, and listen. This holds true whether we are conducting research in the archives, the classroom, the workplace, or the community.

HOW DO WE DEAL WITH ETHICAL CHALLENGES AND DISTURBING DISCOVERIES?

Woven throughout the narratives in this volume are questions of ethics and serendipity: What are our obligations when we come across unexpected opportunities? Bill Endres raises some provocative questions in this regard: Do researchers have an ethical obligation to act on serendipitous opportunities? Do they need to act immediately or at least in a timely fashion? Does a "happy accident" represent an invitation, an opportunity, a responsibility, or an obligation? Should we stop what we are doing, shift trajectories, and devote time when an extraordinary opportunity arises? Endres tells the story of coming face to face with an exceptionally rare opportunity: to digitize a medieval manuscript. All the right components came together—funding, access, and being in the right location at the right time. Endres decided to go for it: to seize the moment and pursue this rare opportunity, even at the risk of compromising his career path—and possibly his livelihood—as a tenure-track faculty member who was expected to publish in more traditional scholarly venues. The answer to Endres's question—whether we have an ethical obligation to seize a *kairotic* moment—turns out to be, I venture to say, "it depends" (as it so often does). It depends on the many facets in a scholar's life—time, space, working conditions, family obligations, financial resources, moral support, and more. Endres's ethical dilemma centered on a historical artifact—a dilemma of a more abstract nature, though no less challenging, than those associated with people's lives. When research involves our contemporaries—students, colleagues, community members—or historical figures, ethical dilemmas can take on an added urgency and complexity (as I have argued elsewhere, "Being on Location"). We have to make choices about ethics and representation and consider how to represent those whom we study thoughtfully and respectfully, with dignity and care, with considerations of impact and consequences (see also Mortensen and Kirsch).

Alongside teaching and celebrating occasions of "serendipity in rhetoric, writing, and literacy," as many authors in this collection do, I propose that we need to be prepared—and help prepare students—for the emotional upheaval, turmoil, or pain that can emerge when research reveals painful secrets or disturbing cultural histories. As scholars wade into the messiness of research, there is a good chance that they might be startled, disturbed, aggrieved, humiliated, or devastated by their discoveries. When researchers make troubling discoveries, the notion of being curious, passionate, and open-minded may not suffice.[2] Rather, we may have to steel ourselves to become strong, resilient, and courageous. This is risky business, especially for researchers in vulnerable positions, such as graduate students, lecturers, and those on tenure-track positions.

A number of authors in this collection tell stories of how adventures can go awry, revealing disturbing cultural histories and reminding readers that the archives—as well as local communities—can reveal pain and suffering, death and dying (Coskan-Johnson, this volume). Such was the case when Shirley Faulkner-Springfield (this volume) discovered the archival records that classify her great-great-grandfather Friday Faulkner as human chattel; or when Gail Okawa discovered, through a bundle of letters kept by her family, the painful past—and shame—experienced by her grandfather who was accused of being an "alien enemy" during World War II, forcefully removed from his home in Hawaii, and interned in New Mexico ("Unbundling"); or when researchers come face to face with disaster and the loss of life in their communities, as was the case for Doreen Piano (this volume). Piano lived through Hurricane Katrina, witnessing death, decay, and willful neglect—a failure of state and federal agencies to act promptly. More than ten years later she continues to confront the legacy of the disaster, a process that has changed her research focus, her research methodologies, and her commitment to community, advocacy, and social justice. How, then, do we prepare ourselves and our students for the potential of facing an emotional upset, an ethical dilemma, or a heart-wrenching, perhaps traumatic event?

The contributors to this volume offer some possible answers. Piano proposes that our research methodologies should adapt and evolve to fit the rhetorical exigency; Gale Coskan-Johnson suggests that anger and outrage might be an appropriate response when researchers encounter xenophobia, violent border crossings, and the fact that "immigrant death is rarely in the news" (this volume, 46); and Zachary Beare reflects on what he calls "serendipitous failure," moments of defeat and rejection that led him to take unexpected pathways through the academic world. As painful and challenging as these journeys may have been for these scholars, they provide an important framework for rethinking the ethical challenges and emotional upheavals researchers can encounter during the research process, especially when they discover that what they thought was a "happy accident" turns out to be an unhappy one.

In the current age of discontent, I argue, it is ever more important that we support, honor, and respect human dignity, especially for those who find themselves in vulnerable positions. As we are enmeshed in the volatile times of the 2016 post-election era, as conversations on campus and around the country have become increasingly divisive and hostile, we need to be particularly mindful of those who feel silenced, disrespected, or threatened. We need to develop rhetorical strategies and ethical moves that help us address, support, and advocate for diversity and social justice in all its forms. Some of the authors in this volume begin to address these issues; in fact, they seem downright prescient: Coskan-Johnson, for example, reflects on the violence and deaths experienced by those who cross borders (and our callous responses to such death and dying). Similarly, Piano explores governmental responsibility (or lack thereof) for rebuilding disaster-stricken communities, and Clary-Lemon explores the opportunities and risks involved in crossing international borders in pursuit of job and research opportunities—all topics that have taken on a new urgency in the current political climate.

How do we speak truth to power when faced with forces that work against an inclusive, diverse vision of citizenship? How do we restore, honor, and acknowledge the humanity of all of us—past, present, and future—regardless of color, creed, religion, gender, sexual orientation, age, ability, and national origin? How do we promote and reaffirm human dignity—imbued in our constitution as well as our professional code of conduct as educators—when we face an increase in backlash, violent speech, and hate crimes? These vexing questions are too large to tackle here; nevertheless, they are precisely the ones we need to keep front and center, I affirm, as we conduct research in rhetoric, writing, and literacy, as we teach students in graduate and undergraduate courses, as we engage in the communities in which we live, and as we try to become advocates and activists for social justice.[3]

Notes

1. These qualities are also attributed to creative scholars, innovators, and entrepreneurs, according to research on creativity. As someone who teaches in the innovation and creativity unit of the Bentley MBA, I have been struck by the parallels between discussions of serendipity in rhetorical studies and those in the literature on creativity, innovation, and design thinking in business education.
2. When adventures go awry, we no longer describe such experiences as "happy accidents," "fortuitous discoveries," or "chance encounters." Instead, we opt for

language that calls attention to their disturbing nature, such as a "nightmare," "journey to the dark side," or "struggle for justice."
3. Some of our professional organizations have begun to take a lead on this front; for example, the November 2016 Statement on Language, Power, and Action by the CCCC declares: "As an organization, CCCC reaffirms its commitments to cultivating thoughtful speakers and writers, to ethical teaching and research, and to classrooms that engage the full range of the power and potential of writers and writing. Acting on these commitments requires respect for diversity, equity, social justice, and intellectual and pedagogical freedom." See also the statements issued by the RSA, WPA, AERA, and MLA after the November 2016 election.

Works Cited

CCCC Statement on Language, Power, and Action. November 2016. Web. 30 Nov. 2016.

Kirsch, Gesa E. "Being on Location: Serendipity, Place, and Archival Research." *Beyond the Archives: Research as a Lived Process*. Ed. Gesa E. Kirsch and Liz Rohan. Carbondale: Southern Illinois UP, 2008. 20–27. Print.

Kirsch, Gesa E., and Liz Rohan. *Beyond the Archives: Research as a Lived Process*. Carbondale: Southern Illinois UP, 2008. Print.

Mortensen, Peter, and Gesa E. Kirsch, eds. *Ethics and Representation in Qualitative Studies of Literacy*. Urbana, IL: National Council of Teachers of English, 1996. Print.

Okawa, Gail. "Unbundling: Archival Research and Japanese American Communal Memory of US Justice Department Internment, 1941–45." *Beyond the Archives: Research as a Lived Process*. Ed. Gesa E. Kirsch and Liz Rohan. Carbondale: Southern Illinois UP, 2008. 93–106. Print.

Ramsey, Alexis E., Wendy Sharer, Barbara L'Eplattenier, and Lisa Mastrangelo, eds. *Working in the Archives: Practical Research Methods for Rhetoric and Composition*. Carbondale: Southern Illinois UP, 2009. Print.

Royster, Jacqueline Jones, and Gesa E. Kirsch. *Feminist Rhetorical Practices: New Horizons for Rhetoric, Composition, and Literacy Studies*. Carbondale: Southern Illinois UP, 2012. Print.

ABOUT THE AUTHORS

MAUREEN DALY GOGGIN is professor of rhetoric in and former chair of the Department of English at Arizona State University. She is the author and editor of nine scholarly books and several editions of a textbook and a pedagogical book. Her latest work includes *Shifting Perspectives: Personal and Political Transformations* (2016), co-edited with three graduate students, and *Women and the Material Culture of Death* (Ashgate, 2013), co-edited with Beth Fowkes Tobin. She has written widely about the history of rhetoric, writing pedagogy, gender, visual rhetoric, and women and material culture in both journals and edited collections. Currently, she is co-editing a collection with Shirley Rose titled *Women's Ways of Making*.

PETER N. GOGGIN is an associate professor in rhetoric (English) and a senior scholar in the Global Institute of Sustainability at Arizona State University. He is the editor of *Environmental Rhetoric and Ecologies of Place* (Routledge, 2013) and *Rhetorics, Literacies, and Narratives of Sustainability* (Routledge, 2009) and the author of *Professing Literacy in Composition Studies* (Hampton, 2008). His articles on literacy, environmental rhetoric, and writing include publication in *Composition Studies, Community Literacy Journal*, and *Computers and Composition*. He is founder and co-director of the annual Western States Rhetoric and Literacy conference, which features themes on sustainability, culture, transnationality, and place.

ELLEN BARTON is a professor in the Linguistics Program and Department of English at Wayne State University in Detroit, Michigan. Her research interests are in medical communication and medical rhetoric, using mixed-methods approaches to explore ethically charged communicative events such as end-of-life discussions, offers to participate in cancer clinical trials, and deliberation on Institutional Review Boards. Her research on Motivational Interviewing has been published in the *Journal of Developmental and Behavioral Pediatrics* and *Patient Education and Counseling*.

ZACHARY BEARE is a PhD student and the Associate Writing Center coordinator at the University of Nebraska–Lincoln. His work focuses on the political, ethical, and affective dimensions of writing instruction and writing program administration, issues of embodiment and performance, and critical (especially feminist and queer) pedagogies and rhetorics. He is engaged in a multi-year project investigating the ways failure, anxiety, and other negative affects impact and shape the teaching and scholarly practices of academics in the field of composition and rhetoric (often in positive ways). He has work forthcoming in *College Composition and Communication*.

LYNN Z. BLOOM recently retired after twenty-seven years as Aetna Chair of Writing and Board of Trustees Distinguished Professor at the University of Connecticut. Many of her happiest professional endeavors have been serendipitous, from writing *Doctor Spock: Biography of a Conservative Radical* (1972) to commuting 2,000 miles weekly from St. Louis to the University of New Mexico after quitting her first tenured job at Butler University in Indianapolis. She addresses other serendipitous phenomena in *Writers without Borders: Writing and Teaching Writing in Troubled Times* (2008) and *The Seven Deadly Virtues and Other Lively Essays* (2008). Her current research on creative nonfiction examines *Lives, Liberties, and Pursuits of Happiness*.

ABOUT THE AUTHORS

JENNIFER CLARY-LEMON is associate professor in rhetoric, writing, and communications at the University of Winnipeg and past editor of the journal *Composition Studies*. Her research interests include writing theory and pedagogy, oral histories, discourse analysis, material rhetorics, and rhetorics of identity. Her recent publications can be found in *Discourse and Society*, *Rhetoric Review*, *ISLS Readings in Language Studies*, *Oral History Forum d'histoire orale*, and *College Composition and Communication*.

CAREN WAKERMAN CONVERSE is a lecturer in the Writing Program at the University of California Santa Barbara, where she earned her PhD in language, literacy, and composition. A native New Yorker, she arrived on the West Coast with extensive experience in the criminal justice field as both a practitioner and an educator. A former probation officer, youth counselor, and secondary school teacher, her research appears in the *Journal of Business and Technical Communication* and in *Across the Disciplines*' special issue on Writing across the Secondary School Curriculum. She is a fellow of the South Coast Writing Project.

GALE COSKAN-JOHNSON is associate professor of rhetoric and writing at Brock University in Canada. She chairs the Writing, Rhetoric, and Discourse Studies Program and is affiliated with the MA in Social Justice and Equity Studies. Her current research project, "(Il)legal, (Ir)regular, (Un)documented: Rhetorics of Sovereignty and Transnational Migration," examines United Nations Convention discourse to explore contemporary rhetorical entanglements of transnational mobility and sovereign power.

KIM DONEHOWER is professor of English at the University of North Dakota, where she researches the relationship between literacy and the sustainability of rural communities. With Charlotte Hogg and Eileen E. Schell, she coauthored *Rural Literacies* (Southern Illinois UP) and co-edited *Reclaiming the Rural: Essays on Literacy, Rhetoric, and Pedagogy* (Southern Illinois UP). Her essays have appeared in *Literacy, Economy, and Power*, *Rethinking Rural Literacies*, and the *Routledge International Handbook of Rural Studies*. Her latest publication, *Re-Reading Appalachia: Literacy, Place, and Cultural Resistance* (UP of Kentucky), was co-edited with Sara Webb-Sunderhaus.

BILL ENDRES is an assistant professor in the English department at the University of Oklahoma. His scholarship intersects the digital humanities, rhetoric, and manuscript studies. Using advanced imaging techniques, he has digitized the eighth-century St. Chad Gospels, presenting the results on the Web through interactive 3D renderings, a viewer for Reflectance Transformation Imaging, and stacked and comparable multi-spectral and digitized historical photographs. He has given invited talks at Trinity College, Dublin, and the National Library of Wales. His essay "A Literacy of Building: Making in the Digital Humanities" is forthcoming in *Making Humanities Matters*, part of the Debates in the Digital Humanities Series.

SHIRLEY E. FAULKNER-SPRINGFIELD is an English instructor at Johnston Community College in Smithfield, North Carolina, where she teaches workplace writing. Her research lies at the intersection of academic, community, and professional writing. Shirley wants to understand the connection among students' identities, literacy practices, and potential professions. She and three pre-medical college students coauthored a manuscript, which is under review, about how their writing course functioned as what Etienne Wenger calls a community of practice. Shirley is writing a manuscript that maps the literacy activities of an eighteen-year-old African American male who acquired literacies at home that formed his identity as an academic writer. She earned a doctorate in English with a specialization in writing and rhetoric from Bowling Green State University. Some of Shirley's publications appear in *C&C Online*, *Feminist Teacher*, and *Reflections*.

About the Authors

LYNÉE LEWIS GAILLET is professor and chair of the English department at Georgia State University. She is author of numerous articles and book chapters addressing Scottish rhetoric, writing program administration, composition/rhetoric history and pedagogy, publishing matters, and archival research methods and is a recipient of an NEH Summer Research Award and an ISHR Fellowship. Her book projects include editor of *Scottish Rhetoric and It Influence* (1998) and co-editor of *Stories of Mentoring* (2008), *The Present State of Scholarship in the History of Rhetoric* (2010), *Publishing in Community: Case Studies for Contingent Faculty Collaborations* (2015), and *On Archival Research* (2016). She is coauthor of *Scholarly Publication in a Changing Academic Landscape* (2014) and *Primary Research and Writing: People, Places, and Spaces* (2015). She is a past president of the Coalition of Feminist Scholars in the History of Rhetoric and Composition and past executive director of the South Atlantic Modern Language Association.

BRAD GYORI has been a film and broadcast instructor since 2007. He also has over twenty years' experience writing and producing for such networks as MTV, VH1, FX, E!, and HBO online. For ten years he was the head writer of the Emmy award–winning *Talk Soup*. He has been nominated for five Emmys and holds a PhD in rhetoric and composition from Arizona State University. His research interests include new media rituals and project-based learning models. His work has been published in the *Journal of Broadcasting and Electronic Media*, *Flow*, and the *Interdisciplinary Journal of Problem-Based Learning*. In 2014 Gyori's play *Desolation Angels* was presented as a staged reading by Chicago's Steppenwolf Theatre.

JUDY HOLIDAY's research interests focus primarily on issues related to postmodern difference. She has published in *Rhetoric Review* and *Composition Forum* and has contributed book chapters to *The WPA Outcomes Statement—a Decade Later* and *What We Wish We'd Known: Negotiating Graduate School*, which she co-edited with Ryan Skinnell and Christine Vassett. She is working on a monograph about violence as a socially constructed, cross-cultural episteme. She teaches in the Writing Program at the University of La Verne.

GESA E. KIRSCH is professor of English at Bentley University, Waltham, Massachusetts. Her research and teaching interests include feminist rhetorical studies, ethics and social responsibility, qualitative research methodology, archival research, and environmental rhetoric. She has authored and edited numerous books, articles, and book chapters. Recent works include *Feminist Rhetorical Practices: New Horizons for Rhetoric, Composition, and Literacy Studies*, coauthored with Jacqueline Jones Royster (Southern Illinois UP, 2012, winner of the Winifred Bryan Horner Outstanding Book Award); *Beyond the Archives: Research as a Lived Process*, co-edited with Liz Rohan (Southern Illinois UP, 2012); and a new edition of *More Than Gold in California*, the memoir of Dr. Mary Bennett Ritter, an early California physician, civic leader, and women's rights' activist (Globe Pequot 2017). Her current research explores the rhetorical strategies, professional networks, and social activism of a group of late nineteenth-century women physicians.

LORI OSTERGAARD is an associate professor and chair of the Department of Writing and Rhetoric at Oakland University in Rochester, Michigan. She researches both current degree programs and histories of composition-rhetoric at midwestern normal schools and high schools. Her research has appeared in *Rhetoric Review*, *Composition Studies*, *Studies in the Humanities*, and *Peitho*.

DOREEN PIANO is an associate professor of English and women and gender studies at the University of New Orleans, where she teaches undergraduate and graduate courses in rhetoric and writing, nonfiction literature, and digital/visual literacy. She has published articles and essays in *College Composition and Communication*; *Reflections: Writing, Service-Learning, and Community Literacy*; *Women's Studies Quarterly*, and *Rhizomes: Cultural Studies in Emerging Knowledge*.

ABOUT THE AUTHORS

LIZ ROHAN is professor of composition and rhetoric at the University of Michigan Dearborn. With Gesa Kirsch she is the editor of *Beyond the Archives: Research as Lived Process* (Southern Illinois UP, 2008). Her research that reflects her ongoing interests in pedagogy, feminist research methods, and America's progressive era has appeared in journals such as *Rhetoric Review*, *Composition Studies*, *Pedagogy*, *JAEPL*, *Reflections*, *Composition Forum*, and *Peitho* and in several book chapters.

RYAN SKINNELL is assistant professor of rhetoric and composition and assistant writing program administrator at San Jose State University. His research interests include rhetoric and composition histories, institutional rhetorics, bureaucracy, and archival methodologies. He is the author of *Conceding Composition: A Crooked History of Composition's Institutional Fortunes* (Utah State UP, 2016) and co-editor of *What We Wish We'd Known: Negotiating Graduate School* (Fountainhead, 2015) with Judy Holiday and Christine Vassett. His scholarship also appears in *Rhetoric Review*, *JAC*, *Composition Studies*, *Enculturation*, the *Journal of Veterans Studies*, and edited collections.

PATTY WILDE is an assistant professor of English and director of composition at Washington State University Tri-Cities. Her work has been published in *Learning and Teaching Writing Online: Strategies for Success*, *Pedagogies of Public Memory: Teaching Writing and Rhetoric at Museums, Archives, and Memorials*, and *Women at Work: Rhetorics of Women and Labor in the US*.

DANIEL WUEBBEN is an assistant professor of English in the Goodrich Scholarship Program at the University of Nebraska Omaha. His teaching and research engage overhead electrical networks, writing with video, and multilingual service learning. His scholarly work has appeared in *Basic Writing e-Journal*, *Victorian Literature and Culture*, and *Computers and Composition*. He is completing a manuscript *Power-Lined: Electricity, Landscape, and the American Mind*.

SUBJECT INDEX

Activity Theory, 73–76
African American, 19, 21, 24, 25, 34, 41(n8), 52, 86, 95, 178, 182, 187
African American–centered, 93
ahistorical, 51
alternating current, Tesla, 141–46
American Academy of Pediatrics, 179, 186
American Embassy, Ankara, 44
American studies, 30
American West, US region, 165
Anglo-Saxon, 221, 227–32
Ankara, Turkey, 44–45
Annals of Ulster, 222
anti-establishment impulse, 243
anti-logic, 242
anti-slavery, 20
archival methods, 67
Arizona Senate Bill 1070, 66, 45
Arizona State University, Tempe, 119–23, 126
arkhe (where things begin), 212
Art of Death (exhibition), 116(n1)
Ashburnham, England, 106–13
Ash Tree Pub, Ashburnham, 111
autoethnographer, 70

backtracking, as in process of discovery, 3
backup plan/project, 229
Bank of America Tower, New York City, 138
Battle, England, 107–11
Battle of Nashville (US Civil War), 26
Beatlemania, 243
Belfast, Northern Ireland, 211–12
Bible (the), 114
Bible study, 96
Biblical, 191
big bang (general reference), 133
Big Bang (the), 134
biopower, 48
black (race) 18, 20–25
black-and-white: family, 22, 24; photography, 226, 230
blockade runner, 165
book club café: women's, 94–98
Book of Kells, 222, 225, 230–31
borderlands, 49–50

boundary crossing, 243
Brexit (Great Britain), 12
British Isles, 221
Bryant Park (New York City), 138–39, 142–43
Bureaucracy: A Love Story (exhibition), 127
burned-out, as in probation officers, 172
by-product, as in death, 48

Camellia Grill, 36–37
Canton, Illinois, 84
career-altering, as in research agenda, 207
Catholic (religion), 212
Catholic-only neighborhoods, 212
Catsfield: England, 106–110; Manor, 109; Post Office and Village Store, 109; White Hart Pub, 110
ceann fa eitil (head-under-wing), 224
Change Talk, in Motivational Interviewing, 179–81
Chapel Hill, North Carolina, 64, 166
Chapter House (Litchfield Cathedral; also Lichfield), 226
Chicago: activism, 84–86; area, 81–84, 85, 87, 141, 162; Barack Obama, 46; Innovation Exchange, 68; University of Illinois, 81, 86
Chichester, England, 116
chi-rho (page that ornamentally presents the first three letters of the Greek word for Christ), 225
Chi-square analysis, 184
chōra (something always ongoing, generated, a beginning), 205–16
Christmas Day, 231
Church of England (the), 24
churchyard, 10, 109–10, 112
Civil War (England). *See* English Civil War
Civil War (US), 10, 26, 164–65, 170, 173(n3), 173(n4)
client-centered, method, 178–79
climate: change, 240; controlled, 155; political, 272; vulnerable, 31
Coastguard Cottages (Fairlight), 108–9
coauthor(s), 67, 98, 176, 177, 182, 183
co-generative (problem solving), 85
colonialism, deconstruction process, 244

Commitment Language, in Motivational Interviewing, 179–81
commonsense, philosophy, 61
communism, 52
communist, 250
Confederate (US Civil War contexts), 11, 167, 169
Confederate Army (US Civil War), 164, 168
Conference on College Composition and Communication, 66, 119, 128(n4), 209, 230
consciousness raising, 249
content-based sub-codes, 185
Cook County Board of Commissioners (IL), 86
cor fa carsan (turn-in-the-path), 224
Cornwall, United Kingdom, 131
corporeality, 207
counterculture, 243
counter-narrative, 21, 38, 243
courthouse, 29, 20, 26
Court of General Sessions of the County of New York, 75
critical discourse analysis, 208, 209
cross-border, 52, 214
cross-carpet, 228
cross-class, 85
cross-cultural, 248
cross-disciplinary, 30
cross-dressing, 164, 168
cross-institutional, 30
cross-pollinating, 240
cutting edge: historical research in Rhetoric and Composition, 59
cyberspace, 24

databases: academic, 252; library, 159–60, 164; medieval, 235; methods, 194–95; newspaper, 167–72
data coding/analysis, 177, 179–83; in Motivational Interviewing, 178–79, 182
data collection: of images, 9; Overboe's process, 84
data-driven studies, 175–76
data gathering, 133
data miners, 244
data set, 177, 265
day-to-day: conversations, 50; materials, 156
dead-ends, 3, 6, 118, 123, 126
Dead Sea Scrolls, 59
Dearborn, Michigan, 81
decentering, as in move, 50
decision-making, as in process, 73, 125
decommissioned, school, 126

deconstruction: cinematic, 239, 242; tactics, 243–44; of text, 242
deep wounding, in sectarianism, 212
dehumanize, of African Americans, 19, 21
delimit, available means, 255(n5)
depersonalize, language, 77
de rigueur (roman), as in literature instruction, 157
destabilize: European Union, 12; methods, 206; text, 243
determinism, 245
Detroit area, 80, 82, 88
dialogism, 93
direct current (Edison), 146
directionless: of scholarly agenda, 207
disaster: aftermath, 31–34, 40, 267; events, 210; natural, 222–23; pedagogy, 29, 35; politics, 33, 41(n9); research, 29–32, 39, 267, 271
disaster-stricken, 272
disconnect, 74, 137(n4), 263
discredited (Tesla), 142
disjunction: in cinematic editing, 238–39
disjunctive strategies, 238–39, 243–44
Donegall Quay (Belfast), 212
double entendre, 207
du jour: of an argument, 245

early medieval, 11, 221–24, 229, 231
early nineteenth century, 63, 104
East Sussex Records Office (Lewes), 106, 116
eBay, 159
eighteenth century, 48, 59, 61, 63, 66, 117
eighth century, 221, 231
electromagnetic, 144
email, as a medium of discovery and serendipity, 24, 35, 54, 121–24, 142–43, 157, 160, 186, 230, 261
end of life care, 177
English Channel, 108–9
English Civil War (seventeenth century), 223–24, 226
English language: news, 44
English Midlands, 221
Enhanced Digital Unwrapping for Conservation and Exploration (EDUCE), 228
enslavement, 20, 22, 25
epiphany, 9, 117
epistemology/epistemological, 19, 22, 35, 61, 85, 248, 254, 261, 276
ethnographic: authority, 92, 93, 97; method, 5; writing, 92
ethnography, 41(n9), 47, 77, 92–93, 97
European Union, 12
Evanston, Illinois, 81

evidence-based assessment, 75
exoticism, 243
exposedness, as in corporeal existence, 207–8
expressionism/expressionist, 237

facades, of buildings post-Katrina, 36–37
facebook (social media site), 177, 184, 252
face to face situations, 40, 270, 271
Fairlight, England, 106–9, 113
fairytale (Persian), 117
Family Records Centre (London), 107, 116
fan edit: as in cinematic deconstruction, 242, 244
Festschrift, 94
fieldwork-based research, 5, 8, 136, 175–76
fifth century, 224
film edit bay, 240
first time, process of discovery, 51, 82, 130, 159, 178, 252, 263
first year writing/composition, 67, 122, 126, 190, 260
floodwaters: Hurricane Katrina, 33, 34, 39
front page news, 46
full-time: enrollment, 260; teaching, 129

gender studies, 30, 31, 255(n2), 254(n3)
genre-jumping, 242
genre theory, 73, 77, 261
geopolitical, border, 50
gestalt, 96, 240
GI Bill, 65
Google, 49, 159
gospel books, Insular, 222–31
Gospel of Luke (Bible), 223
Gospel of Mark (Bible), 223
Gospel of Matthew (Bible), 223
Grand Forks, North Dakota, 96
Great Depression (US), 80, 86
griot, 26
Grosse Pointe, Michigan, 80
Guerra de los Diez Años (Ten Years' War), 170
Gulf Coast (US), 28, 29

Halifax County Courthouse (VA), 17, 18, 23
Hamtramck, Michigan, 80
hands-off, policy, 263
handwritten: correspondence, 29; draft, 161; note, 268
happenstance, 4–9, 12, 61, 64, 66, 130, 132–33, 135, 237
Harriet Vittum Park (Chicago), 84, 87–90
Hastings, England, 107–8

Hemingway Society, 161
high school, 154–56, 159–62
high tech: company, 138; platform, 244
historiography, 101, 250
Houghton, Michigan, 154, 162
Hull House (Chicago), 81, 85–86
human rights (activists), 197
Hurricane Katrina, 9, 28, 30, 271
Hurricane Memory Databank (Katrina), 30
hyper-competitive (space), 257
hyper-cut (film), 238
hyper-visible rhetoric of death, 48

Illinois Association of Teachers of English, 159
impressionism, 244
infrared, in multi-spectral imaging, 229
infrastructure, in conference organizing, 209–10
inlaid garnets, 228
institutional review board (IRB), 124, 199, 207, 214
Insular period (600–850 CE), 221–34
interconnectedness, of serendipity, 11, 250
interconnection, 208, 214
interdisciplinarity, 5, 210, 252, 255(n2)
interdisciplinary, 47, 59, 61, 63, 140–41, 248, 253
interlibrary loan, 159
internet, 17, 63, 159, 193, 194, 202(n5), 203(n9), 230, 250
interpersonal, 96, 248
interracial, 247
interrelationships, 208
interreliability, 183
intersubjective, life/relations, 95, 208
intrapersonal, 248
Irish Association of Manitoba, 207
Irish Troubles (the), 212
Islamabad, Pakistan, 127
Isles of Scilly (Cornwall), 131, 133
Istanbul, Turkey, 44
I Will Fight No More Forever (film), 52
Izmit, Turkey, 44

job training, 85
John and Francis (ship), 23
journal writing, 34
judgment, 61, 114, 145, 195, 269–70

K–12 education, 250
kairos (opportunity; opportune moment), 12, 232, 249, 252–53, 257–59
Katrina-related, 9, 28–40, 271
Kew, England, 107, 116

keywords, 94, 252
kingdom of Mercia (England), 221, 223
knowledge: creation, 135; making, 31, 38, 66, 104, 248; sharing, 131

ladylike (behavior), 243
large scale: disaster, 31; typification, 73
Last Will and Testament, 18, 21, 23, 26
latitudinarian perspective, 191
Lewes, England, 106, 107, 109, 111, 116
Library of Congress (Washington, DC), 169
Lichfield, England, 11, 221, 223, 226–31, 234–35
lifelong: appreciation, 145; heath consequences, 178; journey, 5
life-saving (items), 4
lightning bolt, as in serendipitous insight, 244
Llandeilo Fawr, Wales, 223
long-standing: myth, 238; tradition, 224
Los Alamos National Laboratory (NM), 176
low density housing, 32
lower class, 104
Lower 9th Ward (New Orleans), 33
low income neighborhoods, 32

maintaining chaos, 248, 252–55
Manuscripts of Lichfield Cathedral (website), 235
Marxism, 239, 241
Mary Providence (ship), 23
mashup: as in media, 197, 143
mass (Catholic service), 231
meaning making, 205, 251
medieval: as in manuscripts, 11, 221–35, 270
Mesa, Arizona, 124
mestiza, 49
meta-cognition, 248
metalsmith, 228
metalwork, 228
metanoia (missed opportunity), 12, 258–59
methodipity, 216
micro-ethnography, 29
middle class, 85, 86, 90
Middle Eastern Technical University (Ankara), 44
mini-serendipities, 133
Minnesota Sentencing Guidelines, 74
mise en page (viewing both imagery and written text as visual expression), 224–25
mixed media, 193
mixed methods, 11, 176–78, 181–87

mobcast, 244
modernism, 244–45
monolingual/monocultural, 50
Motivational Interviewing, 178–83
Motivational Interviewing Sequential Code for Observing Process Exchanges, 179
Mount Vesuvius, 228
multidisciplinary, 176, 228
multilingual, 49, 140
multi-modal, 38, 146, 225, 244
multi-spectral imaging, 229
Museum of the Confederacy (Richmond), 167

National Archives of Composition and Rhetoric, 119
National Council of Teachers of English, 159
National Federation of Settlement Archives (Minneapolis), 82
National Geographic Channel, 231
National Institutes of Health (NIH), 11, 177
nationalism, 12
National Science Foundation, 228
National University of Modern Languages (Islamabad), 127
nation-state, 51
Near East (world region), 237
needlework, 93, 104
needleworker, 106
neoclassicism, 242
neo-liberal, 40, 41(n9)
neo-Luddite, 44
neo-Marxism, 241
New Orleans, Louisiana, 28–31, 34, 35–38, 40, 41(n2), 7, 8, 9, 119–21, 121, 123, 126, 127, 165, 267
New Rhetoric (North American Genre Theory), 73
New Testament (of the Bible), 229, 230, 234
New York Public Library Main Branch, 138, 169
New York State Criminal Procedure Law, 71
New York State Division of Probation, 74
New York Stock Exchange, 142
Nikola Tesla Corner (New York City), 142, 143, 148(n1)
9/11 (New York City), 9, 44–45
nineteenth century, 21, 51, 60, 63, 64, 66, 74, 85, 104, 110, 145, 104, 107, 108, 141, 148(n2), 157
Nobel Prize, 5, 197
nominalization, 254

non-conventional, 31
non-elite discourse, 210
non-hierarchical, 234
non-parametric method, 183
non-representational, 237
non-scholarly publications, 7
non-status, 46
non-Western (part of the world), 36
nonfiction, 193, 194, 203(n11)
nonprofit, 41(n9), 86
normal school, 126, 154, 157, 158
North American Genre Theory (New Rhetoric), 73
Northern (US Civil War contexts), 170
Northern Ireland, 211–12
Northpointe Institute for Public Management, Inc., 75
North Star Mining Company, 171
Northwestern Settlement House (Evanston), 85
Northwestern Settlement Organization, 83
Northwestern University Settlement, 82, 83, 85–86, 90
Northwestern University Settlement archives (Evanston), 83, 88
Norton Reader, 195

Oak Park, Illinois, 162
Oak Park and River Forest High School (IL), 160
objectivism, 92
Old Alms Cottages (Ashburnham) 111, 112
Old Coast Guard Cottages (Fairlight), 109
Old Welsh writing, 223
online, 28, 29, 45, 46, 62, 63, 64, 81, 92, 159, 160, 193, 202(n2), 223, 235, 235(n1), 244, 264
ontological, 19, 22, 29, 31, 261
open-ended, 136, 178, 181, 243, 270
openness, 5, 30, 45, 48, 65
Operation Gatekeeper (US-Mexico border), 45, 54(n2)
oral history, 17, 26, 206–8, 209, 211
out-migration, 95
overarching narrative, 32
overdetermining, 253
overwriting, 92

participant observation, 92, 93, 95, 96, 97, 98
Patient Education and Counseling (journal), 186
Person County (NC), 18, 23
Petri dish, 60, 129, 130
phronesis, 6

place-based, 29, 35, 37, 107, 130, 131–32, 133
podcast, 109. 244
"The Poet" (poem by Emerson), 144
polyphonic, 92
polyphony, 92–93
populism, 12
post-bellum, 23
post-Brexit, 12
post-colonialism, 244
post-colonial studies, 32
post-disaster, 31
post-election, 272
post hoc, 177
post-impressionism, 244
Post-It note memorial, 36, 37
post-Katrina, 29, 32, 36, 40
postmodern, 92, 97, 238
postmodernism, 244, 245
post–9/11, 47
post-postmodern, 245
post-process, 192
post-structural, 242
post-structuralism, 244
postwar, 171
post–World War II, 80, 194
predetermined, 75
pre-digital age, 138
pre-Katrina, 36
pre-mediation, 237
premeditation, 238
pre-research, 139
pre-sentence, 9, 70
pre-sentence investigation report, 9, 70
The Prestige (film), 142
Primetime Live (television series), 129
problem solver, 198
problem solving, 85
progressive era, 81, 85; progressive-era, 80, 81, 85, 86
Project Be (Odoms), 38–39
Protestant (religious affiliation), 212
Protestant-only, 212
proto-feminist, 251
proto-postmodern, 251
psycho-geographic, 40
Public Records Office (Kew), 107
Public Records Office of Northern Ireland (Belfast), 212
Puget Sound (WA), 258
Pulitzer Prize, 202(n4)

quasi-religious, 238

reaffirm, 272
real world, 244

284 SUBJECT INDEX

rearrange, 6
reassemble, 239, 242
rebooting, 239, 244
recidivism, 75
recombining, 240
reconfigure, 198, 241
reconstruct, 20, 83, 107
recontextualize, 210
redefine, 73
rediscover, 155
redraw, 215
re-envision, 40, 263
reexamine, 76, 255
reflexivity, 5, 49, 89, 97, 222
Reformation (sixteenth century), 223
reframe, 153
reimagine, 240, 241, 242
reimaging, 8
reinscribed, 26
reinvestigate, 264
re-listen, 96 re-made, 212
remix, 239–41, 244
Renaissance (the period), 226
reorder, 238
repurpose, 104
reread, 49, 76, 95, 96, 167, 177, 181, 197, 251
reshape, 118
reshuffle, 241
restructure, 242
retelling, 8, 241
rethink, 6, 29, 39, 40, 271
Revolutionary War (US), 24
Richmond, Virginia, 166, 167
roadblock, 5, 6
Romantic (era), 148, 201, 263

Santa Fe Institute (NM), 240, 241
Saturnalia (festival in ancient Rome), 243
science-fiction, 142
screenwriter, 240
self-efficacy, 178
self-imposed, 240
self-perpetuating, 254
self-reflection, 248
self-reflexivity, 89, 97
Serbian Orthodox Church, 145
serendipitous: anecdote, 206; circumstance, 62; climate, 190; coalescence, 9; connection/conjunction, 162, 237, 241; consequence, 194, 200; detour/path, 90, 125, 147, 176; discovery, 4, 10, 11, 64, 118, 119, 120, 122, 123, 125–26, 134, 135, 153, 154, 156, 160, 161, 186, 190, 192, 193, 194, 197; encounter, 65, 268; event, 10, 45, 47, 54, 177, 221–24, 233, 252, 265; experience, 9, 59, 60, 251, 259; failure, 271; find, 61, 63, 66, 68, 156, 164, 172, 196; happenstance, 133, 143, 154, 159, 229, 254; interaction, 213; lead, 60, 158; methodology, 216, 255; moment, 7, 8, 9, 10, 30, 65, 77, 96, 132, 133, 153, 162, 207, 208–10, 215, 216, 226–27, 249, 258, 259; nature, 62, 201; occurrence, 130; opportunity, 9, 10, 68, 124, 177, 232, 235, 270; pivot, 176; possibility, 12, 259, 262; preparation, 194; process, 192; quest, 126–27; resonance, 190; rupture, 238; signal, 139; transformation, 8, 248; travelogue, 118
serendipity: as accidental wisdom/sagacity, 6, 133, 135, 268; as art, 5, 238; as catalyst, 11; as chance, 4, 17, 117; and computers, 5; conditions for, 11; and connections/networking, 167, 209, 239; and context, 29, 30, 215, 249; and curiosity, 60, 69; and disaster, 29, 32; as epiphany, 117; and ethical responsibility, 222, 232–33, 270; as exploration, 133–34, 136; and failure, 258, 266; as falling into place, 12, 103, 258; as fate, 237–38; and the future, 12; as happy accident, 132, 191, 213, 221, 232; history of, 5, 85, 117, 175, 176, 177, 198, 222; and innovation, 243; and interdisciplinarity, 5; as intuitive, 65; as journey, 118–23, 126–28, 178; and methodology, 11, 154, 178–86, 205; narratives, 11, 65, 122, 202; and pedagogy, 11, 103, 270, 272(n1); and place, 29, 39, 59; as praxis, 7; preparedness for, 6, 45, 48, 53, 61, 97–98, 112, 118, 136, 191, 205, 249, 251, 255; as purposeful discovery, 130, 191; recognition/predictability of: 129–30, 137(n3), 164, 202, 249; in research, 5–6, 8, 11, 12, 29, 60–68, 77, 81, 94, 132, 154, 157, 186, 191, 197–98, 249; and rhetorical analysis, 139, 232; and risk, 118, 135, 232; as rupture, 4, 258; in scholarship, 47, 172, 190, 215, 222, 232, 244; in science, 4, 5, 135; as stumbling, 4; terminology, 59, 175, 269; as transformation, 98; and unpredictability, 7, 222, 229; 258, 265
seventeenth century, 104; seventeenth-century, 111, 223
sine anticipatio mentis (an open mind), 6
sixteenth century, 128; sixteenth-century, 117, 223
sixth century, 224
small island, 133

Subject Index 285

small-town cafe, 94
social justice, 40, 41(n8), 265, 271, 272, 273(n3)
social media, 45, 137(n4)
socio-cultural imaginary, 50
Southern Historical Collection (of the Wilson Library, Chapel Hill, NC), 166
Southern History Society, 167
South Puget Sound (WA), 260
spatiotemporal disjunction, 239
stand-alone, 132, 241
St. Chad Gospels (ca. 730; Lichfield, England), 222
St. George's Market (Belfast), 212
St. Lawrence Church (Catsfield, England), 109
St. Mary's Island (Cornwall, England), 131
St. Michael's Chapel (Lichfield Cathedral), 226
storytelling, 7, 76
Strange Fruit (book), 247, 248, 249, 250, 251
"Strange Fruit" (song), 249, 250–51
structuralism, 244
subcode, 185
suffragist, 84
suffragist movement, 157
surrealist, 239, 242
sustainability, 95, 131, 133
systemicity, 206

Tacoma, Washington, 259
Tau Beta (women's club), 80, 81, 90
Tau Beta archives, 82
Tau Beta Community House (Hamtramck), 80, 81, 82
Teaching English as a Second Language (conference in Ankara), 44
Technical/Professional Communication, 175
Teflon, 4, 68
Tempe, Arizona, 119
tenth century, 223; tenth-century, 223
Ten Years' War (Cuba versus Spain), 170
tertium quid (third meaning), 240
Tesla Motors, 142
thirteenth century, 226; thirteenth-century, 226
time-consuming, 172, 182
time frame, 124, 135
time span, 194
Titanic Quarter (Belfast), 213
topographical, 50
Toynbee Hall Settlement (London), 85
transdisciplinary, 5, 11, 186, 248, 252, 253, 254

transmedia, 244
transnational feminism, 51
t-test, 183
Tucker Family Papers (Southern Historical Collection), 166
twentieth century, 74, 147, 157, 162, 173(n1); twentieth-century, 154
twenty-first century, 74, 196, 197; twenty-first-century, 21, 193
Two-Year College English Association, 264

ultra-conservative, 23
ultraviolet, 229
un-archived, 131
un-choreographed, 253
uncensored, 255
uncharted, 210
uncontrollable, 210
underfunded archivists, 64
under-prepared writers, 192
under-theorized, 82
unearthed, 228
unending conversation, 5
unfunded researcher, 177
Union (in US Civil War contexts), 166
Union Flag Disputes (UK), 212
United States Census, 19
United Way, 86
University of Wisconsin Digital Collections, 160
unknowing, 6, 47, 115
unmaking, 7, 258
unrefined, 226
unsystematic poll, 194
untenured, 234
untroubled methods, 206
upended, 243
upload, 159
upper-division, 260
upper-middle-class women, 86
Upper Peninsula of Michigan, 154
upscale vacation, 129
urban renewal, 86
usable knowledge, 8; models, 10
US Baselands, 130
US Congress, 35, 131
US Postal Service, 247

Velcro, 4
Victorian and Albert Museum (London), 104, 107, 116
Virginia Company (the), 24
Visibility Project (Phelps), 214
Vittum Park, 84, 87–88, 90
vodcast, 244

water-damaged text and imagery, 229
weight loss, 178–79, 181–84, 186
well-preserved archive, 133
West (US region; world region), 238
West Sussex Records Office (Chichester), 106, 116
westerners, 211
Western feminists, 51; Feminist subject; Narratives, 50; philosophy, 20; savior narrative, 51
white (race), 18, 19, 20, 21, 22, 23, 24, 33, 35, 46, 50, 51, 53, 93, 243, 247
White Hart Pub (Catsfield), 110
whiteness, 25, 250
Will Book 12, 17
Winnipeg, Manitoba, 206, 214, 215
wireless, 138, 139, 140, 142, 144, 146, 147
Woman's City Club of Chicago, 86
women's movement, 197
women's studies journal, 140
Women's Trade Union League (Chicago), 86

working class, 32, 33, 41, 85
workplace, 270; academic, 40; studies, 175; writing, 71, 73
World Cat (search engine), 169, 170
World's Columbian Exhibition (Chicago, 1893), 85
World War I–era, 248
World War II, 200, 271
Worldwide Wireless (Tesla), 138
writing center, 248, 252, 258–60, 262, 263–64, 265
writing process/processes, 6, 20, 192
Wycliffe New Testament, 229–30, 234

xenophilic, 51
xenophobia, 51, 271
X-ray, 4, 134

zero-sum game, 239
zoomorphic, 228

NAME INDEX

Achebe, Chinua, 238, 245
Ackerman, John, 214, 217
Addams, Jane, 80, 81, 84–86, 88, 89, 90
Ahmed, Sara, 50–51, 54
Alemán, Jesse, 165–66, 168, 173
Anderson, Chris, 202, 204
Anderson, Leon, 70, 77, 78
André, Paul, 6, 13
Andrus, Jennifer, 209, 210, 217
Anzaldúa, Gloria, 49, 50, 54
Appadurai, Arjun, 103, 116
Arbenz, Jocomo, 46
Atwell, Nancy, 192, 204

Baca, Damian, 226, 236
Baker, Nicholson, 64
Ball, Aimee Lee, 36, 41
Ball, Edward, 25, 26
Bancroft, Pat, 227
Barber, Elinor G., 5, 6, 13, 133, 135, 137, 188, 191, 204
Bass, Erin Z., 255, 256
Baum, L. Frank, 242
Bazerman, Charles, 73, 76, 78, 139, 140, 146, 148, 188, 236, 261, 266
Beard, William, 171, 172
Becker, Alton, 6, 13
Bernhardt, Stephen, 176, 188
Berryhill, Carisse, 62, 68
Biklen, Sari, 71, 78
Bin Laden, Osama, 9, 46, 48, 50
Blakeslee, Ann, 175, 188
Bloom, Harold, 193
Bogdan, Robert, 71, 78
Bolter, Jay David, 225, 236
Boswell, James, 59
Bowie, David, 142
Brady, Judy Syfers, 196
Brandt, Deborah, 93–96, 98
Brueggemann, Brenda Jo, 97, 98
Buchanan, Lindal, 158, 162
Buford, Harry T., 165, 168, 169
Burgess, John, 5, 14
Burke, Kenneth, 6, 13, 53, 54, 139, 233–34, 236, 251
Burroughs, William S. 239
Butler, Judith, 47, 54, 243, 249, 256

Cahill, Thomas, 224, 236
Calhoun, Craig, 6, 13
Campanella, Rich, 33, 34, 41, 43
Campbell, Alexander, 62, 63, 68, 69
Campbell, Thomas, 62
Carlson, Bernard, 145, 146, 148
Carruthers, Mary, 225
Chamberlain, Essie, 158–61
Cheney, Margaret, 143, 148
Chief Joseph, 52
Clark, Irene, 128, 248, 252–53, 256
Clifford, James, 92, 93. 97, 99
Colby, June Rose, 157–60, 162
Corbett, Edward, 65
Cromwell, Oliver, 223, 226
Crookes, William, 141
Crowley, Sharon, 65, 120–23, 128, 159, 162
Cvetkovich, Ann, 31, 41, 42

Darbellay, Frédéric, 5, 13
Davies, Christian, 168
Davis, Diane, 65, 68, 207, 217
Davis, William, 173
Deegan, James G., 47, 55, 77, 78
Dell, Floyd, 202
Derrida, Jacques, 206, 212, 217, 242–43, 245
Devitt, Amy, 73, 77, 78
Didion, Joan, 192, 193, 196
Donaldson, Sam, 129
Douglass, Frederick, 20
Dove, Mary, 229
Dowie, Ménie Muriel, 168, 173
Düppe, Till, 4, 13

Early, Jubal, 165, 166, 167, 173
Eble, Michelle, 67, 69
Edison, Thomas, 140–43, 146
Edmonds, Sarah Emma, 173
Eisenhower, Dwight, 46
Eisenstein, Sergei, 240, 245
Elbow, Peter, 192, 204
Emerson, Ralph Waldo, 144–45, 148
Enoch, Jessica, 60, 83, 91

Farge, Arlette, 154, 161, 162
Faulkner, David, 24, 25

NAME INDEX

Faulkner, Friday, 17, 18, 21, 24–26
Faulkner, Jacob, 18, 20, 21–24, 26
Faulkner, Jan, 26
Faulkner, Obadiah, 18, 26
Faulkner, Rebecca Harris, 17
Faulkner, Thomas, 23
Felmley, David, 155, 156
Fennell, Stephen A., 71, 78
Fine, Gary Alan, 47, 55, 77, 78, 97, 99
Fine, Michelle, 97, 99
Fischgrund, Tom, 252–53, 256
Fitzgerald, Kathryn, 60
Fleming, Alexander, 60, 68. 129, 130, 134
Ford, Edsel, 81
Ford, Eleanor Clay, 81, 90
Ford, Henry, 81
Franklin, Benjamin, 140
Freud, Sigmund, 51, 241, 242

Gates, Henry Louis, 23, 26
Geertz, Clifford, 76, 93, 99
Gere, Anne Ruggles, 35, 42
Glaser, Barney, 175, 188
Goggin, Maureen Daly, 30, 42
Goggin, Peter, 30, 42
Gold, David, 3, 13, 60, 65, 153, 158, 163, 168, 172–73, 262, 266
Graves, Roger, 214, 215
Green, David, 5, 13
Griffiths, Lily, 104, 116
Grimm, Nancy, 260, 261, 266

Hall, Richard, 165–66, 169, 172, 174
Hall, William N., 71, 78
Halpern, Irving, 75, 78
Hamilton, Sir William, 61
Hardwick, Elizabeth, 193, 204
Harris, Wendell, 195, 204
Harvey, Steve, 93, 95, 96
Hawhee, Debra, 206, 213, 217, 251–55, 256
Haybury, Maria Georgia Pilkington, 110
Hazan, Haim, 5, 13
Heath, Shirley Brice, 92–93, 99
Heber-Percy, Algernon, 228
Helmholtz, Heinrich, 144
Hemingway, Ernest, 159, 160, 161
Henry, François, 224–25, 236
Heraclitus, 3, 13
Herbert, Terry, 228
Hertz, Heinrich, 142
Hertzog, Esther, 5, 13
Hill, Carla, 198, 200, 201, 204
Hill, Helen, 36
Hirsch, Marianne, 36, 39, 41, 42
Hirschman, Albert O., 3, 4, 13, 103, 116

Hoeflich, Michael H., 60, 62, 69
Holiday, Billie, 251
Honig, Bonnie, 50–51, 55
hooks, bell, 25, 26
Horner, Winifred Bryan, 65, 66
Huckin, Thomas, 208, 210, 217
Hutchinson, Coleman, 170, 174

Jackson, Shannon, 87, 91
Jacobs, Harriet, 20
James, Pamela, 222, 236
James, William, 140–42, 145, 148
Jardine, George, 59, 60–64, 69
Jeffrey, Francis, 61
Jenkins, Dafydd, 223, 236
Jenkins, Henry, 243
Jenkins, Pam, 30, 41, 42
Jindal, Bobby, 32
Johnson, Jeffrey, 97, 99
Johnson, Robert Underwood, 145
Jones, J. William, 167, 174

Kafka, Franz, 238, 245
Kankel, Jessica, 68
Kanzler, Josephine Clay, 90
Kaufman, O. Brian, 120
Keizer, Arlene R., 21, 26
Kierkegaard, Søren, 238, 245
King, Martin Luther, Jr., 196
King James I (England), 24
Klein, Naomi, 33, 41, 42
Koritz, Amy, 29, 42

Lacan, Jacques, 242, 245
LaCapra, Dominick, 20, 42
LaCuruba, Craig, 143
Lady Somerset, 223
Lafargue, Paul, 240
Lee, Robert E., 166
Lemon, Moore, 211–15
L'Eplattenier, Barbara, 69, 117, 128, 165, 174, 273
Leonard, Elizabeth, 164–66, 173–74
Lester, Elisha A., 18
Lester, Henderson, 18
Lindblom, Kenneth, 60
Lindemann, Erika, 64, 69
Llewellyn, Nigel, 116
Lloyd-Jones, Richard, 65
Lockhart, J. G., 61
Lowery, Dwayne, 95
Lunsford, Andrea, 215, 263–64, 266
Lyotard, Jean-François, 238, 245

Mach, Ernst, 144
Maguire, Gregory, 242

Mann, Horace, 117
Marcus, George, 92, 97, 99
Marshall, Margaret, 165, 174
Marx, Karl, 239–40, 245
Maxwell, James Clerk, 142
Maxwell, Joseph, 76
May, Sam, 95
McClellan, James E., III, 5, 13
McCulley, George, 176, 188
McCurdy, Patrick, 97, 99
McDowell, Mary, 86
Meeropol, Abel (pen name: Lewis Allan), 250
Merton, Robert, 5, 6, 13, 133, 135, 137, 175–76, 178, 180, 186, 188, 191, 204
Michener, William, 5, 14
Millar, John, 61
Millay, Edna St. Vincent, 202
Miller, Carolyn R., 73, 78
Miller, Janette, 82
Miller, William, 178, 188
Mishler, Elliot, 176, 188
Mizell-Nelson, Michael, 30, 42
Moffett, James, 92, 99
Mohanty, Chandra Talpade, 51, 55
Moody, Zoe, 5, 13
Morse, Samuel F.B., 144, 148
Mortensen, Peter, 60, 271, 273
Mountz, Alison, 40, 42
Mueller, Derek, 214
Murray, Donald, 192, 204
Myers, Kelly, 259, 266

Nardi, Bonnie A., 73, 78
Nash, Edith, 159–60, 163
Newell, Aimee, 104, 116
Newell, William H., 252, 256
Newton, Isaac, 191
Niestepski, Michelle, 120
Nitecki, Alisha, 65
Norman, Michael D., 71, 79
North, Christopher, 61

Obama, Barack, 9, 45–47
Odoms, Brandon, 38
Olbricht, Thomas H., 62–63
Orwell, George, 192, 195, 196, 197
Osundari, Niyi, 32
Overboe, Doris P., 82–84, 85, 86, 87–88, 90, 91
Overboe, Ellert, 82, 91
Owens, Derek, 29, 41, 42

Paré, Anthony, 73, 79
Parker, Elizabeth, 104–7, 109, 112, 116
Pasteur, Louis, 3–4, 14, 103, 116, 186

Peshkin, Alan, 71, 76, 79
Phelps, Louise Wetherbee, 214, 217
Pilkington, Andrew, 109–10
Plath, Sylvia, 202
Pollock, Jackson, 237
Pope, Peter, 71, 79
Porter, Edward Sefton, 74, 79
Powell, Malea, 22, 27
Price, John, 83
Prince, Mary, 20

Rachwalski, Helen, 87
Rachwalski, Michael, 87
Ramsey, Alexis E., 7, 14, 69, 267, 273
Randolph, Charles, 95
Rayfield, Jo Ann, 157
Reid, Thomas, 61
Reynolds, Nedra, 35, 37, 43, 83, 91
Ritter, Kelly, 206, 217
Ritter, Mary Bennett, 4, 29, 30, 164, 173
Rivoal, Isabelle, 5, 6, 14, 269
Robins, Margaret Drier, 86
Rock, Chris, 52–53
Rodriguez, Richard, 196
Roen, Duane, 65, 124, 213, 217
Rogers, Emma, 85
Rogers, Henry Wade, 85
Roosevelt, Eleanor, 247
Roosevelt, Franklin Delano, 247
Rosaldo, Renato, 92, 97, 99
Rose, Mike, 192, 204
Rosecrance, John, 70, 79
Rosenberg, Ethel, 250
Rosenberg, Julius, 250
Rosenberg, Michael, 250
Rosenberg, Robert, 250
Royster, Jacqueline Jones, 83, 91, 235, 236, 269, 273
Rutter, Russell, 70, 79

Said, Edward, 238, 246
Salazar, Noel B., 5, 6, 14, 269
Sanford, Marcelline Hemingway, 160
Sartre, Jean Paul, 238, 246
Sauer, Beverly, 175, 189
Scaife, Ross, 228
Schaefer, Vincent J., 5, 14
Schwalm, David, 123–25
Schwegler, Robert, 119
Sedooka, Ayuko, 5, 13
Selfe, Cindy, 65
Selzer, Jack, 139, 148, 208, 218
Shehadeh, Raja, 38, 43
Simone, Nina, 251
Slemons, William F., 166, 173
Smith, Adam, 61, 116

NAME INDEX

Smith, Lillian, 247–48, 250–52, 256
Smith, Venture, 20
Snell, Hannah, 168
Solnit, Rebecca, 33, 43
Southwick, Fred, 137
Spencer, Edmund, 144
Spinuzzi, Clay, 175, 189
Spivak, Gayatri, 238, 246, 262, 266
Springsteen, Bruce, 52, 55
Stebbins, Robert, 134–35, 136, 137
Steffen, Gabriela, 5, 13
Steinem, Gloria, 195, 196
Stevens, Rick, 68
Stewart, Evelyn S., 80, 91
Stewart, Kathleen, 39, 43
Strauss, Anselm, 175, 188
Stumpf, Carl, 144
Sutherland, Christine Mason, 65, 107, 212, 218

Talbot, Mary Anne, 168
Taleb, Nassim Nicholas, 132, 137
Tesla, Nikola, 138–47, 148
Tirabassi, Katherine E., 120
Townsend, Keith, 5, 14
Tramezzino, Michele, 10
Tucker, John Randolph, 166, 173
Turner, Frederick Jackson, 140–42, 145, 149
Twain, Mark, 169, 174, 193

Uldam, Julie, 97, 99

Van Andel, Pek, 5–6, 14
Vandenberg, Peter, 214, 218
Van Dorn, Earl, 166
Velazquez, Loreta Janeta, 164–72, 173, 174
Vittum, Daniel, 84
Vittum, Harriet E., 82–86, 88, 89–90, 91

Wadman, Robert C., 71, 79
Wakoski, Diane, 106, 116
Wallace, Maurice O., 21, 27
Walpole, Horace, 59, 61, 69
Welty, Eudora, 204
White, E. B., 196
White, Eric Charles, 232, 236
White, Hayden, 240, 246
Whitman, Walt, 144, 149
Wilcox, Peter, 226, 228, 229–31
Wild-Wood, Emma, 5, 14
Williams, Andrea, 214
Wilson, Eric, 148, 149
Wilson, Gregory, 176, 189
Wukas, Mark, 83, 85, 87, 91
Wynsige (tenth-century bishop), 223
Wysocki, Anne, 225, 236

Yeats, William Butler, 197
Yin, Robert K., 71, 79
Young, Elizabeth, 165, 166, 174

Zenger, Amy, 120
Zmaj, Jovan Jovanovic', 145
Zueblin, Charles, 85

www.ingramcontent.com/pod-product-compliance
Ingram Content Group UK Ltd.
Pitfield, Milton Keynes, MK11 3LW, UK
UKHW042122200326
4879IPUK00002B/25